The New York Times
GOURMET
SHOPPER

By the same author:

The Hot and Spicy Cookbook, 1977
Quintet: Five American Dance Companies, 1976
Cooking with Fruits and Nuts, 1973
The Campus Cookbook, 1973
The Raw Food Cookbook, 1971

The New York Times
GOURMET
SHOPPER

A Guide to the Best Foods

By Moira Hodgson

Times
BOOKS

Charts depicting retail cuts of meat in the Beef, Lamb,
Pork, and Veal chapters appear courtesy of the National
Live Stock and Meat Board.

Published by TIMES BOOKS, a division of
The New York Times Book Co., Inc.
Three Park Avenue, New York, N.Y. 10016

Published simultaneously in Canada by
Fitzhenry & Whiteside, Ltd., Toronto

Library of Congress Cataloging in Publication Data

Hodgson,Moira.
    The New York Times Gourmet Shopper.
    Bibliography: p. 355.
    Includes index.
    1. Cookery. 2. Marketing (Home economics) I.
New York Times. II. Title.
TX652.H58   1983   641   82-50041
ISBN 0-8129-1026-5

Manufactured in the United States of America
83 84 85 86 87 5 4 3 2 1

For my parents

Acknowledgments

I should like to thank my editors Annette Grant and Alex Ward at *The New York Times,* and Susan Kane, my editor at Times Books, for their patience and help way beyond the call of duty. I should also like to thank Michael Shulan for his advice, help, and willingness to taste endless recipes. For contributing recipes or ideas I thank Len Allison, John Cage, Anna Teresa Callen, Nicola Civetta, Patrick Clark, Juan Corradi, Mark David, David Diao, Pascal Dirringer, Lawrence P. Forgione, Dennis Foy, Adi Giovanetti, John Gottfried, Maurice Grosser, Daniel Halpern, Karen Hubert, Raeford Liles, Gisèle Masson, Gianni Minali, John Bernard Myers, Leslie Revsin, Robert Russell, Ninno Ruzzier, Rosario Santos, André Soltner, Stephen Spector, Virgil Thomson, Elizabeth Tingson, Robin Tomlin, Madeleine van Breugel, Alfredo Viazzi, and David Waltuck. For helping me with the chicken taste-testing I thank Mary Beth Clarke, and with the vinegar tasting, Jenifer Harvey.

Introduction

What do you do when faced with a choice of over 200 mustards to buy or an entire wall stocked with shelves of honeys, oils, or vinegars? How can you tell which are the best? Are all brands of flour or peppercorns pretty much the same? How old is the leg of lamb or swordfish steak you are buying?

These are just a few of the questions confronting people who shop for food these days. With such a plethora of brand names available at vastly differing prices and a bewildering choice of meat and fish, often packaged and arranged in display cases so that it is hard to judge the quality, it is essential to know what to look for to get the top value for your money.

Good cooking starts with the best ingredients. True, inexperienced cooks can ruin food, but it is hard for a good cook to produce a fine meal with poor ingredients. Anyone who has tried to make a good salad with hard, pale pink supermarket tomatoes or harsh-tasting olive oil, or to produce a fine piece of grilled sole from a frozen fillet can testify to this. On the other hand, the shopper who can discern quality from inferior ingredients, no matter how limited his or her own cooking experience, can often produce simple but superior meals.

During the years I was on the staff of *The New York Times* I had the good fortune to be able to conduct blind tastings of many different kinds of foods. It was fascinating to see how a seemingly bland meat such as chicken, for example, varied in taste and texture after I roasted and tasted over fifty birds at one time in a restaurant kitchen. Or to try every kind of mustard imaginable spread on pieces of bland ham so that their flavors would not be altered. All this intensive tasting revealed, among other things, that the most expensive ingredients are not necessarily the best. And many mass-marketed American products hold up very well against higher-priced imported items.

I was brought up on a variety of cuisines and have shopped in all kinds of places, from the crowded souks of Morocco and the open-air Indian markets of southern Mexico to midwestern supermarkets as big as airplane hangers and a Sunday market in Fishkill, New York, held in a drive-in movie theatre where local German farmers sold fat blackberries and yellow tomatoes and sweet corn with kernels like white pearls.

My father was in the British diplomatic service and as a child and teenager I lived in the Far East, Middle East, and Europe, finally ending up in the United States in the mid-sixties when my parents were posted here. In New York I soon learned where the good food shops were. I used to frequent Hell's Kitchen, the neighborhood along Ninth Avenue by the Port Authority, where Greek, Italian, Puerto Rican, and, more recently, Philippine and Indian shops sell an incredible variety of foods at very reasonable prices. I also made expeditions to Chinatown and to Little Italy, which are not far from Greenwich Village where I lived. By shopping in these neighborhoods I was always discovering new things and saving a considerable amount of money over the prices at my local supermarket, not to mention getting better quality food. But this is not to denigrate the supermarket. In recent years there has been an extraordinary improvement in some chains, where fresh fish, milk-fed veal, and a fine selection of vegetables and unusual delicacies are now available.

This book is an attempt to pass on some of the information I have picked up during my travels, in my shopping expeditions, and in the many comparison tastings I have done. It is based on the experience of someone who has for years shopped on an extremely low budget but who has had the good luck to eat in some of the world's best restaurants and develop a taste for the finest food. This is not a complete encyclopedia — that would be impossible in a book this size. But I have included things that I most usually buy. The word gourmet is used in the title not to sound snobbish but to denote a shopper who is curious and adventurous, not put off by the unfamiliar, and who wants only the best.

Contents

I. THE BASIC STORECUPBOARD

II. FISH

III. POULTRY

IV. MEAT

V. DAIRY PRODUCTS

VI. GRAINS, FLOUR, AND RICE

VII. PASTA

VIII. DRIED PEAS AND BEANS

IX. VEGETABLES

The Basic
Storecupboard

Coffee

We now drink two thirds of the world's coffee, and it doesn't all come in styro-foam cups that we carry to work. Shops specializing in nothing but fresh roasted beans are burgeoning across the country. Many of them roast their beans daily and offer a variety of blends that can be baffling. The names are as enticing as those in a nineteenth-century travel book: Celebes Kalossi, Jamaican Blue Ridge Mountain, Old Java, Sumatran Mandheling, Kenya AA. Yet with all this, the promise of a delicious home-brewed cup is not always fulfilled.

The mystique about coffee making is quite unwarranted. Anyone can make a good cup of coffee by following a few simple rules. Use freshly roasted beans and grind them just before brewing (Balzac used to grind his coffee fresh for each cup from a grinder nailed to his desk). The grind should be right for your method of infusion, and the water you use should be cold and pure. Coffee and water should be used in the right proportions. The most common mistake is to make the brew too weak. Thus the joke in *Punch*: "Waiter, is this tea? Bring me a cup of coffee. Or is this coffee? In that case bring me a cup of tea."

Besides grinding and brewing, it is simply a matter of learning a little about the beans themselves.

Coffee beans are not beans but the seeds of a fruit produced by the coffee plant. They are quite pale before they are roasted. Roasting brings out their flavor and determines the richness of the brew. Light roasts are mild and deli-cate, medium are stronger, full roast stronger still. These are good breakfast coffees. High or continental, French, and espresso roasts are progressively darker, with a rich full kick, and are good for after dinner.

Like wine grape harvests, coffee bean crops vary dramatically in quality from year to year. The trade is extremely complex. In general, coffee is classi-fied by market names, size, shape, and color of the beans, and the altitude in which they are grown. The best and most expensive coffees are of the species called arabica and come from the higher altitudes. Robusta and lierica strains do not have as good a flavor. A good Colombian coffee comes from ripe arabica beans picked manually. Brazilian is a lower grade of arabica and is mass harvested by stripping whole branches, regardless of whether all the beans are uniformly ripe. The flavor is neutral and this coffee is mostly used for blending. Robusta is the cheaper bean, disease resistant, grown at lower al-titudes than the arabicas and generally used for blends and instant coffees.

Some of the best choices on the market include fragrant Costa Rican and mild Guatamalan Antiguan, sharp Colombian, and the fine, straightforward brew produced by Hawaiian Kona, named after the region where the trees are grown in holes in volcanic rock. From Africa comes a particularly good, almost winey coffee, Kenya AA, and the stronger, spicy Ethiopian. Some of the richest and softest coffees come from Indonesia: Sumatran Mandheling, Celebes Kalossi, and Old Java, which is aged and has a fine flavor. From Jamaica comes the rare Blue Ridge Mountain, the most expensive and delicately flavored coffee in the world.

Instant coffee does not have the aroma or subtle tang of freshly made coffee. Freeze-dried coffee is the best of the instants. Both coffees are made from robusta beans.

Water-decaffeinated coffee beans can make fine coffee when freshly roasted and brewed. Flavored beans (such as cinnamon, orange, and almond) are not recommended — they have a flat, stale taste. But coffee can be pleasantly flavored with a fresh lemon peel, a stick of cinnamon, or a couple of crushed cardamom seeds. It can be laced with eau de vie, ouzo, Cointreau, rum, brandy, or whiskey for Irish coffee. The idea of spiking or flavoring coffee is hardly new. Samuel Pepys wrote of concoctions in his day that would be enough to turn anyone into a tea-only drinker. They included "oatmeal, a pint of ale or any wine, ginger, honey or sugar to please the taste. . . . Butter might be added and any cordial or pleasant spice."

Once ground, coffee loses its aroma within a week. It is best ground fresh in a small electric or hand grinder. Keep the beans in an airtight container and refrigerate. Coffee beans can be kept for a month in the freezer.

There are many different methods of brewing coffee, and coffee lovers swear by their own favorite methods. Turkish coffee, a bitter black brew, is made by steeping powder-fine grounds in a long-handled copper or brass pot called an *ibrik*. A slightly coarser grind is used for the Italian Moka Express pot, which works by steam forced through the grounds. Stainless steel Moka pots are better than the aluminum ones, which can add a strange aftertaste to the brew. The Moka machine makes fine coffee, both for after dinner espresso and café au lait, half coffee and half hot milk, for breakfast.

A more aromatic coffee is produced with drip pots or the steeping method such as the Melior. This is one of the best methods, the only drawback being that the coffee can get cold as it is left to steep. Pour boiling water into the pot to heat it before you make the coffee.

With the drip pot, which makes the café filtre you get in restaurants, boiling water is poured into the top of the pot. It seeps through the coffee grounds in the middle. It is similiar in principle to the filter Melitta, in which boiling water is poured onto the coffee in a paper filter. Again, the coffee is excellent but can also get cold. Use a fine grind for these methods, not so fine as to clog or so coarse that the coffee is weak.

The percolator is the worst method of making coffee. It boils the coffee and produces a bitter solution.

Composer Virgil Thomson says his method is best. He brews his coffee in a saucepan and strains the grounds through a sock. "If people only knew about the sock, which costs 50 cents, they wouldn't bother with those other things," he says. He has been making coffee this way for 65 years.

Café Brûlot

YIELD: 4 Servings

8	whole cloves
	Peel of 1 small orange
	Peel of 1 lemon
	Sugar to taste
½	cup brandy
4	cups hot coffee

1. Combine the cloves, orange and lemon peels, and sugar in a warmed bowl. Heat the brandy and pour it into the bowl. Stir until the sugar is dissolved.

2. Ignite the brandy and slowly pour in the hot coffee. Stir until the flames die down, and pour the mixture into warmed cups.

Note: Cointreau may also be added with the brandy. This is attractive made in a silver bowl or chafing dish over a low flame.

Caffè Borgia

YIELD: 4 Servings

4	ounces unsweetened chocolate
	Sugar to taste
4	tablespoons heavy cream
4	cups hot coffee
4	tablespoons whipped cream
1	teaspoon ground cinnamon
2	teaspoons grated unsweetened chocolate for garnish

1. Melt the chocolate in a double boiler. Add the sugar and cream.

2. Pour in the coffee and beat with a whisk until frothy. Pour into cups and top with whipped cream, ground cinnamon, and grated chocolate.

Herbs, Spices, and Salt

It is hard to imagine cooking today without herbs and spices, even when making the simplest dish. A few leaves of fresh tarragon do wonders for a piece of chicken, some crushed juniper berries transform a pork chop, and a handful of basil leaves eaten with tomatoes makes a simple yet perfect summer salad.

To be of any use, herbs and spices must be fresh — even if dried, they should not have been left on the store shelf long enough to lose their aroma. Always buy in small quantities. Spices should have a rich, vibrant color and in most cases are best ground as needed.

The best source for herbs and spices is a local spice merchant. Ethnic stores often have good supplies; otherwise, Spice Islands, sold in most supermarkets, is a good brand. But the freshest and most superior spices I have found come from a mail order house, Select Origins Inc., 670 West End Avenue, Suite 10E, New York, New York 10025.

Herbs such as parsley, chervil, and basil should only be used fresh. Luckily, these herbs are easy to grow in a pot on the windowsill. Oregano and rosemary, on the other hand, also have good flavor dried, provided they have not been sitting around for long. When buying dried herbs, look for green leaves as close to whole as possible. You can test their potency by rubbing some leaves between the palms of your hands. Avoid powdered herbs; they have little bouquet once they have been ground. Also to be avoided are such concoctions as garlic or onion powder. They are unpleasant tasting and useless.

Some fresh herbs, such as basil and tarragon, can be frozen and used to flavor sauces or stews. They will have lost their consistency but will retain their flavor.

Bouquet garni, used to flavor stocks, stews, and sauces, is made from parsley, thyme, and bay leaf tied in a cheesecloth. It is cheaper to make your own than to buy ready-made. It is used for such dishes as basic fish or meat stocks, to flavor bean dishes such as cassoulet or to add a gentle herb aroma to a beef stew.

Do not store herbs and spices near the stove or in sunlight. The best place is the refrigerator, the next best place a cool, dark cupboard where they should be kept in tightly sealed jars. Fresh herbs should be wrapped in plastic bags. Basil or mint that has the roots intact can be kept fresh standing in a jar of water in a cool place. Frozen herbs lose their consistency but can be used in stews or sauces where this is not important. Bay leaves, marjoram, oregano, rosemary, sage, tarragon, and thyme can be dried.

Herbs

Basil

Fresh basil has a wide, flat leaf and a minty aroma. It is indispensable for making pesto sauce to go with pasta and also goes with tomatoes, vegetables, seafood, and stews and in salads. The best basil is grown at home in a pot and cut when needed. Dried basil is not recommended. When buying basil, choose bunches that are firm and green, not limp or wilted.

Bay Leaves

European bay leaves are superior to California bay leaves, which are stronger and oilier. The best come from Turkey. Bay leaves are used for stews, marinades, stocks, and stewed tomatoes. They are usually sold dried, but it is simple to grow your own at home. Fresh bay leaves are good with pasta.

Capers

These are not herbs, but are unopened flower buds of the caper plant. The small green buds lend their sharp flavor to sauces, tuna fish, Skate with Black Butter (page 89) and Steak Tartare (page 141). The best are dried and packed in salt. They should be soaked for about 20 minutes, drained, and dried before being used. Of the capers sold in jars and pickled in vinegar, the small ones are recommended; they have a sweeter taste. These are available in good specialty stores.

Chervil

Chervil is an extremely delicate herb, subtle with a slight hint of anise. It is best grown at home, since few stores stock it fresh and it is no good dried. Use with chicken, seafood, or in salads.

Coriander

Fresh coriander, also known as Chinese parsley, looks like Italian parsley but has a pungent aroma that has been variously compared to orange peel and crushed bedbugs. It can be used with avocado and salads and is often used in Mexican and North African stews and soups. It grows easily in a pot on the windowsill. When buying coriander, avoid wilted or brown bunches.

Dill

The feathery leaves are used often in Scandinavian and Russian dishes, with fish — especially salmon — and cucumbers. The plant grows successfully in pots. When buying dill, make sure the leaves are fresh-looking, neither slimy nor dried out.

Fennel

The thin, feathery leaves and the seeds are similar in taste to anise. The leaves are good with fish. The seeds should be dry-roasted to release their aroma. They go with curries and fish and are also used to flavor an Italian salami called *finocchiona*. Seeds are sold in small jars, dried.

Marjoram

A strong aromatic herb from the mint family, marjoram is good dried and fresh with lamb and beef, in stuffings, salads and pâtés, and with pork or sausages. Fresh leaves are delicious with roast lamb or with feta cheese, tomatoes, and olives.

Mint

Use only fresh mint. It is extremely easy to grow. There are many varieties, the most common of which is spearmint, which has pointed leaves. If buying mint, choose bunches that look bright and fresh, with no brown or slimy leaves. It goes with yogurt and cucumbers, with new potatoes, and in mint juleps.

Oregano

There are two varieties, one grown in the United States and Mexico and another grown in the Mediterranean. American and Mexican oregano has a sharp, bitter taste that goes well with barbecue and chili sauces. Mediterranean oregano is milder and sweeter and goes with pasta sauces, tomato sauces, and stews. The best oregano comes from Greece and is hand picked and dried in the sun. Oregano is not generally used fresh.

Parsley

The best is flat-leaved Italian parsley — it has more aroma than the curly-leaved variety. Choose bunches that are bright green and crisp looking, not wilted or slimy.

To keep parsley fresh for a couple of weeks, wash it, remove the leaves, pat them dry and put them in a large glass or plastic container with a tight fitting lid. Never use dried parsley flakes. They add nothing.

Rosemary

Rosemary bushes grow two to three feet high in the right climate. The best is grown in France in Provence, where it grows wild on enormous bushes. Rosemary also comes from Spain, Portugal, and Albania. The long thin leaves are good both dried and fresh with lamb, chicken, pork, and veal. Fresh rosemary, wrapped in plastic, lasts a couple of weeks in the refrigerator.

Sage

The finest sage is grown on the Dalmatian coast of Yugoslavia and is much mellower than Albanian, Turkish, Italian, or Spanish sage. Fresh sage is easy to grow in a pot on the windowsill and is less pungent than dried, making it a pleasant herb to serve with veal, calf's liver, or chicken. It also goes well with fatty dishes, such as duck or pork.

Summer Savory

The leaves have an aroma similar to that of thyme, but they are longer and pointed. This herb goes with chicken, veal, and rabbit. Use fresh or dried.

Tarragon

There are two kinds, Russian and French. Avoid the Russian; it has very little flavor. To tell which is which, squeeze a leaf and smell it. French tarragon has a fuller, less harsh aroma. The subtle anise flavor of tarragon goes with chicken, eggs, salmon, and salads. A fresh sprig can be put into a bottle of vinegar to add flavor. Fresh or dried tarragon can be used for cooking.

Thyme

The best comes from southern France. Thyme also comes from Italy, Spain, and California. A little thyme goes with almost every savory dish, particularly when the sauce is made with red wine or tomatoes. Lemon thyme, a variety of thyme, is good in stuffing for pork or veal. Thyme can be used fresh or dried.

Spices

Spices release their aroma when crushed and even more when cooked. They should be used judiciously and blended harmoniously with each other and the food. Spices are sold loose or in small jars. They do not last more than six months, and, like herbs, should be kept away from the light. Keep them in the refrigerator or a cool, dark place. A small grinder is useful for grinding spices as you need them so that you'll get the maximum flavor.

Allspice

Allspice is the berry of the allspice tree, which grows in the West Indies. Buy it whole rather than ready-ground, and grind it fresh in a mill or spice grinder. It will have more aroma that way. It has a hint of cinnamon, cloves, and nutmeg and can be used for curries, pâtés, and with spicy beef, lamb, or chicken dishes.

Anise

The seeds come from a plant with long feathery leaves that is native to Middle Eastern countries. It has a licorice taste and is used to flavor curries, stews, cheese dishes, and fish.

Asafetida

Sold in lump or powdered form, it is made with gum resins of various Indian plants. It has a strong, not entirely pleasant smell when powdered. But once cooked, it has a subtle aroma with a hint of onions. It is used in Indian curries and stews.

Caraway Seeds

These tart little seeds are widely used in German, Austrian, and Jewish cooking. They are good with cabbage, sauerkraut, goose, pork, potatoes, and sausages, and are usually sold in small jars.

Cardamom

The dried fruit of a plant belonging to the ginger family, cardamom is a chief ingredient in curry powders and in many Scandinavian dishes. The greenish or straw-colored pods are discarded, and the tiny seeds inside are used with fish, chicken, and fruit dishes. Arabs use it in coffee, the Swedes in mulled wine. Open a pod and make sure the seed inside is shiny and aromatic, not dried up.

Cayenne

Made with ground seeds and pods of peppers, this is a fiery red pepper that is good in small amounts with eggs, fish, and some meat dishes. Buy small quantities, and don't keep it longer than six months.

Celery Seeds

These can be used in soups or stews if you can't get fresh celery. A little is rather nice in scrambled eggs.

Cinnamon

This is a fragrant bark from Ceylon and Malabar. It is sold both ground and in sticks. Use in spicy dishes and with desserts or mulled wine.

Cloves

These are traditionally from Zanzibar, but now Madagascar is producing the more fragrant cloves because it has better growing conditions. Cloves should be used sparingly with apples, fruit, curries, ham, and pork dishes. Cloves are sold whole or ground. They last for about six months.

Coriander Seeds

Grind the seeds in a mill or spice grinder. A basic ingredient in curries, the seeds are piquant and sweetish. They are delicious freshly ground and sprinkled on olives or raw mushrooms. Dry-roast them just before crushing.

Cumin

Cumin seeds are straw colored and should be freshly ground to have the best flavor. They are widely used in Middle Eastern, Indian, and North African cooking, especially with lamb kebabs and chicken. Little bowls of cumin are often placed on the table along with salt and pepper.

Fenugreek

This tiny, reddish-brown seed has a slightly bitter flavor and sweet spicy scent when heated. It is used in Indian dishes, especially in curries.

Ginger

Cochin white ginger is the best and comes from the Malabar region of India. Jamaican ginger is also good, but not as good as Cochin, which is hot, biting, and sweet. Chinese ginger is not as sweet and is much hotter. Fresh ginger is wonderful in Chinese dishes and is good with fish. Choose roots that are not withered or pliable.

Horseradish

A piquant, biting root, it is best bought fresh and grated as needed. Bottled horseradish does not have as powerful a flavor. Choose firm, ungnarled roots. Fresh horseradish is delicious grated and mixed with sour cream for roast beef or tongue, hot or cold.

Juniper Berries

These aromatic and pungent purple berries go with pork, game, pâtés, and red cabbage. Crush in a mortar before using. They should be soft when squeezed, not rock-hard and dried up. They are sold in small jars.

Mace and Nutmeg

Mace is the outer coating of the nutmeg seed, which grows on trees in Sri Lanka, Sumatra, and Malaya. The Moluccas, once under control of the Dutch and known as the Spice Islands, were the original sources of nutmeg.

Mace is mild and fragrant and can be used instead of nutmeg. Use fresh and buy in small quantities.

Nutmeg is good for both sweet and savory dishes. It keeps well whole, and you can grate it in a small grater. Never buy ground nutmeg: It quickly loses its aroma.

Both nutmeg and mace can be used in cakes, desserts, cheese dishes, béchamel sauce, and terrines, as well as with spinach, broccoli, onions in white sauce, and sausages.

Paprika

Hungarian paprika is the best; other kinds are little more than decorative. It comes in three kinds, all powdered: mild, piquant, and hot. Don't try to keep it longer than six months, even in the refrigerator. Use for Hungarian goulash and spicy dishes.

Pepper

Pepper is the most widely used spice in the world. It comes from India, Indonesia, and Malaysia. In the Middle Ages, peppercorns were worth their weight in silver and used to mask the flavor of rancid meat. Later, in the sixteenth century, they were carried by ships as part of a lucrative spice trade.

Peppercorns from the Malabar coast of India are the best. Of these, the pungent and fruity Tellicherry, grown on the north coast, are superior. They are bigger and darker than other peppercorns and are regular in shape. Malabar Black are also good. When buying peppercorns, look for the largest and blackest. Small brown ones will have a harsh taste. Peppercorns should not be so hard that you can't crush them between your fingers.

White pepper is more expensive than black because the outside husk is removed. It does not have as much flavor or aroma but is used for white sauces, mayonnaise, and fish dishes where black specks would spoil the look of the sauce. I personally don't mind the black specks, but some perfectionists say they are like tar on a white beach.

Mignonette pepper is a mixture of the two, coarsely ground together for pâtés.

Pepper should always be ground fresh, never ready-ground. A good peppermill is essential. Avoid cheap decorative ones and buy those with good grinders that last.

Green peppercorns are young peppercorns, and they are generally sold in cans or jars. They have a gentle aroma that wonderfully enhances sauces for fish or meat.

Poppy Seeds

The seeds come in blue-gray and yellow. Blue-gray seeds are very hard to grind, so buy them ready-ground if using them in breads or desserts. Whole poppy seeds can be sprinkled on top. The yellow seeds are used in curries or Indian breads.

Saffron

Saffron, the dried stigmas of a type of crocus, has a penetrating aroma and a pungent taste. The orange and brick-red threads look like pipe tobacco. After saffron has been added to rice, its hue begins to deepen and develop like a print in a photographer's lab. Because the threads have to be harvested by hand, saffron is very expensive. The threads are sold in small tubes at around $2 for 0.20 grams and in powdered form at around $7 for 1.3 grams. Luckily, a little goes a long way. Powdered saffron is sometimes adulterated and is better avoided.

When Charles V made his son Philip the Duke of Milan, initiating nearly two centuries of Spanish rule, saffron from Spain became the craze in Milan. It was so overused by one well-known cook that he was nicknamed Zafferana. When he married in 1574, friends put saffron into every dish at the wedding banquet — quite a feat considering the number of courses that must have been served.

Sesame Seeds

The seeds come in black and brown — brown being the more usually available. Before using them, roast the seeds in a dry pan or in the oven to release the flavor. They can be used on breads and cakes, in salads, or in Chinese foods. Sesame seeds sold in ethnic stores are usually cheaper than those found in supermarkets.

Tamarind

Tamarind is brownish black in color and looks like a dried pea pod when whole. The pulp is sold in small jars in Indian stores or occasionally in speciality shops. It has a sour, slightly bitter taste. It is used in curries and many Southeast Asian and Middle Eastern dishes.

Turmeric

A dried, aromatic root related to the ginger family, turmeric gives dishes a golden yellow color and is the main ingredient in curry powder. It is sold loose in ethnic stores, where it is cheaper than in supermarkets.

Vanilla

Vanilla beans are long, brown, and ribbed. Placed in a jar of sugar, they will give it a vanilla aroma that is pleasant when you use the sugar for making desserts. They can also be infused in hot milk for custards. Vanilla beans will keep indefinitely.

There is no curry powder on this list because I prefer to make mine at home. The secret of a good curry is to grind spices fresh. The hotness of the curry will depend on the amount of red pepper you use. The following dish goes with stewed Mung Dal — yellow split lentils (see page 232) — and rice. Freshly grated coconut, chopped raw onion, and chutney can be served in small bowls on the side. The curry improves upon being left overnight.

1	*teaspoon red pepper, or*
	to taste
1	*teaspoon coriander seeds*
1	*teaspoon cardamom*
	seeds
½	*teaspoon fenugreek*
2	*tablespoons clarified*
	butter (page 205) or
	vegetable oil
1	*medium onion, finely*
	chopped
2	*cloves garlic, minced*
1	*tablespoon chopped fresh*
	gingerroot
¼	*teaspoon ground*
	cinnamon
1	*tablespoon turmeric*
2	*pounds ground lamb*
3	*cups water*
	Coarse salt and freshly
	ground pepper to taste
3	*tablespoons chopped*
	fresh coriander leaves
	or parsley

1. Put all the spices except the cinnamon and turmeric into an electric grinder and grind to a powder, or pulverize with a pestle and mortar. Set aside.

2. Heat the clarified butter or oil in a skillet and gently fry the onion, garlic, and ginger without browning. Add the blended spices plus the ground cinnamon and turmeric and fry for 2 to 3 minutes, stirring constantly.

3. Add the lamb and cook for 1 minute, stirring. Add the water and bring to a boil. Season with salt and pepper, turn down to a simmer and cook for 1 hour. If the curry dries out, add more water. Garnish with coriander or parsley and serve.

Salt

Don't overuse salt, especially if you have high blood pressure. Salt makes the body retain fluid and can therefore be useful in hot climates, but it is not for people leading cool, sedentary lives. It is wise to use less salt and more herbs, spices, lemon, or vinegar in cooking. Salt substitutes have a peculiar flavor brought on by such additives as dextrose and potassium chloride.

Salt comes in various forms, and the quality of the salt you buy makes an enormous difference. Sea salt is the most expensive and the best, made from sea water evaporated by sun, wind, or heat. Its crystals have natural iodine. The very best comes from Malden on the east coast of England; it is even better than French salt from the Mediterranean. Also good is sea salt from Cagliari in Sardinia.

Mediterranean sea salt is the one most often found in our markets. It comes in both coarse and fine grains. I prefer to use sea salt and like to keep a box next to the stove for cooking. For both the table and the kitchen I prefer coarse grains. Sel gris is a coarse, unrefined sea salt with mineral traces left in it and is used in many kitchens in Europe.

Common salt that you find in the supermarkets is made free-running with the addition of magnesium carbonate and is often iodized. It is made from solid sodium chloride found in underground salt mines and dried in a vacuum. If you put rice into the bowl or shaker it will prevent the salt from caking in damp weather.

Kosher salt is coarsely crushed and is the next best thing to coarse sea salt.

At all costs, avoid salt that is seasoned with MSG, onion, garlic, or celery. It will only impart a harsh medicinal taste to the food. The ingredients will be on the label.

Honey

Like mustard, olive oil, and vinegars, honey seems to be available in endless varieties on the shelves of stores these days. Over 200 are made in America alone. The choice is confusing. Some honeys are thin and runny, others creamy or stiff, and some come complete with the comb in a wooden box. The colors vary as much as the textures and range from white to burnished gold and black-brown. How do you choose the best?

Honeys are very much a matter of personal taste. In general, superior honeys will have a clean, clear taste that is not cloyingly sweet. Two of those preferred by connoisseurs include Tasmanian leatherwood from Australia, a smooth light-colored honey, and Greek hymettus, another great honey with the flavor of wild herbs. Herbs such as thyme, rosemary, or sage give a special light aroma to honey, while blossoms, such as those from apple, orange, or lemon trees, add a heavy scent. There are eucalyptus honeys from Australia, in various colors and consistencies; rich, dark Jamaican honey; sunflower honey from Greece or Turkey, and dark buckwheat honey from California.

In buying honey, there are a couple of rules of thumb to go by as you set about choosing a taste that you will like. Blended honeys such as those generally found in supermarkets are best avoided. They are sometimes stretched with non-honey sweeteners and pasteurized for consistency. They have longer shelf life than other honeys but less taste because they have been heat-treated so they won't crystallize. When honey is granular you know it hasn't been pasteurized.

The color, flavor, and scent depend not on the bee but on the nectar that the bee gets from the flower — two million flowers are said to be pollinated for one pot. Killer bees don't make honey any better or worse than other bees — the marketing of their honey is merely a gimmick.

Honey has a special enzyme that helps it counteract mold, so it needs no refrigeration. It is easy to digest, but it is not a health food and, like sugar, should not be eaten in great quantities.

Comb honey, usually sold in a wooden box, is one of my favorites. It is chewy and unadulterated. It is eaten wax and all and is delicious on fresh brown bread. Chunk honey has pieces of comb left in and is also excellent. Some other honeys that are recommended include acacia, a mild, golden honey that remains liquid; dark and creamy New Zealand manuka honey; heather honey, which has an aromatic tang, and smooth and amber honey from lavender, which is popular in the South of France.

Honey crystallizes and hardens with age, but it can be melted down over hot water. It is sweeter than sugar, so use it sparingly when making desserts.

Mustard

Mustard used to be thought of as something to be smeared on hot dogs. Not any more. Now there is a vast choice of French, German, English, and American mustards on the market, in every category and price, and suitable for a multitude of uses, from sauces to coating roasts, from marinades to salad dressings. For those who want to travel further afield, there are now anchovy mustards, peanut mustards, sherry mustards, lime mustards, and pink- and green-peppercorn mustards.

Mustards are packaged in huge crocks sealed with wax, in porcelain jars, in fake Champagne bottles, Mason jars, tin buckets, and tubes. There are, in fact, so many different flavors and brands on store shelves these days that the average shopper may never figure out which is the best for him.

In an attempt to navigate through this deluge of mustards, I tasted 187 different brands from specialty stores and supermarkets. For purposes of comparison, I grouped the mustards by nationality.

American mustards are mild, sweet, and generally rather oily; English mustards are very hot; the Germans are generally sharp, with some slightly on the sweet side. French mustards fall into three main categories: hot Dijon mustard, grainy mustards made with ground and semiground or whole seeds, and mild mustards flavored with red wine, dark and slightly sweet-sour.

I tasted the mustards on their own, eating bread between each taste to clear the palate. Those mustards meant to accompany charcuterie I sampled with ham, boudin blanc, or bratwurst; I also tried the appropriate ones with steak and roast beef. The following are my findings. They reflect, of course, my own taste. The best mustards, I found, were invariably the Dijons — smooth, hot, yellow-gray pastes ranging from subtle to fairly sharp. These all come from Dijon in Burgundy, where half the world's mustard is made. They are frequently used in French cooking, for vinaigrette dressings, mayonnaise (mustard helps the emulsification of egg and oil), and sauces.

Mustard companies keep their recipes a closely guarded secret, but basically, mustard is made from mustard seed milled and mixed with liquid, such as white wine or vinegar, into a paste. Dijon mustard is made only from ground, hulled mustard seeds, white wine, vinegar or verjuice (the juice of green grapes), and spices. By law, no fortifiers, such as mustard oil, flour fillers, or sugar, are allowed in Dijon mustards.

American mustards have much less pure mustard seed than do the French. The American product often contains sugar, flour fillers, mustard oil, and turmeric, a ground spice that gives the ballpark mustards their bright yellow color. German mustards usually have ground mustard seed, vinegar, salt, and spices, with flour fillers and sugar sometimes added. English mustard comes in pure powder form or as a paste with such additives as wheat flour and sugar.

Of 26 smooth Dijon mustards tasted, I found the best to be Les Frères Troisgros, Bourdier d'Auvergne, Fauchon, Paul Corcellet, and Etoile de Dijon, with the less expensive Old Monk, Reine de Dijon, Maille, Maître Jacques, and Amora also quite good. For those on salt-free diets, salt-free Corcellet is particularly recommended.

Grey Poupon Dijon mustard, an American manufactured mustard using the original French Poupon recipe, is not as good as its French counterpart, but it is far less expensive and more readily available in supermarkets.

Two French mustards flavored with wine from the Champagne district were rich and full, slightly less sharp than the Dijons, but also excellent for sauces. These were Florida mustard and Albert Menes Moutarde au Vinaigre et Champagne. There were also two excellent red wine mustards, made by Paul Corcellet and Bourdier d'Auvergne, that would make fine accompaniments for steak.

Grainy mustards — the grains are actually mustard seeds — are not as sharp as Dijon. They go with ham, cold cuts, sausages, and pork, or can be used as a coating for roasts. They are also good with French charcuterie. Of the grainy mustards in crock jars sealed with wax that I tasted, I found none to be outstanding. Pommery, the best selling French crock mustard in America, tasted harsh in comparison with the Maître Jacques and Raoul Gey brands.

The best value was La Charcutière at around $2 a 13-ounce jar. Other pleasing grainy mustards were Les Frères Troisgros Country Mustard, which was rich and dense; Old Monk, a full blend of mustard seeds and white wine vinegar, and two sharp British grainy mustards, Elsenham and Military Mustard.

Corcellet's à l'Ancienne, a coarse mustard, was one of the best, with Crabtree & Evelyn's Old Fashioned and Celine Corcellet's à L'Ancienne, which are similar blends, close runners-up. These were looser in texture than the other grainy mustards and had a sharp but refined flavor. The tiny mustard seeds are left whole in a light aromatic sauce in all three. These are fine mustards to serve with cold meats.

The market for flavored mustards has blossomed in the last year, and some companies now produce as many as 30 varieties. They are a nouvelle cuisine syndrome, combining the unlikeliest ingredients. Occasionally they work well: Crabtree & Evelyn's tarragon mustard, for instance, Albert Menes Herbes de Provence, and a Provençal mustard put out by Aux Amysetiers du Roi, each of which has a thick, creamy texture and tastes generously of fresh herbs. But in most cases, if you want to create unusual mustards, it is cheaper and more satisfying to do it by adding the ingredients, such as herbs, yourself.

Some of the "couture" mustards are alarming in appearance and even worse in taste. They range from dark green, almost like puréed spinach, to a startling fire-engine red. Some of the most unpleasant included a "three-vegetable" mustard (beet, raisin, and tomato), anchovy mustard, peanut mustard, tomato purée, garlic-parsley, Xérès sherry, black olive, and a series of lime and lemon mustards that taste like misfired sherbet.

Of the peppercorn mustards I tried, the best was Pommery, sold in a crock. It is an honest, mild mustard, mixed with the crushed green berries. In general, however, the peppercorn-flavored mustards were unexciting. The pink-peppercorn mustards were disappointing. The green-peppercorn mustards were better but not worth the money (for example, Bourdier brand costs around $9 a 9-ounce jar). Use a regular Dijon and add peppercorns as you need them.

The fiercest mustards are English and Chinese. The familiar Colman's English mustard is a bright yellow blend of powder, wheat flour, and spices — strong enough to lift your head off. The powdered kind should be mixed with cold water about half an hour before being served so the flavor develops. It is delicious with roast beef, ham, sausages, and Cheddar cheese.

Also hot, but not as searing as Colman's, is Far East mustard, less than a dollar a 4-ounce jar, a yellow paste to go with Oriental food and beef.

Among the German mustards, Düsseldorf is hot, and Bavarian mustards tend to be rather sweet and dark. As you'd expect, both kinds go well with German smoked pork and sausages. The Bavarian mustards were too sweet for my taste. I preferred the hot ones: Hengstenberg medium hot was the best, having a clean, sharp taste. Also good was Lion Brand, a buttery, well-rounded Düsseldorf mustard.

Two Swedish mustards sampled were interesting: Slotts Sweet and Slotts Spicy Swedish. Both had a bold orange-brown color. Slotts Sweet was far too sugary, but the spicy version had a pungent sweet-sour flavor and would be good on frankfurters or hamburgers or mixed with dill as a sauce for gravlax.

With the exception of Sabel & Rosenfeld, a syrup-like Canadian mustard made with sugar, I found the sweet mustards to be cloying. For glazing ham or pork it is cheaper and more satisfactory to use Dijon mustard mixed with honey.

American mustards fall into two categories, delicatessen-style brown mustards and bright yellow ballpark mustards, flavored with sugar, vinegar or white wine, and turmeric. Prices for them are generally lower than for imported mustards, but the quality is significantly inferior and lacking in character. Those I tasted included Gulden's Creamy Mild and Spicy Brown, Nance's (high priced for this group), French's Bauers, and Kosciusko. Kosciusko, a pleasant, mild German-style mustard good for hamburgers, hot dogs, and charcuterie, was the best of the American mustards.

Olive Oil

Not long ago only a handful of brands of olive oil were on the markets. Nowadays literally dozens are available, and many cooks are becoming as choosy about their olive oil as wine drinkers are about fine Bordeaux. And they should be, considering the prices some extra-virgin olive oils — those made from the first pressings of the best olives — are commanding. A one-liter bottle of Poggio al Sole, from the Italian province of Tuscany, sells for over $20!

Stores are competing so hard for the attention of the discerning olive-oil user that they dispatch buyers to Europe to scout the small groves for the finest oils. The primary reason for the high cost of many extra-virgin oils is that they are made almost entirely by hand. Only the finest of olives are picked by hand and pressed in a small, manually operated cold-stone press. Then the oil is filtered through cheesecloth. The larger companies — Berio, Bertolli, and Sasso — use hydraulic presses to make their extra-virgin oils, but these can heat up and destroy some of the vitamins and flavor in the oil.

Besides extra-virgin, olive oil comes in two lesser grades: virgin and pure. Virgin olive oil can be pressed from olives of less than top quality. Pure olive oil, the lowest grade, can be made from second or even third pressings, in which the pulp left over from a previous pressing is reused. In the United States, olive oil labeled "pure" may also contain oil chemically extracted from olive pits and pulp; this is not permitted in any other country that produces olive oil.

I conducted a sampling of more than fifty olive oils bought from specialty stores and supermarkets around New York City. They came from France, Italy, Spain, Greece, Portugal, and California, and many of them were extra-virgin. The range in price was from a low of $13.54 a gallon to $20 a liter.

My personal favorites were Italian extra-virgin oils from Tuscany, where Chianti Classico wines are produced: Badia a Coltibuono, Castello di Cacchiano, Colavita, Castello di Fonterutoli, Montorselli, and Poggio al Sole, all selling for close to $20 a liter. The slightly less expensive Col d'Orcia, Olivieri, and Mancianti (the last from Lombardi) were also excellent, if not on a par with the others. Such oils are perfect for salads and vegetable dishes such as Fried Eggplant (page 281) and sliced tomatoes with basil and mozzarella cheese.

Badia a Coltibuono is a rich, unrefined cold-pressed olive oil that even carries a vintage on the label. It is possible to discern a distinct difference between some years — one year may produce an oil that is darker, thicker, and fuller than that of another year. (Vintages on olive oils, however, are something of an affectation. Although harvests do vary from year to year, olive oil tends to lose some of its bouquet after about 18 months in the bottle.)

The most common Italian brands in American markets, Olio Sasso, Berio, and Bertolli, are pure, factory-produced oils. They have a very faint taste of olives and are thin and almost colorless. Lucca oil, packed by Callisto Francesconi, and also readily available to the shopper here, is a very light extra-virgin oil with more flavor than those pure Italian oils, but it lacks the character of the small-farm oils. For cooking, many Italians use a mixed corn-and-sesame oil, *olio di semi*, which is completely tasteless and burns at a higher temperature than olive oil.

The French extra-virgin olive oils are generally lighter in texture, color, and aroma and have a nuttier flavor than the Italian, and I don't always find them as satisfying. However, some that I tasted were particularly outstanding, and can be recommended wholeheartedly for mayonnaises, green salads, and the dishes of Nice and Provence.

Hilaire Fabre Père et Fils, J.B.&A. Artaud Frères, and Crabtree & Evelyn (actually made by Roger Michel, a top French producer of olive oil) are especially good. The Hilaire Fabre is a delicate and fragrant oil that would be ideal in cold fish dishes. Artaud Frères is among the most full bodied and aromatic of the French oils. Other excellent French oils are Bourdier d'Auvergne, Moulins de la Brague, and James Plagniol.

There are also a number of fine inexpensive olive oils on the market, although not one is comparable in quality to the Italian or French extra-virgin products.

If you like a stronger oil, Goya (virgin Spanish) and Mondegão (Portuguese) brands are reliable and inexpensive. Progresso olive oil, a longtime standby in most supermarkets, is a blend of Spanish virgin and pure oils that is a decent and workmanlike — if somewhat bland — product.

Of two California brands, Hain's virgin olive oil, sold in health food stores, is flat. Vine Village, from the Napa Valley, has a strong olive taste that is rather pleasant but not as subtle as the French oils it most resembles. The costs of both California brands were comparable to the French extra-virgin oils.

Crinos, Minerva, and Hermes olive oils from Greece are all robust, pure oils that are quite suitable for cooking.

A few tips on the use and storage of olive oil: Caution should be exercised in using extra-virgin oils, which can overwhelm delicately flavored dishes. They are best for such things as salad dressings, pesto sauce, Provençal and Niçoise dishes, cold pasta, marinated vegetables, or dishes where the taste of olives is complementary. Jean-Jacques Rachou, chef at La Côte Basque, uses it in rouille for bouillabaisse.

Olive oil does not have to be kept in the refrigerator, but it should be kept sealed and in a cool, dark place. A sealed oil can keep for several years, but do not leave oil in an open can; decant it into a capped bottle. Refrigerated oil turns cloudy but will not lose flavor. Put oil in the refrigerator — in the bottom — only in extraordinarily hot weather.

Olive oil, which is completely free of cholesterol, is a "neutral" or mono-unsaturated oil, meaning its use will neither add to the cholesterol in your bloodstream, as will butter or animal fats, nor decrease it, as will some polyunsaturated oils such as corn, soybean, and safflower.

Like other cooking oils, olive oil will decompose quickly when it burns, and it burns at a much lower temperature — about 280 degrees Fahrenheit — than do other vegetable oils, which can take between 380 and 440 degrees, depending on the oil.

Olive oil can be reused, but it is inadvisable to do so more than twice because particles of food may turn it rancid. If you do plan to reuse an oil, it should be strained through cheesecloth immediately after using.

The labeling of olive oil in the United States is confusing. The Food and Drug Administration does not require packagers to distinguish between extra-virgin, virgin, and pure oils. In Europe containers must state the type of oil.

If you buy an oil that has been packaged abroad, you can be certain of what you are getting, but oils packaged in the United States may be described as virgin oil even if they are far from it.

Though in 1979 the F.D.A. filed a notice of intent to change the practice, it does not consider this a high-priority item and may even drop it altogether. Meanwhile, some cheaper products packed here may be made from residue oils obtained chemically from the pits and pulp.

A Guide to the Best Oils

Following is a list of recommended extra-virgin olive oils. Prices, of course, are subject to change.

Badia a Coltibuono   Expensive

From Gaiole, near Siena, in the Chianti Classico region. Labeled by year. It is a dark, thick, and full oil, superb, with a flowery aroma. A rich, unrefined cold-pressed Tuscan oil, it should be used for salads, cold cooked vegetables, cold pasta, and cold sauces (such as pesto or green sauce).

Poggio al Sole   Expensive

A deep green, velvety oil from the Chianti Classico region near Poggio al Sole in Tuscany. It has a powerful aroma, yet is light in taste and texture. Good with cold dishes.

Colavita   Moderate

An elegant olive oil, light in comparison with the other Chianti oils, but with a strong, pungent aroma and very flowery taste. It sells for half the price of the preceding oils.

J.B.& A. Artaud Frères   Moderate

A superb French oil, full-bodied and aromatic, good for salads, mayonnaise, and sautéing where a delicate yet definite olive flavor is called for. Also good for such Niçoise and Provençal dishes as ratatouille, aïoli, pistou (basil paste), grilled fish, brandade, sauce verte.

Crabtree & Evelyn   Expensive

A very pleasant and superior oil made from Nice olives, fragrant and light, made by Roger Michel, who also exports under his own name. Can be used for all of the above dishes.

Castello di Cacchiano   Expensive

From the Chianti Classico region in Italy, this is a rich, complex oil, with remarkable flavor and aroma. Serve with cold dishes. Castello di Fonterutoli, which is not quite as rich as the Castello di Cacchiano, sells at the same price and comes from a nearby vineyard.

Montorselli   Expensive

From the Chianti Classico region, sold in glass cruets with cork top or in small bottles. A dark green, full-bodied, fragrant oil.

Hilaire Fabre Père et Fils   Moderate

This is a little lighter than most of the other French extra-virgin oils. It is a particularly delicate oil, fragrant, smooth, and aromatic, which makes it a good choice for fish dishes and mayonnaise.

Puget

Moderate

A light oil with a pungent flavor and fine bouquet. Good for Niçoise and Provençal dishes.

Old Monk

Moderate

A rich, full-bodied French olive oil that was one of the first to be imported into this country. A very good buy.

Louis de Regis

Moderate

A straw-colored, gentle oil from France. It is light enough for frying and yet aromatic enough for salads.

James Plagniol

Moderate

This light, fairly bland pure oil from Marseilles is the biggest selling French olive oil in this country. It lacks the depth of flavor of the extra-virgins but appeals to many cooks who do not care for a pronounced olive taste in their foods.

BARGAINS

The following oils, while not the equals of the extra-virgin products from Italy and France, are nonetheless strong flavored and full bodied and are quite suitable for use in salads and other dishes.

Crinos

A Greek olive oil from Calamata olives. Other pure Greek brands tested include Minerva, Nissa, and Diana. All are pleasant cooking oils, with a good flavor. They are slightly stronger than the moderately priced, widely available Italian oils. All quart cans around $4.

Goya

Pure imported Spanish virgin olive oil. Excellent value for those who like a strong, pungent oil. Widely available in supermarkets.

Mondegão

Portuguese pure olive oil, very strong and dark, good for salads and for use as a condiment. Available in Italian and Hispanic stores.

Cooking Oil

There are many excellent oils on the market for cooking and for salads. Peanut, safflower, sesame, walnut, and hazelnut oils all give a distinctive flavor to food. They also have the added advantage of having no cholesterol. Some, such as safflower oil, even have the effect of lowering cholesterol in the body. But when buying peanut or vegetable oils, several things have to be taken into consideration.

I usually buy my oils in health food or specialty stores where cold-pressed, unrefined oils are sold. Oils extracted from their sources by cold pressing are better than oils extracted by heat or chemical methods. Over-refined or chemically preserved oils have prolonged shelf life to the detriment of their flavor — these are the ones you will see most on the shelves of supermarkets. This category includes all-purpose mixed vegetable oils, some of which contain cottonseed or soybean oils. These are blanched by being heat treated, deodorized, and often treated with preservatives. Oils that have been cold pressed say so on the label. They are generally mellower in taste than the refined oils.

For frying and sautéing, I usually use a bland cooking oil such as safflower, peanut, light sesame, or corn oil. These have high burning temperatures, while butter and olive oil burn easily.

Safflower oil is very highly polyunsaturated and burns at the highest temperature of all, 510 degrees. It is a golden, light oil and excellent for deep-frying.

Peanut oil can be flavored with fresh chopped ginger, garlic, and scallions and used for frying all manner of meat and fish Chinese style. It doesn't burn until it has reached 440 degrees. Chinese peanut oil has more flavor than Planter's, the brand sold at most supermarkets.

Corn oil is cheap, mild, and all-purpose. It is so bland that it is useful when you don't want any flavor added to the food from an oil. Recommended brands include French Benedicta, Erewhon cold-pressed oil, available in health food stores, and Mazola, 100 percent corn oil sold in supermarkets. These oils smoke at 475 degrees.

Sesame oil burns lower, at 420 degrees. The pale yellow sesame oil often sold in health food, Indian, and Middle Eastern stores has no smell and can be used for frying. The dark brown Chinese sesame oil has a powerful nutty taste and is used for seasoning or in salads. It can also be mixed with lighter oils for frying. It is sold in Oriental markets.

Soybean is also a fine frying oil because it does not burn until it reaches 495 degrees. It has a strong aroma and is high in polyunsaturates. Use it only on foods that can stand up to its flavor, or mix it with other, blander oils such as corn or peanut oils. Delicate foods will be overwhelmed if it is used on its own.

Two oils that I don't recommend in the kitchen are cottonseed and coconut oil. Cottonseed oil is high in saturated fats. It can contain chemical residues from boll weevil sprays, and my advice is to avoid it. It is often used for packing fish, tuna, and sardines and is an ingredient in Wesson oil. Coconut oil is high in saturated fat and is used for baking or in convenience and artificial foods.

You can find superb oils for salads in health food or specialty stores. The rich toasted flavor of hazelnut oil or French walnut oil is wonderful with salads, especially with delicate greens such as Bibb or Boston lettuce or a mixed salad of arugula, endive, and radicchio. Sherry vinegar goes especially well with these oils, as do herbs such as tarragon or basil. Sunflower oil is neutral and can be mixed with these more expensive oils, extra-virgin olive oil, or walnut oil for salad dressings. These oils should generally not be used for cooking — they break down easily when heated — and they, and all other oils, should be refrigerated in hot weather. They may cloud when cold, but that has little or no effect on their flavor.

A clear, pale grapeseed oil for salads and for frying meat is also available in specialty and health food stores. It is very light and is popular in France and Italy. The French use it for fondue Bourguignonne, the party dish in which pieces of steak are deep-fried at the table and served with a variety of sauces and dressings. It has a pleasant toasty flavor.

I rarely cook with margarine, the butter substitute usually made from vegetable oil, except sometimes for baking. If I do use it, I use soft sticks because they are less saturated than the hard ones and are generally made entirely from vegetable oil. The first ingredient listed on the package should be liquid vegetable oil, not partially hydrogenated (and hardened) oil. Hydrogenated oils can increase cholesterol in the body. Solid shortenings are hydrogenated, and I avoid those.

Buy oils in small quantities. Stale or rancid oils are bad for the digestion. You can tell if they have gone rancid by their rank, musty smell.

Don't allow oils to smoke or reuse frying oils. They can become toxic when overheated and should be thrown out.

Sugar and Molasses

America is a sugar-addicted nation. The statistics for its consumption are staggering. A conservative estimate is that the average person eats 100 pounds of sugar a year or over a quarter of a pound a day. This is not to suggest that people are hysterically spooning bowls of sugar into their coffee or piling it on dessert. But they are eating enormous amounts of sugar in ways of which most are entirely unaware. Most of it is in so-called "convenience foods." There is sugar in bottled salad dressings, in ketchup, in frankfurters, hamburger buns, cereals, bread, and in processed, frozen, and canned foods. And most of all, there is sugar in soft drinks. Americans drink over 29 gallons per capita a year of these.

Sugar in small quantities does not do any harm and, indeed, helps to sweeten fruits such as rhubarb that would be practically inedible without it. Of course, like white flour, refined white sugar is a symbol of the well-off, even though it has less flavor than unrefined brown sugar, the darkest of which can have the consistency of fudge.

Brown sugar, if it is the real thing, has more character than white because it retains its molasses. Read the label on the package. It should state the sugar's country of origin. If it doesn't and is simply labeled "light brown" or "soft dark brown," it is refined white sugar that has been tossed in syrup or molasses or decolorized. This sugar does not have much flavor.

Don't be misled into thinking that brown sugar is much healthier than white. The amount of molasses left is so minimal that brown sugar is still little more than calories.

The best brown sugar is made from raw sugar cane and refined by evaporation. It should be soft and moist, but when it has been kept for a while it can go hard and be difficult to use. The best include very dark Barbados or demerara sugar, soft and fine grained, or the lighter turbinado sugar.

Granulated sugar is all-purpose refined sugar. It comes from the juice of plants such as sugar cane or sugar beets and is ground into different consistencies. It is less sweet when cooled, which is why ice cream is made with such large quantities. The standard grain should be used for sweetening tea or coffee and desserts. Superfine or extra fine is small grained and good for baking. My mother used to make vanilla sugar by adding a vanilla bean to the jar. She used the flavored sugar for custards and mousses.

Powdered or XXX sugar is used for baking, but check the label, because some sugars are adulterated with cornstarch to prevent them from caking.

Confectioner's or XXXX sugar is a fast dissolver and is used for sherbets, icing, and powdering cakes.

Preserving sugar has thick crystals so they don't sink in a solid mass when used for jellies and jams.

Raw sugar is made from crystallized remnants of the juice of the sugar cane after sugar and molasses have been removed. It is then purified. But since the bulk of the minerals and vitamins go out with the molasses, it is not much better for you than regular white sugar.

Molasses is a byproduct of sugar. After the sugar has been extracted, the liquid that is left is molasses. Molasses goes through three processes of boiling. The first yields light molasses, the second dark molasses, and the third blackstrap molasses, much beloved by Gayelord Hauser, the famous health food advocate. I once had a record on which Danny Kaye and Groucho Marx sang a song about health foods which had lines that I recall as something like:

"Blackstrap molasses and whole wheat bread

Make you live so long

You wish you were dead."

Molasses can also be made from sorghum. Both kinds of molasses offer more vitamins and minerals than sugar. Molasses is good with pancakes, Boston baked beans, and shoofly pie.

Soy and Other Sauces

Not every sauce can be made to order each time you need it. Some you have to buy. But I don't see the need for buying mayonnaise, for example, America's best-selling sauce, since making it at home is simple (page 196), particularly if you have a blender.

Ketchup, that thick, bright red sauce, is loaded with sugar but is an almost indispensable item in the American kitchen. I use tomato paste instead if I want to intensify the tomato taste in a dish. If you do buy ketchup, avoid brands that are laden with artificial flavoring. Heinz is one of the most reliable.

The only real Worcestershire sauce comes from India. It contains tamarind, molasses, sugar, anchovies, garlic, and salt — all natural flavors. There are many imitations on the market. The best is Lea & Perrins.

Tabasco, so called because the original is from Tabasco in Mexico, is a hot peppery sauce made with red chilies, vinegar, and salt. It can be used for Bloody Marys, eggs, seafood, and Creole dishes. It is stale when brownish and separated. Sauce bottles are often dated in code for final date of sale, so if you are in doubt, ask the store clerk to decipher the codes for you.

Soy Sauce

Soy sauce is made from naturally fermented soybeans and wheat or barley flour. Many commercial brands are chemically fermented, and they do not have the flavor of naturally fermented soy sauce or the natural vegetable protein.

The best soy sauce has a rich, salty, pungent smell. Japanese Tamari and Shoyu, found in health food stores, are pure and among the best. They have no artificial color or flavor. Kikkoman soy sauce is a Japanese sauce available in supermarkets across the country. It is not as good as Tamari or Shoyu, but it is perfectly decent. I prefer the Japanese *usukuchi shoya*, a light and pleasantly flavored soy sauce. Also good is a sweet Indonesian soy sauce, *ketjap manis*.

To test soy sauce, shake the bottle. If the sauce forms a thick foam at the top, it is naturally fermented.

American soy sauce is often sweet, while Japanese is full flavored. Chinese is even stronger than Japanese. In Oriental stores, soy sauce can be light or dark or heavy and sweet — it is a matter of personal taste which one you prefer. Thin soy sauces are lighter but saltier. In any case, soy sauce should be used in moderation or it can overpower food.

Miso paste is made from fermented beans or grains and can be used for flavoring soups and sauces; it is a thick paste that comes in various shades, according to the color of soybeans or grains used. The color ranges from almost black to white, with yellow, dark brown, and red in between. It is sold in health food stores. A spoonful is also delicious added to carrots or brown rice before cooking.

Oyster sauce is made from oysters cooked with soy sauce, and salt is also used to flavor this sauce.

Tea

British people drink more tea than anyone else. It is served first thing in the morning and punctuates the day, providing a lift of the spirits when all else fails, until the final "cuppa" is brewed before bedtime. Ten pounds per person are said to be imported into the British Isles per year, and that, if 300 cups can truly be made from a pound of tea, is 3,000 cups a year, or a little over eight cups a day. This staggering figure is given in *The Pocket Guide to Coffee and Teas*, an excellent handbook by Kenneth Anderson. Tea is consumed worldwide more than any other drink except water, he says, with Americans drinking four cups a day and the prudent Dutch only two.

Apart from herb teas, tea comes from one species of plant, a flowering evergreen that is usually pruned to a height of between three and five feet. Teas vary enormously because of the differences in growing conditions, the kind of leaves used, and how the leaves are processed. As with coffee, the best tea is grown at a high altitude where the leaves mature more slowly than in hot lowlands. Most tea is grown in India, Sri Lanka, China, Taiwan, Japan, Indonesia, and parts of Africa.

Teas generally fall into three categories: black, green, and oolong, which is a brown tea. Like coffee, tea varies according to the region in which it is grown, the sun, rainfall, altitude, soil, season, time of day picked, and the skill of the picker. Black tea is fermented before firing or heat drying. Brown tea, such as oolong, is partially fermented and is not as strong as black tea but has a more assertive flavor than green tea. Green tea, the ceremonial tea of Japan and the tea served in many Chinese and Japanese restaurants, is not fermented. Green teas are lighter than black teas with a less pronounced flavor that can nevertheless be extremely subtle and satisifying.

The names can be confusing. Orange Pekoe has nothing to do with oranges; the term denotes the size of the leaf not the taste of the tea, and it is a black tea. Darjeeling and Assam are not types but are named for the places where they are grown.

Terms for tea tasting are also confusing and certainly baroque. A leaf may be described as common, hairy, tippy, shotty, chesty (a smell caused by inferior tea chest panels), or cheesy (caused by inferior glue on those panels). The brew can be baggy (tainted from sacking), brassy, biscuity, croppy, sweaty, tired, or simply gone-off.

Teas are sold in small, closed tins or loose, in bulk, or in bags. The tins have a long shelf life — up to two years — but bulk tea can lose its flavor fast, especially if the containers in which the tea is stored are not tightly closed.

Tea leaves should crumble between your fingers but should not turn to powder at the first touch. They should be slightly resilient. The best tea leaves are tightly rolled.

Black tea packaged in an airtight container will keep its flavor for about two years, green and brown teas for about six months. But they must be kept in a sealed tin, for, as the head of Twinings, one of the major tea firms, points out, tea absorbs smells like blotting paper. The two best brands generally available are Twinings and Jackson's of Piccadilly.

Herb teas without caffeine are becoming more popular these days. Celestial Seasonings puts out very good herb teas, including blends such as Sleepytime, Red Zinger, and Country Apple. If you have a garden, you can make your own from such herbs as chamomile, mint, borage, comfrey, or lemon balm. Brew them with green tea or steep on their own.

In Morocco meals are always ended with a pot of mint tea. A huge bunch of fresh mint is picked and infused into green tea that is brewed in a metal pot and flavored with spoonfuls of sugar. It is poured from a great height back and forth between a small glass and the pot until the desired strength is reached. After several infusions, the tea is poured and passed around with the toast "B'ssmillah!" "Moroccan whisky!" one Arab boy in the desert once called it, to show that he knew about such things.

Black teas include Assam from India, full bodied and stimulating and good quality. Lapsang Souchong originated in Fujian province in China and is a smoky tea grown in soil rich with minerals. It has large curled leaves. The name Souchong also applies to teas with this size leaf in India, Indonesia, and Sri Lanka.

Formosa oolong is a gentle brown unblended tea from Formosa whose fruity aroma is often compared to that of ripe peaches.

Gunpowder is the world's oldest tea and lowest in caffein and is made from rolled young green tea leaves. It is a mild and astringent tea and goes with Chinese and Japanese food.

China Black is a mellow Keemun tea served in Chinese restaurants.

Some teas are scented with oranges (Constant Comment, for instance), lime, lemon, or cinnamon. Earl Grey is a traditional blend of China and Darjeeling teas with a smoky fragrance that comes from oil of bergamot. It is one of the largest selling teas and one of my favorites.

Jasmine tea is often made with dried jasmine flowers added to green tea leaves from Guangdong Province and is sometimes mixed with black tea.

The aristocracy of Britain and Russia were as fond of tea as anyone. A tea called Prince of Wales is a smooth and rich blend from the northern China province of Anhui, while Queen Mary blend is a mixture of Darjeeling teas, mainly Orange Pekoe. Russian Caravan, said to have been the Czars' favorite, was then a hearty blend of China black and oolong brown teas. It now varies depending on the dealer.

For those who prefer to wake up with tea instead of coffee in the morning, there are breakfast blends. Ceylon Breakfast tea is mild but deep gold in color, with a lovely bouquet. English Breakfast tea is a blend of Ceylon and India leaves, while Irish Breakfast is a pungent blend of Assam and Ceylon teas. All are strong and can stand up to milk and sugar.

The larger the leaf, the milder the brew and the longer the brewing time required. Always use fresh, cold tap water, and don't forget to warm the pot and pour the water into it the minute you add the leaves.

I'm not a fan of tea bags — they are to tea what instant coffee is to real coffee. Why do some of the best restaurants, where infinite trouble is taken over every detail of the food, table setting, wine, and atmosphere, ruin it all by serving tea in a bag? Brewing a small, fresh pot takes very little time.

According to Alexandre Dumas, teacups were first made at Kronstadt, "and the bottom was decorated with a view of that city. When a teahouse proprietor stinted on the tea, this picture could be seen clearly, and the customer would say to him, 'I can see Kronstadt.' Since the proprietor could not deny this, he was caught *in flagrante delicto*. It became customary, then, for tea to be served in teahouses in glasses, at the bottom of which there was nothing to see, let alone Kronstadt!"

Vinegar

The best vinegars can cost $8 to $9 a bottle these days, but most vinegars average $3 to $4. There are so many vinegars on the market that the choice is bewildering. In one store alone I counted over eighty, including the basic red and white vinegars plus a host of concoctions flavored with marigold, raspberry, lavender, green peppercorns, shallots, and even lemon juice. Some of these fancy mixtures are simply gimmicks, expensive ones at that.

Vinaigre means sour wine. It is produced by acid fermentation of fresh wine. Malt vinegar is made from liquor from fermented potatoes or grains; cider vinegar from cider. Chinese and Japanese sweet-sour vinegars are made from fermented rice wine — sake. The best vinegars are allowed to mature naturally and are not pasteurized or treated with chemicals. Cheap vinegars are often inferior, synthetic, and unpleasantly flavored.

Vinegar can be made at home if you have a vinegar "mother." This is a fungus that is alive in wine and will turn leftover wines into vinegar as the bacteria turns the alcohol into acetic acid. Vinegar mothers are not sold in stores; a mother can be made by adding a tablespoon or two of an unpasteurized vinegar, such as an imported French Orleans vinegar, to a wine that has not been treated with preservatives. Jug wines have usually been so treated and should be avoided for this purpose. The best container to use is an earthenware jar with a loose-fitting lid so that air can get in. A film forms on top of the wine and eventually sinks into the liquid, forming a pancake shape. This is the mother. More pancakes form — these are mothers that can be given to friends or saved to start another batch. When the vinegar is ready, it will be absolutely clear with a good aroma. It can then be poured into a bottle and sealed.

Meanwhile, for those who have not the time or inclination to make their own, there are many excellent buys on the market. I tasted over eighty vinegars to find the ones I liked, using a sugar cube dipped into the vinegar to make them palatable.

Red wine vinegars have many uses. They are good for salads and for deglazing the pan after frying calf's liver, veal chops, or chicken. They can be used to cut the oiliness of fish, such as mackerel or bluefish, and to make vinaigrette sauce. They should not be used for pale sauces, such as mayonnaise or hollandaise sauce, because they will turn them a strange pink.

French wine vinegars from Orléans are very pure. In red wine vinegars,

Pommery Bordeaux, Paul Corcellet, and Pikarome are like wine, aromatic and pure. Also recommended are Sasso, Maxims, and Alain Chapel, very rich and smooth, and Vine Village, an American vinegar. Crabtree & Evelyn and Heinz, an inexpensive supermarket brand, are both pleasant. Berio is sweet and, like Troisgros and Desseaux Fils, the favorites of many chefs, lacks the distinguishing winy taste of the Pommery, Corcellet, and Pikarome. But these are good all-purpose vinegars. Bertolli, Spice Islands, and Pouret are well-rounded all-purpose vinegars but a little harsh. Michel Guérard's red wine vinegar is surprisingly harsh, and Madre Siciliani is even harsher.

Of red wine tarragon vinegars, Soleillou is absolutely delicious, with much character and a fresh tarragon taste. Three other pleasant and recommended brands are Vinaigreries du Lion, Crabtree & Evelyn, and Pouret.

There are fewer Italian vinegars, and they are made under strict government supervision and slowly aged in wood. Badia a Coltibuono, made from Chianti Classico wine, is aged a minimum of three years in oak and is a superb vinegar, one of my favorites.

In addition, there are rich, red Italian vinegars, so mellow that they don't interfere with the taste of wine. When mixed with Tuscan olive oil they need no other flavorings on a green salad. Some people even use them on strawberries sprinkled with pepper. They come from Modena and are aged in wood barrels for ten to twenty years, becoming a dense, deep, rich brown color. By law the vinegar must be at least twenty years old when it is sold. Of these, the one I like best is Monari. It is the least sweet of the three tasted, which included Fini, my next best choice, and Duke of Modena, a light *balsamico*.

The best sherry vinegars come from Spain. They are aged in wood, some as long as twenty-five years, and have a distinctive flavor that goes well with oils such as walnut or hazelnut for salads. Recommended brands include La Bodega, Fernández Sherry vinegar, and Racimo Vintage Sherry wine. Jerez de la Frontera makes a fine twenty-five-year-old vinegar that is sold in numbered bottles and is excellent for making gazpacho. The French firm of Pommery also makes a top-quality sherry vinegar sold in a crock bottle.

White wine vinegars are used for mayonnaise, béarnaise, hollandaise, and horseradish sauces. There are many good ones flavored with tarragon on the market. The best are made by Fines Herbes, La Taste, and House of Herbs, all very tarragony and pleasant. Desseaux Fils from Orléans and Pikarome are also mild and sweet. Heinz white wine vinegar, an inexpensive supermarket brand, ranked with the much higher-priced Michel Guérard's and Crabtree & Evelyn, both pleasant. I did not like Raoul Gey or Maxims, both medicinal and harsh.

In general, it is better to make your own herb vinegars by putting fresh tarragon, thyme, mint, or basil into a jar of white wine vinegar. Vinegar flavored with chilies steeped in it for a couple of weeks is good for shellfish.

Green peppercorn and garlic are two popular combinations that are appearing on the market these days, but they are a waste of money. You are better off flavoring your own — cheaper with superior results. Fruit vinegars such as raspberry, blueberry, or pear are good for sauces or salad dressings. You can make these yourself by macerating fruits in vinegars, straining, and storing them. They will keep for months. Paul Corcellet's raspberry vinegar, however, is recommended. It is delicious on salad and with calf's liver.

Rice vinegars are used in Japanese and Chinese cooking. Rice vinegar is sweet and is good in cucumber and radish salads and on Japanese rice. A recommended brand is Ka-Me.

Distilled spirit vinegar is a tasteless white vinegar used for pickling. It is very inexpensive and basic.

Cider vinegar can be used for pickles and chutneys but does not do for salads or sauces. Beaufor makes a pleasant one from French cider.

Malt vinegars, made from barley grain and cider vinegar, can either lack character or have too much. Recommended ones are HP Malt or Elleseys. Malt vinegar is good for pickling and is colored brown with caramel, not from aging.

In England, vinegar is still served in a cruet on the tables of cafes and is sprinkled liberally on fish and chips.

Fish

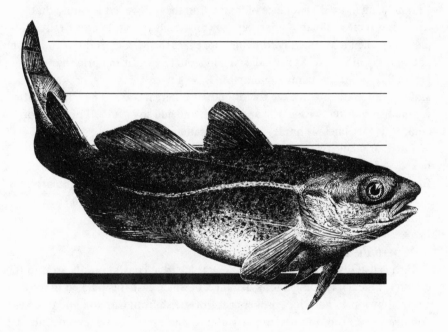

Introduction

Americans are slowly becoming fish eaters. In recent years there has been a steady increase in the consumption of fish, especially of once-ignored varieties, because fish is both low in fat and cholesterol and easy to digest. Yet the choice in many supermarkets is still limited to frozen fish sticks despite the fact that there are over five hundred species of fish and shellfish in wholesale markets in the United States.

Not only is fish high in protein and low in fat, it is also extremely versatile for cooking. When it's really fresh — straight out of the water — there's nothing like fish cooked absolutely plain, brought sizzling to the table and served with nothing more than a piece of lemon. But the fish we eat is rarely that fresh, and there are many other ways to enhance its flavor. White-flesh fish is delicious when marinated before it is cooked, as the Mexicans do — in lemon and orange juice — or Moroccan style, in a mixture of fresh coriander and garlic. Spices such as cumin, cinnamon, fresh ginger, tomatoes, onions, garlic, and soy sauce all enhance the flavor in their different ways. The Chinese stir-fry the fish quickly, with garlic and ginger, and add soy sauce. This kind of cooking is fast, cheap, simple — and non-fattening.

Large or whole fish such as red snapper or striped bass can be scored and baked after being marinated first in lemon or lime juice, or in a mixture of fresh ginger and garlic in soy sauce. Fresh tuna and swordfish can be broiled, basted with oil, and served plain or with an herb butter. Small fish such as whiting are good deep-fried and served with lemon.

Where Fish Comes From

Fish is usually brought to the cities by truck from coastal points around the country, unless it is going a long distance, in which case it is packed in ice and shipped by air. In addition, brokers get frozen fish from Canada and overseas countries — European ones, in particular — and store it in warehouses for sale by local dealers or wholesalers.

Fresh salmon is brought to cities in the United States by air from the West Coast and Norway; trout comes from Colorado by air or is trucked in, often live, from local trout farms.

If the fish are large they are usually eviscerated on the ships at the moment they are caught, because spoilage starts in their stomachs. Florida red snapper, for example, is gutted right on the fishing vessel and sometimes ice is then placed in the stomach cavity. Local fish is not always gutted if it is not being shipped out of the area.

In the Market

Fish is sold whole, with head, scales and intestines intact, or eviscerated, without the entrails and sometimes without the gills. It can also come without the head, tail, or fins, skinned or partially skinned, in fillets or steaks.

Most fish have a shelf life of about five days if caught within forty-eight hours of delivery. But fish can take ten days or more before reaching the store from the moment it is caught, because it is sometimes stored chilled on the fishing boat. So the fish in our stores is not always as fresh as it might be, and it can sometimes be very stale when it gets to the market even though it will have been kept properly on the boat.

One of the most disconcerting experiences I ever had was in Hammerfest, Norway, a town that subsists on its fishing industry. It was impossible during the two days I spent to get fresh fish anywhere. All of it was frozen on the boats at sea. Luckily, this is not the case here, but neither is it usually possible to run down to the harbor or wholesaler and get absolutely fresh fish caught only a few hours earlier.

When you walk into a fishmonger's, the store should have the fragrant sea-weedy smell of fresh seafood, not a stale, fishy smell. So be sure to buy from a reliable fishmonger who has a good turnover.

The eyes of a whole fish should be brilliant and clear. If they are cloudy, dimmed, or sunken, the fish is not fresh. Bloody eyes mean the fish has been mishandled or badly stored. The exception is red snapper, which has naturally red eyes.

Fish should always smell fresh, not fishy. Lift up the gills — the flaps behind the eyes — if you are at all in doubt about a whole fish. They should be bright red. As the fish gets staler, the gills turn pink, then brown or even green-gray. The skin should be shiny and unblemished, and if pressed should leave no indentation mark. The scales should be glistening and firmly attached, not loose, the flesh firm and resilient. When you hold a fish it should be stiff, not limp.

It is more difficult to tell if fillets are fresh. They should smell fresh, be firm textured, and look translucent. They are very perishable — sometimes they are dipped in brine to keep them fresh looking — and are more expensive than unfilleted fish. It's a better buy to get the fish whole and fillet it yourself or have the fishmonger do it for you. Or cook it whole; the bones will give the flesh more flavor.

When buying steaks look for center cuts; they are more tender than the tail. The surface should be moist, not dried out, and there should be no brownish tinge at the edges.

Avoid frozen fish because it will not have the flavor or texture of fresh. But if you must buy it, make sure the package is solid. If it is misshapen it may have thawed and been refrozen. This could happen for a variety of reasons;

perhaps the boxes stood at room temperature before being put in the freezer, for example.

If you have asked the fishmonger to cut off the head and tail, take them with you for making court bouillon (see below), soup, or sauces.

Avoid fish that has been buried in ice in the display case. The ice can cause "burns" on the flesh. Fish that has been frozen and thawed will have opaque, not translucent, flesh and will be dry and textureless when cooked.

In supermarkets fish are often dated with an expiration date of one day after they have arrived. Thursday and Friday are the best days for buying fish, because there is more demand on those days. Monday is the worst because fish is not generally delivered to the stores on weekends.

In the Kitchen

The most appealing thing about many fish dishes is their simplicity. Most of the recipes are quick and easy and are excellent for people who must cook dinner after a day's work.

When you have brought your fish home, rinse it in cold water, pat it dry with paper towels, and squeeze lemon juice on it. Place it in a covered dish and refrigerate until you are ready to use it, preferably as soon as possible.

When broiling whole fish, if it is thick fleshed, make three slits in the skin so that it does not burst while cooking. Paint the fish with oil and turn only once. Be careful not to overcook or the fish will fall apart. Be sure to brush with oil or the fish may stick to the rack underneath. Broil in a thoroughly preheated oven.

For cooking fish à la meunière, in hot butter, be careful not to get the butter too hot or it will lose its nutty flavor and burn. On the other hand, if the butter is not hot enough, the fish won't fry but will steam and become soft. The fish should be golden brown when cooked. Getting this perfect is simply a matter of practice. Serve the fish with parsley and lemon.

For poaching fish, the essential thing is a court bouillon that will impart flavor to the fish while it cooks. Great care must be taken not to boil the fish or it will fall apart. The water should merely "shudder." With the exception of turbot, which is cooked in a white court bouillon (milk is added), the following court bouillon is suitable for any kind of fish to be poached. The quantities will vary according to the size of fish and the size of the kettle you are poaching it in.

Court Bouillon

1	onion, coarsely chopped
2	carrots, sliced
	Herb bouquet
	Coarse salt and freshly ground pepper to taste
5	cups water
1¼	cups white wine
1	tablespoon white wine vinegar

1. Bring all ingredients to a boil in a fish kettle and simmer, covered, for 30 minutes. Allow to cool.

2. When ready to cook the fish, put it into the cool court bouillon and bring gently to a shudder. Turn down heat and simmer very gently until the fish is cooked.

Note: If possible, add fish heads or other parts to this and simmer. Remove them before adding the fish.

Bass and Red Snapper

Bass and red snapper are tailor-made for the table. Cooked whole on a bed of seaweed, broiled on fennel stalks over coals, or baked with oranges, lemons, or herbs, they are easy to prepare and make a simple course for a dinner party. They have sweet, firm white flesh and are easy to stuff, the cavity held together with toothpicks or even left open. They can also be poached in a court bouillon and served simply with maître d'hôtel butter or hollandaise sauce.

Red snapper is found in the Pacific, the Gulf of Mexico, and in the Atlantic. There are 250 species in this family, which includes the gray snapper and yellowtail snapper, but the one with the most flavor is the red.

When buying red snapper, don't be put off because the eyes are red. This is their natural condition and does not mean the fish isn't fresh. Smaller snapper are sold whole, and they should be firm and slithery, with no fishy smell. Larger snapper are sometimes cut into steaks or fillets. These, too, should smell fresh and be firm and springy to the touch.

Along with red snapper, striped bass (called rockfish in the South) is one of our most popular fish. It can be baked and served with beurre blanc or with a simple sauce such as fines herbes butter (using chopped herbs such as parsley, chives, chervil, tarragon, and watercress) melted and swirled over gentle heat with heavy cream. Use about half a cup of cream to a quarter of a pound of butter. Season with salt, pepper, and lemon juice to taste.

Striped bass is an inshore fish that is found all along the coast from the Gulf of Mexico to the Gulf of St. Lawrence. Unfortunately, bass caught in polluted waters off metropolitan areas can sometimes have a peculiar taste, even though it may be perfectly fresh. Because this fish manages to survive in the worst waters, it can sometimes take on the unappetizing flavor of oil slick or fuel oil. Not long ago, such a fish was served in one of Manhattan's finest restaurants. It could not have been fresher nor more perfectly cooked and presented, cold and jellied with a ring of thinly sliced cucumbers, fennel leaves, and green mayonnaise. But the taste of oil overpowered it, and it was virtually inedible — to the distress of both the diners and the chef. If the chef had known exactly where the bass had been caught, this might have been avoided. The best bass comes from the least polluted waters. PCB contamination is also a factor and can affect bluefish, white perch, white catfish, and American eels.

Alice B. Toklas once made a stuffed bass for Picasso, the recipe for which she gives in her cookbook. When he saw it he remarked sadly that he thought it was a beautiful dish that would have been much more appropriate for Matisse.

Striped Bass Baked in Lettuce

YIELD: 4 Servings

1	3-to-4-pound striped bass
	Juice of 1 lemon
¼	cup chopped basil or tarragon
	Coarse salt and freshly ground pepper to taste
2	heads Boston lettuce
1	tablespoon peanut or vegetable oil
¼	cup chopped shallots
1	tablespoon butter
1	lime, sliced
	A few extra basil or tarragon leaves for garnish

1. Preheat oven to 350 degrees. Wipe the bass dry with paper towels and squeeze lemon juice inside and out.

2. Place the basil or tarragon leaves, salt, and pepper in the cavity.

3. Blanch the lettuce leaves in boiling water. Drain. Wrap the bass in the lettuce leaves so that it is entirely covered except for the tail.

4. Oil a baking dish and sprinkle with half the shallots. Place the fish on top and sprinkle with remaining shallots. Dot with pieces of butter.

5. Cover with foil and bake for 20 to 30 minutes or until the fish flakes when tested with a fork. Serve garnished with lime slices and basil or tarragon leaves.

Note: This dish is good served with a Hollandaise Sauce (page 197).

Baked Fish Yucatan Style

YIELD: 4 Servings

1	3-to-4-pound red snapper or striped bass
	Juice of 1 lemon
	Juice of 1 orange
	Coarse salt and freshly ground pepper to taste
½	cup olive oil
1	small onion, coarsely chopped
1	clove garlic
4	tomatoes, peeled
2	green chilies, peeled
	Dash of ground cinnamon
	Dash of ground cloves
1	cup water
2	teaspoons capers
6	pimiento-stuffed olives, sliced

1. Marinate the fish in the lemon and orange juice, salt, and pepper for 1 hour.

2. Meanwhile, in a blender, combine the remaining ingredients except the capers and olives. Reduce to a purée. Put the mixture in a saucepan and simmer for 10 to 15 minutes or until thick.

3. In a heavy pan large enough to hold the fish easily, put some of the purée. Arrange the fish over the top and cover with the rest of the mixture. Simmer the fish, uncovered, until cooked. Remove to a heated dish, pour on the sauce, and decorate with capers and olives. Serve with rice.

Whole Baked Fish Moroccan Style

YIELD: 4 to 6 Servings

1	bunch fresh coriander
2	cloves garlic
2	tablespoons white wine vinegar
	Juice of 1 lemon or lime
1	tablespoon paprika
1	tablespoon ground cumin
½	teaspoon red pepper flakes
	Coarse salt and freshly ground pepper to taste
2	tablespoons olive oil
1	4-pound whole fish, such as striped bass or red snapper, head and tail intact
1	lemon, sliced

1. Reserve a few sprigs of coriander for garnishing and combine all the ingredients except the fish and lemon in an electric blender and mix until smooth. With a sharp knife, make three slashes in the skin. Smear the mixture in the fish cavity and over the skin. Marinate at room temperature for about 2 hours.

2. Preheat the broiler. Broil the fish for about 10 minutes on each side, depending on the thickness of the fish, or until cooked. Arrange on a serving platter and garnish with coriander and lemon slices.

Steamed Red Snapper with Tarragon

YIELD: 4 Servings

1	3-to-4-pound red snapper
2	lemons
1	bunch fresh tarragon
	Approximately 1 cup dry white wine
	Coarse salt and freshly ground pepper to taste

1. Wipe the snapper dry inside and out. Squeeze the juice of 1 lemon over the surface and cavity. Place half the tarragon, including the stalks, inside the fish.

2. Steam the fish over the white wine until cooked. Season with salt and pepper, garnish with the rest of the tarragon and lemon wedges, and serve.

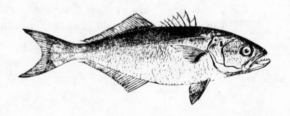

Big Fish (Swordfish, Tilefish, and Tuna)

In the summer, big fish are especially good eaten as steaks or kebabs, broiled outdoors over coals. The big three we see most often in the market are swordfish, tuna, and tilefish. To a lesser extent, there is mako shark. Shark steaks, like those of the other three, can be marinated in olive oil and herbs, grilled and served with lemon juice. Mako shark is sometimes sold as swordfish, but its flesh is darker and not as delicate. Whole swordfish steaks can be distinguished from mako shark steaks by their dark, fatty spots and firmer textured flesh.

Swordfish has white, firm, fine-grained flesh. It swims in all the great oceans and can be recognized by its long sword, dark back, and silver belly. It is in season during the summer and fall.

Swordfish steaks can be broiled with garlic butter or olive oil and lemon juice or served garnished with anchovies, tomatoes, and olives. Marinate the steaks first in herbs and olive oil.

Tilefish is a North Atlantic fish with sweet, succulent flesh that tastes almost like lobster. Its skin is spotted like a pointillist painting. Tilefish feed on lobster and red crabs, which give their flesh its flavor. Their steaks are similar to those of halibut and respond well to strong, spicy sauces. Small tilefish are sold whole, while larger ones, weighing 7 to 40 pounds, are cut into steaks.

Tuna, found in the Atlantic and the Pacific, is a member of the mackerel family and is a huge fish with silver skin. It is available all year round. Americans tend to be prejudiced against the red meat variety. They like the albacore tuna best, and this is used largely for canning because of its white meat.

Raw tuna looks like raw beef. It can be poached, baked, or cooked like meat. Don't overcook it or the meat will become dry. It is good raw for sushi or sashimi, but it must be very fresh. Cut it thinly against the grain and serve with *wasabi*, Japanese green horseradish, and thinly sliced fresh ginger. It is also good raw with a vinaigrette dressing made with olive oil, mustard, and red wine vinegar.

Sautéed Tunafish Steak

YIELD: 2 Servings

1	pound tuna
	Flour for dredging
2	tablespoons olive oil
3	green peppers, sliced
3	tomatoes, chopped
1	tablespoon chopped fresh parsley
¼	teaspoon thyme
2	teaspoons paprika
	Coarse salt and freshly ground pepper to taste
1	cup dry white wine

1. Dredge the tuna in flour. Heat the oil in a large skillet and brown the tuna on both sides. Remove and set aside.

2. Add the peppers and tomatoes and cook until the peppers have softened. Return the tuna to the pan and add the parsley, thyme, paprika, and salt and pepper. Cook 10 minutes and add the wine. Cover and simmer for 30 minutes.

3. Place the tuna on a serving dish and pour the sauce over it.

Broiled Swordfish Steaks

YIELD: 4 Servings

2	swordfish steaks, 1½ inches thick, about 2 pounds in all
1	clove garlic, minced
1	teaspoon rosemary
¼	cup olive oil
	Freshly ground pepper to taste
1	lemon, quartered

1. Marinate the steaks in a mixture of the garlic, rosemary, oil, and pepper for 1 hour.

2. Heat the coals in an outdoor grill. Broil the steaks for about 6 minutes on each side or until the flesh flakes when tested with a fork. Take care not to dry out the steaks. Serve with the lemon quarters.

Tuna, Swordfish, or Tilefish en Brochette

2 pounds tuna, swordfish, or tilefish
8 mushroom caps
1 small onion, quartered
2 green peppers, sliced in eighths
½ cup olive oil
Juice of 2 lemons
Coarse salt and freshly ground pepper to taste
Sauce
1 cup plain yogurt
¼ cup finely chopped fresh coriander or basil
Juice of 1 lemon or lime
Coarse salt and freshly ground pepper to taste

1. Cut the fish into 1½-inch cubes. Thread on large skewers, alternating fish and vegetables.

2. Combine the olive oil, lemon juice, salt, and pepper in a small bowl. Brush the fish with the mixture and marinate for 30 minutes. Meanwhile, get the coals ready or heat the broiler.

3. Broil for 5 minutes on each side.

4. Serve the fish on skewers or slide the kebabs off onto a serving plate. Combine the sauce ingredients and serve the sauce separately.

Tilefish Steak Creole Style

1½ tablespoons olive oil
1 large onion, finely chopped
1 clove garlic, minced
2 sweet peppers, sliced
1 or 2 hot green or red chilies, minced
1 cup peeled and seeded tomatoes, with their juice
¾ pound okra, trimmed
1 1½-to-2-pound tilefish steak, halved vertically
Coarse salt and freshly ground pepper to taste
2 tablespoons chopped fresh parsley

1. Heat the oil in a large heavy skillet and gently sauté the onion with the garlic, peppers, and chilies until the onions have softened.

2. Add the tomatoes and okra, cover, and simmer for 10 minutes, stirring occasionally.

3. Add the tilefish. Spoon the sauce over the fish so that it is covered. Cover the skillet and simmer for another 10 to 15 minutes or until the fish is cooked.

4. Season with salt and pepper, transfer to a heated dish, sprinkle with parsley, and serve.

Note: This recipe works well with halibut steaks.

Caviar

"If you must give yourself the illusion that you are impressing everyone by serving caviar, then you must do so in the grand style by providing your guests with half a dozen tins of the stuff into which they can dip freely, even if they are a little bit sick afterwards." So says André Launay in *Posh Food* (Penguin, 1964), and I agree. One of the most enjoyable parties I ever went to was given by a friend who owns an art gallery. Every year one of his rich clients would send him a pound tin of beluga. After a few mouthfuls the select group of guests could no longer keep up the pretense of not being greedy, and we ate until we thought we could eat no more, yet kept on eating until there was nothing left.

Mr. Launay, who was writing in 1964, brings up the price of caviar — a subject most people would not discuss today. Beluga in England in those days cost 20 shillings — around $2 an ounce; sevruga, 15 shillings. "Over the counter it is usually sold in glass or earthenware jars which are usually return-able (they cost about 12 shillings themselves). Pressed caviare is sold in tubes, like toothpaste, but without free gift offers."

Those were the days. Today, beluga runs closer to $30 an ounce.

Caviar is best eaten plain with buttered toast. If it is top quality it needs no lemon, chopped onion, or hard-boiled eggs. Lumpfish caviar, on the other hand, can be improved by these additions. Champagne or vodka are the most complementary drinks. Danish akvavit goes well with lumpfish caviar.

Fresh caviar does not come in vacuum-sealed jars. The caviar in these has usually been "cooked" by being pasteurized and is often heavily salted and chewy.

Fresh caviar is sold in tins or small jars. It should not smell metallic, stale, or fishy — it should have no smell at all. The eggs should be glistening and firm, not mushy, milky, or dull. The cans have codes for color: 000 for lightest, 00 for medium, and 0 for darkest. The lightest gray is usually the most prized, but caviar varies so much from batch to batch that color is not ultimately a good criterion for judging it. Ask for the can to be opened before you take it home so that you can look for yourself.

Here is a brief guide to the various kinds of caviar on the market.

Beluga Caviar

This is the highest priced caviar and comes from a high grade of sturgeon, originating in the Caspian Sea. It has the largest eggs of all the black caviar. The color ranges from bluish-white to deep black. The best grade is malossol, meaning lightly salted.

Osetra Caviar

Some people prefer this caviar over beluga. It has smaller eggs, and the color varies from golden brown to dark green or gray.

Sevruga Caviar

This caviar comes from the roe of the smallest sturgeon. The eggs are very dark green or near black.

Saltwater Salmon Caviar

One of the less expensive types, this caviar has large red eggs and comes from Russia, Alaska, and the Pacific.

Freshwater Salmon Caviar

These eggs are paler and more orange in color than saltwater salmon caviar. This caviar comes from salmon that are caught during migration upriver.

Pressed Caviar

Because the eggs are squashed, this is slightly cheaper than whole-egg caviar. Pressed caviar is in a solid mass, it is saltier than malossol but more intense.

American Caviar

Much less expensive than Russian or Iranian and less salty, American caviar comes in black and golden colors and is less pronounced in flavor.

Blini, Russian buckwheat pancakes, are delicious with red or black caviar, melted butter, and sour cream, served with champagne. I love them on New Year's Eve.

Blini with Red Caviar

YIELD: 6 to 8 Servings

1½	cups milk
1	package granular yeast
1½	cups unbleached white flour
½	cup buckwheat flour
½	teaspoon salt
1	teaspoon sugar
4	eggs, separated
¼	pound butter, melted
6	ounces red caviar
2	cups sour cream

1. Scald the milk and set aside.
2. Dissolve the yeast in ¼ cup warm water.
3. Sift the white flour into a bowl, add the buckwheat flour, salt, and sugar.
4. Beat the egg yolks until thick and sticky. When the milk has cooled to lukewarm, add the yolks and 3 tablespoons of the melted butter. Add the yeast. Mix well and pour into the flour. Mix thoroughly, removing any lumps. Set aside in a warm place for about 2 hours, or until doubled in bulk.
5. Whip the egg whites until they stand in stiff peaks. Fold them into the batter.
6. Lightly butter a small frying pan. Pour in just enough of the pancake mixture to coat the bottom of the pan. When the mixture begins to bubble, turn the pancake over and cook lightly on the other side.
7. Wrap the pancakes in a napkin and keep them warm in the oven while you cook the others. Serve in a pile, wrapped in a napkin.
8. Serve the caviar, the sour cream, and the remaining melted butter in small bowls on the table.
9. Each person puts a pancake on a plate, butters it, adds sour cream and caviar, and rolls it like a crêpe.

Codfish and Haddock

Cod is a large, handsome fish with a poor image. It is often ruined by institutional cooking — overcooked until mushy and served with a floury sauce, making the sick feel even worse.

But cod has large, firm flakes and keeps its texture well. It is good lightly poached or fried in batter and served with sauces flavored with dill, fines herbes or mustard, or beurre blanc, or cold with aïoli, garlic-flavored mayonnaise (page 197). Fish pies, croquettes, and fish cakes are also excellent made with cod.

"There are grounds for thinking that the European colonization of North America was prompted to a large extent by the existence of large stocks of cod on that side of the Atlantic," writes Alan Davidson in *North Atlantic Seafood*. "Cape Cod was of course named for the cod; and Boston, 'the home of the beans and the cod,' has an effigy of the 'sacred cod' from which the city derived much of its wealth, hanging in the State House. . . . Shed, therefore, any ideas that the cod is an ordinary fish and invest the next piece of cod you buy with the exciting qualities which are its by right."

The cod family is a large family of white-fleshed fish that includes haddock. These cold-water fish are at their best in winter, and they should be very fresh. Codfish has a greenish-tinged and mottled-brown skin, with a white belly. It is usually sold as steaks and fillets. Avoid those with pinkish or yellow patches. Frozen cod does not have as good a flavor as fresh.

Cod is the most important salt-water fish besides herring, and salt cod has almost forced fresh cod off the market. Once dried and salted, it keeps for months. Overfishing threatens cod, with the trawlers dragging the sea bed clean and leaving no younger fish to grow. Salt cod, however, remains an excellent and cheap source of fish and is generally to be found in ethnic markets. Choose plump, soft pieces and be sure to soak them overnight and rinse them thoroughly in several changes of water before cooking them. Avoid stringy tail ends of dried cod; sometimes they never lose their tough, leathery quality when cooked.

Haddock, also victimized by overfishing, is light and firm and similar to cod in appearance, although the skin is grayer. Many people think it superior to cod. It is at its best in winter and early spring. Cooking methods for cod can be used for haddock.

Haddock is also sold smoked and is sometimes known as finnan haddie, after Findon, in Aberdeen, where the method of smoking this fish was first developed. Avoid those fillets that are an unlikely bright yellow; they have been dyed and treated with artificial smoke flavor. Properly smoked haddock has just a faint smoked hue. Smoked haddock is broiled or poached in water or milk and served dotted with butter.

Spicy Fish Cakes

1 pound fresh cod, cooked and flaked
1 pound potatoes, cooked and mashed
2 tablespoons butter
Coarse salt and freshly ground pepper to taste
1 small green chili, diced
1 egg, beaten
1 cup fine bread crumbs
½ teaspoon cayenne pepper
Approximately ½ cup peanut or vegetable oil

1. Combine the cod, potatoes, butter, salt, pepper, and chili in a bowl and mix well.

2. Form the mixture into slightly flattened balls about 2 inches in diameter. Roll in beaten egg and bread crumbs seasoned with cayenne.

3. Heat the oil in a skillet and fry the fish cakes until golden on all sides.

Frittura Mista

(Deep-fried Baccala and Vegetables)

1 pound thick baccala (salt cod)
1 head cauliflower
2 medium zucchini
2 or 3 stalks celery, cut into 1-inch pieces
3 large eggs, separated
3 tablespoons flour
Water
Coarse salt and freshly ground pepper to taste
Vegetable oil for deep frying
1 small piece bread
3 tablespoons vinegar
Lemon wedges

1. Soak the salt cod overnight in several changes of water. Rinse thoroughly and cut into 2-inch pieces.

2. Divide the cauliflower into flowerets. Cut the zucchini into quarters lengthwise and cut each strip into four pieces.

3. Blanch the cauliflower, zucchini, and celery and drain.

4. In a mixing bowl, beat the egg yolks. Add the flour and enough water to make a soft batter. Season with salt and pepper. Whip the egg whites until stiff and fold into the batter. Do not stir rapidly or the batter will fall.

6. Heat the oil. Soak the piece of bread in the vinegar and drop it into the oil. When it rises to the surface the oil is ready (this will also purify the oil).

7. Dip the vegetables into the batter and drop them into the hot oil without crowding. Fry until golden, remove with tongs, and drain on paper towels. Then cook the fish the same way. Keep warm until all the pieces are done. Serve with lemon wedges.

Flat Fish (Flounder, Halibut, Sole, and Turbot)

Within this odd-looking family — their flat bodies shaped like the sole of a shoe, underbellies white and eyes that both lie on the same side of the head — there is enormous variety. These strange fish lurk on the seabed half buried in the sand — "all profile," as Jean Cocteau said. In order better to watch what is going on above, their eyes are placed on top of their heads. When flat fish are alarmed, they burrow further, "sanding," fishermen call it. And once these fish have sanded they are well nigh impossible to catch.

Dover sole and turbot are the sweetest and most delicate of flat fish and are available year round, flown in from Europe because they are not found on the American side of the Atlantic. But these are by no means the only small flat fish worth eating. The more common of the lesser strains, known collectively in America as flounder, includes dab, plaice, winter and summer flounder, and gray or lemon sole. These fish sell for less than half, or even a third, the cost of their aristocratic cousins.

Perhaps the most underrated flat fish, often overlooked in favor of the more glamorous and expensive members of its family, is the larger fish, halibut. Sole and turbot cost twice the price and are most frequently to be found on the tables of high-priced restaurants. Halibut, however, is a delicate and close-textured fish, the taste less refined than either sole or turbot but much better than its budget cousin, flounder. A lean and non-fatty fish, halibut is available all year round.

Dover sole and turbot are the inspiration for some of the greatest French classic dishes. They are best cooked unfilleted because the bones add flavor, but even without the bones they remain the kings of flat fish. They can be simply fried in butter à la meunière and sprinkled with fresh herbs, poached in white wine, and, if you like, served Florentine style on a bed of fresh spinach. But sole and turbot dishes should be simple, not, as some French cookbooks suggest, served with foie gras and truffles or what-have-you — "A mere plinth for a mound of 100 franc notes," says Alan Davidson.

Dover sole can be recognized by its sepia-colored skin marked by dark blotches. Turbot has a mottled dark gray skin and can grow to a huge size. Sometimes turbot are too big to buy whole so they are sold in fillets. Whenever buying fillets, avoid pieces with a bluish tinge. They will be stale. There is no point in buying frozen flat fish; it will be dry and tasteless.

Of all the flat fish, halibut is far and away the largest. It can weigh as much as 600 pounds and measure 6 feet long. This is exceptional, though; most of the big ones weigh around 100 pounds or less. The smaller fish weigh as as little as 3 pounds. Halibut is found only in northern waters and is a darkish brown color on top with a white belly.

The fine texture of halibut makes an excellent ceviche for summer dinners. Marinate cubes of the fish in lemon juice and olive oil with chopped fresh green chilies, coriander or parsley, and red or green peppers. This fish takes well to strong seasonings, such as garlic, onions, capers, and rosemary or thyme, and is especially good in spicy sauces. It can be poached or baked in the oven.

Cold poached halibut can be made into a salad with diced boiled potatoes, hard-boiled eggs, pickles, and pimiento-stuffed olives and dressed with olive oil and lemon juice or a mustardy mayonnaise.

Madame Prunier, whose famous Paris fish restaurant attracted the richest and most fashionable of the epoch, including Sarah Bernhardt, César Franck, Oscar Wilde, and Clemenceau, discovered the pleasures of halibut when she opened a branch of her restaurant in London in 1935. "This fish, which is very little known in France, is very much appreciated in England and Holland for the sake of its delicate and palatable flesh," she writes in *Madame Prunier's Fish Cook Book*. "It is a little like brill in appearance, but longer, its shape being more like that of a very large lemon sole. The various ways of preparing small turbot and the different preparations of sole and fillets of sole can be applied to the halibut."

Large halibut make superb steaks; a thick steak will serve two for dinner. And fresh herbs, such as rosemary, tarragon, and basil, are perfect complementary herbs.

Broiled Halibut Steaks with Rosemary YIELD: 4 Servings

2	medium halibut steaks, about 2 to 2½ pounds, 1½ inches thick
¼	cup olive oil
	Freshly ground pepper to taste
2	teaspoons fresh rosemary (or 1 teaspoon dried)

1. Preheat the broiler or charcoal grill.

2. Brush the steaks with the olive oil, and grind on liberal amounts of pepper. Press the rosemary into the flesh on both sides.

3. Broil the steaks for 6 to 7 minutes on each side, turning once.

Note: These steaks may also be baked in a preheated oven at 400 degrees for 15 to 20 minutes without being turned.

Halibut with Anchovies

3	tablespoons olive oil
1	small onion, finely chopped
2	flat anchovy fillets
2	tablespoons chopped flat-leaf parsley
	Freshly ground pepper to taste
2	halibut steaks, 1 inch thick (about ¼ pound each)
	Flour for dredging

1. Heat 1 tablespoon oil in a small frying pan and sauté the onions without browning until soft. Add the anchovies and parsley and sauté, mashing the anchovies with a wooden spoon until they have mixed thoroughly with the onions. Season with pepper.

2. Meanwhile, dredge the steaks lightly with the flour, shaking to remove excess. Heat remaining oil in a separate frying pan and fry the steaks until golden on both sides, taking care not to overcook them.

3. Remove the steaks from the pan with a slotted spatula and place on a heated serving dish or individual plates. Pour the anchovy-onion mixture over the top and serve.

Ceviche

YIELD: 4 Servings

1½	pounds fresh, firm-fleshed white fish fillets
1	cup fresh lime juice
1	Bermuda onion, thinly sliced
1	fresh green chili, diced
6	tablespoons olive oil
	Coarse salt and freshly ground pepper to taste
3	tablespoons chopped fresh coriander

1. Slice the fish thinly against the grain into 1-inch pieces. Arrange in a glass or china serving dish and toss with the lime juice.

2. Arrange the onion slices over the fish and sprinkle with the chili, olive oil, salt, pepper, and coriander.

3. Refrigerate, covered, for several hours or overnight, until the fish has turned opaque. Serve with salad, fresh bread, and chilled white wine.

Stir-Fried Fish Fillets

2   pounds fish fillets

4   tablespoons vegetable,
    peanut, or sesame oil

2   tablespoons chopped
    fresh ginger

1   clove garlic, finely
    chopped

4   scallions, including green
    part, chopped

1   green pepper, seeded and
    chopped

3   tablespoons soy sauce

1. Dry the fish fillets with paper towels and slice into pieces about 2 inches long. Heat the oil in a frying pan or wok and fry the ginger, garlic, scallions, and peppers for about 3 minutes, stirring so they don't burn.

2. Add the fish and fry for about 3 minutes or until it turns opaque. Add the soy sauce, stir well, and remove the mixture to a heated dish. Serve with rice and a green vegetable.

Poached Fish with Sorrel Purée

½   pound sorrel leaves

2   tablespoons butter

4   tablespoons heavy cream

1   small onion

    Bay leaf

    Strips of peel from 1
    lemon

    Black peppercorns

    Coarse salt

1   cup dry white wine

2   pounds flat fish, skinned,
    with heads on

1. Wash the sorrel leaves, pat dry, and sauté them in the butter. Put them in the blender with the cream and set aside.

2. Simmer the onion, bay leaf, lemon peel, peppercorns, and salt in the wine for about 5 minutes, covered. Add the fish and poach, at a very gentle simmer, for about 10 minutes or until cooked. Remove heads and bone — it is easy when fish is cooked. Keep warm.

3. Add enough of the poaching liquid to the mixture in the blender to blend until smooth. Reheat without boiling and serve either over the fish or separately. Boiled new potatoes go well with this dish.

Sole with Tarragon

1	tablespoon butter
6	shallots, chopped
1	cup tarragon leaves
8	fillets of sole
½	cup brandy
1	cup dry white wine
	Coarse salt and freshly ground pepper to taste

1. Preheat the oven to 350 degrees. Butter a shallow fireproof dish and add the shallots and tarragon.

2. Place the sole on top and pour in the brandy and white wine. Season with salt and pepper and bake, covered, for 20 to 30 minutes.

3. Place the sole on a serving dish. Pour the sauce into a small saucepan and reduce. Pour over the sole and serve.

Poached Turbot

1	3-to-4-pound turbot
	Approximately 1 cup milk
	Approximately 5 cups water
1	tablespoon butter
	Coarse salt and freshly ground pepper to taste
	Fresh parsley for garnish
1	lemon, sliced

1. With a sharp knife, make a deep incision along the backbone (the dark side) of the turbot. Place it on a rack in a fish steamer.

2. Combine the milk with the water and pour in just enough to cover the turbot. Slowly bring to a boil and simmer gently, not boiling but merely shuddering; otherwise the fish may fall apart.

3. Cook for 7 to 10 minutes a pound. Gently slide the fish off the rack onto a heated serving platter. Dot with the butter and season with salt and pepper. Garnish with parsley and lemon slices.

Note: This dish is good with Hollandaise Sauce (page 197) and boiled potatoes.

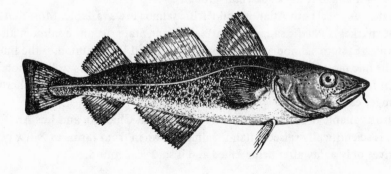

Fresh/Saltwater Fish
(Salmon, Shad, and Trout)

Salmon

Salmon was once a cheap fish and as prevalent on the table as chicken is today. It was so plentiful that servants in colonial America had clauses in their contracts stipulating that they could not be served salmon more than a certain number of times a week. Two centuries before, Elizabethan servants had objected to too many oysters. No wonder you can't get help these days.

Only in the last 25 years, because of dwindling numbers, has salmon climbed the culinary scale to become a luxury. At elegant spring and summer dinner parties it appears garnished with truffles and lobster sauce or in brilliant aspics on the buffet table. In New England, poached salmon, fresh green peas, and boiled new potatoes are a traditional Fourth of July treat.

Salmon steaks are served hot with hollandaise sauce or cold with cucumber salad. One of the new dishes which appeared on the menus of New York restaurants recently is raw salmon, cut paper-thin and served with a mustard dill sauce — or even plain, nouvelle-cuisine style, with nothing but lemon and freshly ground pepper.

Salmon used to glut rivers, lakes, and streams. They have traveled the Seine, the Thames, and the Rhine in quantity, and were even found in the Hudson. In the spawning season, salmon jammed the rivers of the Pacific Northwest so densely that one of the first traders there contended that he could cross on their backs.

Nowadays, pollution and overfishing have threatened the fish with extinction. The laws regulating fishing seasons have been made stricter, and efforts are being made to restock spawning grounds.

In the summer, both Atlantic and Pacific salmon are available. Most that is on the market is Pacific salmon from Washington State. Atlantic salmon, also known as Eastern salmon and including Scottish and Irish salmon, is the finest and the one most often sold smoked. The best Pacific salmon is troll salmon, caught from the sea where it has been feeding and not from the rivers, where it no longer eats when on its way to spawn.

Also available in major cities, such as New York, Chicago, and Los Angeles, is scientifically raised Atlantic salmon flown in from farms in Norway. It arrives only a day after being killed and is sold year round.

The season for Atlantic salmon starts in June and usually lasts until shortly after July 4. The Pacific salmon normally start their run in May and remain in season into the fall; by then the quality will have deteriorated. The usual size for fresh salmon is 7 to 12 pounds, with an average length of 4 feet. They are sold whole or in steaks or larger pieces cut to order for fillets. Small whole salmon from Washington State weighing about 2½ pounds are good for poaching whole; they serve four to six people.

The salmon are usually eviscerated after being caught and shipped packed in ice by air to major cities across the country or, if being sent to nearby destinations, packed in ice in trucks.

Most fishmongers sell salmon cut into steaks. These are good for broiling or sautéing. Salmon tails or small whole salmon can be baked or poached. I prefer salmon with the bones in, because they give the flesh flavor and they are not difficult to extricate when eating. But if you want fillets, the fishmonger will certainly cut them for you, usually for a small charge.

When buying whole salmon, choose those with a small head, broad shoulders, and a plump belly. The scales and eyes should be bright, the skin a silvery color. The upper side will be a light bluish gray with black spots. The flesh should be rose pink, with a buttery whitish substance between the flakes. Since salmon get soft and dull quickly, the most important clue is firmness: A fresh salmon is springy and firm to the touch.

The small coho salmon, not much larger than trout, are sometimes found in the markets, and they are delicious broiled, the cavity flavored with fennel or dill leaves. Larger salmon, sea bass, and striped bass may also be cooked this way.

Whole poached salmon, served hot or cold, is an ideal party dish. The salmon is skinned and decorated with lemon, parsley, dill, cucumber, hard-boiled egg, and tomatoes or coated with aspic and garnished.

To poach the salmon, use a fish kettle that will hold it comfortably. Never let the liquid boil; bring it to a shudder, cooking the salmon fast and gently, otherwise you will end up with dry, flaky meat. If you do not have a kettle, you can bake the fish whole in foil. Salmon is also good cut into chunks, brushed with oil or melted butter, and broiled over hot coals.

Hot salmon goes with hollandaise sauce, sauce mousseline, beurre blanc, beurre fines herbes (with tarragon and parsley), or anchovy butter. Steaks can be braised in red or white wine, or they can be broiled and served with sorrel sauce and new potatoes and steamed fresh green fava beans.

Cold salmon goes well with green mayonnaise, rémoulade sauce, or fresh horseradish mixed with whipped cream, all served with thinly sliced cucumbers and new potatoes. Leftover salmon is good for mousses, soufflés, croquettes, and quenelles.

There are innumerable recipes for salmon, and many early ones, perhaps to dress up this poor man's fish, are baroque. Salmon was served garnished with crawfish, quenelles of truffled forcemeat (stuffing), truffles "fashioned like olives," tiny *goujons* of sole, and small fried smelts. Escoffier, who gives a litany of such dishes in his cookbook, said he liked the fish best served plain.

The following recipes are simple and quick to make. The steaks and raw or marinated salmon require little preparation. The salmon in red wine takes a little longer to prepare, as does the poached salmon, because fish stock and garnishes are involved.

Chilled white wines are an excellent complement: Chablis, Montrachet, Meursault, Muscadet, Gewürztraminer, Vouvray, Pouilly-Fumé or Pouilly-Fuissé, Sancerre, and rieslings or chardonnays.

Salmon, whose battle with industrial waste and deep-sea fishing still goes on worldwide, are being raised artificially in parts of Europe, but no one has yet managed to produce one with the taste of wild salmon. In the Paris newspaper *Le Figaro*, Jean Le Coquet, the food editor, wrote of his disappointment with ranch-raised fish: "This salmon was no longer a hard-bellied athlete. You could sink a finger into its flesh as if it were an eiderdown coverlet. Salmon are like men: too soft a life is not good for them."

Salmon Ceviche

YIELD: 4 Servings

(Raw Marinated Salmon)

1½	pounds salmon
1 or 2	hot green chilies, seeded and thinly sliced
4	scallions, including green part, sliced
1	tablespoon olive oil
	Juice of 3 limes
	Coarse salt to taste

1. Skin and carefully bone the salmon. Cut into ½-inch pieces.

2. Put the salmon into a serving dish and add the chilies, scallions, oil, and lime juice. Toss and refrigerate to marinate for 1 hour before serving, or overnight.

3. Season with salt and serve with brown bread and butter as an hors d'oeuvre.

Saumon Cru

2 pounds fresh salmon fillets
1 lime, cut in half
Coarse salt and freshly ground pepper to taste
2 tablespoons finely chopped fresh chives
2 tablespoons olive oil
8 thin strips of chives, about 4 inches long

1. With a very sharp knife, cut the salmon horizontally into paper-thin slices. Have six plates ready. Squeeze lime juice on each plate, sprinkle the plate with salt and pepper, and arrange the salmon slices on top. Season the top of the salmon with salt and pepper and sprinkle with the chopped chives and more lime juice.

2. Sprinkle with olive oil, and with the back of a spoon smooth the oil into the salmon. Arrange 2 long strips of chives in a V pattern on each serving. Refrigerate.

3. About 5 minutes before serving, remove from the refrigerator so that the salmon is nearly room temperature when you serve it.

Darnes de Saumon Chambord

(Salmon with Red Wine)

4 salmon steaks, about 2 pounds in all
Coarse salt and freshly ground pepper to taste
4 tablespoons butter, at room temperature
6 shallots, finely chopped
¼ pound mushrooms, finely chopped
¼ teaspoon thyme
3 sprigs parsley
1 bay leaf
2 cups dry red wine, preferably Burgundy
¼ cup brandy
2 teaspoons flour

1. Preheat the oven to 350 degrees. Season the salmon steaks with salt and pepper. Grease a baking dish with 1 tablespoon butter. (Use a dish that can be used both in the oven and on top of the stove and is large enough to hold the steaks in one layer.)

2. Put the salmon into the dish and surround with shallots, mushrooms, thyme, parsley, and the bay leaf. Add the wine and brandy. Cover and bake for 20 to 25 minutes.

3. Mix 2 tablespoons butter and the flour together in a small bowl, making a *beurre manié*. Set aside.

4. Remove the salmon from its poaching liquid and keep warm. Add the *beurre manié* and, over a high flame, reduce the sauce to about 1 cup. Remove from the heat, stir in the remaining tablespoon butter. Correct the seasoning. Pour the sauce over the steaks and serve with boiled new potatoes.

Barbecued Whole Salmon

1	2½-to-3-pound whole salmon, cleaned
	Coarse salt and freshly ground pepper to taste
	Juice of 1 lemon
1	tablespoon olive oil
3	sprigs fresh dill or tarragon
¼	cup chopped fresh dill or tarragon
2	tablespoons chopped fresh parsley
3	tablespoons unsalted butter, at room temperature

1. Heat barbecue coals. Meanwhile, place the salmon on two pieces of foil. Season the cavity with salt, pepper, lemon juice, and olive oil. Place the dill or tarragon sprigs inside and leave for 1 hour before cooking.

2. Meanwhile, combine the dill or tarragon and parsley with the butter. Season with salt and pepper. Shape into a cylinder and put into the freezer.

3. When barbecue coals are hot, place the salmon, on its foil, on a rack. Grill for 5 to 7 minutes. Using the inside piece of foil, lift up the salmon and turn it over, placing it on top of the outer piece of foil. Discard the inner piece. Grill for 5 to 7 minutes.

4. Put the fish on a serving platter. Remove the skin from the upper side of the salmon. Using a metal spatula, pull the salmon meat away from the backbone. Remove the backbone. Remove the skin from other side of the salmon. Slice the herb butter into eight pieces. Put a slice or two of butter on each helping of salmon.

Note: This dish is good with grilled sweet corn and boiled new potatoes. Steamed fiddlehead ferns or asparagus also go well with it. Salmon steaks may also be broiled in the oven this way. It is better to undercook the salmon; when undercooked inside it is still delicious, but when overcooked the texture becomes dry.

Salmon Steaks with Sorrel Sauce

YIELD: 4 Servings

2	pounds sorrel
4	tablespoons butter
½	cup heavy cream
	Coarse salt and freshly ground pepper to taste
4	salmon steaks, about 2 pounds in all
1	lemon, sliced

1. Preheat the broiler. Wash the sorrel, pat dry with paper towels, and remove the stems. Heat 2 tablespoons butter in a frying pan and fry the sorrel until limp. Add the cream, a little at a time, and stir over low heat for 5 minutes. Season with salt and pepper. Pour the sauce into a gravy boat and keep warm.

2. Butter the salmon steaks with remaining butter and broil for about 5 minutes on each side or until barely cooked through. Do not overcook or they will dry out. Arrange on a serving dish, garnish with lemon slices and serve the sauce separately.

Note: Serve with new potatoes and steamed fresh green fava beans or peas.

Poached Fresh Whole Salmon

YIELD: 6 Servings

1	3-to-3½-pound salmon, cleaned
	Coarse salt and freshly ground pepper to taste
	About 4 to 5 quarts court bouillon (page 41)
2	cups dry white wine
	Lemon slices for garnish
	Fresh herbs for garnish

1. Season the salmon cavity with salt and pepper. Put the fish on the rack of a fish kettle and lower into the kettle.

2. Pour in enough court bouillon and wine to barely cover the fish. Slowly bring to a shudder, not a full boil. Simmer gently for 15 to 20 minutes (about 5 minutes a pound).

3. Remove the rack with the fish and let stand.

4. Before serving, peel the skin from the serving side. Arrange the salmon on a platter and garnish with lemon slices and herbs.

5. Serve hot with a hollandaise sauce or cold with homemade mayonnaise, plain or green, flavored with herbs (including tarragon).

4	*small coho salmon, or 3½ to 4 pounds salmon, striped bass, sea bass, or red snapper in one piece*
	Coarse salt and freshly ground pepper to taste
2	*small lemons*
2	*large heads fennel*
2	*tablespoons butter*
1	*tablespoon olive oil*

1. Preheat the oven to 350 degrees. Season the fish with salt and pepper and the juice of half a lemon and place the leaves from the fennel bulbs in the cavity. Dot with butter and close the cavity. Set aside at room temperature.

2. Cut the fennel into quarters lengthwise. Butter a baking dish, add a dash of oil, and cover with a piece of foil. Cook the fennel for about 20 minutes or until browned and tender.

3. When the fennel is almost done, broil the fish for a few minutes on each side (the length of time will depend upon the thickness of the flesh). Serve on a large, heated platter, with the pieces of fennel and lemon wedges arranged around the fish.

Shad

"The shad," wrote the French author Grimod de la Reynière, "reclines on its bed of sorrel like a beauty on the ottoman of her boudoir." This sweet, delicate, white-fleshed fish with its spectacular roe is in season in the spring.

Shad has wire-like bones like those in a nineteenth-century corset. They are so tiny and persistent that tweezers are sometimes needed to remove them. Because of this, the French traditionally cook shad stuffed with sorrel. As the author Waverley Root points out, the "oxalic acid softens and indeed seems all but to dissolve the bones, so that you eat them embedded in the flesh without being aware of their presence." Shad can also be served with fresh tomato sauce or beurre blanc.

The fish is a member of the herring family and lives both in fresh and salt water. Out of season shad is scrawny and thin, but in season it is plump and succulent. It is sometimes sold boned.

Shad and its roe are good served broiled with lemon wedges and bacon.

Florida shad are the first to run. They go up river to spawn when the water starts to get warm. As the rivers get progressively warmer, the shad start spawning up to Georgia, then to the Carolinas, Virginia, Delaware, all the way to the Hudson and up the Connecticut River. The fish come in from the sea, spawn and go back. The young fish grow in the river and then go out to sea.

Most shad we buy comes from Virginia and from the Carolinas. It is caught in nets fastened to poles driven into the bottom of the river. These nets are set

4 to 6 feet above the bottom and the same distance below the surface of the river so only a portion of shad is caught and the others can go through; otherwise the species would be decimated. During the nineteenth century more than 4.5 million pounds a year were fished from the Hudson alone, compared with an estimated 100,000 today.

Shad is usually sold in fillets because it is so bony. The fillets should be translucent, with no fishy smell.

In the 1880s shad were so common that H.L. Mencken wrote of his mother's outrage at being charged extra for the roe, which the fishmonger used to give away free with the fish. When buying shad roe, in season in the spring, avoid pieces that are dried up or discolored. The roe should be sparkling and moist, with a fresh glow. Frozen shad roe lacks the texture of fresh and tends to become watery and mushy when cooked. The roe is good sautéed or broiled in butter and served with bacon — a Victorian breakfast dish still served in Britain today.

The shad is a sensitive fish. An Englishman, Francis Day, wrote in 1880 that in Germany it was "terrified at storms and troubled waters, delighting in quiet and musical sounds. Therefore, to the nets are fastened bows of wood, to which are suspended a number of small bells which chime in harmony together on the nets being moved: The fish are thought to be thus attracted to their destruction, and as long as the alluring sounds continue they cease all efforts at escape."

Trout

At the beginning of April a yearly ritual takes place when fishermen of all ages try their luck for trout in brooks and streams. Experienced fly fisherman and small boys with rods and fresh worms celebrate the end of winter by trying to catch this supremely sweet fish.

There is nothing quite like trout cooked within minutes of being caught. These freshest of trout can be poached au bleu in water with a little vinegar in it and served plain with lemon or with a hollandaise or mousseline sauce.

The best trout is wild brook trout; the least interesting is rainbow trout, artificially raised in hatcheries around the country. Brown, steelhead, cutthroat, and lake trout from streams and lakes across America also make good eating. Sea trout is a brown trout that, like salmon, spends part of its life in the sea, in this case the western Atlantic. It is not common in American streams. Just to be confusing, seatrout, spelled as one word, is also called weakfish and is found along the Atlantic seaboard. It has a fragile white flesh and should be eaten as soon as possible after being caught since it spoils rapidly. The fillets can be cooked much as flatfish is (page 56).

Hatchery trout is now widely available in fish stores and supermarkets. It can be good when very fresh but it does not have anything like the flavor of trout caught in the wild. Some fish markets have trout swimming in tanks, and these are of course the freshest you can buy. You can have them in the pan within the hour of their being killed. They are expensive, but they are infinitely better than the trout that has been in the display case for a while. When trout loses its freshness it becomes flabby and limp. Thus, it is generally better, unless your supermarket has an especially good fish section, to buy from a fishmonger. Supermarkets usually stock frozen rainbow trout, and these have very little flavor.

Although the best way of cooking brook trout is the simplest — a quick pan fry or poaching — there are many other recipes that work extremely well with the trout sold in the market. A court bouillon gives the fish flavor. It is also good à la meunière — dredged in seasoned flour and sautéed in butter. I've never seen the point of trout with almonds. But it is very good stuffed with sorrel, spinach, or herbs or served with a purée of gooseberries. It is also delicious baked with cucumber as in the following recipe. Small Kirby cucumbers are particularly sweet and go very well here. They should be cooked until they are bright green and have just lost their crunchiness before being baked with the trout.

Baked Trout with Cucumber

YIELD: 4 Servings

2	pounds cucumbers
4	tablespoons butter
4	trout
4	tablespoons chopped fresh dill
	Coarse salt and freshly ground pepper to taste
	Juice of 1 lemon
	Sprigs of dill for garnish

1. Preheat the oven to 375 degrees.

2. Peel the cucumbers and cut into thin strips about 3 inches long. Melt 2 tablespoons butter and sauté the cucumber for 5 to 10 minutes or until it turns bright green and begins to lose its crunchiness.

3. Butter an ovenproof dish. Sprinkle the trout cavities with dill, salt, and pepper and squeeze the lemon juice inside and over the trout. Arrange the cucumber over the top and around the trout. Bake for 10 to 15 minutes or until the trout flakes when pierced with a fork.

4. Garnish with fresh dill and serve with boiled potatoes.

Trout in Court Bouillon

YIELD: 4 Servings

2	cups dry white wine
1	cup water
1	onion, coarsely chopped
	Coarse salt and freshly
	ground pepper to taste
2	whole cloves
4	sprigs parsley
3	tablespoons butter
½	cup bread crumbs
4	trout
2	tablespoons finely
	chopped parsley for
	garnish

1. In a pan or poacher large enough to hold the trout, simmer the wine, water, onion, salt, pepper, cloves, and parsley, covered, for 10 minutes. Meanwhile, melt the butter in a small pan and fry the bread crumbs until golden.

2. Drop the trout into the court bouillon and poach for 5 to 7 minutes or until they are cooked. Remove to a heated plate and sprinkle with the bread crumbs and their butter and a little parsley. Serve hot.

Trout Stuffed with Herbs

YIELD: 4 Servings

4	trout
1	cup fresh bread crumbs
¼	cup chopped fresh
	tarragon
¼	cup chopped fresh chives
¼	cup chopped fresh parsely
	Coarse salt and freshly
	ground pepper to taste
3	shallots, minced
2	tablespoons olive oil
1	cup dry white wine
1	tablespoon tarragon
	leaves for garnish

1. Preheat the oven to 375 degrees. Dry the trout inside and out with paper towels.

2. In a bowl, mix together the bread crumbs, tarragon, chives, and parsley. Season the mixture with salt and pepper and stuff into the trout cavities. Secure with toothpicks and place in a greased flameproof baking dish.

3. Sprinkle with shallots, brush with olive oil, and bake for 10 minutes. Remove to a warm serving platter. Pour the wine into the baking dish and bring to boil over high heat. Scrape up the cooking juices and pour over the fish. Garnish with tarragon and serve.

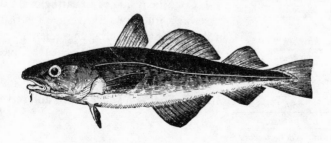

Oily Fish (Bluefish, Herring, Mackerel, and Sardines)

Bluefish

Bluefish are the gangsters of the marine world. They are voracious foragers and go on the rampage in schools, attacking and consuming all fish around, even those almost their own size. These orgiastic fishes are found off the Atlantic Coast and are usually in season in the South from December to April and in the North from May to October.

Besides being good eaters themselves, bluefish are great eating. They should be very fresh because their oils make them spoil fast. They make especially tasty sashimi.

Because bluefish are oily, they go well with foods that cut their oiliness. They can be served with limes, lemons, and oranges or vegetables, such as tomatoes and onions. Large bluefish can be filleted, broiled, or cooked whole in the oven or over coals and served with a tart sauce.

A whole bluefish that can serve four to eight people may be wrapped in foil and baked with slices of lime or lemon, garlic, and dill or parsley.

Alan Davidson in *North Atlantic Seafood* gives a recipe from the Portuguese of Provincetown that is an unusual way to serve this fish if you are not eating it immediately. I give an adaptation of the recipe below.

Vinha Dalhos

YIELD: 4 Servings

(Bluefish Portuguese Style)

1 to 2	tablespoons olive oil plus oil for frying
2	pounds bluefish fillets
1	cup wine vinegar
1	cup dry red wine
4	cloves garlic, crushed
1	teaspoon ground cumin
	Coarse salt to taste
½	teaspoon cayenne pepper

1. Coat the inside of an earthenware or glass casserole with olive oil. Arrange the fish fillets in it, combine remaining ingredients, and pour the mixture over them. Leave overnight, turning occasionally.

2. Pat the fish dry and pan fry in ¼-inch olive oil. Drain on paper towels and serve.

1	bluefish, 3 to 4 pounds
	Juice of 1 lemon
1	tablespoon olive oil
1	onion, thinly sliced
2	tomatoes, sliced
1	sweet green pepper, sliced
	Coarse salt and freshly
	ground pepper to taste
1	lemon, quartered

1. Preheat the oven to 350 degrees. Pat the bluefish dry and squeeze the lemon juice inside and out.

2. Oil a casserole with the olive oil and place the fish in it. Arrange the onion, tomatoes, and pepper over the fish. Cover with foil and bake for 30 to 45 minutes or until the fish flakes when tested with a fork.

3. Season with salt and pepper and serve with lemon quarters.

Herring

Fresh herring — called green herring — are plump and sweet and are eaten raw. The silvery fillets are traditionally dipped into chopped onions, held up by the tail and gulped down in a few bites. With them the drink is ice-cold neat Dutch gin or beer. The herring are flown into the U.S. in the spring.

In Holland, the annual herring run starts around the end of May or the beginning of June when the water warms up. The first catch of the herring fleet is marked by a celebration and is given to the Queen. The fleet makes several runs in its brightly painted herring boats. Butterflied and lightly salted, it is a popular snack sold on little wooden carts in the streets of Amsterdam and Scheveningen.

The food writer Waverly Root lived in Holland for two and a half years and observed the Dutch as they solemnly devoured the first herrings, never with knife or fork, but by dripping the fish whole into their mouths. The skill, he says in *Food*, must be innate, since few foreigners ever master it. "Head bent back as far as it will go, mouth strained open, each herring fancier hoists a small fish deftly by the tail, suspends it for a split second over the gaping gullet and lowers it into the expectant orifice without losing a single one of the little chips of onion sprinkled over it. More dangerous still are herring that are dunked into a drippy creamy sauce in preparation for this act of levitation. I am convinced that no foreigner should attempt this feat except when wearing his oldest clothes."

8	fresh herring
1	cooked beet, diced
3	tart apples, diced
½	pound boiled new potatoes, sliced
1	small onion, chopped
¼	cup olive oil
2	tablespoons red wine vinegar
	Coarse salt and freshly ground pepper to taste
2	hard-boiled eggs, sliced
2	tablespoons chopped fresh parsley

1. Bone the herring and cut the flesh into thin strips. Combine in a salad bowl with the beet, apples, potatoes, and onion.

2. Mix the oil and vinegar in a small bowl and season with salt and pepper. Pour the mixture onto the herring and toss lightly. Garnish with eggs and parsley.

Mackerel

The pleasure of contemplating shiny mackerel, with their brilliant silver and blue-black skins and firm, svelte bodies, is even greater when you realize how little they cost. They are among the least expensive of fish and make excellent eating. Yet because they are cheap, they are often overlooked. In Victorian times, they were a great delicacy, grilled so their skins turned a crisp brown and served with a mustard or tart gooseberry sauce. The French like mackerel with gooseberries, too, so much so that *groseilles à maquereau* is the French word for these fruits; *groseilles* alone means red currants. Curiously, *maquereau* is also the French for pimp. Its etymology is moot.

Since gooseberries aren't as common in France as they are in England, the French often serve mackerel with a purée of sorrel instead. Its acidity cuts the oiliness of the fish. The mackerel can be broiled while the sorrel leaves are simply tossed in butter until they form a purée. The purée can then be thinned with a little cream and served separately. Tart fruits such as rhubarb or cranberries, simmered as are the gooseberries in the recipe given below, are also delicious with mackerel.

Mackerel is an extremely versatile fish. Instead of being grilled, it can also be rolled in oatmeal and pan-fried like herring, or poached in a court bouillon and served cold. Fennel sprigs blanched and served with a velouté sauce flavored with a little nutmeg also go well with this fish. And for people with facilities for home-smoking, it is perfect, taking on a beautiful golden hue after about ten minutes in the smoker.

Mackerel is sold whole and usually weighs about a pound, enough for one person as a main course. Buy it only if the fish is shiny and firm. If it is dull and limp it is not fresh. It deteriorates quickly because it is a fatty fish; therefore, freshness is very important. Mackerel is widely available.

Alexandre Dumas described mackerel as one of the most beautiful and courageous of fish. "When it is taken alive from the line into the boat, it seems made of azure, silver and gold," he wrote in his *Dictionary of Cuisine*. "A Norwegian historian tells of a seaman who suddenly disappeared while swimming in the ocean. When his body was found ten minutes later, it had already been devoured by mackerel."

This is the only record of mackerel ever eating people.

Mackerel with Gooseberry Sauce   YIELD: 4 Servings

1	pound gooseberries
3	tablespoons sugar, or to taste
1	tablespoon butter
1	egg, beaten
	Freshly grated nutmeg
2	large or 4 small mackerel
1	tablespoon olive oil
	Coarse salt and freshly ground pepper to taste
2	tablespoons chopped fennel leaves for garnish (optional)

1. Cook the gooseberries, covered, with the sugar and butter until tender. Put through a sieve into a saucepan.

2. Over low heat, add the beaten egg and cook just enough for the sauce to thicken. Do not boil or it will curdle. Season with nutmeg and set aside.

3. Preheat the broiler and brush the mackerel with oil. Broil, turning once, until cooked. Arrange on a plate, season with salt and pepper, and garnish with fennel. Serve the sauce separately.

Grilled Mackerel with Mustard   YIELD: 4 Servings

2	large or 4 small mackerel
1	onion, chopped
2	tablespoons butter
2	tablespoons Dijon mustard
	Coarse salt and freshly ground pepper to taste
1	tablespoon olive oil
2	tablespoons chopped fresh parsley

1. Rinse and dry the mackerel. In a small pan, soften the onion in the butter. Add the mustard, salt, and pepper. Remove from heat and mix well.

2. Preheat the broiler or charcoal grill. Stuff the fish cavities with the mustard mixture, sprinkle with oil, and broil, turning once, for 5 to 10 minutes or until the fish flakes when tested with a fork.

3. Sprinkle parsley over the fish and serve.

¼	cup olive oil
1	medium onion, finely chopped
½	cup pine nuts, toasted
¾	cup white bread crumbs
½	teaspoon ground coriander seeds
2	tablespoons currants, soaked and drained
	Coarse salt and freshly ground pepper to taste
4	small mackerel, cleaned
1	cup court bouillon (page 41) or dry white wine
	Chopped fresh coriander for garnish

1. Preheat the oven to 425 degrees. Heat the oil in a skillet and gently fry the onion until soft. Remove from the heat, add the pine nuts, bread crumbs, ground coriander seeds, and currants and mix thoroughly. Season with salt and pepper and stuff into the mackerel cavities.

2. Place the mackerel in a baking dish and add the court bouillon or wine. Cover loosely with foil and bake for about 20 minutes or until the fish flakes when tested with a fork.

Sardines

The best sardines I ever ate were at Essaouira in Morocco. The blue and white fishing boats were moored in the harbor and at the water's edge people had set up trestle tables and benches. The sardines were placed in a double-sided rack and grilled over hot coals in a charcoal brazier. We ate them with nothing but lemon and loaves of fresh bread.

Most sardines sold in America are canned. They are briefly cooked, then packed in small tins with soybean or olive oil, sometimes with chili powder or mustard added. I like to eat canned sardines on toast. The toast is spread with a little mustard and butter, the sardines sprinkled with lemon and cayenne pepper, and the whole thing put under a broiler until it is sizzling.

Sardines are members of the herring family and their name is often used to denote all the small fish of this school, including herring, pilchards, and sprats. Sardines are not often on the market when fresh because they spoil easily. But once in a while they will be, and my fishmonger calls to let me know. I either grill them plain or prepare them the following way for lunch. They are good hot or cold. If you are serving them cold, combine 4 teaspoons olive oil with 1 teaspoon vinegar and coat the sardines wtih this mixture. The following day, serve the cold sardines with sliced red onion, brown bread, and butter.

Sardines in White Wine

1	cup dry white wine
1	teaspoon salt
1	teaspoon lemon juice
1	drop Louisiana red hot sauce
2	teaspoons pickling spices
6	teaspoons olive oil
1	teaspoon white wine vinegar
8	fresh sardines

1. Bring the wine, salt, lemon juice, hot sauce, pickling spices, and 2 teaspoons olive oil to a simmer in a skillet. Poach the sardines for 2 to 3 minutes. Remove and drain.

2. Combine the remaining olive oil with the vinegar and pour over 4 sardines. Cover and refrigerate for later.

3. Serve the hot sardines with mustard, pickles, brown bread, and butter.

Shellfish (Crabs, Lobster, Clams, Mussels, Oysters, Scallops, Sea Urchins, and Shrimp)

Crab

America has a huge choice of crabs in its waters. There are blue crabs from the Atlantic and the Gulf Coast, stone crabs from Florida, Dungeness from the Pacific coast, the rock crabs of New England and California, and king crabs from Alaska.

Crabs should be bought live and used on the day you buy them. They are at their peak in warmer months. Shelled, cooked crab meat sold in tins is not as good as crab meat you prepare yourself, but it is better than that in vacuum-packed cans or the frozen and is certainly time saving. It should have no off smell and should not be darkened or yellowed.

Lump crab meat is the most expensive and the best quality, coming from the body of the crab. Backfin comes in smaller pieces, and claw from the pincers. Flake crab meat is made with the smallest pieces from any part of the crab.

Blue crabs come in two forms, soft shell and hard. Soft-shell crabs are crabs that have molted their hard shells and are caught before they have had time to grow new ones. They are normally at their best in late June and early July. If the water warms up, they molt earlier. Around Labor Day the quality starts to deteriorate because the shells get too hard with the cold weather.

Chesapeake Bay in Maryland yields more crabs for food than any other body of water in the world. With the first signs of warm weather, the crabs settle in the marshes to molt. Crabs that have molted must be collected at once before their soft carapaces toughen. They are packed in wooden boxes lined with seaweed, which lets them breathe.

When buying soft-shell crabs look for those with translucent, pearl-gray skin, white underbellies, and pink tips on their claws. They must be alive. They should be plump and springy to the touch, with no trace of hard carapace. The fishmonger will clean them or show you how if you wish to clean them at home.

The smaller crabs are the best. "Prime" grade crabs are about 4 to 4½ inches across; "hotel prime" (sold mostly to restaurants) are about 2½ inches. Choose crabs of equal size. "Jumbo" crabs, about 6 to 8 inches across, have a tendency to become mushy when cooked.

Kill the crab by cutting off the front of its head with a pair or scissors. Turn over and cut off the apron and remove the messy intestines and gray gills. Rinse and dry.

The traditional way to cook the crabs is to dust them lightly with flour and fry them for 3 to 5 minutes on each side in a small amount of butter or oil and serve them hot with lemon wedges. They develop their own nutty flavor and don't need the slivered almonds that restaurants often add.

To deep-fry, dip them in seasoned flour then in a mixture of beaten egg and milk, then roll them in fresh fine bread crumbs. Fry them until golden in vegetable oil (olive oil is too heavy) and serve them with lemon wedges.

They are also excellent pan-fried in a mixture of butter and oil (flavored with a little garlic if you like), drained, and sprinkled with chopped parsley and lemon juice. French-fried potatoes and a green salad are good accompaniments.

The artist Raeford Liles, who has been a soft-shell crab devotee since his childhood in the South, cooks his in a skillet and flambés them with ouzo. He's been preparing crabs that way for twenty years and it is his favorite method.

"You must wear glasses to protect your eyes when you fry soft-shell crabs," he warns. "No matter how thoroughly you've dried them they tend to pop and sputter. I cover the skillet at an angle for a few minutes at first so that the fat doesn't spray all over the place, but I don't cover it completely or the crabs get soft."

He does not use flour. "I think it makes the dish too heavy," he says. "I don't even use lemon, it's too sharp against the subtle and faint minty flavor the ouzo gives to the crabs." Nor does he use salt and pepper. "The crabs have so much flavor they don't need it."

He cautions against flambéing the ouzo if cooking in a confined place. So, instead of applying a match, simply bring the ouzo to a boil to evaporate the alcohol.

6	medium-size "prime" soft-shell crabs, cleaned
¼	pound unsalted butter
⅓	cup ouzo or Pernod
	Chopped fresh parsley for garnish

1. Pat the crabs dry with paper towels.

2. Melt the butter in a skillet over medium heat. Do not turn heat up too high or the butter will burn. Add the crabs back side down. Cover the skillet with the lid at an angle to prevent butter from spattering, but do not cover tightly. Cook for 3 to 4 minutes.

3. Turn the crabs over. The butter will now be browning. Cook for an additional 3 minutes, making sure the butter does not burn as it browns.

4. Add the ouzo all at once. Put a match to the ouzo and stand well back as the flames flare up. Serve the crabs immediately on a heated platter with pan juices poured over. Garnish with parsley.

5. Serve with rice and chilled Muscadet wine.

Lobster

During the summer no one wants to spend hours in the kitchen, sweltering in front of a hot oven. This is the perfect time for serving the occasional luxury food, such as fresh lobster, that can be cooked without enormous fuss and eaten out of doors, cold with homemade mayonnaise or hot with drawn lemon butter and accompanied by a dry white wine.

The very best lobsters are those that are bought live and cooked just before being eaten. They are at their peak during the warm months, from May to October. They come from Maine and Nova Scotia and from year-round lobster farms; some are so big they look like horror-film monsters. The complicated structure of their shells requires the skill of a third-year biology student for all the meat to be extracted from inside. You need a nutcracker for cracking the claws and a pick to get the meat out from the most difficult parts.

Lobsters should be bought live and plunged into boiling salted water or sea water. Choose lobsters that are heavy for their size, with both claws intact; the best meat is in the claws. But fishmongers usually give a good discount on lobsters that have only one claw, and for serving a large number of people, these are an excellent buy. Smaller lobsters are usually the most tender, although I have had some delicious giants.

To cook the lobsters bring a large pot of heavily salted water to a boil. Plunge the lobsters in head first and quickly put the lid on. This seems more humane and a quicker way of killing lobsters to me than putting them in cold water and bringing it to the boil. This method is preferred by some cooks who contend that the lobster gets dopier as the water heats up. But once I tried this with crabs. I'd read that crabs can lose a claw when in pain or frightened. I carefully put six of them into an enormous pot of salted water that I slowly brought to the boil. When I opened the lid, all of the crabs had thrown a claw. So thereafter, I opted for the quick method.

When the water has come back to a boil after the lobsters have been plunged in, cook them for no more than 15 minutes for the first pound, 10 minutes for each pound thereafter. Be careful not to overcook or the meat will be tough and chewy. Remove with slotted spoons and drain.

Many fishmongers sell cooked lobsters but these are often overcooked and tasteless. If you do have a reliable source, remember always to choose cooked lobsters that are heavy for their size, firm and bright red. Their tails should spring back into their original position when pulled. If in any doubt of freshness at all, smell the lobsters.

The following recipe is extremely simple and is a splendid main course for a summer dinner. It can be prepared in advance. The lobsters look very attractive arranged on a large serving plate and garnished with slices of lemon. I add nasturtium leaves from the garden and arrange the flowers in the middle, their color reflected in the orange-red of the cooked lobsters.

Melon, figs, or ripe peaches with prosciutto make a fine first course for this meal. With the lobster, cucumbers, sliced very thin and dressed with oil and vinegar, go nicely. You don't need to add dill or herbs because there are plenty in the mayonnaise. Follow with salad and goat's cheese.

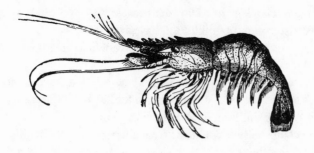

6	*1-pound lobsters*
2	*egg yolks*
¼	*teaspoon dry mustard*
1	*cup safflower oil*
	Approximately ½ cup
	olive oil
	Juice of 1 lemon
	Coarse salt and freshly
	ground pepper to taste
4	*tablespoons Pernod*
2	*tablespoons chopped*
	fresh chives
2	*tablespoons chopped*
	fresh parsley
2	*tablespoons chopped*
	fresh tarragon

1. Cook the lobsters and drain them. Set aside.

2. Beat the egg yolks in a small bowl until they are thick and sticky. Add the mustard. Little by little, beat in the safflower oil, adding it gradually; otherwise, the mayonnaise may curdle.

3. Continue beating and adding the olive oil, little by little, until you have a stiff mayonnaise. Add the remaining ingredients. If the mayonnaise is too thin, thicken it with more oil, added gradually. Season with salt and pepper. Serve in two small serving bowls.

Clams

Clams are in season all year round, at their best from September through May. They should feel heavy in the hand, and the shells should always be tightly closed. Throw away any open ones. Scrub clams with unsoaped steel wool if you plan to use the liquid in which they are cooked.

On the East Coast, quahog or hard-shell clams are the most widely sold. Within this species, littleneck are the best for eating on the half shell; they are the sweetest and most delicate. Cherrystones are good both for eating and cooking. The biggest clams go into chowder because they are tough when raw. Soft-shell clams, also common in the East, have a siphon — a neck that sticks out like a little rubber hose. These clams are also known as steamers and are extremely popular in New England.

In the Pacific, there are pismo clams, which have the best flavor, and the razor, which has a long shell like a flat razor, in the hard-shell category. The soft-shell in the West is similar to that of New England.

When buying clams be sure you do so from a fishmonger with a high turnover. Avoid clams that have broken shells or that feel oddly light for their size. When tapped, the clams should close their shells tightly. If they have a siphon, it should contract. They should not have any unpleasant smell.

Fresh raw clams are best eaten with lemon juice and pepper, and sometimes with horseradish or cocktail sauce.

1	onion, chopped
6	tablespoons olive oil
3	stalks celery, chopped
2	tablespoons tomato paste
2	cloves garlic, chopped
2	tablespoons chopped
	fresh basil
½	teaspoon oregano
	Coarse salt and freshly
	ground pepper to taste
36	clams, scrubbed

Sauté the onion in the olive oil until soft. Add the remaining ingredients except for clams and simmer over low heat, covered, for about 1 hour. Add the clams and cook for no more than 6 minutes.

Mussels

Mussels are found year round on both coasts and can be picked off rocks and piers. The blue mussel is the most common; it has a black-blue shell and plump flesh. These mollusks are more expensive in mid-winter, though, because they are difficult to harvest in cold waters. But they are not as good in late spring and summer because they spawn at this time and are not as plump.

When buying mussels avoid those with broken shells or that feel unusually light or heavy for their size. The heavy ones may be filled with sand. When the mussels are tapped, they should close, otherwise they are probably dead.

Buy more than you need because, no matter how careful you are, some will inevitably have to be discarded. If collecting your own, make sure you are not doing so in polluted waters.

Mussels with Salsa Verde
YIELD: 6 Servings as an appetizer

2	cornichons
1	tablespoon capers
1	small dill pickle
1	clove garlic
1	bunch flat-leaf parsley
1	anchovy fillet
1	hard-boiled egg
½	teaspoon Dijon mustard
1	tablespoon red wine vinegar
⅔	cup extra-virgin olive oil
	Dash of Worcestershire sauce
	Coarse salt and freshly ground pepper to taste
42	large fresh mussels

1. Chop the cornichons, capers, dill pickle, garlic, parsley, anchovy, and egg very fine.

2. Combine the mustard, vinegar, and olive oil. Add Worcestershire sauce.

3. Add the chopped ingredients, mix thoroughly, and season with salt and pepper. Set the sauce aside (it will keep refrigerated for up to a week).

4. Scrub the mussels thoroughly, removing as much grit as possible from the shells. Put them in a pot with ¼ inch of water and steam for 2 to 3 minutes or until the shells open.

5. Debeard the mussels and pour out the juice of each one, making sure there is no grit inside. Discard the juice (it is salty and too strong to go with the sauce) and half the shells. Return the mussels to the shells. Chill until ready to serve.

6. To serve, arrange 6 or 7 mussels on each plate and spoon a little sauce onto each one.

Oysters

When I was a teenager, a boastful young man anxious to impress described a skill he had learned in Paris. Blindfolded, he could tell a Belon from a Portugaise, an Ostend from a Marenne verte. His fashionable friends would set before him a plate of many different kinds of oysters. A napkin was tied about his eyes and bets exchanged. As each creature went to its doom, it was correctly and triumphantly identified.

The story made a deep impression on my untutored mind, since at that time an oyster to me was simply an oyster, one kind. It was a depraved creature that my grandfather said he'd once dropped live into a glass of brandy to see if the two would mix well in the stomach. I had never eaten one myself; in fact, I had never seen one.

My first oyster slipped down in the easeful company of my mother at the counter of the Oyster Bar and Restaurant in Grand Central Station and was followed by another novelty, cheesecake. I had arrived in New York from England on the Queen Mary that morning. It was my first meal in America and perhaps the most exciting I have ever eaten. But I still wasn't sure exactly what an oyster was.

"The oyster is the most disinherited of mollusks," wrote Alexandre Dumas. "Being acephalous — that is to say, having no head — it has no organ of sight, no organ of hearing, no organ of smell. Its blood is colorless. Its body adheres to two sides of its shell by a powerful muscle that it uses to open and close it. Neither has it any organ of locomotion. Its only exercise is sleep; its only pleasure, eating."

Oyster-eating goes back to the Romans, who were particularly fond of them. Seneca is said to have consumed 1,200 a week, saying that they "are not really food, but are relished to bully the stomach into further eating." American Indians ate oysters, and in New York, Diamond Jim Brady bullied his stomach with a daily helping of three dozen for breakfast and eight dozen every night.

The best way to eat oysters is plain with lemon juice and freshly ground pepper. Some oysters, such as Cotuits and Chincoteagues, have enough flavor to stand up to a mignonette sauce made with tarragon vinegar, pepper, and shallots. Red cocktail sauce and horseradish are too strong for any oyster. The best drink with oysters is white wine, such as Muscadet, Chablis, California chardonnay, or Champagne.

Oysters come from states along the Chesapeake Bay (which produced 20.8 million in 1980), from the Gulf Coast and the Atlantic. There are brown Belons from Maine; bluepoint and box — large, firm Long Island oysters good for cooking; Malpeque from Prince Edward Island, and others by the name of Kent Island, Wellfleet, Chatham, Chincoteague, Cotuit, and golden mantel .

A new kind of oyster has recently appeared on the market, raised in farms in Hawaii. Hawaiian oysters are free of sand and don't have to be rinsed. They are raised without risk of pollution and are among the sweetest tasting oysters I've ever had. They are available year round. They also have a thinner shell, which makes them easier to open, and a deeper bowl than other oysters, so you get a higher meat-to-shell ratio. Inside they are plump and firm, with a delicate nectar.

"No other country in the world can compare with America as far as oysters are concerned because we have more shoreline," says George Morfogen, the fish buyer at the Oyster Bar and Restaurant in Grand Central Station in New York where 40,000 oysters are shucked a week.

While oysters were once eaten only in months with an "r," modern refrigeration has made them safe all year round. "Beds are categorically listed for safe digging," says Mr. Morfogen. "Most cases of sickness from shellfish are caused by bootleggers or amateurs digging in water that is off limits. They think because it looks clear, it must be safe. But each bushel that comes in is tagged with the date the oysters were dug and the name of the body of water they came from."

When buying oysters make sure they are tightly closed. They can be opened three to four hours ahead and refrigerated. They should not be rinsed, or their liquid and flavor will be lost. Unopened, they can be kept for several weeks at 35 to 40 degrees in a container covered with a wet cloth from which they will drink water.

One oyster is known to have brought fame and fortune to its owner. A century ago, André Launay wrote in *Posh Food*, the owner of a London restaurant was awakened during the night by repeated whistling from the kitchens. He went down armed with a stick, and traced the whistle to a barrel of oysters in the corner. One oyster had a small hole in its shell . When it breathed, water was forced through this hole, causing the whistle.

"The next night," Launay goes on, "the oyster set fashionable London alight, and its owner was host to Thackeray and Dickens, among a stream of other celebrities who came to listen to the musical mollusc while gobbling up dozens of its less talented cousins."

Poached Oysters with Cream

YIELD: 4 Servings

1	carrot
1	leek
24	bluepoint or box oysters
2	tablespoons chopped shallots
¼	cup dry white wine
¼	cup heavy cream
12	tablespoons unsalted butter, cut in small pieces
	Juice of ½ lemon (or to taste)
	Freshly ground white pepper to taste
	Chopped fresh parsley for garnish

1. Cut the carrot and leek into julienne strips and blanch for 30 seconds in boiling water. Cool in ice cold water.

2. Open the oysters over a strainer lined with a cheesecloth set over a bowl. Filter the juice through and reserve. Put the oysters in another bowl. Wash half the shells and set aside.

3. Combine the shallots and the white wine in a small saucepan and bring to a boil. Cook until the wine has almost completely reduced, about 3 to 4 minutes.

4. Add the cream. When the mixture starts to thicken add the butter pieces. When the butter has melted remove from heat and keep warm.

5. In a small pan, poach the oysters for 20 seconds in the strained juice. Meanwhile, reheat the vegetables over a low flame in a steamer.

6. Put the shells on four warmed plates. Put the poached oysters on the shells. Add a teaspoon of the poaching liquid to the cream sauce, season with lemon juice and white pepper. Heat through and pour a teaspoon of the sauce onto each oyster. Sprinkle vegetables on each oyster. Garnish with parsley and serve.

Note: This dish is served at the Odeon Restaurant in New York, where oysters are, of course, opened on the spot. When oysters are opened in advance at the fish market, much of their juice can be lost in transit. If there is not enough juice for poaching, substitute ¼ cup of dry white wine.

Scallops

It used to be said that people should be wary when buying scallops because half of the time they would be getting nothing more than shark meat punched out into tiny circles and selling for a sum. These days, however, it is doubtful that anyone would go to the trouble to do all this, now that shark meat is a delicacy, too, and fetches a high price on the market. But shark meat is not really as finely textured as scallops nor as subtle in flavor.

There are two kinds of scallops on the market: the small, delicate bay scallops the size of a penny, and sea scallops, larger and coarser, measuring an inch and a half — and even two inches — across. The latter are not as subtle as the bay scallops, but they can be cooked in similar ways provided they are cut to an equal size so that all will cook evenly.

Scallops, like clams and oysters, are mollusks and are culled along the coast. The only part that is marketed is the single adductor muscle that opens and closes the large fan-shaped shell it lives in. The roe, which is wonderful to eat and golden as that of sea urchins, is thrown away because it spoils so fast. Some expensive restaurants occasionally take the trouble to fly in whole scallops and serve them in their shells complete with the roe. Don't miss an opportunity to try them.

Both kinds of scallops make excellent ceviche marinated overnight in lemon or lime juice and served raw with chopped onion, tomato, peppers, and chilies. Chopped parsley, coriander, or basil can be added after the scallops have marinated. The larger scallops can also be broiled, threaded on skewers alternately with pieces of chopped bacon. They are also good broiled over hot coals after they have been marinated in olive oil and orange juice with chilies. Thread them alternately with pieces of onion and tomato. Garnish with fresh basil leaves.

One of the most attractive ways to serve scallops is in scallop shells, as the French serve the classic dish Coquilles St. Jacques, for a first course. Simmer the scallops in vermouth with a few slices of onion, lemon, and parsley for 2 to 3 minutes. Drain them and toss in a homemade green mayonnaise. The mixture looks very pretty in the scallop shells, garnished with basil leaves or parsley.

When buying scallops, choose those that are firm and fresh with no off odor. Avoid any that are too watery, indicating that they have been lying around for a while. Avoid, too, those that smell strong. Scallops go very well with pasta. The following dish can be served hot or cold, as an appetizer or as a main course.

Scallops with Tomatoes and Pasta   YIELD: 4 Servings

2	pounds scallops
	Flour for dredging
2	tablespoons butter
1	pound tomatoes, peeled, seeded, and chopped
½	cup heavy cream
1	pound green pasta (penne or fusilli), cooked and drained
4	tablespoons chopped fresh basil
	Coarse salt and freshly ground pepper to taste

1. Rinse the scallops and pat dry. Dredge in flour.

2. Heat the butter in a skillet. Fry the scallops on both sides until golden.

3. Add the tomatoes and cook another 5 minutes. Add the cream and continue cooking until you have a smooth sauce.

4. Meanwhile, cook the pasta until al dente.

5. Place the pasta and the scallops in a bowl. Add the basil, salt, and pepper, and toss thoroughly. Correct seasoning. Serve hot or cold.

Ceviche   YIELD: 6 to 8 Servings as an appetizer

2	pounds scallops
3 to 4	hot red or green chilies
1	cup lime juice
	Coarse salt and freshly ground pepper to taste
4	tablespoons chopped fresh coriander
1	medium onion, cut into rings

1. If using sea scallops, cut into even-sized pieces. Chop the chilies finely and put in a bowl with the lime juice. Add the scallops, season with salt and pepper and mix thoroughly. Refrigerate, covered, for several hours or overnight if possible.

2. To serve, add coriander and onion rings and toss thoroughly.

Steamed Scallops with Fennel

YIELD: 6 Servings

2	cups white wine
1	head fennel, cut julienne
2	pounds scallops
2	tablespoons butter
	Coarse salt and freshly
	ground pepper to taste
3	tablespoons chopped
	fennel leaves

1. Put the wine in the bottom half of a steamer. Bring to a boil.

2. Place the fennel in top half of steamer and top with the scallops. Place on top of lower half of steamer and steam, covered, for 5 to 7 minutes.

3. Remove the scallops and fennel from the steamer. Place in a bowl. Toss with butter, salt, and pepper. Place in scallop shells and sprinkle with fennel leaves.

Sea Urchins

Because of their spikes, these hedgehogs of the sea are a menace to bathers. But their coral-colored roe, protected by a fierce, bristly shell, is a great delicacy, comparable to caviar or the finest oysters. Only the roe is edible, and it makes a delicious first course when eaten raw from the shell, accompanied by fresh French bread and cold white wine such as a Muscadet or a Chablis or a California chardonnay. The taste is so subtle that nothing more is needed than a drop of lemon juice, if that, and the roe is carefully scooped out with a small spoon.

In recent years sea urchin roe has become enormously fashionable and is on the menus of nouvelle cuisine restaurants puréed in sauces or served in a rich soup. A classic recipe to be served as an hors d'oeuvre combines the roe of thirty-four urchins with an equal amount of béchamel sauce in light pastry barquettes.

Picking out sea urchins that are just right is a tricky business. The quills on fresh sea urchins are green and sharp; if the quills are matted and dark brown the urchins are old. But it is difficult to tell which have the best roe. Whatever their size, pick the heaviest in that particular size, because those that are light may be bad. However, size in itself is no indication of the amount of roe; the small ones may have a good supply.

To serve, cut the urchins in half with a sharp knife or scissors. Do not rinse them.

Fresh roe flown in from Japan is also available in some speciality stores and fish markets. The Japanese, who along with the French are the largest consumers of sea urchins in the world, use the roe for a delicious sushi item called *uni,* served in many sushi bars in New York and often available by the piece. Sea urchin roe imported from Japan is sold fresh in boxes. It is expensive but much larger than the roe from American urchins and is good for sauces or for eating raw.

In France sea urchins are displayed in large baskets outside fishmongers and restaurants. On top sits an opened sea urchin with an especially plump roe that will tempt the customers to buy.

Shrimp

My friend Raeford Liles, a painter, is a great cook even though he has only an electric skillet to work with. When the shrimp in the market are fresh and cheap, he invites me to his studio overlooking the Lincoln Tunnel in the part of New York known as Hell's Kitchen. There we have had many a wonderful lunch of fresh shrimp piled in a pyramid on newspaper and served with home-made mayonnaise and chilled white wine. We sit peeling, shelling, and eating the shrimp — which Raeford cooks in white wine in the skillet with their shells on.

Most of the shrimp on sale in American markets has been frozen and thawed. This is not always the case with shrimp sold with its head still on, but if the flesh is opaque rather than translucent, it probably has been frozen. The flesh inside the shell shrinks as the shrimp gets older, so avoid those with loose shells. Shrimp should not smell of ammonia or fish; they should smell fresh. Color is not an indication of quality. Shrimp can be pale pink, red, translucent with green, white, or blueish tinge.

Jumbo shrimp are the most expensive, yet they are less sweet than smaller shrimp and can sometimes be tough. But they are easier to prepare since there is less shelling to do. The dark thread-like vein that runs along the back of the tail just under the shell should be removed. Be careful not to overcook shrimp; they may toughen or become woolly.

The smaller shrimp with the heads on are often sold at bargain prices, but even if they are not, remember to take the heads into account when comparing prices.

Shrimp heads and tails make an excellent stock. Cook them for an hour with onion, carrot, leeks, bouquet garni, and celery. The stock can then be strained and used for sauces for fish, shrimp, or other seafood.

In the following dish the shrimp is "cooked" by being marinated overnight in lemon juice together with spices and chilies. Shrimp becomes especially juicy prepared this way; it is very good served with drinks before dinner.

Mexican Shrimp Ceviche

1	pound medium shrimp, peeled
¾	cup olive oil
2	tablespoons red wine vinegar
	Juice of 1 lemon
½ to 1	teaspoon ground red chilies (according to taste)
1	medium Spanish onion, sliced into thin rings
2 or 3	green chilies, sliced thin
½	cup chopped fresh coriander
	Coarse salt and freshly ground pepper to taste

1. Put the shrimp into a china or glass bowl. Combine the olive oil, red wine vinegar, lemon juice, and red pepper and mix thoroughly. Toss the shrimp in this mixture.

2. Add the onion, chilies, and coriander and toss. Season to taste, cover, and refrigerate overnight.

Note: Mexican tortillas go well with this dish.

Barbecued Butterfly Shrimp

2	pounds large shrimp, in their shells
4	tablespoons olive oil
	Coarse salt and freshly ground pepper to taste
	Juice of 1 lemon

1. Slice the shrimp, shells on, from head to tail without cutting all the way through. With your fingers, remove the dark intestinal vein down the back.

2. Combine the olive oil, salt, pepper, and lemon juice. Pour the mixture over the shrimp and leave to marinate for 1 hour. Meanwhile, heat the coals of the barbecue so they are extremely hot.

3. Thread the shrimp on skewers and broil for 3 minutes on each side, brushing with lemon and oil as they cook. Serve hot.

Trinidad Shrimp Curry

1	teaspoon ground cumin
1	teaspoon coriander seeds
1	teaspoon whole mustard seeds
1	teaspoon turmeric
½	teaspoon crushed hot red pepper
1	teaspoon black peppercorns
1	bay leaf
2	tablespoons peanut oil
1	onion, finely chopped
1	clove garlic, minced
2	cups chopped peeled tomatoes
	Juice of 1 lime
	Coarse salt and freshly ground pepper to taste
1	cup water, or more as necessary
2	pounds medium shrimp, peeled and deveined

1. Grind the spices and bay leaf in an electric grinder or pound them in a mortar until fine.

2. Heat the oil in a large, heavy frying pan. Add the onion and garlic and sauté until softened without browning. Add the spices and sauté for 2 minutes without browning.

3. Add the tomatoes and lime juice; season with salt and pepper. Add the water, bring to a boil, and simmer gently, uncovered, for 30 minutes, adding water if the sauce becomes too dry.

4. Add the shrimp and cook, covered, for 3 to 5 minutes. Be careful not to overcook them. They should be juicy and pink. Serve immediately.

Note: Serve this with rice and mango chutney.

Shrimp in White Wine

YIELD: 4 Servings

2	pounds medium or small shrimp, in their shells
1	bay leaf
1	small onion, quartered
1	cup dry white wine
½	cup water
2	slices lemon
6	black peppercorns
1	cup mayonnaise (page 196)
2	tablespoons chopped fresh dill (optional)

1. Wash the shrimp thoroughly in cold water.

2. Combine the bay leaf, onion, wine, water, lemon, and peppercorns in a skillet. There should be about ½ inch of liquid. If more is needed, add water. Bring to a boil.

3. Add the shrimp and cook for 3 or 4 minutes, so that they turn pink but do not overcook. Remove with a slotted spoon and serve on a plate. Do this in two batches.

4. Mix the mayonnaise with dill. Peel the shrimp and dip them into the sauce as you eat them.

Skate

Skate, or rayfish, is less well known in America but enormously popular in France. It is a strange-looking kite-shaped fish that is traditionally served in French bistros in a bubbling nut-brown butter sauce garnished with capers. Skate is at its best in the autumn and winter months. Succulent and sweet-fleshed when ready to cook, it should not be too fresh or it will be tough. If it is very fresh, keep it for a day or two before cooking it. Most fishmongers will keep it for a couple of days before selling it. It may have a very slight ammonia smell, which will disappear entirely when the skate is cooked.
Skate is sold in skinned wings. The flesh easily separates from the cartilage when cooked. This fish is found in Atlantic waters.

Raie au Beurre Noir

YIELD: 4 Servings

(Skate with Black Butter)

1	onion, sliced
3	sprigs parsley
1	lemon, sliced
1	teaspoon black peppercorns
3	pounds skate, cut into 4 portions
4	tablespoons butter
1	tablespoon white wine vinegar
2	tablespoons capers
	Coarse salt and freshly ground pepper to taste

1. Put about 2 inches of water in a large frying pan. Simmer the onion, parsley, lemon, and peppercorns for about 5 minutes. Add the pieces of skate and simmer gently for 15 minutes. Remove and drain, place on a serving dish, and keep warm.

2. Heat the butter in a small pan until the butter turns golden brown. Pour the butter over the fish. Add the vinegar and capers to the saucepan, season with salt and pepper, bring to a boil, and pour over the fish. Serve immediately.

Note: This dish goes well with boiled potatoes.

Small Fry

Those tiny fish that appear from time to time in the markets are among my favorite dishes when tossed in flour, deep-fried until golden, and eaten with the fingers. This group includes whitebait — actually baby herrings or sprats, measuring about an inch and a half long — and the larger smelts, that measure about seven inches long.

Also delicious cooked this way are fresh baby eels from Maine, about two inches long. Once in a while they make an appearance in fish stores. They are as tiny as the ones in seaside restaurants of Oualidia, near Tangier, where they are served along with miniature octopus and whitebait, fried until crisp, and served in sizzling heaps with lemon halves and bottles of cold Oustalet rosé wine.

Smelts are unusual fish. When very fresh they smell of cucumber. They are best threaded on small skewers, dipped in milk, then flour, and deep-fried. Drain the fish on paper towels, season with salt and pepper, and serve with lemon wedges and fresh parsley. They go very well with sauce tartare. Smelts are in season mostly in the fall, winter, and spring. Fresh anchovies, when they make their rare appearances in stores in the winter, are also delicious this way. All these fish should be absolutely fresh and silvery.

I once served a pile of whitebait to a large, bearded, and highly neurotic poet from England who said he couldn't eat them with their heads because of the look in their eyes. So he proceeded to ruin everyone's dinner by decapitating each little fish one by one and tossing the heads, which were no bigger than the nail on your little finger, into a pile on the side of his plate.

Sauce Tartare

2	hard-boiled egg yolks
1	teaspoon dry mustard
	Coarse salt and freshly
	ground pepper to taste
2	teaspoons vinegar
1	cup olive oil
1	tablespoon chopped
	capers
1	tablespoon chopped fresh
	chives
1	tablespoon chopped fresh
	parsley
2	pickles, chopped

1. Mix the egg yolks into a paste with the mustard, salt, and pepper. Add the vinegar and mix well. Gradually work in the olive oil, as for mayonnaise.

2. Stir in the capers, chives, parsley, and chopped pickles.

Fried Anchovies

1	pound fresh anchovies or
	other small fry
3	cups peanut or vegetable
	oil
1	cup flour
1	teaspon cayenne pepper
	Coarse salt and freshly
	ground pepper to taste
2	lemons, quartered
2	tablespoons chopped
	fresh parsley for garnish

1. Carefully remove the intestines from the anchovies. Rinse the anchovies and pat dry.

2. Heat the oil in a deep-fryer. Dredge the anchovies in flour and cayenne, shaking loose any excess. Fry about 5 at a time in the hot oil, turning once, for about 3 to 4 minutes in all.

3. Remove and drain on paper towels. When you have cooked all the anchovies, serve them immediately, garnished with lemon and parsley.

Note: This dish is good with french fries.

Fried Baby Eels

2 pounds baby eels
Flour for dredging
Coarse salt and freshly
ground pepper to taste
Peanut or vegetable oil
for deep-frying
2 small lemons, quartered

1. Wash the eels and pat dry with paper towels. Put the flour into a large bowl and toss the eels until coated. Shake off excess flour. Sprinkle the eels with salt and pepper.

2. Heat the oil in a deep-fryer until very hot (if the oil is not hot enough, the eels will be mushy).

3. Add the eels, a handful at a time, and deep fry for 2 to 3 minutes or until golden and crisp. Drain on paper towels and serve at once with lemon quarters.

Poultry

Chicken

Americans now consume a pound of chicken a week, according to the U.S. Department of Agriculture, so it's small wonder that poultry producers compete for customers with the same intensity as promoters of designer jeans. Across the country, we are subjected to a barrage of advertisements in city subways, on radio and television, and in newspapers and magazines as poultry producers try to corner the market.

You would think that given the similarities in their rearing conditions and feed — which is based largely on soybean and corn — our chickens would be very similar, despite the claims of the brand-name advertisers. But there is a surprisingly wide range in the quality of chickens on the market. None has the remarkable flavor of free-range farmyard chickens unless raised on a farm, and those are hard to find. Only the occasional butcher or health food store sells them. In general, the modern American chicken is a pretty bland bird as far as flavor is concerned. Has it become conveyor-belt food to be put on the table without high hopes?

Where Chicken Comes From

Arkansas is America's largest broiler-producing state, Georgia second. The "broiler belt," as it is called in the industry, stretches from eastern Texas through Louisiana, Arkansas, Mississippi, Alabama, Georgia, North Florida, the Carolinas, and into the Delmarva peninsula. People living far away from these areas in, say, Seattle, get their chicken a little later and at slightly higher cost than a close metropolitan area such as New York City, which is supplied overnight. According to the National Broiler Council, chickens normally arrive overnight in most large cities. For faraway cities, two days on the road is the longest.

Broiling chickens, weighing 2½ to 4 pounds, are not injected with hormones because of their fast growth rate. But there are antibiotics in almost all commercial feeds. To prevent coccidiosis, a parasitic disease, broiling chickens are treated with drugs on a regular schedule. The birds are put on non-medicated feed for five days before slaughter.

Large chickens of 6 to 8 pounds, however, are sometimes injected with estradiol palmitate, a hormone compound that helps them to put on weight. The hormones can be injected only after a chicken is six weeks old, and the chicken cannot be processed until twelve weeks old. According to the U.S. Department of Agriculture, the hormone has no side effects other than changing fat deposition.

All poultry-processing plants that ship their products out of state have a U.S. Department of Agriculture inspector on the premises, and each chicken inspected carries a tag saying so. In addition to the U.S.D.A. gradings, some plants hire additional inspectors to grade their chickens A, B, or C. The process is entirely voluntary, and the grading is based on appearance, not taste or freshness. Grade A birds are usually full fleshed and attractive, with no lacerations of the flesh and no pin feathers. Grade B birds are not as good looking, and grade C birds are used for processed foods.

Of course, chicken is at its best fresh, but the desire of producers to increase the birds' shelf life has led to innovations that do nothing for freshness or taste. Ninety percent of all broiler-fryer chickens are sold as fresh and are shipped after being ice packed, CO_2 packed, or deep chilled. The rest are frozen or fully cooked.

The best mass-produced chicken is ice packed and shipped surrounded by ice shavings. When a chicken is CO_2 packed, carbon dioxide "snow" is used to keep the chicken cold. This process is similar to ice packing.

But increasingly, chicken producers are "chill packing" chicken. After the bird is slaughtered, it is shipped at about 28 to 32 degrees. The problem is that the chicken is partly frozen and develops a crust of crystals on the skin. Sometimes the wings become frozen, the drumsticks semi-frozen. Inside, the temperature remains between 32 and 43 degrees. Many supermarket chains prefer this method because, if held at 28 to 32 degrees, chill-packed chicken lasts two weeks longer than ice-packed, which lasts only for a week. But at 30 degrees it's hard — and since it has been partially frozen, the chicken will not have the same texture as ice-packed birds once it is cooked.

In the Market

There are three places I go for the best chicken: a reliable butcher, a live poultry market, or a health food store with good free-range hens. In New York I buy Bell & Evans chickens. These are sold in butcher shops and come from a variety of small farms. The quality is generally excellent. These chickens are not yellow but have a creamy white skin and a good flavor.

The two largest selling supermarket brands in the country are Gold Kist and Holly Farms, supplying mostly the Southeast and Southwest. Other predominant brands include Country Pride, Cookin' Good, Perdue, Paramount, and Foster Farms.

The only way to get the best of the brands is to look carefully at the chicken and know what you are looking for. The color of a chicken's skin, so prominent in its advertising, is no indication of its flavor, nor is its plumpness. The color depends on the feed. Bright yellow birds have usually been fed marigold petals or food coloring. A plump breast does not mean better flavor. Some chickens are bred to give a larger breast.

A chicken may look good but taste medicinal. This suggests that there were plenty of chemicals in the feed, and you'll probably want to avoid this brand in the future. Fish meal is a part of most chickens' diet, but some have been fed such a high proportion of this that they actually taste fishy. I know one restaurant where the chef serves his chicken breasts stuffed with crabmeat. This may seem unusual but his reasoning was sound. "Since the chicken tastes like fish, why not go all the way instead of pretending it doesn't?" he said. And, in fact, the dish was delicious.

When buying chickens, look for those that are are rather rigid, plump but not flaccid. You can tell how old a bird was when it was killed by pressing down on the tip of the breastbone. A springy breastbone indicates a young bird, which will be more tender than an older one. A chicken's skin should be fairly taut, smooth, and soft with no mottled or rough dry spots.

A fresh chicken should have no off smell and should not be slimy but should be satiny and moist. You can ask the store to open the package if you want to be sure the chicken smells good. Watch out for pieces of ice inside the cavity or a gush of water pouring out of the bag when you open it. This indicates that the chicken was frozen, then thawed.

Chickens sold in supermarkets are wrapped in plastic so that it's possible to see the condition of the skin. But there is no way of telling how old birds are by looking if they are packed in opaque bags.

Supermarket packages usually have expiration dates on the price tag. You cannot tell by looking whether the chicken was chill packed or ice packed. There are no Federal laws governing the period of time within which a slaughtered bird must be sold, but they usually reach markets within a day or two of being slaughtered. Chill-packed chickens can remain in the cooler for over a week before being shipped out. Some poultry companies, such as Holly Farms, are now putting an expiration date on the label, but this is seven days after the chicken was shipped, not slaughtered. To add to the confusion, many stores are dating their chickens after they have arrived in the store. Again, this can be misleading. You cannot know how old the chicken was when it arrived.

Most butchers sell their chickens unwrapped and wrap them in butcher paper when they are sold. Most supermarkets sell them wrapped in plastic, often on trays, and this makes it hard for the shopper to tell how fresh they are. Sometimes I have bought a chicken at the supermarket and opened it at home to find that it had spoiled.

The freshest chickens are those sold at live poultry markets where customers can pick out the live bird of their choice. But chicken should not be eaten the day it is killed or the meat will be tough. Anyone who has tried to eat a chicken or turkey the same day that it is slaughtered knows what it's like to eat rubber; these birds have to sit for a day, long enough for the muscles to relax, before they can be properly cooked. Kosher chickens are also usually very fresh because they are killed locally. But although these chickens are fresh, how much flavor they have depends on what they have been fed.

There are several kinds of chickens on the market. The smallest is the Rock Cornish game hen, which is an immature chicken about five to six weeks old, weighing not more than 2 pounds. A broiler or fryer is a young chicken, usually under thirteen weeks old, with a breastbone cartilage that is more pliable than that of older chickens. A roasting chicken is usually three to five months old. A capon is a neutered male chicken, usually under eight months old. A hen, fowl, or baking chicken is usually more than ten months old and has a nonflexible breastbone tip. A cock or rooster is a mature male chicken with toughened, darkened meat. Old birds have more flavor than younger ones, but they can be tougher.

It is always cheaper to buy a whole chicken than to buy parts. The carcass can be used for stock. Don't be misled by advertisements that try to persuade you to buy parts rather than whole chickens. There is much more profit in selling parts.

In the Kitchen

Chicken is certainly a remarkably versatile bird. Because it has a fairly bland taste, it goes with almost any kind of flavor, with fresh herbs such as basil or tarragon, with Oriental spices, or with expensive black truffles. It can be stuffed and roasted and served with roast potatoes and brussels sprouts, or simmered with red wine, carrots, and onions. It takes well to fruits such as apples, pears, apricots, or prunes, and the carcass always makes a fine stock. Chicken breasts can be coated with a mayonnaise-tuna dressing for a summer dinner party. The legs are delicious coated with mustard and grilled over hot coals until crisp and almost charred.

If a chicken does not have much flavor but is young, it can still be good roasted with herbs and spices. Marinating chicken before you cook it does a lot to improve the flavor. If you have an older bird and you supect it may be tough, use it for soup or stew.

If you freeze chicken, it will keep up to three months, but will have lost its texture — it turns mushy — and much of the flavor. Chicken is best not frozen. Leave the chicken loosely wrapped in the refrigerator in waxed or butcher paper, not in plastic.

If you are planning to roast a chicken you will get a silky, taut skin if you "air dry" it first. Leave it to sit unwrapped in the refrigerator for a couple of hours so that the air can circulate around it. After being roasted, the chicken should rest up to an hour at room temperature before being served so that the juices develop.

If you want a medium-done bird (with an internal temperature of 150 to 155 degrees), evenly cooked through, with a golden but not browned breast, the majority of the cooking time is done breast down so that the juices flow into the breast as it cooks, preventing it from drying out. However, with this method the breast does not become very brown. If you want a brown breast, cook it at a higher temperature and turn the chicken over breast up for the last half hour of cooking.

Chicken is also delicious roasted in a casserole in butter with a whole head of garlic separated into cloves but unpeeled. This sounds like a lot of garlic, but cooked this way the cloves are roasted and become soft and golden. They impart a very delicate flavor to the chicken.

If you want to keep raw chicken for a day or two, rub it with lemon. It also keeps well marinated in wine, lemon, or vinegar, which breaks down the tissues and helps to tenderize the meat. Yogurt, olive oil, or chopped garlic and lemon juice are good marinades for chicken that is to be braised; a mixture of mustard, garlic, lemon juice, and oil goes well with chicken to be barbecued. An unusual spicy marinade can be made with lemon juice, garlic, green chilies, ground cumin, basil, parsley or mint, and yogurt, all puréed in the blender.

After you have cooked a chicken, simmer the bones in water with a chopped onion, a couple of celery stalks, a sliced carrot, thyme, bay leaf, and peppercorns, The strained stock can be frozen. It can also be kept in the refrigerator for a week, provided it is brought to a boil every two or three days. It is extremely useful to have on hand for soups and sauces — indispensable, in fact.

The following recipe suggests letting the chicken rest for 1 hour after it is roasted. This may seem like a long time, but you will be amazed at how much juicier the bird will be. Roast chicken does not have to be piping hot.

Breast-Down Roast Chicken   YIELD: 4 to 6 Servings

1	3-to-4-pound roasting chicken
¼	cup melted butter

1. To get a crisp skin and to keep moisture in the bird, air dry the chicken, completely unwrapped, in the refrigerator, for 2 hours before cooking it. Place a plate on the shelf below to catch blood.

2. Preheat the oven to 500 degrees. Wipe the cavity dry with a paper towel. On a V-shaped roasting rack, which holds the legs next to the breast, roast the chicken breast down for 10 minutes.

3. Turn the temperature down to 225 degrees. Baste the chicken with melted butter, using a pastry brush. Roast for 30 minutes, breast down.

4. Turn, baste, and continue roasting breast up until the chicken has reached an internal temperature of 150 to 155 degrees at thickest part of thigh or breast. Approximate roasting time at 225 degrees is 15 minutes per pound.

5. Let the chicken rest at room temperature for 1 hour before serving to allow the juices to redistribute themselves. If it is carved immediately, the chicken's juices will be lost.

Crisp-Skin Roast Chicken

YIELD: 4 to 6 Servings

1	3-to-4-pound roasting chicken
¼	cup melted butter

1. Sear, breast up, for 20 minutes at 500 degrees, baste with melted butter, and turn breast down. Turn oven down to 225 degrees and roast for 30 minutes.

2. Baste and turn breast up. Raise heat to 500 degrees. Finish roasting breast up until the chicken has reached an internal temperature of 165 to 175 degrees at thickest part of thigh or breast. Allow the chicken to rest before serving.

Römertopf Roast Chicken

YIELD: 4 to 6 Servings

1	3-to-4-pound chicken, including heart, liver, and gizzard
3	lemons
4	slices fresh ginger
5	cloves garlic, peeled
½	cup tamari soy sauce

1. Wipe the chicken dry with paper towels. Place in the Römertopf and squeeze on the juice from the lemons. Place the lemon skins inside the cavity.

2. Place a slice of ginger and a garlic clove between the wing joints and where the legs join the chicken. Place a garlic clove in the cavity.

3. Sprinkle with soy sauce. Slice the heart, liver, and gizzard and place around the chicken.

4. Cover the Römertopf and put into a cold oven. Turn the oven to 425 degrees and roast the chicken for 1 hour. Take the lid off and brown for 15 minutes.

Note: A Römertopf is a Dutch oven made of clay. It seals in the moisture of foods while baking.

Spicy Marinated Chicken

YIELD: 4 to 6 Servings

⅔	cup plain yogurt
2	tablespoons olive oil
2	cloves garlic, minced
	Juice of 1 lemon
	Freshly ground pepper to taste
2	green chilies, coarsely chopped
½	cup fresh basil, parsley, or mint leaves (reserve extra leaves for garnish)
1	3-to-4-pound chicken

1. Combine all ingredients except the chicken, and purée in the blender. Coat the chicken thoroughly with the mixture. Leave overnight or for 2 days in a covered china or glass bowl before cooking.

2. To cook, preheat the oven to 350 degrees. Place the chicken in a covered casserole and roast for 1 hour or until tender. Garnish with the extra leaves and serve.

Coq au Vin

YIELD: 6 Servings

1	3½-to-4-pound chicken, cut up
1	medium yellow onion, coarsely chopped
1	carrot, coarsely chopped
	Coarse salt and freshly ground pepper to taste
2	herb bouquets (thyme, parsley, and bay leaf tied in a cheesecloth)
2½	cups water

1. Make the chicken stock by putting the giblets and chicken wings into a saucepan with the onion, carrot, dash of salt, a few grindings of pepper, and 1 herb bouquet. Add water, cover, and simmer for 20 minutes. Remove the vegetables, and set the stock aside.

2. Meanwhile, pat the chicken pieces dry with a paper towel.

3. Cut the salt pork or bacon into ¼-inch cubes. Heat 1 tablespoon each of oil and butter in a heavy casserole large enough to hold the

¼	pound salt pork or lean bacon, in a chunk
1	tablespoon olive oil
2	tablespoons butter
18	small white onions
¼	cup cognac
3	cups red wine such as Burgundy, Beaujolais, or Côtes du Rhône
2	cloves garlic, crushed
½	pound fresh button mushrooms
1	tablespoon flour

chicken pieces without crowding and sauté the salt pork until lightly browned. Remove with a slotted spoon to a plate.

4. Peel the onions by dropping them briefly into boiling water, draining them and slipping off their skins. Sauté them in the butter and oil until browned. Remove with a slotted spoon to a warm place, such as the back of the stove.

5. Place the chicken pieces in the casserole, skin side down, and brown lightly, turning so that they are done on all sides. Season with pepper.

6. Heat the cognac in a small saucepan and pour it onto the chicken. Set it alight and agitate the casserole until the flames die down. Add the onions and bacon.

7. Add the wine, garlic, and a fresh herb bouquet. Add enough stock to cover chicken, place lid on casserole, and simmer gently for 30 minutes.

8. Meanwhile, wash and thoroughly dry the mushrooms. Leave them whole if they are small, quarter them if large. Add them to the casserole and cook for 5 minutes.

9. Meanwhile, mix the remaining butter and flour into a paste.

10. With a slotted spoon, remove the chicken, vegetables, and salt pork cubes to a heated dish and keep warm in the oven.

11. Add the butter-flour mixture to the casserole and stir over low heat. Bring to a boil and stir, simmering for 15 minutes or until sauce is thick enough to coat the spoon.

12. Arrange chicken, bacon cubes, and vegetables in the casserole and spoon the sauce over them. Dot with small pieces of butter.

13. Just before serving, heat through for about 5 minutes.

Chicken Breasts Tonnato

	Juice of 1 lemon
4	chicken breasts, boned and skinned
	Coarse salt and freshly ground white pepper to taste
4	tablespoons butter
2	egg yolks
½	teaspoon dry mustard
1	cup extra-virgin olive oil
3½	ounces canned tuna, drained
8	canned flat anchovy fillets
3	tablespoons capers, drained
3	tablespoons chopped fresh tarragon or basil leaves

1. Squeeze the juice of half the lemon over the chicken breasts and season them with salt and pepper. Heat the butter in a skillet until foaming; turn the chicken breasts in the butter to coat. Lower the flame and cook, turning once, for about 3 minutes on each side, without burning. Cool to room temperature.

2. In a mixing bowl, beat the egg yolks with a wire whisk. Add the mustard and remaining lemon juice. Mix thoroughly, then little by little add the oil and make a mayonnaise. Add salt and pepper and more lemon juice if necessary. If the mayonnaise curdles, beat an egg yolk in another bowl and gradually beat in the curdled mixture until the yolk has absorbed it and you have a smooth mayonnaise.

3. Pound the tuna in a mortar with a little coarse salt. Mix into the mayonnaise.

4. Put the chicken breasts into a bowl and pour on the mayonnaise. Cover and refrigerate. Put on a serving dish when ready to serve and decorate with strips of anchovies, capers, and fresh herbs.

Note: This is good with Artichoke Hearts with Fava Beans (page 235).

Chicken with Sesame Seeds and Pears

1	large (4 to 5 pounds) or 2 small (2 to 3 pounds) chickens
	Coarse salt and freshly ground pepper to taste
½	cup sesame seeds
½	cup sesame oil
½	teaspoon ground cinnamon
½	teaspoon ground ginger
2	cloves garlic, minced
1	medium onion, sliced
4	Bartlett pears

1. Wipe the chicken with paper towels and sprinkle the cavity with salt and pepper. Set aside.

2. Preheat the oven to 350 degrees.

3. Brown the sesame seeds either by baking them briefly in a moderate oven or toasting them in a heavy skillet.

4. Oil the inside of a deep casserole just large enough to hold the chicken. Add the chicken and sprinkle with cinnamon, ginger, and garlic. Arrange onions on top, season with salt and pepper, cover, and bake for 30 minutes.

5. Peel and core the pears and cut into eighths. Remove the casserole from the oven and arrange the pear pieces over the chicken. Sprinkle sesame seeds on top. Return the casserole to the oven. Continue baking 20 to 30 minutes or until the chicken is done. Serve with rice and steamed vegetables.

Chicken with Fresh Coriander and Garlic

YIELD: 6 Servings

2	medium-sized chickens (about 2½ to 3 pounds each)
1	bunch fresh coriander
6	cloves garlic
	Coarse salt and freshly ground pepper to taste
1	teaspoon ground cinnamon
1	teaspoon ground cumin
1	tablespoon peanut or vegetable oil

1. Preheat the oven to 400 degrees.
2. Wipe the chickens inside and out with paper towels.
3. Trim the stalks off the coriander and chop the leaves.
4. Peel the garlic, cut in half lengthwise, and discard the center core.
5. Place the garlic and coriander in the chicken cavities and sprinkle with salt, pepper, cinnamon, and cumin. Sprinkle the skin with the oil.
6. Roast the chicken for 45 minutes or until the chicken is cooked so that the juices run rosy when the chicken is pricked with a fork.

Chicken Breasts in Mustard Cream Sauce

YIELD: 4 Servings

4	boned chicken breasts
1	cup dry vermouth
2	large cloves garlic, finely chopped
2	teaspoons dried tarragon
½	cup chicken stock
½	cup heavy cream
1	heaping teaspoon Dijon mustard
	Coarse salt and freshly ground pepper to taste

1. Slice chicken breasts in half horizontally.
2. Heat vermouth in frying pan and add garlic and 1 teaspoon tarragon. Bring to a boil, add chicken, turn heat down to low, and poach gently for about 7 minutes, removing pieces as they finish cooking. It is very important that the chicken should not be overcooked. The center should be pink. The chicken will continue cooking even after it has been set aside.
3. Add the remaining ingredients except mustard to pan and cook over moderate heat, stirring constantly, so that it reduces to the consistency of heavy cream.
4. Stir in mustard and return chicken to sauce and serve. This dish can also be served cold or with the chicken breasts at room temperature and the sauce hot.

Broiled Chicken Legs

YIELD: 4 to 8 Servings

8	whole chicken legs
1	cup red wine vinegar
2	cups sweet vermouth
2	teaspoons dried tarragon
3	large cloves garlic, coarsely chopped
	Coarse salt and freshly ground pepper to taste

1. In a large bowl, marinate the chicken legs in a mixture of ½ cup vinegar, 1 cup vermouth, and the tarragon and garlic for 5 hours or overnight.

2. Place the chicken and marinade in a large frying pan and cook over moderate heat, turning chicken often.

3. When the chicken is almost fully cooked, in 10 to 15 minutes, transfer the legs to a broiling pan. Preheat the broiler.

4. Add the remaining vinegar and vermouth to the marinade and bring to a boil, reducing over high heat until almost syrupy (to about ¾ cup).

5. Meanwhile, place the chicken under the broiler and turn the pieces until very crisp.

6. Return the chicken to the sauce and serve.

Hangover Soup

YIELD: 8 Servings

2	small chickens (about 2½ pounds each), chopped in 2-inch pieces
½	pound bacon, diced
	Juice of 8 lemons
1	tablespoon Tabasco sauce, or more to taste
	Coarse salt and freshly ground pepper to taste
1	large onion, chopped
1	tablespoon thyme
2	quarts water

Combine all ingredients except the water in a large pot and leave to marinate for about 1 hour. Add the water and simmer, covered, for 30 minutes. Correct seasoning.

Chicken Liver

When buying chicken livers, look for those that are plump and shiny with no smell. They should be bright in hue, not brown or dingy. Trim away the connecting gristle and pat the livers dry before cooking them.

Chicken Livers with Tagliatelle

YIELD: 4 to 6 Servings

1	pound chicken livers, trimmed
3	tablespoons butter
1	tablespoon olive oil
1	small onion, finely chopped
1	teaspoon crumbled sage leaves
1	bay leaf
1	slice prosciutto, cut julienne
2	cups canned plum tomatoes
¼	cup Marsala (or dry red wine)
	Coarse salt and freshly ground pepper to taste
1	pound tagliatelle
	Freshly grated Parmesan to taste

1. Quickly brown the livers in 2 tablespoons butter and the oil. Remove to a plate.

2. Add the onion, sage, bay leaf, and prosciutto. Cook until the onion has softened, stirring occasionally.

3. Add tomatoes with their juice and the Marsala. Season with salt and pepper and simmer gently for 10 minutes. Meanwhile, bring 4 quarts water to a boil for the tagliatelle.

4. Add the chicken livers to the sauce and cook until they are just pink inside. Do not overcook them. Keep the sauce warm while you cook the pasta until al dente. Drain the pasta and toss with the remaining tablespoon of butter.

5. Place in a heated dish and pour sauce over the top. Serve the cheese separately.

Chicken Livers with Green Peppercorns

1	pound chicken livers, trimmed
	Flour for dredging
1	tablespoon safflower oil
½	cup port wine
2	tablespoons green peppercorns, drained
1	tablespoon fresh ginger, chopped
¾	cup chicken stock
	Coarse salt and freshly ground pepper to taste
¼	cup heavy cream
2	tablespoons butter, cut into small pieces

1. Dust the livers with flour. Heat the oil in a skillet and brown the livers quickly. Set aside.

2. Add the port, peppercorns, ginger, and stock. Season with salt and pepper, bring to a boil, turn down heat, and reduce to ½ cup.

3. Return the livers to the pan. Add the cream and cook until it has thickened and the livers are heated through. Whisk in the butter and serve.

Note: Be careful not to overcook the livers. They should be pink in the center. Serve with rice.

Duck

Duck is no great bargain. It is a bony bird with little flesh for its size and an enormous amount of fat. But roasted to a shiny mahogany color, duck looks especially attractive served with wild rice and green vegetables, such as peas or watercress, and orange salad. The rich, meaty flavor is a perfect foil for fruit sauces made with apples, cranberries, cherries, or oranges, and goes with potatoes roasted or puréed with turnips or celery root. Turnips can also be placed around the duck to roast in the fat that comes off it while it cooks.

Where Duck Comes From

The market for duck has been growing fast in recent years, with an 80 percent increase since 1965. In 1981, 18.2 million ducks were sold, bringing the industry its fifth record year in a row. But despite all this, per capita consumption of duck is only three quarters of a pound a year, compared with almost a pound a week for chicken. People are still nervous about the bird, unsure of how to cook it or even how to buy it.

The most widely sold duck is the white Pekin, which was brought to the United States from China over a hundred years ago. This is a very fatty bird. It accounts for about 99 percent of the market, according to the National Duckling Council. The major producers of Long Island duckling — white Pekin — are in Indiana and Wisconsin. Long Island produces only about 4.4 million ducks a year. The Long Island Farm Cooperative is a cooperative of about twenty farms. Long Island Pekins are generally not sold under a brand name, so the only way to be sure of getting the best is to find one you like and go back to the same source for more.

Barnhard Farms near Williamsburg, Virginia, and Concord Farms in Concord, North Carolina, also supply the eastern United States with white Pekins. But more than two thirds of the ducks on the market are raised in the Midwest. Maple Leaf farms in Milford, Indiana, and their subsidiary, C & D in Wisconsin, produce around nine million white Pekins per year and ship them nationwide. Reichardt Duck Farms near San Francisco supplies the Chinese market in San Francisco with fresh white Pekins dressed Chinese style — complete with head and feet — put on cracked ice and shipped into Chinatown within hours of slaughter. Sometimes they are shipped live so the Chinese can do their own slaughtering.

The ducks are fed a high-protein diet that includes corn, soybean, and fish meal. They are usually slaughtered after six to seven weeks and weigh an average of 4½ to 5 pounds. White Pekin or Long Island ducks are fattier and juicier but do not have as rich a flavor as Mallard and Muscovy ducks.

Mallard and Muscovy ducks are produced on a much smaller scale than white Pekin. They are the most flavorful ducks on the market but are in small supply, and not everyone takes to their gamy taste. Pietrus Foods in Sleepy Eye, Minnesota, is the largest supplier, and its biggest market is in New York and Chicago. The birds are slaughtered in the fall, frozen, and supplied to supermarkets and butchers. They are at their best in late fall and throughout the winter. Mallard duck, a flying bird native to North America, is the ancestral parent of all domestic ducks. It is small, weighing on the average between 1½ and 3 pounds, and is marketed at 12 weeks. This is one of the best ducks, with very little fat and a rich gamy flavor.

Muscovy duck is native to South America and also has very little fat. The female can weigh from 2½ to 6 pounds, the male from 5 to 10 pounds. Muscovy is much beloved by the French and is perhaps the best of all, with its broad, plump breast and firm, dark, gamy meat.

Even though the majority of duck is frozen, the trend is toward fresh. Major supermarket chains in New York, Cleveland, Chicago, Detroit, Milwaukee, and Minneapolis are now featuring special fresh Pekin duck sales. The ducks are slaughtered and arrive by truck in the stores the following day. According to the National Duckling Council, duckling is much easier than chicken to handle fresh because its fat protects it from deteriorating.

In the Market

Duck prices have come down considerably in recent years. Good ducks can now be found in supermarkets for as little as 99 cents a pound. They freeze well because they have so much fat, and, unlike chickens, they retain their juiciness when defrosted. Duck can be kept in the freezer for three to four months. Thaw a frozen duck slowly, 24 to 36 hours in the refrigerator, and do not put it into the oven until it is thoroughly thawed, both inside and out.

The best way to be sure of getting good duck is to buy from a reliable butcher or supermarket. Look for a plump skin, and if the duck is frozen, it should be frozen solid. The color varies slightly with the breed. Mallard and Muscovy duck should be creamy yellow or ivory, and white Pekin, the most widely available, pinkish white or white. The skin should not be mottled or rough with dry patches, and the color should be even.

Ducks are federally inspected, just as chickens are, and are graded, like chickens, according to appearance with grades A, B, or C. If the skin is torn or there is a part missing, they won't get a Grade A. Almost all the whole ducks you'll find in the stores will be Grade A.

Fresh ducks come chill-packed and frozen from Wisconsin, Virginia and North Carolina, arriving in the stores two or three days after slaughter. Long

Island ducks are also available fresh, chill-packed and frozen, but supplies have dwindled in recent years because of high energy costs and increasing encroachment on farmland by real estate developers.

Mallard and Muscovy are the most expensive, but there is less waste in fat. Pekin ducks, which have a lot of fat, are good for steaming or roasting.

When buying duck in a supermarket, check the expiration date on the package. Avoid packages with a deposit of liquid, which indicates that the duck has been frozen then defrosted or has been in the package for some time. Many brands of duck are sold in opaque vacuum packs, making it impossible to tell if they are fresh by looking or smelling.

In the Kitchen
Duck is very greasy, and it is important to get rid of as much fat as you can. There are several ways to do this. First of all, prick the skin all over with a fork and rub it with salt. Then the duck can be browned under the broiler on all sides so that the fat runs out. I also discovered a strange but highly effective method of degreasing duck from my friend John Bernard Myers. He boils the duck for a few minutes and then dries it with, of all things, an electric hand-held hair dryer. The hot air opens the pores so that the fat runs out. Another good way is to steam the duck before roasting it. These last two methods make the skin almost as crisp as that of duck cooked Peking-style in Chinese restaurants. Remove some of the fat near the cavity before cooking. Don't throw away any of the fat — it is marvelous for frying potatoes.

Mallard and Muscovy ducks should not be cooked well done; they are at their best medium rare. If they are overcooked, the meat dries out. The breast is the best part; the legs and thighs can be tough and are better kept for soup or stock.

The painter Monet was particularly fond of duck. One of his eccentricities was to cut off the wings of roast duck, sprinkle them with salt, pepper, and nutmeg and send them to the kitchen to be grilled as a special treat.

1   duck, about 5½ pounds, with liver
6   tablespoons coarse salt
2   teaspoons freshly ground pepper
2   teaspoons finely ground sage
2   teaspoons finely chopped rosemary

1. Set the duck liver aside. Boil the duck in water to cover for 7 minutes. Drain.

2. Preheat the oven to 450 degrees.

3. With an electric hand-held hair dryer, dry the duck inside and out for 8 minutes.

4. Using two small bowls, put equal amounts of salt, pepper, sage, and rosemary into each and mix.

5. Using a mortar and pestle, pound the raw duck liver with the salt-herb mixture from one of the bowls. Rub the duck cavity with the resulting mixture. Close the opening with skewers or sew closed with cotton thread.

6. Rub the duck skin with the spices from the second bowl.

7. Place the duck in a roasting pan, breast side up, and roast for 30 minutes. Lower the temperature to 375 degrees. Turn the duck over, breast side down, and roast for an additional hour.

8. Remove the duck from the oven and place it on a dish. Open the cavity and allow the juices to flow out. Scrape out the herb-liver mixture from the cavity. To make a sauce, put the juices in a small pan, add the herb-liver mixture, mix, and heat through.

9. To cut into serving pieces, use a cleaver, Chinese-style, cutting through the bone and meat. Serve with the sauce poured over the pieces.

10. Serve with a purée of potatoes and turnips (page 286).

Two-Way Duck Salad

2	5½-to-6-pound ducks
	Coarse salt and freshly
	ground pepper to taste
2	tablespoons fresh
	rosemary leaves
3	oranges
1	small Spanish onion
2	tablespoons chopped
	fresh mint
4	sprigs fresh mint
1½	cup dried flageolets
6	cups water
	Herb bouquet
1	medium onion, peeled
	and quartered
1	cup dry white wine
4	ripe tomatoes, seeded and
	chopped but not peeled
4	tablespoons olive oil
1	tablespoon red wine
	vinegar

1. With a mortar and pestle, mash the duck livers with salt, pepper, and 1 tablespoon rosemary. Salt the duck cavities and smear the mixture inside.

2. Prick the ducks all over lightly with a fork and rub with salt. Put one of the ducks, breast up, in a colander or steamer. Cover with foil so that no air escapes, and steam over boiling water for 40 minutes. Remove foil and let sit while the other duck cooks. (If you have two steamers, both ducks can be cooked — separately — at the same time.) Prick the skin again lightly with a fork to allow more fat to flow out. Allow the second duck to rest for 15 minutes before roasting.

3. Preheat the oven to 550 degrees. Pat the ducks dry with paper towels. Put them on a roasting rack in a pan big enough to hold them both. Roast for 15 to 20 minutes or enough to brown the skin.

4. Remove from oven and pour the juices from the cavity into a small bowl. Cool and proceed with the following recipes.

Duck Breast with Oranges

1. Separate the breasts from the bone and slice them. Set aside.

2. Peel 2 of the oranges and chop coarsely, removing pith and seeds. Cut the remaining orange in half and slice thinly. Peel the Spanish onion and slice into thin rings.

3. Arrange the pieces of duck breast on a plate with the orange and onion. Season with salt and pepper and sprinkle with chopped mint. Garnish with mint sprigs.

Note: This is good with fresh peas and a mixture of white and wild rice, served hot or cold.

1. Cook the flageolets in the water with the juices from the duck cavity along with the herb bouquet, onion, salt, and pepper, and simmer, covered, for about 2 hours or until tender. If there is still liquid in the beans, turn up heat and boil down. Cool. Remove the herb bouquet.

2. Remove the legs and thighs from the duck. Bring the wine to a simmer and cook the legs and thighs in the wine for 10 minutes. Set aside to cool in the wine, about 15 minutes.

3. Remove the meat from the legs and thighs, chop coarsely, and mix into the beans. Refrigerate until needed.

4. Mix the tomatoes, the leg meat, and the beans. Mix the oil and vinegar and add, along with the remaining tablespoon of rosemary leaves. Correct seasoning.

Note: Mixed green or arugula salad is a good accompaniment for this dish.

Broiled Duck with Orange-Glazed Turnips YIELD: 2 Servings

1	4-to-4½-pound duck
1	orange
½	teaspoon rosemary
	Coarse salt and freshly ground pepper to taste
1	large turnip, cut in walnut-sized pieces
2	teaspoons sugar
4	tablespoons butter
1	tablespoon chopped fresh parsley

1. Cut the duck in half lengthwise with poultry shears, working up from the tail and down the center, or have it cut in half by the butcher. Remove as much fat as possible from the carcass. Prick the skin lightly all over with a fork so the fat will pour off as the duck cooks.

2. Peel the orange thinly and set the peel aside. Squeeze the juice from the orange and pour it over the duck meat. Sprinkle with rosemary, salt, and pepper.

3. Heat the broiler to medium-hot. Place the duck halves on a broiler rack, bone side up, and broil 4 inches from heat for 15 minutes. Drain off the fat and turn the duck pieces so the skin side is up. Season with salt and pepper. Broil for 20 minutes or until the skin is browned and crisp. Be careful not to burn the skin. If it cooks

too fast, move the broiling pan farther from heat. The duck is done when the juices are pink.

4. While the duck is cooking, bring the turnips to a boil in water to cover. After 5 minutes add the orange peel. When the turnips are almost tender — after about 10 minutes — drain off all but ½ cup of water. Add the sugar and butter and cook until glazed, turning occasionally with a wooden spoon. Meanwhile, cut the orange peel into julienne and add to the turnips. Correct seasoning.

5. Serve the turnips in a heated dish and the duck halves on heated individual plates. Garnish with parsley and serve.

Duck with Coriander Rice

YIELD: 2 to 3 Servings

1	4-to-5-pound duck
	Juice of 2 lemons
1	tablespoon ground cumin
	Coarse salt and freshly ground pepper to taste
1	can dark beer
1	can light beer
2	cups Patna rice
1	cup shelled peas
1	cup chopped fresh coriander

1. Prick the skin of the duck all over with a fork. Rub it with the lemon juice, cumin, salt, and pepper. Leave for a couple of hours at room temperature or refrigerate overnight.

2. Brown the duck on all sides in a hot frying pan or under the broiler. Pour off the fat (keep it for frying potatoes). Put the duck into a heavy pan and add the beer. Cover and simmer for 1 hour or until cooked.

3. Remove the duck. Add the rice to 3½ cups of the liquid and simmer, covered, over low heat for about 20 minutes or until cooked. Meanwhile, put the duck into a hot oven to get crisp.

4. Cook the peas in a separate pan in 1 inch of water.

5. When the rice is cooked, stir in the peas, coriander, salt, and pepper. Arrange the duck on a serving dish with the rice.

Goose

One Christmas my grandmother surprised us by serving goose instead of turkey. We sat down to the meal with some trepidation, for neither my sister nor I, schoolgirls at the time, had ever eaten goose. There were only the three of us at this meal since my parents were posted abroad, too far for us to go for the brief Christmas holiday. Buying a whole turkey for our small Christmas dinner seemed extravagant to my grandmother, and anyway, she knew we'd already had turkey at school. She made a wise choice. The goose was exquisite, stuffed with apples from the garden and roasted so that the skin was crisp and browned, served with roast potatoes, brussels sprouts sprinkled with nutmeg, and a port-and-red-currant-jelly sauce. We thought she had made a radical departure from tradition, but she could hardly have been closer.

In Europe, goose, with its rich flesh and delicate fat, has always been popular in the lean winter months around Christmastime. It is traditionally eaten on November 11, Martinmas (the feast of St. Martin), and September 29, Michaelmas (the feast of St. Michael). It shows up again at Christmastime and at the New Year. During the Middle Ages goose was served on Twelfth Night, Epiphany, which was marked by special entertainments, plays, music, and, of course, a lavish banquet.

In England in 1663 a modest Twelfth Night feast was held at Ingatestone Hall, the Essex county seat of Sir William Petrie, the Secretary of State. According to the household accounts, over seven pounds of meat per person were served to a hundred guests. The menu included roast beef (weighing thirty pounds), a haunch and a leg of pork, two legs of veal, a whole young pig, a loin and breast of veal, two rabbits, two mutton, and four sides of venison. These dishes were decribed as "very great." The remainder of the menu consisted of three geese, two capons, two partridges, three woodcock, two teal, and twelve larks, plus sauces, dressings, stuffings, pastries, and bread.

Where Goose Comes From

Americans now consume an average of four million geese a year — one goose for every five hundred people — not much, compared with a pound of chicken a week.

The major goose processors are in Minnesota and South Dakota. The largest, Pietrus Farms of Sleepy Eye, Minnesota, produces over 120,000 a year under the brand name Sleepy Eye. In South Dakota there are three: Schultz

Processing Plant in Sissiton, Wenks Produce in Madison, and Dakota Producers in Watertown.

The geese are raised on small farms and fed vitamins, corn, soybean meal, meat scraps, and vegetable protein. The most popular size for goose is around 8 to 9 pounds, so most birds are slaughtered at sixteen weeks of age when they will have reached this weight gutted. Larger geese, twenty to twenty-four weeks old when slaughtered, are fed grass in addition to the regular diet, but this seems to have little effect on their flavor. These geese weigh about 13 to 17 pounds when dressed and for four weeks before slaughter are put on intensive feed to increase their volume of fat. Goose fat, which many people throw out, is highly prized among Jewish, German, and Eastern European ethnic groups, who, incidentally, buy more goose than any other group.

To encourage the geese to start laying during the winter, lights are turned on them from the beginning of February. They lay the most eggs during cold weather and stop when it gets hot. Curiously, geese that have hatched late put on weight more quickly than the early ones. The geese are slaughtered and shipped from July through the middle of December.

Once the geese are slaughtered, most are frozen and shipped by truck to distributors in every major city and points in between. Most go on the market within a month of slaughter, but many distributors hold them frozen until Thanksgiving or Christmas when the demand is high. In early spring it is virtually impossible to find goose in the stores. Geese are federally inspected and graded the same way as chickens. The grades A, B, and C are based on appearance — pin feathers or missing parts will not earn a rating of grade A.

In the Market

During the winter, local farms supply a small quantity of fresh geese to local butchers, but almost all goose is sold vacuum-packed and frozen. It is impossible to see what those geese look like, because you can't see through the bags. But generally the quality will be pretty consistent — with the smaller geese leaner and less fatty than the larger ones — if you stick to a brand you like. When buying a fresh goose at the butcher, make sure that it is plump and well formed, with a smooth, moist, unblemished skin and no pin feathers.

Wild goose has less fat and more flavor than domesticated goose but should only be eaten young or it will be tough.

Although in France you can buy geese at live poultry markets, it is impossible to do so in the United States. The reason is that geese molt at various stages in their life and at those times feathers can be plucked easily. The breast feathers are not discarded but are used for pillows and the ubiquitous down coat. But if you try to pluck them at other times, it can be a nightmare. As one processor put it, "You end up roasting the goose as is and skinning it!" The French, though, have years of experience in the matter.

Like ducks, geese have a large carcass, and when it comes to carving, the amount of meat can turn out to be less than overwhelming. When buying geese choose those with a soft, apricot-colored skin and plump breast. Do not buy a goose over 10 pounds or it will be tough. If you are planning to serve more than six people, buy two small geese rather than one large one. There is much less meat on a goose than on a chicken.

In the Kitchen

An excellent dinner for twelve people can be made with two roast geese, each with a different stuffing. One can be stuffed with prunes and fresh chestnuts, the other with sage and bread crumbs flavored with tangerine peel.

For the Czechoslovaks (and Hungarians, too), goose roasted to a crisp is a favorite New Year's dish. The Czechoslovaks serve it with an aromatic sauerkraut dressing and springy bread dumpling shaped like a loaf and sliced. The giblets and wings are roasted underneath the goose and their juices are scraped up into a rich brown sauce.

Two 8-pound geese placed side by side on a rack will fit in a regular oven. Line the floor of the oven with foil to catch any drips and put a large roasting pan underneath the rack. Potatoes can be roasted in the goose fat that drips down from the birds while they are cooking.

Goose fat makes the best roast potatoes ever — a fact that must have been known by the German burglars who once broke into our house when we lived in Berlin. They neglected many items of value but made off with a jar of goose fat from the refrigerator.

To prepare the goose, pull out the fat from just inside the cavity and reserve it for the potatoes. Put the fat in the roasting pan, and while it is melting, boil the potatoes until they are half done. Then add them to the pan, turning frequently so that they are browned on all sides.

The night before you prepare the meal, remove the package containing the livers and gizzards from the cavity. Put the geese on a rack, unwrapped. Leave them overnight in a cool place if there is not enough room in the refrigerator. The skin will become dry and taut and will turn very brown and crackling when roasted. As the geese are cooking, splash them with cold water during the last hour to make the skin crisp.

Roast the geese in a preheated 450 degree oven for fifteen minutes per pound, or more if you like them well done. With the geese, steamed brussels sprouts are a pleasant traditional accompaniment.

If you are cooking for six, use one of the stuffings below and cook only one goose.

Prune and Chestnut Stuffing YIELD: Stuffing for an 8-pound goose

1	pound prunes, pitted
1	cup port
2	pounds fresh chestnuts
2	tablespoons butter
1	medium onion, chopped
2	cloves garlic, chopped
6	stalks celery, chopped
4	tablespoons chopped fresh parsley
	Coarse salt and freshly ground pepper to taste

1. Soak the prunes for 1 hour in the port. Meanwhile, prepare the chestnuts. Make a slit in the top of each one with a sharp knife. Put them in boiling water and simmer for 10 minutes. Remove a few at a time with a slotted spoon. Wearing clean rubber gloves to protect your fingers, slip off the outer and inner skins. Place the chestnuts in a large bowl.

2. Melt the butter in a large skillet and add the onion, garlic, and celery. Cook without browning until the onion has softened. Add the chestnuts and prunes with the port they have been soaking in and simmer gently for 30 minutes.

3. Stir in the parsley, season with salt and pepper, and stuff the mixture into the goose cavity. Sew up the cavity and truss the goose.

Sage and Apple Stuffing YIELD: Stuffing for an 8-pound goose

2	tablespoons butter
1	large onion, chopped
1	clove garlic, minced
4	stalks celery, chopped
	Goose liver, heart, and gizzard, finely chopped
4	large apples, peeled, cored, and chopped
2	cups white bread crumbs
1	tablespoon ground dried tangerine peel
1	cup fresh sage leaves, loosely packed, or 4 tablespoons dried
	Coarse salt and freshly ground pepper to taste

1. Melt the butter in a large skillet and add the onion, garlic, and celery. Cook without browning until the onion has softened. Add the goose liver, heart, and gizzard. Fry for a couple of minutes, then add the apples, bread crumbs, and tangerine peel.

2. Chop the sage leaves, reserving a few to garnish the goose. Add to the mixture in the skillet. Season to taste and stuff the mixture into the goose cavity. Sew up the cavity and truss the goose.

Czechoslovakian Roast Goose

1	8-to-10-pound goose
1	tablespoon caraway seeds
	Coarse salt to taste

Sauerkraut Dressing

2	pounds fresh sauerkraut, rinsed
1	teaspoon caraway seeds
	Coarse salt to taste
1	medium onion, chopped
½	pound bacon, sliced
1	teaspoon sugar
1	teaspooon red wine vinegar or tarragon vinegar

Sauce

1	tablespoon flour
1	cup chicken stock

1. Preheat the oven to 450 degrees. Chop the wings off the goose. Spread the caraway seeds and salt liberally over the goose. Place in a roasting pan with the gizzards, neck, liver, and the chopped wings underneath. Roast for 2 hours or until cooked, basting frequently and pouring off the fat.

2. Rinse the sauerkraut and put into a heavy pot. Add the caraway seeds and salt and simmer for 15 minutes. In a separate pan, sauté the onion with the bacon. Drain and add to the sauerkraut. Season with sugar and vinegar to taste. Cook for 5 more minutes.

3. Arrange the goose on a serving dish and keep warm. Pour off the fat, leaving the cooking juices in the roasting pan. Stir in the flour, cook for a minute, then add the stock. Bring to a boil, season, and serve separately in a gravy boat. Serve the sauerkraut in a bowl.

Pheasant

Pheasant is a small and exquisitely flavored bird. Elizabeth David has called it the bird that inspires fantasies in the kitchen. Indeed, you only have to look at pheasant and the most exotic combinations come to mind. It goes with all sorts of flavorings, especially those that hint of autumn: cranberries, bitter oranges, juniper berries, and chestnuts or that sublime fall luxury that comes in fresh from Italy, white truffles. Roast pheasant can be served with vegetables such as brussels sprouts or roast potatoes flavored with rosemary.

It is available fresh in many markets and can be a feast for two, prepared without much bother. The birds generally weigh about 2 to 2½ pounds. Because they are lean and tend toward toughness, they should be wrapped in fat or bacon before being roasted so they will not dry out. Some butchers will lard the pheasant under the skin for you, and this helps keep them moist while allowing the breast to brown.

Where Pheasant Comes From

The major pheasant reserves are in New Jersey, Pennsylvania, Connecticut, and upper New York State in the East; in South Dakota, Minnesota, and Illinois in the Midwest. Fresh and frozen pheasant is available in fall and winter.

Pheasant is raised on corn and vegetable scraps, a feed similar to that given chickens. They are slaughtered at anywhere from three weeks to six months. The majority weigh 2 to 2½ pounds when gutted. They are shipped fresh by air freight or frozen and shipped by truck to major cities.

In the Market

The farm-raised pheasant sold in American stores is not as gamy and tender as wild pheasant available in Europe, where it is hung anywhere from six to fourteen days. Here, since the pheasant is not wild but ranch raised, if it is not prepared properly it can be stringy and disappointing, tasting rather like a dry chicken (in fact, it is closely related to chicken). But while chickens are better fresh, the flesh of pheasant develops flavor when it has aged, and this is something you can do yourself (see below). Frozen pheasant, like frozen chicken, tends to be tough.

Look for meatiness, plumpness, and some degree of fat. Pheasants are not federally inspected or graded like chickens, but they must be tagged to indicate where they come from and to show that they have been farmed with a license, not poached. They are sold in butcher shops.

In the Kitchen

One difference between pheasant and chicken is that pheasant develops flavor and becomes more tender when aged. To age pheasant, leave it unwrapped in the refrigerator for a couple of days. The skin will come to look like shoe leather, but don't be alarmed. It will tauten and become crisp when roasted, and the flesh will be more tender. If you like, put a sprig of rosemary in the cavity. Frozen pheasant can be thawed in the refrigerator and aged for two days. Pheasant will be juicier if it is covered when being cooked.

Chestnuts are a natural accompaniment to game birds. Combined with chestnuts and braised in a casserole, pheasant comes out very tender and absorbs the flavor of the vegetables. Anna Teresa Callen, a Manhattan cooking school teacher and cookbook author, remembers pheasant stuffed with truffles as a regular autumn treat when she was a child in her native Abruzzi area of Italy. If the truffles are very fresh and pungent, Mrs. Callen marinates them in a quarter cup of cognac and two tablespoons of Marsala before stuffing them into the pheasant. The marinade is then added to the cooking juices.

Fresh truffles are expensive, indeed, but as Brillat-Savarin says in *The Philosopher in the Kitchen*, "Whoever says 'truffles' utters a great word which arouses erotic and gastronomic memories among the skirted sex and memories gastronomic and erotic among the bearded sex. This dual distinction is due to the fact that the noble tuber is not only considered delicious to the taste, but is also believed to foster powers the exercise of which is extremely pleasurable."

Fagiano Tartufato

YIELD: 2 Generous Servings

(Pheasant with Truffles)

1	2-to-2½-pound pheasant
3	tablespoons prosciutto fat, at room temperature (see note)
1	white truffle, thinly sliced
1	tablespoon olive oil
	Coarse salt and freshly ground pepper to taste
4	slices fatty bacon
¼	cup heavy cream

1. The day before, wipe the pheasant dry with paper towels. Chop and mash the prosciutto fat until it is the consistency of thick cream. Smear it over the cavity of the bird. Fill the cavity with truffle slices. Truss the legs and wings with string.

2. Put the pheasant into a glass or china bowl, cover tightly with plastic or foil, and keep in a cool place (not in the refrigerator) overnight. The aroma of the truffle will permeate the pheasant. If refrigerated, the pheasant will be too cold for that to happen.

3. The following day, preheat the oven to 425 degrees. Rub the pheasant with olive oil, place on a rack in a roasting pan, sprinkle with salt and pepper, and cover the breast and legs with bacon slices.

4. Roast the pheasant for 25 minutes, basting frequently.

5. Turn down the heat to 375 degrees, cover the pheasant loosely with foil, and roast

another 20 minutes or until the pheasant is tender. Let stand on a rack.

6. Add the cream to the cooking juices and mix thoroughly.

7. Cut the pheasant into four pieces, using poultry shears, and arrange on a heated serving platter. Heat the juices and cream through and pour over the pheasant. Serve immediately.

Note: While Italians use poultry shears for cutting up the pheasant, the bird may also be carved the traditional way. Prosciutto ends are available at lower prices than regular prosciutto at Italian or speciality stores.

Braised Pheasant with Chestnuts

YIELD: 2 Servings

1	cup stock made from pheasant neck and gizzard
1	onion
1	carrot
1	celery stalk with leaves
	Herb bouquet (thyme, bay leaf, and parsley tied in cheesecloth)
	Coarse salt and freshly ground pepper to taste
1	tablespoon butter
2	carrots, chopped
4	shallots, chopped
½	pound small white turnips, peeled and trimmed to walnut size
1	tablespoon flour
1	2½ pound pheasant, larded under the skin
½	pound chestnuts
½	cup dry red wine
	Pheasant liver, chopped

1. Make the stock by simmering the pheasant neck and gizzard with the onion, carrot, celery, salt, pepper, and herb bouquet for 20 minutes. Set aside.

2. Melt the butter in a casserole large enough to hold the pheasant surrounded by vegetables in one layer. Sauté the carrots, shallots, and turnips in the butter until they are golden brown. Sprinkle the flour on the pheasant and brown in the butter. Place breast up. Turn down heat, cover, and leave to cook.

3. Meanwhile, make a short vertical slit through the top of the chestnuts toward the bottom. Simmer for 5 minutes in boiling water. Remove one at a time with a slotted spoon and peel while hot. If you allow the chestnuts to cool, the inner skin will stick to the chestnut. Use rubber gloves if you cannot peel the chestnuts with your bare fingers.

4. Add the chestnuts to the casserole. Add the wine and 1 cup of stock. Cover and cook for 30 minutes. Test the pheasant for doneness and season with salt and pepper. Remove the pheasant to a serving dish. Add the chopped liver to the sauce and cook for 2 minutes. If the sauce is too thin, bring to a boil and reduce. If it is too thick, add more stock.

5. Arrange the vegetables and sauce around the pheasant and serve hot.

Quail

Fresh quail, once enjoyed only by hunters, is now available in many stores across the country. The difficulty of eating quail, with their intricate little bones, has not proved a deterrent any more than lobster shells have discouraged people from eating lobsters. Quail has become our most popular game bird, with production increasing at an enormous rate at farms around the country. It is even appearing on the menus of some restaurants in a dish called "steak and quail" that is rapidly replacing the once ubiquitous "surf 'n' turf."

One winter I spent a weekend at the Griggstown Quail Farm in New Jersey where in two years sales to New York City had increased from six quail a week to more than six hundred. Several chefs stopped by one afternoon and each one cooked quail his or her own way. The recipes, two of which I have adopted for this chapter, were remarkable in that they were each so totally different. And late that night, when you would have thought that we could eat no more, at 2 A.M. our host, Stephen Spector, deep-fried a whole batch of quail, half of which we ate on the spot and the rest of which we wrapped and took to a dog show the following day. We sat on the grass devouring the little birds and enjoying a bottle of Cabernet Sauvignon as Scotties paraded past, nostrils flared in frustration as they smelled our quail.

Where Quail Comes From

Quail is now available fresh year round. It is supplied to butchers fresh from local game farms or fresh and frozen from North Carolina and Canada.

It can also be ordered frozen by mail from Manchester Farms, P.O. Box 97, Dalzell, North Carolina 29040. Tel. (800) 845-0421.

There are two kinds on the market, small Pharaoh quail that weigh 3 to 4 ounces, and larger bobwhites that weigh 5 to 7 ounces. The birds cost between $2 and $3 each. Quail are usually fed high protein feed, a diet of grains and corn and fresh vegetables. The bobwhites are slaughtered when ten to twelve weeks old, the Pharaoh quail at six weeks.

Those that are shipped frozen are vacuum-packed and shipped in dry ice to cities around the country.

In the Market

When buying quail choose those that are plump and silky, with no mottled or dry patches on the skin. They should smell fresh, with no off odor. The delicate quail does not need to age the way other game birds do. As with chicken, the breastbone of young quail will be soft and pliable and the flesh more tender than that of older birds.

Frozen quail have a tendency to be tough and dry, but if they are soaked in water as they thaw and are larded well with bacon fat or simmered in liquid, they can be very good.

In the Kitchen

Methods of cooking quail are endlessly imaginative. They can be deep-fried, cooked with shallots and tarragon, or with bacon, red wine, and mushrooms. Quail can be split in half and broiled after being marinated in gin, herb mustard, and crushed peppercorns, or simply deep-fried until they rise to the surface, golden and ready to eat.

All quail has to be cooked with plenty of moisture or larding because it can quickly toughen or dry out. If using frozen quail defrost them in cold water. The water restores moisture. One large or two small quail are enough per person. Roast quail is good with shoestring potatoes and watercress salad.

Roast Quail with Madeira Sauce

YIELD: 4 Servings

8 quail
8 pieces of bacon to fit over the breasts
8 tablespoons unsalted butter
8 sprigs parsley
Coarse salt and freshly ground pepper to taste
Madeira Sauce
2 tablespoons butter
The quail livers (if unavailable, substitute 4 chicken livers)
1 cup chicken stock
¼ cup Madeira
2 tablespoons chopped fresh parsley

1. Preheat the oven to 450 degrees. Wipe the quail dry and cover each breast with bacon. Put 1 tablespoon of butter and a sprig of parsley in each cavity. Season with salt and pepper. Place the birds on a rack in a roasting pan and roast for 15 minutes.

2. Remove the bacon and place it in the pan. Baste the birds thoroughly, season, and roast for 5 minutes.

3. Meanwhile, heat the 2 tablespoons butter in a small frying pan and lightly sauté the livers. Remove and chop finely.

4. Put the quail on a heated serving platter. Pour off excess fat from the roasting pan and set the bacon strips aside. Add the livers and stock and bring to a boil. Add the Madeira and simmer for 5 minutes, scraping up the cooking juices from the pan. Season with salt and pepper.

5. Pour the sauce over the birds and garnish with parsley and crumbled bacon.

Braised Quail with Juniper, Bayberry Leaves, and Pomegranates

12	quail
	Coarse salt
16	bayberry leaves (or 4 bay leaves torn in quarters)
3	cloves garlic, cut in quarters
1	tablespoon juniper berries, crushed
¼	teaspoon white peppercorns
1	teaspoon whole coriander seeds
1	tablespoon brandy
½	cup diced carrot
½	cup diced onion
½	cup diced celery
½	cup diced leek
1	clove garlic, crushed with the flat side of a knife
1½	tablespoons rendered duck fat or mixture of butter and olive oil
1½	cups dark, dry red wine
1½	cups game, veal, or chicken stock
4	sprigs thyme (or ⅓ teaspoon dried)
1	sprig rosemary (or ⅛ teaspoon dried)
6	tablespoons unsalted butter
½	cup white bread crumbs, preferably homemade
2	pomegranates, peeled
	Juniper branches for garnish, if available
	Extra bay leaves for garnish

1. The day before, in the cavity of each quail put a little salt, a bayberry or quartered bay leaf, and a quarter of a clove of garlic. Truss the quail.

2. In a large bowl big enough to hold the quail, combine ½ teaspoon salt, the juniper berries, and whole white peppercorns. Crush the coriander seeds in a mortar and add. Add the brandy. Toss the quail in this mixture, cover tightly, and refrigerate overnight.

3. The following day, preheat the oven to 325 degrees. In a large casserole big enough to hold the quail, brown the carrot, onion, celery, leek, and crushed garlic in ¾ tablespoon duck fat or in the oil and butter mixture. Remove the vegetables and set aside. Add the remaining fat and carefully brown the quail a few at a time.

4. Return the vegetables to the pan. Add the wine and the stock. Bring to a boil and skim off any impurities that may rise to the surface. Add the remaining bayberry leaves or bay leaf quarters, thyme, and rosemary and cover tightly. Lower the heat and cook for 45 minutes. The quail are done when they are very soft. Test with a fork or thin skewer. If they are not cooked long enough they will be stringy.

5. Meanwhile, brown 4 tablespoons butter without burning, and brown the bread crumbs in the butter. Set aside.

6. Remove the birds from the pan. Strain the cooking juices into a saucepan and reduce to 1½ cups. Season with freshly ground pepper and salt if needed. Stir in remaining 2 tablespoons butter. Pour the sauce over the birds and sprinkle with bread crumbs.

7. Garnish the plate with branches of juniper and peeled pomegranates, lacing them in and among the birds. Sprinkle with bay leaves.

Note: Bayberries grow wild all over the East Coast. Regular bay leaf can be substituted, but it is stronger; a quarter is plenty for each quail.

Turkey

Turkey has become less of a feast-day dish and more of an everyday one. Americans now eat 11 pounds of turkey per person a year, and the average consumption is increasing slowly but steadily as people buy parts instead of whole birds. Rolled breasts, drumsticks, sliced turkey, and even turkey hams are now available year round, and the delicate breast meat is often substituted for veal.

But the biggest selling time for turkey is of course at Thanksgiving, when it is traditionally served with sweet potatoes, creamed onions, and cranberry sauce. At Christmas during my childhood the classic accompaniments were roast potatoes, brussels sprouts and chestnuts, bread sauce, and gravy. We used to roast baby sausages and rolls of bacon with the potatoes around the bird. After dinner the wishbone was put on a doorsill to dry, the ends facing up so that the luck wouldn't run out. And in the middle of the night we would come downstairs for turkey sandwiches.

For years it seemed to me a sacrilege to eat turkey prepared in any but the traditional way, but when I lived in Mexico I came across turkey "mole poblano," turkey served in a rich, spicy brown sauce that is one of the highlights of Mexican cooking. Spices such as anise, cloves, cinnamon, coriander, and all manner of dark red, wrinkled chilies were ground by hand — our cook refused to use the blender. She loved making mole above all else, grinding the spices on a *metate*, a piece of limestone that was exactly like the ones her pre-Columbian Mayan ancestors used centuries ago. She always made extra quantities of the sauce, which we would use in enchiladas.

Where Turkey Comes From

The major areas for turkey production are North Carolina, Minnesota, California, Missouri, and Arkansas. Young turkeys are fed on soybean meal and corn, supplemented with vitamins and minerals. As they get older, their diet is shifted to corn. A hen turkey will grow to 10 to 14 pounds in about sixteen weeks. It takes five months to raise an 18- to 22-pound turkey.

After they are slaughtered, most turkeys are frozen or chill-packed in Cryovac after being dipped in a chlorine wash. Smaller processors do not freeze, chill-pack (at 28 to 32 degrees, partly freezing the bird), or use Cryovac but ship the turkeys packed in ice so that they remain unfrozen. These turkeys are likely to be fresher because they cannot remain for long in the display case. The smaller processors usually produce the best turkeys, raising them specially for holidays.

Like chicken, turkey is federally inspected and is graded A, B, or C. The grading is voluntary and is based on the bird's appearance — its shape, whether it is missing parts, and whether it has skin abrasions.

Fresh turkeys are frequently available on both the East and West coasts. But they are still hard to come by in the Midwest. If the turkey has a crust on the outside, it has been chill-packed. If it has a deposit of juices at the bottom of the bag, it has probably been frozen and thawed or has been in the bag for a while.

In the Market

A fresh turkey has a plump, smooth, white skin, pearly white rather than purple or blue, with no withered or dry patches. Like ducks, turkeys are often sold in Cryovac, making it impossible to tell freshness. The best bet is to ask the meat seller for a recommendation, then stick to a brand you are pleased with. Fresh turkeys are best hung at the butcher shop for three days to develop their flavor. Frozen turkeys do not have the flavor of fresh ones and can be mushy. If you can get only frozen turkey, thaw it in the refrigerator for a day or two, depending on its size.

Larger birds are less expensive and every bit as tender as smaller, lower-priced birds, and they also provide more meat and less bone per pound. The most frequently available whole turkey is frozen and weighs 8 to 16 pounds. Fryer-roaster turkeys generally weigh 5 to 8 pounds.

The most flavorful turkeys on the market are wild turkeys, and these are sold at superior butchers. They don't look as perfect as the regular birds, but they have a much better flavor. Next in line for value are fresh, large non-self-basting turkeys — ranch raised, if possible. Contrary to what you might think, the larger the turkey the meatier and juicer it will be.

Read labels carefully when buying turkey that has been in any way processed. Rolled breast meat, shaped like a loaf of bread, may contain a variety of chemicals plus artificial color, sugar, modified vegetable protein, and phosphate salts. Avoid those called self-basting: they have been injected with cheap oils, sodium tripolyphosphate, or other chemicals.

Turkeys these days are bred to give plumper breasts because white meat seems to be more popular, even though dark meat has more flavor. Because turkey breast is solid meat it is a very economical buy and can be perfectly good if given a heavy dousing of spices to perk it up.

In the Kitchen

The best way to roast turkey is to start it breast down so that the white meat will have less tendency to dry out. You can also cover the breast with bacon or foil, which can be removed toward the end of the cooking time to allow the breast to brown. Ignore the directions on packages for roasting times; you will get overcooked, dry meat. Measure the oven before ordering the turkey, and order from a reliable butcher. Allow the turkey to rest for about 15 minutes before carving.

Roasting Times

6-8 pounds .... 2½-3 hours	14-16 pounds .... 4½-5 hours
8-10 pounds .... 3-3½ hours	16-18 pounds .... 5-5½ hours
10-12 pounds .... 3½-4 hours	18-20 pounds .... 5½-6 hours
12-14 pounds .... 4-4½ hours	

Roast Turkey with Celery and Walnut Stuffing

YIELD: 8 to 10 Servings

1	8-to-10-pound turkey
3	tablespoons butter
2	medium onions, chopped
6	stalks celery with leaves, chopped
3	apples, peeled, cored, and chopped
2	cloves garlic, minced
2	cups fresh homemade-style white bread crumbs
1	cup chopped walnuts
½	cup chopped fresh parsley
1	egg, lightly beaten
	Coarse salt and freshly ground pepper to taste
½	cup heavy cream
8	strips bacon

1. Preheat the oven to 325 degrees. Clean the turkey. Melt the butter in a heavy skillet and gently fry the onions until soft but not browned. Add the celery and apples and cook until the apples are soft.

2. Combine in a mixing bowl with remaining ingredients except bacon. Season and bind with cream, adding more if necessary. Stuff into the bird's cavity.

3. Cover the turkey breast with the bacon and roast for 3 to 3½ hours, basting frequently.

8	stalks celery with leaves
1	7½-pound wild turkey, larded with salt pork (see note)
1	medium onion, halved (reserve the skin)
1	medium carrot, halved
2	whole cloves
1	bay leaf
1	teaspoon thyme
1	bunch Italian parsley, coarsely chopped
1	lemon
	Outer lettuce leaves (optional)
	Coarse salt and freshly ground pepper to taste
½	cup brandy

1. Cut the leaves from the celery and reserve. Remove the neck, giblets, and last two wing joints from the turkey. Put these in 2 cups of water with the onion, carrot, 4 celery stalks cut in coarse chunks, cloves, bay leaf, thyme, and parsley and bring to a boil. Reduce heat to simmer and cook about 1 hour, uncovered. Strain the broth through a cheesecloth. There should be about 1½ cups. This liquid will provide basting juice and a base for pan gravy.

2. Preheat the oven to 400 degrees.

3. Wash the turkey inside with the juice of the lemon; put remaining 4 stalks coarsely chopped celery inside.

4. Put the turkey in an open roasting pan and surround it with the onion skins, celery tops, and outer lettuce leaves.

5. Cook the turkey for 1¼ hours undisturbed.

6. Remove the salt pork, any strings, and surrounding leaves. Reduce heat to 350 degrees and cook for 1 hour or more, or until the juices run clear and yellow, basting frequently with the broth and pan fat.

7. Remove the turkey to a heated platter and keep warm while preparing the gravy.

8. Skim off excess fat from pan, add broth, and bring to a boil. Season with salt and pepper and add the brandy. Bring to a boil and pour into a gravy boat. Do not use any flour or thickening. Serve with Braised Celery Hearts or Endive (page 309) and Wild Rice (page 216).

Note: The butcher will normally lard the turkey for you. You can also do it yourself by placing strips of salt pork neatly over the turkey breast and legs to keep it moist while cooking.

1	8-to-10-pound turkey, cut in serving pieces
	Water to cover
5	dried ancho chilies
5	dried mulato chilies
5	dried pasilla chilies
¼	cup lard
2	slices homemade-style white bread
4	ounces shelled almonds
4	ounces shelled peanuts
2	medium onions, chopped
½	pound tomatoes
3	cloves garlic, chopped
½	teaspoon ground cinnamon
½	teaspoon anise seeds
½	teaspoon ground cloves
½	teaspoon ground coriander
¼	cup pumpkin seeds
½	cup seedless raisins
1	teaspoon sugar
1	1-ounce square unsweetened chocolate
	Coarse salt and freshly ground pepper to taste
¼	cup toasted sesame seeds

1. Simmer the turkey pieces in water to cover for about 1 hour. Drain and pat dry. Reserve the stock and soak the chilies in enough hot stock to cover for 30 minutes.

2. Heat the lard in a heavy skillet and brown the turkey pieces. Remove and drain.

3. In an electric blender, combine the chilies with their soaking liquid, bread, almonds, peanuts, and onions.

3. Peel the tomatoes by charring them over a gas flame, then removing the skin. Add to the blender with the garlic and blend to a coarse purée. Add the next 5 ingredients and blend.

4. Put the mixture into the frying pan in which you browned the turkey. Fry for 5 minutes in the lard remaining in the skillet, stirring constantly.

5. Add 2 cups turkey stock, raisins, sugar, chocolate, salt, and pepper. Bring to a boil. Add the turkey pieces and coat with the sauce. Turn down heat and simmer gently for 30 minutes. Sprinkle with sesame seeds before serving.

Note: Dried chilies are available in Latin markets and specialty stores.

Meat

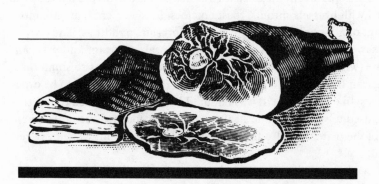

Beef

Colette, in her novel *Prisons et Paradis*, describes a meal of *boeuf à l'ancienne* prepared by Madame Yvon, a Cordon Bleu cook of her acquaintance. It was "an old style beef stew which overwhelmed at least three senses out of five, for, besides its dark and velvety flavor, its melt in the mouth consistency, it shone with a bronze caramelized sauce, ringed around the very edge with a light golden fat." Colette asked what the dish might be. "It's beef," she was told. Colette was amazed. "But there is in this dish a mystery, a magic. One should be able to put a name on such a marvel."

"To be sure," replied Madame Yvon. "It's beef."

Carême, the nineteenth-century French chef and father of *Grande Cuisine*, called beef the soul of cooking. But the French, despite their daubes, tournedos, and médaillons de boeuf, are nowhere near such great beef eaters as Americans. More beef is eaten in the United States than in any other country in the world.

When I was a child in England, roast beef was our favorite Sunday lunch, served with brussels sprouts, roast potatoes, fresh horseradish and, most important of all, small, puffed-up, golden Yorkshire puddings. The only steak I ever saw was on the menu of a pretentious local restaurant and was called entrecôte (which the English pronounce awntra-coat). It was so small that American friends would eat two; they said English steak had to be ordered in doubles, like our drinks. It was not until I came to the United States that I became used to seeing T-bone steaks so large they touched the table on either side of the plate, and also that I discovered that a martini was not sweet vermouth.

Nowadays, beef consumption has dropped slightly as people try to cut back on foods that contain cholesterol. The 20-ounce steak is slowly becoming a thing of the past. But although we are eating beef less frequently, we still enjoy the occasional steak or stew as much as ever. Dr. Johnson may have been right when he said, in his inimitable fashion, "Anyone would rather kill a cow than not eat beef." And my mother, upon reading this, would add, "How I hate Dr. Johnson!"

Where Beef Comes From

Most American beef is grown on large farms in Iowa and Kansas. Most often the meat is "boxed," transported from the Middle West to markets across the country in airtight, vacuum-sealed bags packed in boxes and shipped at a temperature of 28 degrees. These vacuum packs come in various sizes: The beef is usually divided into primal cuts — round, arm chuck, rib, and loin — or further processed into smaller cuts weighing between 15 and 20 pounds. Most vacuum packs are marketed under the trade name Cryovac, a product of W.R. Grace & Company.

After the animal is slaughtered, the meat is chilled for twenty-four hours. Sometimes it is sprayed with a solution containing chlorine to reduce the bacteria count. Industry spokesmen say that only the outside of the carcass is sprayed, and they contend that this does not affect the taste of the meat.

Meat processors and supermarkets like vacuum-packing because meat packed this way is cheaper to transport, easier to store, and has a longer shelf life than a carcass. When meat is shipped in whole carcass form, it is hung on racks and transported in refrigerated trucks. The meat is then cut up when it reaches its destination or hung for longer in a refrigerated chamber to age. When meat is shipped in Cryovac, however, the excess fat and bones are removed at the plant and the supermarket butchers have little more to do than open the package, slice the meat, and put it on the counter.

Smaller meat cuts, such as steaks and roasts, may soon appear in individual vacuum packs that will allow them to stay in the display case for up to six weeks.

By removing the oxygen, which encourages the growth of bacteria, vacuum-packed meat can be kept for as long as four to six weeks, depending on the cut and type of meat. The lack of oxygen causes vacuum-packed meat to turn dark purple and develop a gassy smell. But once the pack is opened at the store the color, or bloom, as it is called in the industry, returns to the meat as oxygen reaches it. Supermarket spokesmen contend that the smell quickly goes away, but many butchers say that meat left longer than a few days in vacuum packs can develop a sour taste that doesn't disappear even when the meat has been aired, and that such beef does not have the firmness of aged beef. They also say that there is no date on the package, so the retailer does not know how old it is, and they add that you can't age meat when it's packed that way because the fat covering has been cut off. To age meat properly it must be hung in refrigerated chambers for a week or two, encased in a protective layer of fat. If the meat is cut into, it can go bad.

To age their beef, many butchers prefer to hang carcasses in carefully controlled refrigerated chambers at the warehouse or in the store. Enzymes break down the meat, giving it flavor and making it more tender. Most beef is aged about two weeks. According to the U.S. Department of Agriculture, the nutrient value of meat is not altered by aging. However, aged meat loses moisture when hung and shrinks, in addition to losing the outer parts that have to be trimmed away. This makes it expensive to produce, and so most of it is sold to restaurants that age their own beef or to a city's best butchers.

All meat sold in this country, if it crosses state lines, must be inspected by the Agriculture Department. It does not have to be graded by the inspectors, but most wholesalers choose to have their beef graded for the marketplace. The grades — prime, choice, good, and utility — do not indicate whether meat has been aged but apply to its quality, texture, firmness and fat content, shape, marbling, and age when slaughtered. A cut from a younger animal will be marked prime, an older one choice. The best prime beef is marbled with tiny flecks of fat that break down during cooking and make the meat juicy and full of flavor.

In the Market

In my experience, the best beef is always to be found at a reliable butcher. By getting to know your local butcher (and butchers seem to be making a comeback these days), you can be sure he won't risk losing a customer by trying to palm off a second-rate piece of meat on you. You may pay more for some cuts than you would in a supermarket, but in the long run it pays off. You can buy exactly the amount you want, and you aren't in for any nasty surprises when you open the package at home.

If you have only a supermarket, however, all is not lost. They usually have a butcher on the premises who will answer questions and even make special cuts for you.

I have not yet found a supermarket that ages its beef. Most of the beef in our markets is chilled and packed in vacuum bags and not aged at all. If you have a good butcher, it is possible to get properly aged meat — at a price. Steaks and roasts are infinitely better when they have been aged. Cuts for stews and braised dishes have more flavor, so aging here is not as important. The meat will become tender through slow cooking with liquids. When buying beef it is essential to get the cuts that best suit the way they are to be cooked. Remember that the toughest parts of the animal will be those that have worked hardest, such as the neck and the legs. Long, slow cooking suits these cuts of meat. The tender parts, such as sirloin, have less flavor than the tough ones, but they can be cooked fast and remain tender. The loin provides the best steaks. The tougher cuts, such as bottom round, have more connective tissue than fat. So if you want to roast this cut, lard it or marinate it, and cook it slowly in liquid. Ground round is good for hamburger because it is not too fatty.

Shoulder or chuck cuts can be braised or stewed or used for pot roasts and hamburger. Skirt and flank steak are good marinated and broiled or braised. Use brisket for boiled beef, and the shank for soups or stock. The rich, glutinous texture of the tail is wonderful in stews or soups.

Whenever it is possible, beef should be sliced or ground to order. If you are buying beef for stewing, buy a whole piece, if possible, and cut it up yourself or have the butcher do it for you. Precut stewing meat is often fatty and tough and sometimes has been frozen. Ask the butcher for bones that you can add to soup or stew for flavor.

If you are buying wrapped cuts in a supermarket, check for the expiration date on the package. There is no law governing the length of time meat may be kept in a display case after it has been delivered to a store, but prepackaged meats usually carry an expiration date stamped on individual packages by the retailer. The date gives no indication of how old the product actually is, only how long the store will keep it on sale after it has arrived. Beef is usually given about three days in the display case. It is impossible to tell exactly how fresh the meat is because the plastic conceals smell. Most stores are pretty strict about their cutoff dates for meat, but sometimes — if you go shopping on a Sunday, for example, and there hasn't been a delivery for a few days — the meat can be pretty stale. It's very much up to the store manager. If he or she is alert, the meat should be fresh.

In fact, color is the best indication of freshness, freshness here meaning the length of time the meat has been cut from the carcass, whether aged or packed in Cryovac. The meat should be bright red, firm, and without an excessive amount of fat. If beef has been exposed to air for a day or two it will deepen to a brownish red. Ground meat tends to spoil quickly; so, if possible, it should be ground to order and eaten the same day. Avoid beef that is flabby or that is wet on the surface; it has probably been frozen.

Good guidelines to follow are these: Look for a moist, satiny patina to the skin, a vibrant color, and a springiness in the flesh. Beware of meat that is wet to the point of being sodden; that usually means it has been frozen and then thawed or that it has been stored for too long. Avoid bloody cuts; blood will turn rancid before the meat does.

When buying steak, buy only prime or choice grades. Tenderloin, fillet steaks, T-bone, porterhouse, rib, and sirloin are the best. They should be not less than an inch thick, in order to be juicy inside when cooked, and should have a good layer of fat around them. The fat helps to seal in the meat's juices while it is cooking.

In the Kitchen

Once you've got your piece of beef home, be very careful how you store it. Put it into the refrigerator loosely wrapped in butcher paper or cheesecloth, which will keep the surface dry. Steaks, chops, and roasts can be kept refrigerated for up to four days. Ground meat should be used within a day.

Don't leave meat in plastic bags. If meat is left in a bag for a few days, the surface becomes soaked in blood, which can get sour. Even when the meat has been aerated, the sour taste doesn't disappear. Steak should be at room temperature when you cook it. Do not salt it until after cooking or the juices will be drawn out by the salt. When broiling steak, first sear it to seal in the juices.

Then cook it until it is done as you like it, turning down the heat if necessary.

I like to serve broiled steaks with a slice of savory butter on top. You can flavor the butter with minced garlic, tarragon, parsley, chives, or mustard, and if you serve the steak with baked potatoes, the butter is good on them too. Chill the butter until just before you serve it so that it can be sliced. One of my favorite butters is made with beef marrow baked and mashed with chopped shallots, butter, and parsley. My butcher gives away the marrow bones free. The rich yet easily digested marrow is a great delicacy, and in Victorian times the bones were served on a white napkin and the marrow eaten with a long, thin, silver spoon. I also love steaks sautéed with green peppercorns or broiled with a mustard coating.

Although prime cuts are the best for steaks, choice chuck steak is excellent sliced thin and marinated in soy sauce, garlic, and ginger for a couple of hours. Stir-fry the slices very fast, so that they are rare in the middle, and serve them with steamed cabbage and rice. This way the meat does not toughen.

Cubed steak is never satisfactory, because the meat is punctured and lacerated to make it tender. As a result, most of the juices escape during cooking and the meat comes out stringy.

Stewing is one of the simplest and most economical ways to cook beef. Long, slow cooking with vegetables, herbs, and stock brings out the best in the cheaper cuts of beef such as shoulder or chuck. A stew should never boil; it should simmer gently. To get the best results, use a deep, heavy pan with a tight-fitting lid. When adding liquid, always add it hot.

Beef brisket, boiled and served with horseradish sauce, is a warming dish on a cold day. The beef is simmered in water with an onion, carrots, celery, and spices. It is sliced hot and served with a sauce made of fresh grated horseradish mixed with sour cream and a little Dijon mustard. Boiled potatoes sprinkled with parsley are the best accompaniment. Boeuf Bourguignon, beef cooked in red wine with carrots and onions, or carbonnade de boeuf, a stew flavored with beer to make a rich, dark sauce, are both fine dinner party dishes.

In the summer I love to cook spareribs outdoors on a rack over an open fire with sweet corn and potatoes baked in the ashes underneath. I usually cut the ribs up and marinate them overnight in a mixture of soy sauce, olive oil, chopped ginger, and garlic. Another excellent marinade is made with lemon juice, thyme, olive oil, and garlic.

If you are lucky enough to sit down to a first-rate prime roast of beef, beautifully marbled and perfectly cooked, don't wreck it by bad carving. Remember Chesterton's letter to his son, written in the eighteenth century: "Do you use to carve adroitly and genteely, without hacking half an hour across a bone, without bespattering the company with the sauce, and without overturning the glasses into your neighbors' pockets?"

Goulash soup, a Hungarian specialty, is a terrific midnight pick-me-up or beginning to the evening meal. This rich, dark red soup-stew is spiced with paprika and caraway seeds and laced with little dumplings.

Use only true Hungarian paprika or the soup will not have the proper flavor. In Hungary, hot cherry peppers are often added at the end. Tiny green hot peppers, deveined under cold running water, can also be added. At the Red Tulip restaurant in New York, regulars order extra hot peppers, which are served in a small bowl with a spoon.

Gulyás Soup with Galuska

YIELD: 6 to 8 Servings

(Goulash Soup with Little Dumplings)

2	medium onions, finely chopped
2	tablespoons lard
1	clove garlic
1	teaspoon caraway seeds
2	pounds stewing beef, cubed
3	tablespoons Hungarian paprika
	Approximately 6 cups hot beef stock or water
3	large potatoes, peeled and cut in ¾-inch cubes
3	Italian green peppers, seeded and cut into ¼-inch strips
1	ripe tomato, peeled and chopped
1	large carrot, sliced
	Coarse salt and freshly ground pepper to taste

Galuska

3	tablespoons flour
	Dash of salt
1	large egg

1. In a large, heavy casserole, sauté the onions in the lard until glossy and golden. Meanwhile, mince the garlic with the caraway seeds. Add to the casserole with the beef. Sauté for 5 minutes, stirring frequently.

2. Off heat, add the paprika. Stir thoroughly. Add enough hot stock to cover the meat. Bring to a boil, cover, and simmer gently for 1 hour. Add more stock as necessary.

3. Add the potatoes and cook for 10 minutes. Then add the green peppers, tomato, carrot, salt, and pepper. Add enough stock to cover. Cook for 30 minutes longer. Correct seasoning.

4. Meanwhile, prepare the dumplings. Sift the flour into a bowl with the salt. Make a well in the middle and add the egg. Mix together to make a smooth dough. Roll out ½ inch thick.

5. Just before serving the soup, pinch off tiny pieces of dough about ½ inch square and drop them into the soup, a few at a time. They are done when they rise to the surface.

Note: If you are making these dumplings for the first time you may wish to cook them separately in boiling water to make sure they are properly cooked. They should be springy to the touch but still soft when they are done.

Carpaccio

(Cold Sliced Beef)

½ pound tenderloin, sliced paper-thin across the grain
2 tablespoons olive oil
Juice of ½ lemon
Freshly ground pepper to taste
1 tablespoon chopped capers
Coarse salt to taste

1. Arrange the beef slices on a plate. Sprinkle with olive oil, lemon juice, pepper, capers, and salt.
2. Serve with bread (semolina bread is recommended) and sweet butter.

Roast Beef and Yorkshire Pudding

4 pounds rib roast
2 tablespoons olive oil
Yorkshire Pudding
¾ cup flour
½ teaspoon salt
¾ cup milk
2 eggs

1. Preheat the oven to 450 degrees. Place the roast on a rack and rub with the olive oil. Cook for 1¼ hours for rare beef. If you prefer it medium done, cook for 1½ hours. Baste frequently.
2. Meanwhile, make the Yorkshire pudding. Sift the flour and salt into a mixing bowl. Make a well in the center and add the milk. Mix with a wooden spoon.
3. In a separate bowl, beat the eggs. Add them to the flour mixture and refrigerate for 30 minutes. This whole process can be done in a blender.
4. When the meat is done, allow it to rest for half an hour on a heated serving plate in a warm place (such as the back of the stove).
5. Beat the batter briefly. Pour the cooking fat from the beef into a muffin pan or a baking pan about 8 inches square. Add the batter and bake for about 10 minutes at 450 degrees. Reduce heat to 350 degrees and bake 5 minutes more if making small puddings, 10 if making a large one. The pudding is done when it has puffed up and is brown. Serve immediately.

Boiled Beef with Horseradish Sauce

YIELD: 4 Servings

2½	pounds beef brisket, in one piece
1	large onion, coarsely chopped
2	carrots, coarsely chopped
	Bouquet garni
	Coarse salt and freshly ground pepper to taste
4 to 6	tablespoons freshly grated horseradish (or to taste)
1	cup sour cream

1. Simmer the beef in water to cover with the onion, carrots, bouquet garni, salt, and pepper for 1½ hours.

2. Combine the horseradish and sour cream. Season to taste with salt and pepper.

3. When the beef is cooked, remove it from the broth. Serve immediately, passing the sauce separately.

Note: The vegetables cooked in the broth will be overdone for eating. Carrots, turnips, and potatoes can be cooked separately and served on the platter, arranged around the beef.

Steak with Marrow Bones

YIELD: 4 Servings

4	marrow bones
4	tablespoons butter, at room temperature
3	shallots, finely chopped
2	tablespoons finely chopped flat-leaf parsley
	Coarse salt and freshly ground pepper to taste
4	individual steaks

1. Preheat the oven to 350 degrees. Wrap the marrow bones carefully in foil and bake for 30 minutes. Remove and, when cool enough to handle, spoon out the marrow into a small bowl. Add the butter, shallots, and parsley and mix thoroughly. Season with salt and pepper. Shape into a cylinder and set aside.

2. Broil the steaks to desired doneness. Arrange on a heated serving platter or individual plates. Slice the butter and place a round or two on each steak.

Pepper Steak with Cream and Cognac

YIELD: 4 Servings

2	teaspoons black peppercorns
4	entrecôte steaks
1	teaspoon olive oil
½	cup heavy cream
2	tablespoons cognac
	Coarse salt to taste
2	tablespoons chopped fresh parsley

1. Crush the peppercorns with a mortar and pestle. Rub the steaks with the olive oil and press the peppercorns into the steaks.

2. Heat a heavy iron frying pan until hot and add the steaks. Cook them over high heat until done as you like them. Keep warm on a heated dish.

3. Swirl the cream and cognac into the pan, season with salt, and allow to reduce slightly. Pour over the steaks, sprinkle with parsley, and serve immediately.

Moroccan Style Meatballs

2	pounds ground beef
	Coarse salt and freshly ground pepper to taste
1	tablespoon olive oil
2	onions, chopped
2	garlic cloves, chopped
1	pound tomatoes, peeled and chopped
½	cup water
1	tablespoon ground cumin
1	tablespoon paprika
4	tablespoons chopped fresh coriander

1. Put the ground beef into a bowl and season with salt and pepper. Shape into balls the size of a golf ball. Set aside.

2. Heat the oil in a large heavy frying pan and fry the onions and garlic until softened. Add the tomatoes and ½ cup water and simmer for 5 minutes.

3. Arrange the meatballs over the tomatoes and onions. Sprinkle with cumin and paprika. Cover and simmer for 1 hour, basting frequently with the juices that will thicken into a sauce. If the sauce gets too dry, add a little more water.

4. Sprinkle with coriander and serve.

Moroccan Kefta

2	pounds ground beef
1	large onion, grated
1	tablespoon ground cumin
1	tablespoon paprika
1	teaspoon ground coriander
	Coarse salt and freshly ground pepper
1	bunch parsley or coriander, finely chopped

1. Heat the coals in an outdoor grill 1 hour before cooking. Put the meat into a mixing bowl and add the remaining ingredients. Knead thoroughly. Set aside for 1 hour.

2. Take a piece of meat the size of a golf ball and wrap it around a skewer, shaping it into a small sausage about 3 inches long. Make sure the ends are firmly packed down onto the skewer. Repeat, using up all the meat.

3. Grill over hot coals quickly so the kefta are crisp on the outside and juicy inside.

Spiced Beef with Cauliflower

2	tablespoons peanut or vegetable oil
3	pounds stewing beef, cut into 1-inch cubes
1	medium onion, chopped
¼	teaspoon turmeric
	Coarse salt and freshly ground pepper to taste
1	teaspoon ground ginger
1	tablespoon paprika
1	teaspoon ground cumin
¼	teaspoon cayenne pepper
1	large head cauliflower, broken into flowerets
	Juice of 1 lemon

1. Heat the oil in a large, fireproof casserole and brown the meat on all sides. Remove to a side dish.

2. Add the onion and cook until soft. Turn the heat down and return the beef to the casserole with the turmeric, salt, pepper, and remaining spices. Moisten with a little water and simmer for 1½ hours, adding more water if the stew becomes too dry.

3. Steam the cauliflower in a separate pan about 5 minutes or until al dente.

4. Add the cauliflower to the beef stew with the lemon juice, cover, and cook for 5 minutes. Serve immediately.

Note: This dish is good with rice or mashed potatoes.

Steak Tartare

1	2-ounce can flat anchovy fillets with their oil
½	small onion, coarsely chopped
1	tablespoon red wine vinegar
	Tabasco sauce to taste
	Worcestershire sauce to taste
1	egg, lightly beaten
4	tablespoons small capers (or large ones, chopped)
	Coarse salt and freshly ground pepper to taste
1	cup finely chopped fresh parsley
1	pound coarsely ground sirloin

1. Put half the can of anchovies, with the oil, in the jar of a blender. Add the onion, vinegar, Tabasco sauce, and Worcestershire sauce, and blend until smooth.

2. Add with the remaining ingredients except the reserved anchovies to the meat and mix thoroughly. Correct the seasoning. Mound the steak tartare on a plate. Chop the remaining anchovies, arrange attractively on top, and serve.

RETAIL CUTS OF BEEF

CHUCK

② Boneless Chuck Eye Roast

Blade ②
Roast or Steak

Boneless Shoulder
Pot-Roast or Steak

① Beef for Stew

③④ Chuck Short Ribs

Arm ③
Pot-Roast or Steak

Cross Rib ④
Pot-Roast

① Ground Beef

RIB

② Rib Roast

② Rib Steak

② Rib Steak, Boneless

② → ← ②
Rib Eye (Delmonico)
Roast or Steak

SHORT LOIN

①②③ Top Loin Steak

② T-Bone Steak

①②③ Porterhouse Steak

①②③ Boneless
Top Loin Steak

②③ Tenderloin
(Filet Mignon) Steak or
Roast (also from Sirloin 1a)

SIRLOIN

① Pin Bone Sirloin Steak

② Flat Bone Sirloin Steak

③ Wedge Bone Sirloin Steak

①②③ Boneless Sirloin Steak

ROUND

④ Heel of Round

① Boneless Rump
Roast (Rolled)

③ Cubed Steak

Ground Beef

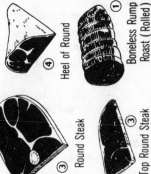

③ Round Steak

③ Top Round Steak

③ Bottom Round
Roast or Steak

③ Eye of Round

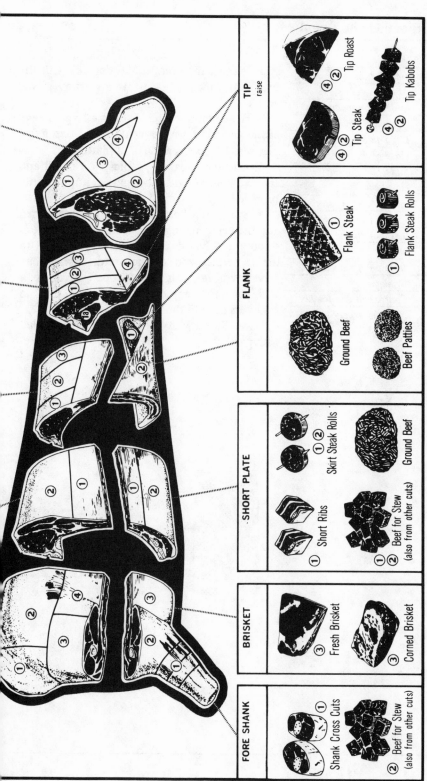

FORE SHANK

① Shank Cross Cuts

② Beef for Stew
(also from other cuts)

BRISKET

③ Fresh Brisket

③ Corned Brisket

SHORT PLATE

① Short Ribs

② Beef for Stew
(also from other cuts)

①② Skirt Steak Rolls

② Ground Beef

FLANK

① Flank Steak

① Flank Steak Rolls

Ground Beef

Beef Patties

TIP
raise

④② Tip Steak

④② Tip Roast

④② Tip Kabobs

This chart approved by

National Live Stock and Meat Board

Carbonnade de Boeuf

2	pounds bottom round of beef
3	tablespoons peanut or vegetable oil
2	large onions, chopped
1	clove garlic, minced
1½	tablespoons flour
2	cups beer
1	tablespoon prepared mustard
1	teaspoon thyme
2	bay leaves
1	tablespoon red wine vinegar
	Coarse salt and freshly ground pepper to taste

1. Preheat the oven to 300 degrees. Cut the beef into 1-inch cubes, trimming away gristle and fat.

2. Heat 2 tablespoons of oil in a large, heavy casserole and brown the meat on all sides, a few pieces at a time. Set aside on a plate.

3. Add the remaining tablespoon of oil and fry the onions with the garlic until lightly browned.

4. Stir in the flour, cook for 1 minute, then add the beer, stirring well. When the mixture is smooth and has thickened, return the meat to the casserole with the mustard, thyme, bay leaves, vinegar, salt, and pepper. Bring to a boil, put into oven, and bake, covered, for 2 to 2½ hours or until the meat is tender.

Note: Serve with boiled potatoes sprinkled with parsley.

Ham

One of the best hams I ever ate was responsible for turning a close friend of mine into a vegetarian. It was a Tennessee country ham, and I bought it when en route by car from New York to southern Mexico. In Dorset, where I was born, the traditional family menu on Easter Sunday had included baked ham with parsley sauce followed by steamed pudding with golden syrup. My friend and I found a motel with a kitchenette and I decided to repeat the treat, since the following morning was Easter Sunday. We celebrated with a 10-pound ham for two. The pudding that followed was not as light as the yellow sponge of my youth, and my companion fell asleep with his boots on.

For the next ten days, using an electric skillet, in motel rooms across the United States and Mexico I served the ham in every conceivable way: in sauces flavored with tomatoes, cream, onions, garlic, mustard, and herbs; I fried it, secreted it under poached eggs on toast, shredded it in pasta, hid it in our tortillas, and masked it with chilies and hot sauce. When we arrived at our destination we hurled the bones to a dog in the street. My friend has not touched meat since.

Where Ham Comes From

The major hog production area in the United States is the Middle West, with processing centers in Iowa, Minnesota, Nebraska, Missouri, and Indiana. The hind legs of the hogs provide the ham.

The best ham comes from pigs that have been fed a diet that contains such delicacies as peanuts, acorns, chestnuts, or peaches. Unfortunately, most pigs are now given a special feed — the exact makeup of which is not disclosed by the producers — that makes them put on weight and retain water. This does nothing positive for the taste or texture of the ham but rather produces meat that is often watery and insipid.

Country hams have the most flavor. The best are made from pigs fed a superior diet. The hams are dry-cured, smoked, and aged. They fall into three main categories. Virginia, North Carolina, and Georgia produce very long-aged cured hams, often aged a year or more. Those of Kentucky and Tennessee are less dry and less aged, about three to six months. The least dry of all come from Missouri, where hams are generally aged around three months.

Of the country hams, Smithfield in Virginia produces among the best. All Smithfield hams bearing the name are processed in Smithfield, Virginia. They are made from pigs that are fed a substantial amount of nuts and usually allowed to forage. Other hams are known as country hams and are generally identified by their state — Tennessee, for example.

Hams are cured to preserve them. There are three main curing methods for ham: dry, sweet pickle, and injection. Dry-cured hams are usually cured with salt, sugar, and sodium nitrate or nitrite or a mixture of both. In some areas pepper is also used. The curing ingredients are rubbed on the surface of the meat over a period of ten days while the ham is held on racks at about 45 degrees. Then the hams are brought down from the racks and the remainder of the cure is applied. Nitrites and nitrates are used to protect and preserve the flavor and the color, but they are still under investigation as possible carcinogens.

Once the hams are cured they may then be smoked over hickory or mixed hardwood fires and sometimes hung for another 30 to 45 days to allow the salt level to balance out throughout the meat. Westphalian hams are heavily smoked, often over sawdust and juniper berries. Smoking helps preserve the meat to some extent, but it is done primarily to add flavor. Prosciutto hams are not smoked but are rubbed with pepper and allowed to air dry.

Regular "urban" hams, the kind sold in supermarkets and by many butchers, cost less than country hams and are mild-cured. These hams are cured either by "sweet pickling" — submerging in a sugared, seasoned brine — or by injection, the most widely used method of curing hams. A mixture of sodium nitrate and nitrite, salt, sugar, and water is injected into the hams. They are easier to prepare in the kitchen because they don't need to be soaked, but they are generally bland and watery. Few are smoked at all, and if they are, it is only barely. They are rarely aged, because aging causes shrinkage and thus lowers profits.

Some hams have their bone removed and are placed into a mold and cooked in water. These are not smoked and have little flavor. Ham may also be boned and put back together in netting or a casing and smoked. Better quality hams are sold without the shank meat, which has tough connective tissue. The ham hocks or shank (the lower portions of the leg) are cut off, cured and smoked, and sold separately. They are tough and are best stewed.

Sectioned and preformed hams are deboned and totally defatted, then put back together in various shapes — square, round, or to fit a can. The flavor varies according to how the hams were smoked or cured. In general it is not particularly intense.

Recently the industry has been experimenting with low-salt hams. With refrigeration it is not necessary to use as much salt in the processing as in the old days, when hams were stored in larders or cellars. Flavorings such as cloves, mustard, paprika, or artificial smoked flavor are sometimes pumped into the hams in a soluble extract, a practice that would not be necessary had the hogs been fed the kind of feed that would give them maximum flavor.

With the mass market hams it is often hard to tell whether they have been smoked or not. The length of smoking time varies anywhere from a few hours to a month or more. The wood used is nonresinous wood such as hickory or maple (resinous wood exudes resin when burning), although some concerns use sawdust. The more the ham has been smoked, the more flavor it will have.

In the Market

The best way to get a good ham is to buy from a reliable butcher. Aged country hams usually come in a cloth bag, and their skin usually has a coating of mold and pepper that must be scraped off before you soak and cook the ham. They are often very salty and must be soaked in several changes of water, preferably for twenty-four hours. Don't be put off by the mold. It acts like a blotter and controls moisture loss. Whole country hams do not have to be refrigerated unless they are cut. Smithfield and Southern hams are usually eaten cooked. Prosciutto, on the other hand, is eaten raw — although in Italy it comes both raw and, less frequently, cooked. As noted, it is dry-cured and air-dried but not smoked.

The best prosciutto is a deep, moist pink, not dry or salty. Don't be misled by labels saying "Imported Parma ham." This ham comes not from Parma, where the best prosciutto in the world is made, but probably from Canada or Switzerland. Italian pork products cannot, at the time of this writing, be imported into the United States because of foot-and-mouth disease. The Italian firms of Citterio in Pennsylvania and John Volpi & Sons are two of the top producers in America.

American prosciutto can be too greasy or salty because it has been insufficiently aged — and often frozen rather than hung — or too watery because of the way the pigs have been fed. If you have a cool, dry place, you can age your own whole prosciutto. Remove the wrapping, tie the ham in a clean cloth and hang it to dry for a month or two.

When buying prosciutto in slices, choose those that are pinkish gold with firm, white fat, not too pink (indicating an excess of nitrates) or dried out.

Other raw hams include dark, rich Westphalian and Black Forest from Germany, and excellent varieties of these hams are produced by Schaller & Weber in New York, who ship them around the country.

Canned hams are mild-cured and not usually aged. Pasteurized canned hams from Holland, Denmark, and Poland do not have much flavor. Sectioned and preformed canned hams are to be avoided; they include inferior pieces of ham.

When buying fresh ham, it is hard to tell by looking whether a ham has been aged or how long it has been in the package. Whole hams usually come in opaque vacuum packs, so it is hard to judge the quality by looking. But whole hams and sliced hams, like other meats, usually have an expiration date on the store label indicating how long the store is willing to sell them. Sliced hams are visible through the plastic wrap. They should be firm and plump with fine-grained, rosy flesh. Many hams come with the word "premium" on the manufacturers' labels. This means nothing except that the manufacturers have decided to put it there — but presumably they have done so because they consider these their best. Hams with "water added " on the label have gained extra weight from the brine they were cured in.

In the supermarket, you will find mostly "urban" and canned hams. Butchers sell these hams, too, but they also usually stock country hams.

In the Kitchen

Although the "urban" hams have nothing like the taste of a country ham, they can be good if prepared with some embellishment. Simply boiled or roasted, they are rather insipid. But one of these hams braised in the French way in Madeira wine, white wine, or vermouth, with carrots and onions to add more flavor, is transformed.

To go with braised ham, sweet potatoes can be mashed, baked, or sliced and dotted with butter, brown sugar, and rum and glazed in the oven. Celery braised in a little chicken stock is also a good accompaniment, as are fresh beets. They can be baked in their skins whole and eaten hot with butter. (Do not pierce the skin before baking them or they will leak.) The leaves can be cooked separately, stir-fried in oil with garlic.

Vegetables cooked together with ham can make some excellent main courses. Leeks are good baked with chopped ham in butter or olive oil in the oven. Endive can be cooked with small pieces of ham and served as a main course with baked potato, or stewed in butter with cubes of bacon or ham. Or serve endive or celery as a vegetable to accompany a thick slice of ham, fried and served on top of tomatoes freshly cooked in olive oil and spiced with garlic, pepper, and herbs.

With prosciutto, unsalted butter and bread, and fresh ripe figs or melon are the best accompaniments. Pumpernickel goes with the German hams.

Braised Ham with Madeira Sauce

1	8-to-10-pound ham, country or regular
1	onion, sliced
1	carrot, sliced
2	stalks celery, sliced
1	bay leaf
1	tablespoon black peppercorns
1	cup Madeira
1	cup dry white wine
1	cup chicken stock
1	tablespoon dry mustard
¾	cup dark brown sugar, loosely packed
	Whole cloves
1	teaspoon arrowroot
	Coarse salt and freshly ground pepper to taste

1. If using a country ham, scrub well and remove all traces of mold. Soak for 24 hours in several changes of cold water. If using a regular ham, wipe with paper towels.

2. Place the ham in a large stockpot and add the onion, carrot, celery, bay leaf, and peppercorns. Simmer for 3 hours, partly covered, adding more water if necessary. Cool in the liquid.

3. Preheat the oven to 350 degrees.

4. Skin the ham and partly trim the fat. Score it with a knife in a crisscross pattern.

5. Place the ham in a roasting pan. Reserve 1 tablespoon of Madeira. Pour the rest of the Madeira, the white wine, and the chicken stock over the ham. Roast, basting regularly, for 45 minutes.

6. Remove the ham from the roasting pan and pour the juices into a saucepan and set aside.

7. When the ham has cooled enough to handle, coat it with a mixture of mustard and brown sugar. Stud at intermittent spaces with cloves. Increase heat to 425 degrees and return the ham to the oven to glaze for about 10 minutes.

8. Meanwhile, mix the arrowroot with the reserved tablespoon of Madeira and add to the pan juices in the saucepan. Bring to a boil, stirring, until the mixture thickens. If a thicker gravy is desired, add a little more arrowroot mixed with Madeira. Taste and correct seasoning.

9. Remove the ham to a heated platter and serve the gravy in a warm bowl or gravy boat.

Lamb

Although lamb has long been the principal meat in Middle Eastern and North African countries and Greece, in America it has never been as popular as beef. But in recent years, lamb has become rather glamorous, appearing more and more frequently as the centerpiece of dinner parties. Rack or leg of lamb, roasted so that the meat is moist and pink inside, and served with roast potatoes or stewed white haricots, has become almost as popular here as in France.

People are also discovering lamb shoulder, boned and roasted in the French style with rosemary and garlic, and the beauty of a crown roast filled with a pilaf of bulgur (cracked wheat) with pine nuts or buttered green peas and onions.

Where Lamb Comes From

Most of our lamb comes from Colorado and Utah and is raised on grazing land. After slaughter, lamb arrives in the market within a week. The carcass is shipped complete with its "fell," a thin exterior membrane, because it protects the meat and prolongs its storage life. It is usually removed when the lamb is cut up, except from the leg. It should be left on while the leg is cooked because it helps to keep in the juices.

Lamb that is slaughtered when it is less than six months old, usually between March and the first of October, is stamped "genuine spring lamb." The best are slaughtered between two and four months. At springtime it is often possible to find lamb young enough to have whitish-pink and meltingly tender flesh — lamb that has just been weaned. These lambs are the most highly prized. But to confuse matters, "spring lamb, " slightly cheaper than "genuine spring lamb," is merely lamb that is less than six months old and may have been slaughtered between November and February. It is hard to tell the difference between the two except by price, but genuine spring lamb is considered by some to be superior, with a more delicate flavor. Lamb can be called lamb until its first birthday, whereupon it becomes mutton — a rarity in this country.

New Zealand lamb, which is grass fed, is less expensive and comes frozen. It lacks the taste and texture of fresh lamb but is perfectly adequate for stews and roasts.

Lamb is graded in the same way as beef at the request of the slaughterhouse. The grades are based on the appearance of the carcass, and the better grades have the most tender and delicately flavored meat. The grades are stamped on the carcass with purple ink. Most lamb in supermarkets is choice. Prime lamb goes to butcher shops, some of which even age their lamb for a few days before selling it to make the flesh more tender.

In the Market

When buying lamb, make sure it has rosy flesh, slender red bones, and white fat. Choose the leanest pieces and avoid any that are discolored.

You can tell how old the animal was by the color of the meat, which will be paler pink the younger the animal, and the size of the leg and bones. A 6-pound leg will be from a younger animal than a 9-pound leg, for example, and the chops of a younger animal will be correspondingly smaller.

I prefer to buy fresh lamb from a butcher. One of the main reasons for this is the awkwardness of American cuts.

Richard Olney in *Simple French Food* points out the problem: "American habits of cutting lamb are a windfall to the stew maker and a disaster for the roaster. The shanks (easily the best pieces for flavor, moistness and leanness) are chopped off both the legs and the shoulders, a 'leg of lamb' being often composed only of the upper half of the leg plus a section of the saddle, creating a bizarre form and a complicated bone structure at the heart of the roast that render both decent presentation and elegant carving out of the question; the animals are usually split open and often cut up in advance, thus destroying the double saddle, one of the handsomest and, when kept pink, finest of roasts. . . . If you have a good butcher and order in advance, everything can be arranged."

Greek, Italian, or top-quality American butchers will often supply whole baby lamb on order in the spring, or get you the cuts you want.

In America the leg is the most popular cut. A spring leg of lamb will weigh not more than 7 pounds. Winter lamb leg weighs around 8 or 9 pounds. Since the leg is often sold in half legs, choose the shank portion of the leg. It has more meat on it and is well worth the extra cost. The meat is not as tender as the sirloin portion, but it is easier to carve and has much less bone and fat. The leg itself can be boned and cubed for shish kebab.

Sirloin roast and chops are cut from the larger end of the whole leg. The roast usually weighs around 2 to 3 pounds, bone-in, or it is sold as individual chops. Sirloin chops are more tender and meaty than shoulder lamb chops, and those closest to the loin section are the best and can be cut into single or double chops.

Neck of lamb has plenty of flavor and is good for stews; the shoulder makes excellent shish kebab when cut into cubes. Lamb chops from the shoulder are best used in stews because they have especially good flavor but are rather bony. They may also be broiled or braised. Shoulder can also be boned and rolled (it can also be stuffed) for an excellent roast. Lamb breast has an enormous amount of fat but is usually an economical buy and is useful for barbecuing or stuffing and roasting. Small lamb shanks — the foreshanks — weigh about 1½ pounds and are good one-person meals. They are best stewed or braised because they can be tough.

The rack of lamb lies along the animal's back between the loin and shoulder. A single rack usually weighs 2½ to 3 pounds and serves two to three people. A double rack comes from both sides of the carcass. You can buy two or three racks and tie them into a circle for a crown roast that will feed around eight people. Rib chops cut nearest the loin are the most tender. The thicker they are, the juicier they'll be. Avoid lamb chops that are less than an inch thick.

When buying lamb in the supermarket look for the expiration date on the package. It is usually stamped on the label that states the price. Avoid packages with a deposit of liquid, indicating that the lamb has either been frozen and thawed or has been there for a while. Avoid lamb that is sold ready ground in packages. There is no way of telling which cut it comes from, and you will usually find that it has too much fat. You are better off buying a shoulder of lamb, trimming away the fat, and grinding it yourself or asking your butcher to do it for you.

In the Kitchen

Leg of lamb can be marinated in yogurt for a few days so that the flesh is exceptionally tender when cooked. Boned and cubed, the leg makes delicious shish kebab served with salads of mint leaves, tomatoes, and bulgur, or with cucumbers in yogurt with pita bread. Do not overcook lamb; it should be underdone, pink in the middle, and juicy.

The neck and shoulder cuts make fine stews, particularly in spring, when young vegetables are in season. Chops can be served with anchovy, béarnaise, or hollandaise sauce and should be cooked so that they are pink in the middle.

The gamier winter lamb can be served with the same garnishes you would use for venison — cranberries or red currant jelly — and marinated in red wine with juniper berries.

For the following crown roast the bones should be "frenched." In other words, the fat should be trimmed from the tip of the rib bone. The racks are tied together in a ring to form a crown shape and the pilaf is piled in the center. Cover the ends of the ribs to prevent them from becoming charred, and put a cushion of foil in the center of the crown so that it keeps its shape while cooking.

Crown Roast of Lamb with Bulgur Pilaf
YIELD: 6 Servings

Bulgur Pilaf

1	medium onion, chopped
2	cloves garlic, chopped
3	tablespoons olive oil
2	cups bulgur
4	cups chicken stock
	Coarse salt and freshly ground pepper to taste
	Dash of cayenne pepper
½	cup pine nuts
¼	cup raisins
½	cup chopped parsley
	Juice of 2 lemons

Crown Roast

1	crown roast of lamb, 2 or 3 racks to make 12 chops in all
2	cloves garlic, peeled and crushed
1	teaspoon rosemary
	Coarse salt and freshly ground pepper to taste

Bulgur Pilaf

1. Sauté the onion and garlic in the oil until soft, without browning. Add the bulgur and cook for 2 minutes, stirring.

2. Add half the chicken stock, salt, pepper, and cayenne and simmer gently for 10 minutes. Add remaining stock and continue to simmer over very low heat for 20 minutes or until the bulgur is fluffy and the grains separated. Stir in the pine nuts and raisins. Add the parsley and season with lemon juice. Serve inside the crown roast.

Crown Roast

1. Preheat the oven to 350 degrees. Rub the roast with the garlic and rosemary. Cover the tips of the chops with foil to prevent them from burning. Roast for about 15 to 20 minutes or until the chops are pink in the middle.

2. When ready to serve remove the foil from the tips of the chops, put the bulgur pilaf in the center, and serve.

Note: Zucchini, eggplant, or a green vegetable, such as peas, goes well with this dish.

Lamb Stewed with Okra
YIELD: 4 Servings

1	tablespoon olive oil
2	pounds shoulder or neck of lamb, cut in 2-inch pieces
1	onion, sliced
2	garlic cloves, minced
½	teaspoon ground cumin
½	teaspooon turmeric
2	cinnamon sticks
2	cups canned tomatoes with their juice
1½	pounds okra, trimmed
	Coarse salt and freshly ground pepper to taste

1. Heat the oil in a heavy casserole. Brown the lamb on all sides. Add the onion, garlic, cumin, turmeric, cinnamon sticks, and tomatoes. Cover and simmer gently for 1 hour.

2. Add the okra and simmer for an additional 30 minutes. Season with salt and pepper. If the stew seems too dry, add a little hot water.

Lamb Kefta

(Moroccan Lamb Meatballs)

2 pounds freshly ground lamb
1 onion, grated
¼ teaspoon ground allspice
½ teaspoon ground cumin
½ teaspoon ground coriander seed
½ teaspoon paprika
Dash of cinnamon
Coarse salt and freshly ground pepper to taste
4 tablespoons chopped fresh coriander or parsley

1. Put the lamb into a mixing bowl and add the remaining ingredients. Mix thoroughly. If the lamb is not properly mixed, the kefta will fall apart on the skewer.

2. Form the lamb into small patties about the size of a walnut. Mold the patties tightly around a long skewer so they form small ovals. Four or five will fit on a skewer.

3. Heat a broiler or charcoal coals and grill the kefta, turning once, for about 6 minutes or until they are golden brown.

Note: These go with pilaf, steamed rice, or with couscous steamed over a combination of such vegetables as potatoes, chick peas, zucchini, turnips, or tomatoes, with raisins and saffron.

Roast Leg of Lamb with Anchovies

1 8-pound leg of lamb
¾ cup plain yogurt
3 cans flat anchovy fillets with their oil
2 cloves garlic, minced
Freshly ground pepper to taste

1. Trim away any loose fat from the lamb and wipe the leg dry with paper towels. Marinate in the yogurt for a couple of hours at room temperature or, refrigerated, for two days or overnight.

2. Preheat the oven to 425 degrees. Arrange the anchovies over the lamb, sprinkle it with their oil, garlic, and pepper.

3. Roast the lamb for 12 to 15 minutes per pound, according to how you like it.

4. Remove from the oven and let rest for a few minutes. Slice thin and arrange the slices on a heated platter. Pour the juices over the slices and serve.

Note: Serve with Stewed White Beans (page 229).

Lamb Chops with Anchovy Butter

YIELD: 4 Servings

4	thick-cut lamb chops
1	tablespoon olive oil
⅔	stick unsalted butter, at room temperature
4	flat anchovy fillets
1	clove garlic
3	tablespoons chopped fresh parsley
	Coarse salt and freshly ground pepper to taste

1. Trim excess fat from the chops and rub them with olive oil.

2. In a blender, combine the butter, anchovies, garlic, parsley, salt, and pepper and blend thoroughly. Shape the mixture into an oblong and put on a plate in the freezer.

3. Broil or pan-fry the chops until they are done to your taste. Put on a heated plate. Remove the butter from the freezer and slice in 4 pieces. Arrange the pieces on the chops.

Note: These chops are good with boiled, mashed, or baked potatoes.

Marinated Raw Lamb with Cornichons

YIELD: 2 Servings

2	thick-cut loin lamb chops
2	shallots
1	tablespoon capers
4	cornichons (baby gherkins)
1	tablespoon red wine vinegar
1	teaspoon Dijon mustard
2	tablespoons olive oil
	Coarse salt and freshly ground pepper to taste

1. With a very sharp knife, trim the fat and the bone from the lamb meat. Slice the meat thin against the grain. Arrange the slices on a plate.

2. Chop the shallots and the capers and sprinkle over the lamb. Arrange the cornichons on the plate. Mix the vinegar, mustard, and oil, and season to taste.

3. Pour the mixture over the lamb and refrigerate for 15 minutes before serving. Serve with bread or Tabbouleh (page 212).

RETAIL CUTS OF LAMB

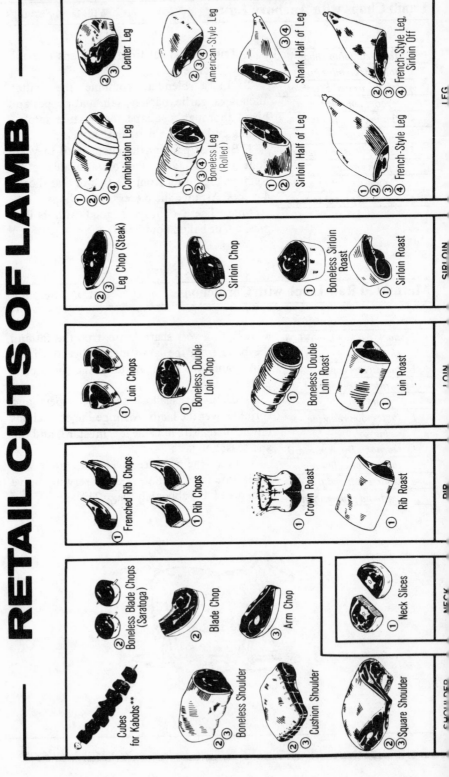

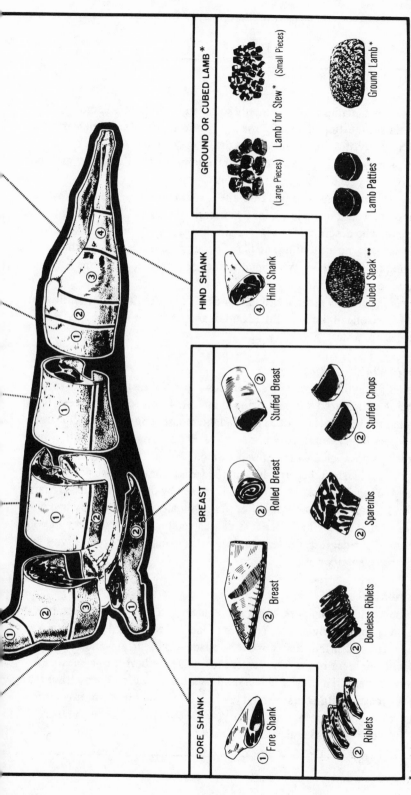

FORE SHANK

① Fore Shank

② Riblets

② Boneless Riblets

BREAST

② Breast

② Rolled Breast

② Stuffed Breast

② Spareribs

② Stuffed Chops

HIND SHANK

④ Hind Shank

GROUND OR CUBED LAMB *

(Large Pieces)   Lamb for Stew *   (Small Pieces)

Cubed Steak **

Lamb Patties*

Ground Lamb*

* Lamb for stew or grinding may be made from any cut.

**Kabobs or cube steaks may be made from any thick solid piece of boneless Lamb.

This chart approved by

National Live Stock and Meat Board

© National Live Stock and Meat Board

Pork

The pig is much maligned. "It is rightly so called," said Samuel Johnson, "for it is indeed a disgusting animal." Jews and Moslems consider it unclean and so, until recently, did the Japanese. But the Chinese, many Americans, and Europeans have long been great pig eaters, finding it one of the most efficient sources of food because it has the least waste.

Every part of the pig is edible, from the tip of the snout to the feet. "Without him there would be no bacon and therefore no cooking," wrote Grimod de la Reynière, who described the pig as a walking repast. "There would be no ham, no sausage, no andouilles, no black puddings and no pork butchers. Everything in him is good. What ingratitude has permitted his name to become a word of opprobrium?"

The pig is perfectly clean if properly looked after and not left to wallow in mud. It is also one of the most intelligent of animals — clever enough to dig out truffles, for a start.

Where Pork Comes From

Most of the nation's pork comes from Iowa and Nebraska and is cornfed. After being slaughtered it is cut up and shipped in boxes to the markets. It is not graded the way beef is. Although slaughterhouses could ask for the grading — Agriculture Department numbers 1, 2, and 3 — most don't bother because there is not such a wide difference among pigs as there is among cattle. The age of cattle when they are slaughtered varies, but most pigs are butchered very young. The pork is, of course, inspected by the Agriculture Department for disease. Trichinosis parasites cannot usually be detected by inspectors, but trichinae are killed at an internal temperature of 150 degrees. If you cook pork to 185 degrees, the temperature given in many cookbooks, you will have overcooked, dry pork.

In the Market

The best place to buy pork is at a good butcher. In the supermarket, be careful to choose the right cuts. The loin is one of the best and is cut into blade, center, and sirloin roasts or chops. Blade-end or sirloin-end roast is normally sold whole for roasts. The center loin makes the best chops because it has more tenderloin muscle and less fat. It is usually sold in chops rather than whole for roasting. Butchers will sell it whole if you ask for it, but it is more expensive than blade or loin-end roast. Ask the butcher to loosen the backbone from the ribs. This makes carving easier.

A spectacular dinner can be made with a crown roast of pork using one to three rib-end racks curved into a circle, the tips covered with foil to prevent them from burning during roasting.

Avoid rib roasts in which the bones have been sawed perpendicular to the backbone. Sometimes they have been sawed right down into the meat so that the juices will escape during cooking and you'll get a dried-out roast. If you are shopping in a supermarket for a roast, ask the butcher, who is usually in the back behind the meat counter, to provide you with a piece that has not been sawed, and ask him to loosen the backbone from the ribs for you.

The tenderloin is the most expensive and tender cut and can be braised, sautéed, or roasted.

In the supermarket, cuts of pork are clearly marked "center-cut" or "blade-end roast" or whatever. The expiration date on the package is put there by the management according to the store's guidelines on how long to keep the pork in the display case. Pork should be eaten within a week of slaughter, and most supermarkets give the meat from one to three days in the display case, depending on the cut.

Much of the pig is sold smoked. The hind legs and the picnic shoulder are sold as fresh or smoked hams (see Ham, page 145). The flank may be smoked as bacon or salted as salt pork. The shoulder is not as tender or as lean as the loin.

The best pork is pearly pink with resilient white fat. Any skin that may be attached should be thin and creamy.

Avoid cuts that are dry and dark pink with yellowed fat. The smaller the cuts for the type, the younger the animal, and subsequently the more tender the meat. When it comes to ribs, make sure that there is an even distribution of fat and lean and that the bones are pinkish white and soft. If the bones are brittle and dry looking and the meat has brownish stains, it is not good quality. Good pork has no odor.

In the Kitchen

Pork is an inexpensive meat, mellow and rich without being too heavy. Its subtle flavor goes well with rosemary, caraway seeds, fennel, sage, juniper berries, thyme, apples, chestnuts, and even truffles. Vegetables that suit it are sweet and sour red cabbage, little carrots or turnips, leeks, or sautéed green cabbage. The fat is absorbed by starchy vegetables, such as potatoes, beans, lentils, and dried peas. One of the of the nicest of dinners, a simple pork chop followed by a green salad, is also one of the most difficult dishes to get right. I find that the most reliable way to cook the chops and be sure they will remain juicy is to fry them. Rub them first with oil, garlic, freshly ground pepper, and thyme. Heat vegetable or peanut oil in a heavy frying pan and sear the chops, then lower the temperature and cook them until they are done. Season with salt just before serving. Frying a 1-inch pork chop takes about 15 minutes, a 2-inch about 25 minutes.

Chops are also good baked in the oven with a cup of cider and garnished with capers just before serving, or braised in a sauce of onions and tomatoes. Apples, sliced and sautéed in butter, make a delicious accompaniment. Braised in white wine with garlic and onions, chops go wonderfully with mustard and green peppercorns, served with buttered noodles.

Pork chops have long been thought to be especially nourishing. Such was their reputation that the actress Mrs. Patrick Campbell, engaged in a furious row with the die-hard vegetarian George Bernard Shaw during a rehearsal of one of his plays, finally ended the conversation by saying, "Shaw, some day you'll eat a pork chop and then God help all women."

One of the best dishes I have found for large dinner parties is loin roast cooked with prunes and pieces of garlic placed between the chops on the loin. It is incredibly easy to prepare and goes well with potatoes mashed with celery root. If I can, I like to buy pork with the skin on. You have to order it in advance from a butcher. The skin makes a wonderful crisp crackling when cooked. Roast it in the oven.

Pork should not be roasted at too high a temperature. At 325 degrees for 30 minutes plus 15 minutes for each pound of weight, juices should be starting to run clear and the center should have just a blush of pinkness. Let it rest for 20 minutes before you carve it.

The shoulder is better for stews but makes a fine roast if you have the butcher bone it for you since the placement of the bones makes it difficult to carve.

The ribs are delicious baked or grilled, sprinkled with lemon juice, garlic, and rosemary for an hour or two before being cooked. I also like them with homemade barbecue sauce or cooked over an open fire in the summer.

Whole roast suckling pig, sweet and tender, is a fine dish for a special occasion such as Christmas or New Year's. It is usually sold to order and the best to buy is medium-sized — around 10 pounds — not so big that it will not be tender or so small that it won't have any meat on it. Cubans serve lechón — suckling pig — in a lavish spread that may include mashed yucca sprinkled with garlic, plantains fried to a golden crisp, black beans, and white rice. It is also good stuffed. When properly prepared the skin turns a shiny brown. Before cooking a suckling pig, measure your oven and make sure it is big enough. The first time I cooked one, it was too big to go in whole. I had to cut it in half and roast it in two pieces, the front end on the top rack and the rump on the bottom. Before serving, I surrounded its waist with a bellyband of flowers and nobody knew the difference.

Pork Chops with Green Peppercorn Sauce   YIELD: 4 Servings

4	pork chops
	Flour for dredging
1	tablespoon peanut or vegetable oil
1	tablespoon Hungarian paprika
1	small onion, diced
1	clove garlic, minced
½	teaspoon thyme
1	cup dry white wine
1	tablespoon Dijon mustard
1	tablespoon green peppercorns
	Coarse salt and freshly ground pepper to taste
1	tablespoon chopped parsley

1. Wipe the pork chops dry with paper towels. Dredge them with flour, shaking off the excess.

2. Heat the oil in a pan large enough to contain the pork chops without crowding. Brown the chops on all sides. Add the paprika, onion, garlic, thyme, and white wine. Bring to a simmer, turn heat down, cover, and cook slowly for about 30 minutes or until the chops are pale whitish pink in the center. Be careful not to overcook them or they will become dry and tough.

3. Remove the chops to a heated serving platter. Stir the mustard and peppercorns into the sauce. Add salt and pepper and spoon the sauce over the chops. Sprinkle with parsley and serve.

Note: This dish goes with noodles.

Pork Chops with Sauerkraut   YIELD: 4 Servings

4	thick slices bacon
4	pork chops
1	medium onion, sliced
1½	pounds sauerkraut, washed
1	tablespoon caraway seeds
1	teaspoon freshly ground pepper
1	cup beer
	Coarse salt to taste

1. Fry the bacon in a heavy skillet until golden. Remove and drain on paper towels. Pat the chops dry with paper towels and brown in the bacon fat. Add the onion, sauerkraut, bacon strips, caraway seeds, and pepper. Cover the chops well with the sauerkraut.

2. Add the beer and bring to a boil. Turn down heat and simmer gently for 25 minutes or until the pork chops are cooked.

Note: Serve this with Düsseldorf mustard and boiled potatoes.

Pork Chops Niçoise

YIELD: 4 Servings

4	pork chops
	Flour for dredging
1	tablespoon vegetable oil
1	cup canned Italian plum
	tomatoes, chopped
2	cloves garlic, minced
1	small onion, finely
	chopped
1	green pepper, seeded and
	chopped
2	tablespoons chopped
	fresh basil
½	cup black olives, pitted
	Coarse salt and freshly
	ground pepper to taste

1. Wipe the chops dry with paper towels and dredge lightly with flour.

2. Heat the oil in a heavy skillet large enough to hold the chops without crowding. Brown the chops on all sides.

3. Add the tomatoes, garlic, onion, green pepper, and basil and simmer for 20 minutes, turning the chops once. Add the olives and cook for 10 minutes or until the chops are tender but not dried out. Season with salt and pepper. Serve hot.

Note: This is good served with rice.

Pork Chops with Cider

YIELD: 4 Servings

4	pork chops
	Flour for dredging
1	tablespoon vegetable oil
1	clove garlic, minced
4	shallots, finely chopped
2	apples, peeled, cored, and
	cut in eighths
1	cup dry (not sweet) cider
	Coarse salt and freshly
	ground pepper to taste
1	tablespoon chopped fresh
	parsley

1. Wipe the chops dry with paper towels and dredge lightly with flour.

2. Heat the oil in a heavy skillet large enough to hold the chops without crowding. Brown the chops on all sides.

3. Add the garlic, shallots, and apples and cook for 2 minutes, stirring to prevent burning.

4. Pour in the cider. Cover and simmer for 20 to 30 minutes, turning the chops once, until the chops are tender but not dried out. Season with salt and pepper, sprinkle with parsley, and serve.

Note: Calvados also goes with this dish; a jigger can be added with the cider.

Stewed Pork in Red Wine

YIELD: 4 Servings

1	tablespoon olive oil
1	onion, chopped
1	clove garlic, minced
2	pounds pork loin, cut in 1½-inch pieces
4	tablespoons red wine vinegar
¾	cup dry red wine
4	flat anchovy fillets, diced
1	ounce dried mushrooms, soaked in 1 cup hot water
½	teaspoon marjoram
1	bay leaf, crushed
3	tablespoons juniper berries, crushed with a mortar and pestle
	Coarse salt and freshly ground pepper to taste

1. Heat the oil in a heavy casserole. Cook the onion and garlic gently, without browning, until soft. Add the pork, turn up heat, and brown quickly.

2. Add the vinegar and wine and bring to a boil. Turn down heat and add the anchovies, mushrooms, marjoram, bay leaf, and juniper berries. Season with salt and pepper, cover, and cook over low heat for 1½ hours.

Lechón Asado

YIELD: 12 to 14 Servings

(Roast Suckling Pig)

2	large onions, chopped
¼	pound butter
	The pig liver, kidneys, and heart
3	cups cooked rice
3	cups cooked black beans
½	cup diced guava paste (see note)
½	cup chopped parsley
	Coarse salt and freshly ground black pepper to taste
1	suckling pig, about 12 pounds
	Olive oil

1. Preheat the oven to 350 degrees. Sauté the onions in the butter until soft. Add the diced liver, kidneys, and heart and sauté for 2 to 3 minutes. Add the rice, beans, guava paste, and parsley. Season with salt and pepper. Mix thoroughly and correct seasoning.

2. Stuff the pig loosely with the mixture and sew the cavity or secure with skewers. Place the pig on a rack in a roasting pan and rub with olive oil. Roast for 3½ to 4 hours or until an internal temperature of 155 to 160 degrees is reached.

Note: Guava paste is obtainable in Hispanic grocery stores.

Marinade

4	cups dry red wine
1	cup red wine vinegar
4	carrots, sliced
2	large onions, sliced
4	cloves garlic, crushed
6	bay leaves
1	bunch parsley
1	teaspoon thyme
1	teaspoon marjoram
½	cup black peppercorns
16	juniper berries, crushed
	Coarse salt to taste

1	leg pork, about 9 pounds
4	tablespoons olive oil
4	tablespoons flour
4	cups chicken stock

1. Combine the marinade ingredients in a large saucepan and simmer for 5 minutes. Cool.

2. With a sharp knife, score the fat on the pork to allow the marinade to penetrate deeply. Put the pork in a large non-aluminum container and cover with the marinade. Cover and refrigerate or leave in a cool place for 4 days, turning occasionally.

3. Preheat the oven to 325 degrees. Remove the meat from the marinade. Wipe it dry.

4. Heat the oil in a large, heavy braising pan and brown the meat on all sides. Meanwhile, in a separate saucepan, bring the marinade and its vegetables to a boil.

5. Remove the meat from the braising pan and stir in the flour over high heat. Gradually add the marinade through a strainer. Stir until smooth and add enough stock to make a thick sauce (about 4 cups). Return the meat to the pan.

6. Cover and cook for 3 to 4 hours or until the pork is coming away from the bone. Transfer to a heated serving dish.

7. Pour off excess fat from the sauce and pour the sauce into a small saucepan. Bring to a boil and reduce slightly. Correct seasoning and serve in a gravy boat.

3	pounds spareribs, cut up
	Juice of 2 lemons
2	cloves garlic, minced
2	tablespoons rosemary
1½	tablespoons extra-virgin olive oil
	Freshly ground pepper to taste
	Coarse salt

1. Put the ribs into a large, shallow dish. Add the remaining ingredients except the salt and toss thoroughly. Cover and leave to marinate overnight.

2. Broil over hot coals on an outdoor grill for about 10 to 15 minutes, turning so that all sides become crisp. Salt lightly.

Note: These are good with baked potatoes and sweet corn.

RETAIL CUTS OF PORK

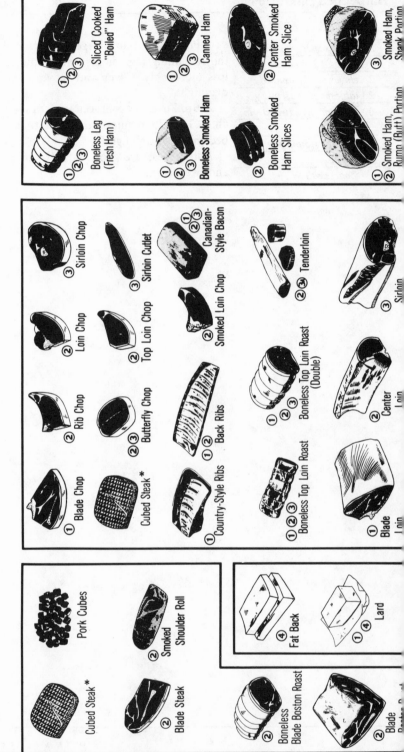

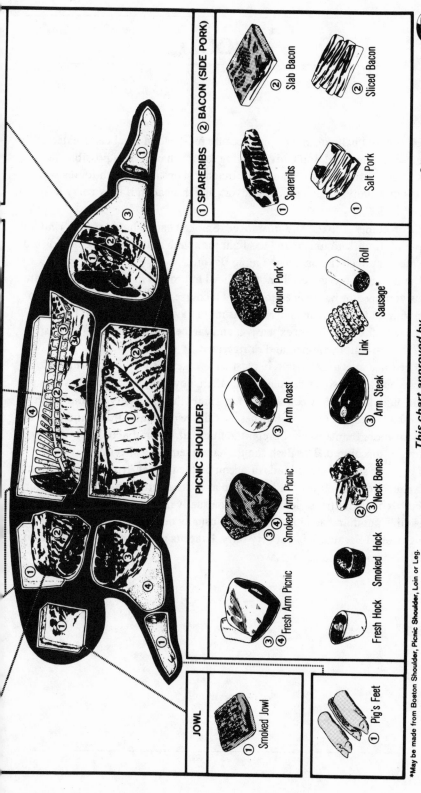

JOWL

① Smoked Jowl

① Pig's Feet

PICNIC SHOULDER

③ Fresh Arm Picnic   ④ Smoked Arm Picnic   ③ Arm Roast   Ground Pork*

Fresh Hock   Smoked Hock   ② ③ Neck Bones   ③ Arm Steak   Link   Roll

Sausage*

① SPARERIBS   ② BACON (SIDE PORK)

① Spareribs   ② Slab Bacon

① Salt Pork   ② Sliced Bacon

This chart approved by

National Live Stock and Meat Board

© National Live Stock and Meat Board

*May be made from Boston Shoulder, Picnic Shoulder, Loin or Leg.

Bacon

Bacon is cured belly or loin of pig. Because most bacon has been treated with nitrates and nitrites, I don't advise eating too much of it. It is possible, however, to get nitrite-free bacon in some butcher shops and health food stores. They will usually make a point of advertising this bacon if they carry it. If not, ask.

Bacon comes smoked and unsmoked. Smoked bacon has a golden rind and deep pink flesh, and unsmoked has light pink flesh and a cream-colored rind. The more smoked the bacon, the more flavor.

The best bacon is generally not presliced but comes in a slab that you can cut as you need or have sliced to order. Of course, the slab has to be good to start with, but slab bacon generally has more flavor than presliced bacon. It comes with the rind, is less expensive, and can be stored longer — up to six weeks — carefully wrapped and refrigerated.

Sliced bacon is usually sold in plastic packages with a window through which you can see some sample slices. Often, however, the lean slices that you see through the window conceal the remainder that is largely fat and water. Sliced bacon comes in three thicknesses, thin, regular, and thick, and does not keep for more than a week. I prefer the thick cut. Avoid bacon that is slimy, moldy, or discolored. The flesh should have a tempting sheen.

There are several other kinds of bacon on the market. Irish bacon contains both loin and belly. It is usually smoked and has a better flavor than regular sliced bacon. Country-style bacon is also usually thickly sliced and well smoked. Canadian bacon is smoked and usually needs fat such as butter when being cooked because it is not very fatty. Pancetta is Italian-style bacon, also highly recommended for its flavor.

Sausages and Salami

The best way to cook sausages is over an open fire in which you have baked a potato to go with them. However, for those without fireplaces or outdoor grills, the stove or the oven will do. Sausages can be pricked with a fork to keep the skins from bursting, then brushed with oil or butter and broiled or fried. To bake them in the oven, place them in an earthenware dish with oil or butter and sprinkle with chopped shallots or scallions.

Sausages are also good poached whole and eaten with horseradish cream sauce. Diced apples and bacon are delicious cooked with country, Italian, or blood sausages accompanied by potatoes baked in the oven. Split the cooked potatoes, coat them with butter and Parmesan cheese, and brown them briefly under the broiler.

A pleasant garnish for all sausages can be made with red or green peppers sautéed in olive oil with chopped shallots, then simmered in dry white wine. Pour this sauce over the sausages and serve with crisp fried bread or mashed potatoes. Also good with sausages is a tomato cut in half, sprinkled with olive oil, chopped garlic, and chopped parsley and baked along with a potato. An onion baked whole in its skin, the juices slightly caramelized, is one of the great accompaniments for sausages. Cook the onion on a piece of foil because the juices leak, and serve with plenty of butter.

Sausages are made from fresh pork or beef or even veal. The best sausage casings are natural ones; they do not burst as the artificial kind do. Jones sausages are recommended among the widely available commercial brands because they do not contain inordinate amounts of preservatives. Preservatives aside, most sausages are high in saturated fats and salt and should not be eaten every day.

Ethnic markets are the best places to get good sausages. Immigrants to America have brought in every kind of sausage. Among the choices are German weisswurst and bratwurst made from veal, garlicky and spicy Polish kielbasa, British "bangers" made with cereal and pork (an aquired taste for those who have not grown up on them), Italian sweet and hot sausages and luganega, a thin pork sausage. Zampone is an Italian pork sausage stuffed into a pig's foot. The French have brought in andouilles made with tripe and chitterlings, and black boudin, a blood sausage. The Chinese sausages are like salami, and are sliced and stir-fried. Chorizos, Spanish hot sausages, are good fried, removed from the pan, and finished in the oven with a little stock or water.

Frankfurters generally contain pork and beef unless labeled kosher, in which case they contain only beef. The best are fresh, sold individually or in pairs. Those in plastic packages are not as good.

When buying sausages look for those that are firm and fresh smelling. They should not be slimy or moldy, and their skins should not be punctured. The brighter red a sausage, the more chemicals it probably has. Always read the label.

Cooked Salami and Slicing Sausages

The best of these are sliced to order or bought whole. Those sold already sliced in plastic packages are not nearly as good.

Salamis usually consist of a mixture of lean pork and pork fat. Sometimes beef is mixed in or veal or wild boar is used. Red or white wine, garlic, fennel, paprika, and peppercorns are often used as flavorings. Italians, Germans, Hungarians, and the French all have their own special styles. Italian salamis include salami Napolitano made from pork and beef and spiced with chili pepper and garlic, salami finocchiona made from pork and flavored with fennel seeds, and, of course, famous Genoa salami made of veal and pork fat. German salami is moister than the Italian. Hungarian salami is spiced with peppers and paprika. Danish salami is an artificial pink and bland. Spanish chorizos, although they can be cooked like sausages, are fully cooked and smoked and very spicy.

Salami should be fresh looking, not too pink, and not brownish or greasy. Avoid dry pieces or salamis with punctured skins. If the meat is too bright a pink, it has too many chemicals in it. Keep salami wrapped.

Soft sausages include Italian mortadella, made from finely ground pork, sometimes flecked with pistachio nuts, and German liver sausage and Hungarian brawn. Again, try to avoid prepackaged sausage, and check the labels for preservatives.

Choucroute Garnie

2	1-pound packets of sauerkraut, rinsed
4	pounds pork neck bones
2	onions, chopped
2	cups chopped carrots
2	celery stalks, coarsely chopped
4	cloves garlic, finely chopped
	Bouquet garni (thyme, parsley, and bay leaf tied in cheesecloth)
1	hard green cooking apple, diced
2	teaspoons poppy seeds
2	crushed juniper berries (or ½ cup gin)
1	cup dry white wine
1	cup chicken stock
2	cups V-8 juice
	Coarse salt and freshly ground pepper to taste

1. Preheat the oven to 350 degrees.

2. Arrange all the ingredients in a large, heavy casserole in layers in the order given except for the bouquet garni, which should be dropped in midway. Season the layers with salt and pepper as you go. Cover, place the casserole in the oven, and bake for 3 hours. Check frequently to make sure the juices have not evaporated; add more stock if necessary. Be sure to remove the bouquet garni when finished.

3. Serve with hot sausages and buttered boiled potatoes, followed by a Grapefruit Salad (page 319).

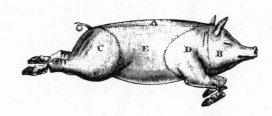

Variety Meats

In France and other Mediterranean countries variety meats such as brains, sweetbreads, kidneys, and liver are given special respect. But in America these meats are often overlooked, and as a result they can be a bargain. I never buy organ meats in the supermarket unless the meat department is an unusually reliable one. I prefer the butcher shop.

Brains

Brains are a succulent and delicate meat. The best are calf's brains. These should be very fresh; always buy them from a reliable butcher on the day you intend to use them since brains are extremely perishable. They should be bright and pinkish white in color with no odor. Sometimes they are sold fresh on "special" in supermarkets. Check to make sure that there is no deposit of juices in the package, indicating that the brains have been frozen and thawed or have been sitting around for a while. Frozen brains are more widely available in supermarkets, but they have neither the flavor nor texture of fresh ones.

Before cooking brains, soak them in water to cover with a couple tablespoons of white vinegar for an hour or two. Then carefully peel away the membrane and blood vessels. The brains should then be rinsed thoroughly in cold running water.

The French poach brains in chicken or veal stock and then fry them quickly in brown butter. They have a superb, nutty, sweet-sour flavor and are a favorite bistro dish. The Italians roll them in bread crumbs and then fry them in oil so that they develop a crisp, golden coating. Both ways make a splendid spring dinner served with new potatoes and asparagus.

Cervelles au Beurre Noire

(Brains in Black Butter)

1½	pounds calf's brains, soaked and trimmed
4	cups chicken or veal stock
4	tablespoons butter
2	tablespoons capers
	Juice of 1 lemon
	Coarse salt and freshly ground pepper to taste

1. Poach the calf's brains in the stock for 20 minutes. Drain and cool.

2. Heat the butter in a frying pan until it turns a nut-brown color. Add the brains and fry, turning carefully so that they are browned on all sides. Add the capers and squeeze on the lemon juice.

3. Season with salt and pepper to taste and serve immediately.

Italian-Style Fried Brains

1½	pounds calf's brains, soaked and trimmed
4	cups veal or chicken stock
1	egg, lightly beaten
1	cup dry bread crumbs
	Peanut or vegetable oil ½ inch deep in pan
	Coarse salt and freshly ground pepper to taste
2	lemons, cut into wedges

1. Simmer the brains in the stock for 20 minutes. Drain and cool. When they are cool, refrigerate for 10 minutes so that the brains become firm.

2. Cut the brains into pieces a little bigger than a golf ball. Dip the pieces into the egg and then into the bread crumbs.

3. Heat the oil in a skillet and fry the brains until golden, turning once. Drain on paper towels, season with salt and pepper to taste, and serve at once with lemon wedges.

Sweetbreads

What part of the animal sweetbreads actually come from is a mystery for many people. In fact, they are the thymus glands from the throat and upper chest or can be the pancreas; either can be used in a sweetbreads recipe. The best are veal sweetbreads, and they should have no smell and be pale pink in color. Choose those that are plump and glossy and buy them on the day you are going to cook them since, like brains, they are extremely perishable.

Like brains, too, they have to be soaked before being cooked so that they will lose their pinkness and turn white. Then they are simmered for two minutes to make them firm. After you have drained them, trim away any skin and gristle.

They are delicious coated with flour or egg and bread crumbs and fried in butter, or poached and cooked with shallots, mushrooms, port, and cream.

Braised Sweetbreads   YIELD: 4 Servings

2	tablespoons butter
3	veal sweetbreads, soaked and blanched
1	leek, sliced
2	carrots, sliced
1	large onion, chopped
	Bouquet garni
1	cup chicken stock
½	cup dry white wine
	Coarse salt and freshly ground pepper to taste
1	teaspoon arrowroot

1. Preheat the oven to 350 degrees. Melt the butter in a heavy casserole and brown the sweetbreads. Remove with a slotted spoon and set aside.

2. Add the leek, carrots, and onion and sauté until the onion is golden but not browned. Add the bouquet garni, sweetbreads, stock, and wine. Season with salt and pepper and bring to a boil.

3. Cover and bake in the oven for 30 minutes.

4. Remove the sweetbreads and cut them into slices. Keep warm on a serving platter. Remove the herb bouquet and bring the sauce to a boil. Mix the arrowroot with 2 tablespoons water until you have a smooth paste, and add. Bring to a boil. When the sauce has thickened, correct seasoning and spoon it over the sweetbreads. Serve immediately.

Note: This is good with new potatoes.

Liver

The best liver comes from milk-fed calves. It should be very pale and should have no smell. Grass-fed veal liver is darker and not as delicate. Lamb's liver, darker than calf's, is rather stronger in taste but can be cooked in similar ways. Pork liver is very dark and good for patés. Beef liver is the coarsest, and I find it too strong for eating although some people like it braised with onions.

If possible, get liver sliced to order. The membrane should be removed and the liver should be cut in paper-thin slices.

Nobody does liver and onions better than the Venetians. The secret of *fegato alla Veneziana* is long, slow cooking of the onions so that they are almost caramelized, and the quick frying of the liver, which must be very fresh and thinly sliced. With this the Venetians eat slices of polenta, cooked yellow cornmeal that often takes the place of bread. It is cooked, cooled, and cut into squares that can be grilled, fried, or even baked with butter and cheese or tomato sauce (see Polenta, page 212).

Fegato alla Veneziana

4 tablespoons olive oil
2 pounds onions, coarsely chopped
Coarse salt and freshly ground pepper to taste
3 tablespoons butter
1½ pounds calf's liver, sliced paper thin

1. Heat the oil in a heavy frying pan. Add the onions, salt, and pepper. Cover and cook, stirring frequently, for about 45 minutes. The onions should be golden and not too browned. Remove them to a heated dish and keep warm.

2. Turn up the heat and add the butter to the frying pan. When it has melted, add the liver and cook very quickly for about 1 minute on each side. The pieces should be pink in the middle and browned on the outside. Arrange on a dish with the onions. Serve at once.

Kidneys

They should have no smell and should be glossy and fresh-looking. If you are buying fresh kidneys wrapped in plastic, make sure that there is no deposit of juices in the bottom. This could mean that they have been frozen and thawed. Kidneys that have been frozen lack the flavor and texture of fresh ones.

Veal kidneys are the most delicate. Lamb kidneys are also delicate and tender and much cheaper than veal kidneys. I find beef and pig's kidneys too strong.

Be very careful not to overcook kidneys. They should be served pink in the middle, otherwise they will be tough.

Kidneys in Mustard Sauce

4 veal kidneys
4 tablespoons butter
1 tablespoon vegetable oil
1 tablespoon Dijon mustard
½ cup brandy
½ cup heavy cream
Coarse salt and freshly ground pepper to taste
2 tablespoons chopped fresh parsley

1. Remove the fat and membranes from the kidneys. Melt the butter with the oil in a saucepan and add the kidneys. Cook for 3 to 4 minutes, turn, and cook on the other side for 3 to 4 minutes. Remove with a slotted spoon when pink.

2. Add the mustard, brandy, and cream and scrape up the cooking juices.

3. While the sauce is reducing, cut the kidneys into slices a quarter of an inch thick and return to the sauce with their juices. Mix thoroughly, season with salt and pepper, and sprinkle with parsley. Serve immediately.

Note: This goes with rice.

Tripe

I want to make a case for tripe. I know it lacks allure. The uninitiated, unsure of its origins, tend to avoid it altogether. Being inexpensive, it has no appeal to food snobs. Worse still, nouvelle cuisine has found no role for it. Tripe is bistro food. It belongs with cassoulet, brains in black butter, or grilled pig's feet — comforting, old-fashioned, and hearty. Its mild, delicate flavor and soft, slightly chewy consistency make it an excellent vehicle for fragrant savory sauces.

Until Les Halles was torn down, in Paris bistros around the markets, steaming bowlfuls of tripe "à la mode de Caen," laced with Calvados, were consumed at dawn by *jeunesse dorée* in the hope of preventing imminent hangovers. In London tripe was — and still is — eaten by people in full evening dress at the counters of far-flung workers' cafes, and in Mexico it remains an essential dish on New Year's Day, cooked in a spicy sauce thickened with chilies and hominy grits. Italians love it, too, and eat it al dente, like pasta, served in tomato sauce.

Tripe is the lining of beef or calf stomach. Elizabeth David, in *Italian Food*, tells of a woman at Genazzano in Calabria at the public fountain "washing what appeared to be a large white fur or woollen blanket; it was an entire ox tripe, and she was bashing it against the marble basin of the fountain."

Tripe is white and about half an inch thick. It comes in two patterns, honeycomb — the best — and smooth, and should be quite white and fresh. Cook it within a day of buying it. Many Americans avoid it simply because they do not realize how easy it is to cook. In fact, it is sold partially cooked in butcher's shops and, when available, in supermarkets. Otherwise, cooking could take 10 to 12 hours.

Tripe with Fresh Tomato Sauce   YIELD: 4 Servings

1	pound tripe
1	tablespoon olive oil
2	tablespoons butter
1	large onion, chopped
1	clove garlic, minced
1	pound fresh, ripe
	tomatoes, peeled
1	teaspoon marjoram
	Coarse salt and freshly
	ground pepper to taste
3	tablespoons freshly
	grated Parmesan cheese

1. Simmer the tripe for an hour in water to cover. Drain, cut into 2-by-½-inch strips, and set aside.

2. Meanwhile, heat the oil and butter in a skillet and gently sauté the onion and garlic without browning until the onion is soft. Add the tomatoes, marjoram, salt, and pepper. Simmer for 20 minutes.

3. Add the tripe and cook for 1 hour or until the tripe is slightly al dente. Do not overcook it.

4. Sprinkle with Parmesan and serve.

Veal

Veal has been called the "chameleon" of the kitchen. This meat adapts to almost any flavor, including sage, rosemary, thyme, tarragon, lemon, orange, tomatoes, white wine, Marsala, cream, prosciutto, and Parmesan cheese. If these ingredients suggest Italy it is hardly surprising, considering that Italians eat the most veal of any nation, 15.4 pounds a year per person (compared with 4 pounds for Americans).

"The charm of veal for Italians is the opportunity it gives them to utilize their culinary artistry to the full," writes Waverly Root in *Food*. "Meats with more individualistic flavor refuse to enter with becoming modesty into the harmonious blends which are the triumph of Italian cooking. In France, a sauce is an adornment, even a disguise, added to a dish more or less as an afterthought. In Italy, it is the dish, its soul, its raison d'être, the element which gives it character and flavor."

Where Veal Comes From

Veal comes from the same breed of cattle as good beef. There are two kinds: milk-fed and grass-fed. Milk-fed veal has, in rare instances, been allowed to nurse on its mother's milk. You won't find it available unless you have a special source, such as a local farmer who raises his own calves. Most often it has been fed a formula based on dried milk. There is a premium for this milk-fed veal because it never is allowed to graze and spends its short life in a darkened stall. Some veal, the kind that often goes to supermarket chains, has been grazed. Once it has been allowed to graze, its flesh becomes darker, the chief cause being the iron in its diet. This meat is really baby beef, several months old, reddish pink and tougher and much less delicate than true milk-fed veal. It is often sold at veal prices and is not worth the expense. But if it is reasonably priced, it is good for the longer-cooked veal dishes such as ragout, stew, braised veal, and veal Marengo.

Milk-fed veal is creamy pale pink and tender, with a very delicate flavor. These veal calves are fed a formula that was invented in the Netherlands. Deprived of iron and confined in pens so small that they cannot develop muscles, the calves become anemic.

There are about half a dozen major Dutch-method producers in this country and they include Primine veal, and Berliner & Marx, who produce Plume de Veau in Brooklyn. But the Dutch method, although it produces pale cream-colored veal, is not as good as veal fed on mother's milk. The formula is not as rich as cow's milk, and the calves raised this way are not slaughtered until they are twelve weeks old and are therefore less delicate than milk-fed calves slaughtered at ten to twelve weeks. And somehow the veal yields an inordinate amount of moisture when cooked.

Most of our veal, except Berliner & Marx Plume de Veau, comes from the Middle West. Some of it is shipped in carcass form. Because the veal is so delicate, the skin is left on to protect it. Other packers prefer to pack the veal, skin off, in Cryovac as with beef.

Veal is between one and three months old. Between four and twelve months it is baby beef. It doesn't become good beef until eighteen months. Then it is sold, of course, as beef.

In the Market

Veal is expensive, but it has little fat so there is almost no waste. It is not readily available in rural areas. It is usually found in towns with an Italian population or in large cities.

Avoid cuts of veal that are gray, brown tinged, dry, or excessively moist. The meat should have a fresh smell, no marbling, and only a little fat around the outside. If packaged veal contains a deposit of liquid in the package, it has probably been frozen and thawed. Look for a moist, satiny patina to the skin and a vibrant color and a springiness in the flesh.

Veal scallops, thin boneless slices that are used for making scaloppine, should be cut from the upper part of the leg, sliced against the grain. They should consist of the cross section of one, not two, muscles, otherwise they will separate when cooked. Sometimes the loin muscle is sliced into scallops, but these are not nearly as good and curl up when cooked. Steaks also come from the leg and are cut thicker than scallops. Rump roast should be boned and rolled. The shank, which usually weighs between 4 and 8 pounds, should be braised; otherwise, it will be tough.

The loin is sometimes sold as a roast in top butcher shops, but more often it is cut into chops. The best chop is the porterhouse cut; it is lean with the most tender meat. Rib chops are best braised; those closest to the loin section are the most tender. A standing rib roast can also be boned and rolled. A crown roast, made with two or three racks of veal, is a spectacular party dish.

Veal shoulder is good tied into roasts for braising. The foreshank makes osso buco. Veal bones contain collagen, a thickener, and as a result make very good stocks and sauces.

Breast of veal is bony, but you can do many things with it. It can be stuffed, braised, cut into spareribs, stewed, or ground for pâtés.

Veal is cheapest in spring.

In the Kitchen

When storing veal, wrap it loosely in butcher paper so that the air circulates around it. Use scallops and ground veal immediately; chops, cutlets, and roasts can be kept for a day or so. Do not freeze veal; it loses flavor and moisture.

Veal must not be cooked too long or it will dry out. If roasting veal, as for the recipe below, lard it or have your butcher do so, and baste it frequently. A roast should be at room temperature when put into the oven, so leave it out of the refrigerator for an hour beforehand. Potatoes, carrots, and small onions can be placed around the roast while it is cooking.

One of my favorite veal dishes is osso buco, veal shanks braised in a rich tomato sauce and served with saffron risotto. Use Italian Arborio rice, cooked until creamy, golden, and slightly al dente.

Pound scallops between plastic wrap or waxed paper before cooking them.

Be aware that veal when cooked often yields a great deal of moisture. Also, be extremely careful to cook scaloppine fast and lightly over a medium-high flame or you will end up with shriveled meat. Spinach and string beans go well with veal scallops.

Veal chops are also good dredged with flour and fried in vegetable oil so that they develop a brown crust and are moist inside. For best results, brown over a high flame, then turn heat to medium.

The following recipe produces a roast that is tender and juicy, slightly pink in the middle. Serve with glazed baby white onions and carrots.

Roast Veal with Rosemary and Potatoes

YIELD: 6 Servings

1 tablespoon vegetable oil
1 5-pound loin of veal, boned, rolled, larded, and tied
8 cloves garlic, unpeeled
2 pounds potatoes
1 tablespoon rosemary
Coarse salt and freshly ground pepper to taste
1 cup veal or chicken stock
½ cup dry red wine

1. Preheat the oven to 325 degrees. Put the oil in the bottom of a large roasting pan. Place the veal in the pan with the garlic and cover with aluminum foil. Roast the veal for 1 hour, basting frequently.

2. Peel the potatoes and cut them into 1½-inch pieces. Cover with water and set aside.

3. Dry the potatoes with paper towels and, after the veal has roasted for 1 hour, place them in the roasting pan around the veal. Sprinkle with rosemary and roast for 1 hour. The veal will have cooked 2 hours in all.

4. Remove the veal to a heated serving dish and surround with potatoes. Sprinkle with salt and pepper. Pour the fat from the roasting pan and add the stock and wine. Bring to a boil. Simmer for a couple of minutes until the sauce has thickened slightly. Correct seasoning and serve in a heated gravy boat.

Osso Buco

1	*tablespoon vegetable oil*
1	*onion, sliced*
1	*clove garlic, minced*
4	*veal shanks*
	Coarse salt and freshly ground pepper to taste
2	*cups canned tomatoes*
2	*cups chicken or veal stock*

1. Heat the oil in a heavy, fireproof casserole. Gently sauté the onion and garlic until soft, without browning.

2. Add the remaining ingredients, cover, and simmer for 1½ hours. If more liquid is needed, add more stock.

Note: Serve this with Risotto alla Milanese (page 216). The marrow spooned from the bones is a great delicacy.

Veal Chops with Anchovy Sauce

4	*large veal chops*
	Flour for dredging
2	*tablespoons vegetable oil*
1	*clove garlic, minced*
2	*tablespoons butter*
4	*flat anchovy fillets, chopped*
2	*tablespoons chopped parsley*
	Coarse salt and freshly ground pepper to taste

1. Wipe the chops dry with paper towels. Dredge with flour.

2. Use two frying pans large enough to hold two chops each without crowding. Heat 1 tablespoon oil in each pan and fry the chops, turning once, for about 7 minutes on each side or until the outside is brown and the inside pink and juicy.

3. Meanwhile, in a small pan, sauté the garlic in the butter until golden but not browned. Stir in the anchovies and parsley and cook for 2 minutes. Turn off heat and keep warm.

4. When the chops are ready, place them on individual heated plates and spoon some anchovy sauce on each one.

Note: This is good with potatoes and puréed spinach.

Veal Scaloppine with Mushrooms

4	tablespoons butter
½	pound mushrooms, sliced
	Coarse salt and freshly ground pepper to taste
4	veal scaloppine, pounded thin (about ¼ pound each)
	Flour for dredging
1	tablespoon vegetable oil
½	cup heavy cream
¼	cup Calvados or Marsala

1. Heat 2 tablespoons butter in a frying pan and add the mushrooms. Season with salt and pepper, turn heat down, and allow to simmer for 5 to 10 minutes so that the juices exude.

2. Dredge the scaloppine lightly in flour, shaking off excess.

3. In a separate pan large enough to hold the scaloppine two at a time without crowding, heat the remaining butter and the oil. Quickly sauté the scaloppine so that they are browned on the outside and pink in the middle. Remove from the pan and keep warm.

4. Add the cream to the mushrooms, bring to a boil, and add the Calvados or Marsala. Season with salt and pepper and add to the pan that the scaloppine cooked in. Return the scaloppine to the pan, bring the mixture to a simmer, remove from heat, and serve. Be careful not to overcook the scaloppine.

RETAIL CUTS OF VEAL

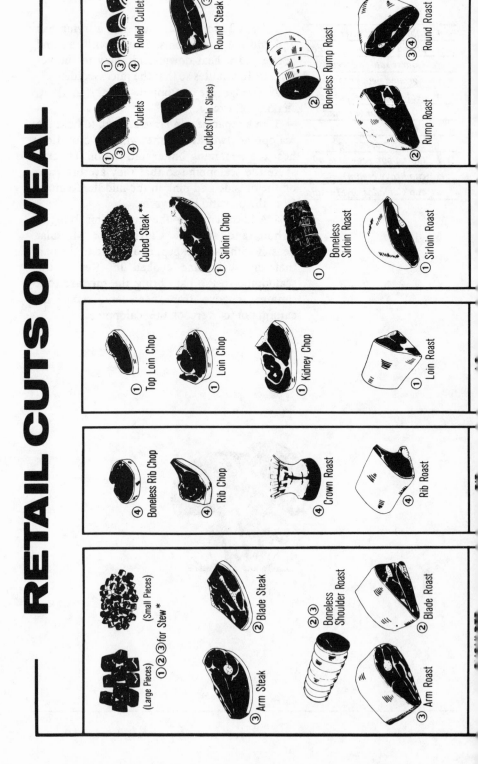

(Large Pieces) ①②③for Stew*

(Small Pieces)

③ Arm Steak

② Blade Steak

②③ Boneless Shoulder Roast

③ Arm Roast

② Blade Roast

④ Boneless Rib Chop

④ Rib Chop

④ Crown Roast

④ Rib Roast

① Top Loin Chop

① Loin Chop

① Kidney Chop

① Loin Roast

Cubed Steak**

① Sirloin Chop

① Boneless Sirloin Roast

① Sirloin Roast

① ③ ④ Rolled Cutlets

③ ④ Round Steak

① ③ ④ Cutlets

Cutlets(Thin Slices)

② Boneless Rump Roast

③④ Round Roast

② Rump Roast

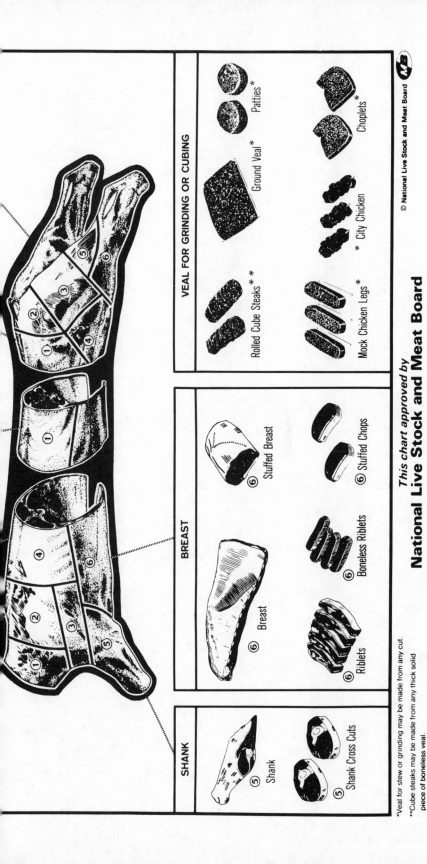

VEAL FOR GRINDING OR CUBING

Ground Veal *

Patties *

Choplets *

City Chicken

* City Chicken

Rolled Cube Steaks **

Mock Chicken Legs *

BREAST

Stuffed Breast

⑥

⑥ Stuffed Chops

Breast

⑥

Boneless Riblets

⑥

Riblets

⑥

SHANK

Shank

⑤

Shank Cross Cuts

⑤

*Veal for stew or grinding may be made from any cut.
**Cube steaks may be made from any thick solid
piece of boneless veal.

This chart approved by
National Live Stock and Meat Board

© National Live Stock and Meat Board

Dairy Products

Cheese

Several summers ago a friend and I took the Orient Express from Paris to Venice. We had decided to splurge on a luxurious dinner in the train's dining car, an establishment long familiar to us from old movies. What a treat it was going to be to eat at a table surrounded by carved wood paneling and *fin-de-siècle* frosted glass, dining on the best French food as the landscape sped by. Alas, this was not in the cards.

We had planned to meet in Paris and catch the train from the Gare du Nord. Since we were early we stopped for coffee in a cafe near the station. I had just arrived from the States and longed at least to look at a French food shop. My companion, who was in the middle of reading Dante's *Inferno* in Italian with the aid of a dictionary, showed no interest. So I went off alone and lost my head, buying several goat's cheeses, some Bleu d'Auvergne, Roquefort, and fresh cream cheeses, along with several baguettes and four bottles of wine. Looking up from the woes of the damned, my companion was horrified. When were we going to eat all this? Sooner, it turned out, than we thought.

Once on the train, we walked from our wagon-lit all the way to the front, and then all the way to the end, without finding the restaurant car. Somewhere in the middle there was a stand-up bar with stale sandwiches in drawers, Horn & Hardart style. This could not be the restaurant. But it was. The old man who was in charge of the wagon-lit explained. They had taken the restaurant car off the season before, he said sadly. He'd worked there for forty years. So out came the cheeses and the wine, and the three of us had a spectacular meal. Now I hear that the dining car has been reinstated, but whenever I take a train for a long ride, I always bring cheese and wine.

There are over a thousand cheeses in the world today. To end a meal, few things can match a sharp goat's cheese and a glass of cold Sancerre wine, or a regal blue-veined Stilton served with port and famous Bath Oliver biscuits (imported from England and sold in some specialty stores). For lunch, my favorites include a thick wedge of aged Cheddar with pickles and a pint of ale or a slice of Greek feta served with black olives and pita bread.

In one chapter it is not possible to go into detail about every cheese, but there are some guidelines that should be followed if you are going to get the best. First of all, shop if you can at a good cheese store or the cheese department of a specialty store you like. You can almost always ask for samples, and the cheese will be cut to order. In these stores, cheeses are usually kept so that they are allowed to ripen naturally — something they cannot do under refrigeration. Some supermarkets also have cheese departments where you can taste before buying.

The main categories of cheese, for the purposes of shopping, are fresh, goat's, hard, blue-veined, soft, and semi-firm. Most are made from cow's milk: skimmed, partly skimmed, or enriched with cream. In smaller quantities, cheeses are also made from the milk of goats, ewes, buffalo, and even from camels, mares, and reindeer.

There are many imitation cheeses, cheese spreads, and processed cheeses on the market, all inferior to the real thing and confusing to the buyer. Someone who reads a recipe calling for Gruyère and buys foil-wrapped wedges of "Gruyère" processed cheese will wonder why the dish comes out like glue, or why sliced "Swiss" cheese in plastic wrap tastes so different from that imported from Switzerland and sliced to order. Cheese that is sold wrapped in plastic or foil in the dairy departments of most supermarkets is likely to be disappointing.

Real cheese is made by the addition of a bacterial starter or rennet — or both — to fresh or pasteurized milk. When the milk starts to curdle, whey separates from the curds. These are then broken up, drained, and pressed or molded or heated to various temperatures to make them more solid.

The best cheese is made from unpasteurized milk. Cheese made from pasteurized milk will not mature and develop flavor because much of the bacteria will have been killed by the pasteurization.

Processed cheese is made from inferior natural cheese that is emulsified, stabilized, and often combined with artificial color and flavoring. It does not ripen or age, and it has no rind. It is not recommended.

Fresh Cheese

Fresh cheeses are simply made from the curds of sour milk or milk that has been cured with rennet. The whey drips through a cheesecloth and the curds form the cheese. This category includes cottage cheese, made from milk that has naturally soured, then been put into a cloth and allowed to drain. Pot cheese is allowed to drain further. Farmer's cheese is almost identical except that it is put into a mold. Some of these cheeses are pretty bland, but they go with fruit or fruit purées. They should be white and very moist, with no fermented taste or sharp smell. Most fresh cheese is stamped with an expiration date by the processor or the store.

Mozzarella is a round, fragile Italian cheese and should be eaten very fresh. In Italy they sell it when it is only hours old. Don't keep it for longer than a week. When buying mozzarella, avoid any that is dry, rubbery, or yellow. Supermarket mozzarella is rubbery enough to bounce and extremely salty (for preservation). It is suitable only for cooking. Imported Italian mozarrella made from buffalo's milk is available in a few specialty stores in the United States. It is so delicious that it is generally used for a first course or a cheese course. Fresh mozzarella made locally from cow's milk is also available in Italian and specialty stores. For a summer first course, serve fresh mozzarella with fresh or sun-dried tomatoes and fresh basil leaves. Dribble extra-virgin olive oil, preferably from Tuscany, over the top.

Mascarpone, flown in from Italy, is an extremely delicate, light and perishable cheese that goes with fruit such as pears, raspberries, or strawberries and is sometime sold layered with Gorgonzola. It should be fresh-looking and moist. See the recipe below for mascarpone with pasta.

Ricotta, a soft white cheese produced in Italy and also manufactured in the United States, is bland and fresh. It is often used as filling for pasta or as a dessert. It is very perishable and should be used within a day or two if it is freshly made. In Italy the best fresh ricotta is eaten with sugar and fruit.

Fromage blanc, a smooth cheese made from skimmed milk, and cream cheeses such as Petit Suisse or coeur à la crème go well with summer fruit, strawberries, and raspberries. Boursin is a French cream cheese, often flecked with herbs or cracked black pepper. It is often sold in carboard boxes. Open the box and make sure the cheese inside is plump and moist. Neufchâtel is made from whole cow's milk and comes both young and ripe, with a slight bloom on the skin.

Brown Mysost is a fresh goat's cheese from Norway that is also sold cooked and called Gjetost. Gjetost is sweet and rich, like fudge, and goes well with pears or apples.

Greek feta is salted and preserved in brine and made from sheep's or goat's milk. It can be sharp or mild and is good served with olives or crumbled in salad. Choose pieces that are moist and shiny and that have been stored in brine.

Soft Cheese

A soft cheese ripens when the bacteria on the rind move into the center. This category includes such cheeses as Camembert, Brie, and Coulommiers from France. These have a white or orange rind, the surface of which is sprayed with bacteria that will penetrate to the center of the cheese. The rinds can be cured with brine, Marc de Bourgogne (a brandy), wine, or spices. The best of these cheeses are made from unpasteurized milk.

Choose those that are plump and soft, but with a slight spring when pressed. If the cheese is precut, look at the inside. If it has a chalky white line running horizontally along the center, it is not yet ripe. Conversely, if it is way too runny with a rank or ammonia smell, it is overripe. Avoid cheeses that are shrunken, oozing too much, and smelling of ammonia. There is a saying in French that a Camembert is ripe "quand il s'abandonne" (when it abandons itself). The cheese should bulge at the sides and run slightly when cut. These cheeses won't ripen once cut.

Creamy cheeses, such as Explorateur or Chaource, are velvety and soft. They should be plump and full, not shrunken or withered. They are excellent served with salad and fruit or on crackers.

Then there are the "monastery" cheeses such as Pont l'Evêque, Reblochon, and Tête de Moine. They are called "washed rind" cheeses because they are washed from time to time with brine, beer, cider, whey, or wine. The rind remains soft and the center moist. They smell too strong when they are overripe, and their rinds become sticky. Pont l'Evêque should be stamped with the words *lait cru* or *non pasteurisé* to show it comes from unpasteurized milk and is the genuine article.

One of the best American cheeses is Liederkranz, which ripens to a fine, strong flavor. It is never as strong as Germany's Limburger cheese, which tastes much better than it smells. In *Eugene Onegin* Pushkin describes the hero's dinner at St. Petersburg's famous Talon's restaurant. Only a poet's imaginary hero could stomach this menu. It consisted of foie gras en croûte, truffles, roast sirloin of beef, fresh pineapple, and very ripe Limburger cheese.

Blue Cheese

This category includes some of the finest cheeses available, such as Roquefort, Stilton, and Blue Cheshire. These cheeses are mottled with blue veins that are produced by the injection of penicillin. The best have a strong flavor and wonderful taste and vary from smooth and mellow to very sharp. They should not be dry or salty or too young. Young pieces have few blue veins. Avoid pieces that are precut and prewrapped. They won't be as fresh as cheese cut from the whole piece. Cheeses that are cut into will not ripen and develop flavor. They will start to spoil, especially the more delicate soft or blue cheeses. Don't buy Stilton in earthenware jars; these usually contain mashed-up, second-rate cheese. The rind of the whole cheese should never be cracked or dried out. The only way to get the best blue cheese is to ask to taste it. Keep pieces well wrapped in plastic or in a damp cloth if the cheese is whole.

Roquefort, made from ewe's milk, is one of the world's great cheeses, rich and creamy with blue veins. To end a meal, it is exquisite served with a chilled sweet wine such as Sauternes or Château d'Yquem. Other good blue cheeses include Gorgonzola from Italy, which is creamier and often more pungent than Roquefort or Stilton. Gorgonzola makes a pleasant hors d'oeuvre served spread on slices of fried or grilled polenta (page 212). Stilton is at its best in whole, ripe wheels, eaten with Bath Oliver biscuits and accompanied by a glass of port. Danish Blue is made from cow's milk. It is more buttery than Roquefort and is good in salads. Blue Cheshire, also from cow's milk, is hard to find. This is an orange cheese, crumbly, rich, and blue veined.

Goat Cheese

These are among my favorite cheeses and come in all shapes and sizes, some small enough for one person, others in long cylinders coated with edible vegetable ash; some with hard crusts and pungent interiors, others soft and delicate, shaped into pyramids or rounds. Some can be very intense and creamy with a peppery, slightly tart edge. The milder ones can be eaten with fruits such as raspberries or pears. Those with soft rinds can be served in extra-virgin olive oil and sprinkled with thyme.

Goat's cheese is fragile and doesn't keep well. As it drains and dries it becomes more pungent. When it is old it becomes hard and ammoniacal. Don't buy cheeses that are shrunken or have tough-looking, withered skins.

American goat's cheeses from California are a fairly new phenomenon. They are not as strong as French goat's cheeses but are very good.

Semi-Firm

This category includes Cheddar, Gouda, French Cantal, Cheshire, Leicester, and the cheeses with holes such as Jarlsberg, Swiss Emmenthaler, and Gruyère. Fontina from the Val d'Aosta in Italy has many rubbery imitations. The real stuff can be recognized by its purple-inked trademark.

There are many kinds of Cheddar on the market. This cheese varies in flavor from very mild to sharp. The best comes from England, Canada, New York, Oregon, Vermont, and Wisconsin. Cheddar is aged from three months to a year or more. Young Cheddar is smooth, bland, and mild. Aged Cheddars develop a fuller, more pronounced and nutty flavor and a smooth, firm texture. The best are from unpasteurized milk. There are also many imitations around, flavored with chemicals and artificially colored.

Swiss cheese has many copiers. Emmenthaler, a true and superior Swiss cheese, comes from cows that have grazed in the Emme Valley in Switzerland. It has a honey-colored rind and large holes. Imported Swiss is not necessarily from Switzerland; it can be from Finland or Austria. Look for imported Swiss from Switzerland.

Gruyère has smaller holes and a brownish rind and is made in Switzerland and France. Appenzeller is similar but a little sharper.

In all these cheeses the holes should glisten. Always ask to taste. Avoid those that are dried out or that have cracked rinds. If they have darkened near the rind they have not been wrapped properly. Precut cheeses do not have the flavor of fresh cut.

Hard Cheese

Hard cheeses are primarily used for grating. They are aged from two to twelve years or more. These include two Swiss cheeses, Sbrinz, which is granular and dry like Parmesan and aged around three years, and Saanen, which is aged for five or six years. Parmigiano (which we also call Parmesan), Grana Padano, and Pecorino Romano of Italy are among the best hard cheeses. True Parmesan cheese is made under strict regulations. Some twelve-year-old Parmesans are crumbly and granular, superb eaten on their own or grated. Parmesan should be straw yellow, moist, and not too salty. White pieces are either stale — especially if covered with white crystals — or too young.

Once Parmesan is grated it immediately starts to lose its flavor. Don't bother with ready-grated Parmesan sold in bottles. It has practically no taste. In many Italian households, Parmesan is grated at the table, each person grating the cheese directly onto his pasta or rice. Grana Padano is cheaper than Parmesan and comes from Piedmont and Lombardy.

Pecorino is a hard grating cheese made from sheep's milk and is sharper than Parmesan. It is a favorite among Romans. In spring they have picnics along the roadside and drink Frascati wine and eat fresh fava beans sprinkled with this cheese. For cooking, it should be used only in spicy dishes because it is very strong.

Other good grating cheeses include Kefalotyri from Greece, aged Dutch Gouda, and dry California jack.

Buy hard cheese in small amounts and store them wrapped in foil in a plastic container with a tight-fitting lid. The cheese must be kept moist. If the cheese whitens and dries out, wrap it in a piece of damp cheesecloth and leave overnight in a plastic container. Then remove the cheesecloth and use for grating.

Cheddar or Gruyère Cheese Soufflé

YIELD: 4 Servings

2	tablespoons butter
1	tablespoon flour
1	cup warm milk
½	cup freshly grated Parmesan cheese
4	egg yolks, beaten
	Coarse salt and freshly ground pepper to taste
6	egg whites
	Freshly grated nutmeg to taste

1. Preheat the oven to 400 degrees.

2. Melt the butter in a saucepan and add the flour. Cook for 1 minute, stirring, then add the milk gradually. Keep stirring over low heat and add the Parmesan. Stir well, add the egg yolks and cook, stirring all the while, over low heat until thickened. Season with salt and pepper. Set aside.

3. Butter a soufflé dish. Whip the egg whites until they stand up in peaks. Fold the cheese mixture into the egg whites and pour into the soufflé dish. Sprinkle with nutmeg.

4. Bake for 20 to 25 minutes.

Pasta with Mascarpone and Walnuts

YIELD: 4 to 6 Servings

1	pound pasta shells (conchiglie)
2	tablespoons butter
½	pound mascarpone cheese
⅓	cup freshly grated Parmesan cheese
½	cup chopped walnuts
	Coarse salt and freshly ground pepper to taste

1. Cook the pasta shells until al dente. The time will vary according to the kind of shells.

2. Meanwhile, melt the butter in a saucepan big enough to hold the pasta. Add the mascarpone and heat gently until it is melted.

3. When the pasta is cooked, drain and add to the mascarpone. Add the Parmesan cheese and walnuts. Toss thoroughly, season with salt and pepper, and serve.

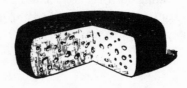

Eggs

The best eggs I ever tasted were sold by a Chamula woman at the market in San Cristóbal in southern Mexico. They came with thick, filthy shells and were carefully wrapped in a woolen shawl to be put one by one (they were sold singly) into your basket. Inside they had yolks of the deepest orange I have ever seen. The omelets made with these eggs were so full of flavor that I kept them quite simple, cooked in a nutty brown butter, either plain or with nothing more than a few fresh herbs. Some enterprising merchant from Mexico City introduced eggs that were a gleaming white with clean shells and sold in plastic cartons. None of the Indians would buy them. They came from factory-raised hens in Mexico City and tasted of fishmeal. These hens had been raised indoors with artificial lighting and fed commerical feed. The ones we had been eating were from local chickens, of course, that were allowed to scratch around happily in the yards of the nearby villages.

Of all the foods, eggs have the most universal appeal. My sister Philippa for years would only tolerate two dishes, frozen fish sticks and a "bald" egg with toast. By the time she had grown up the fish sticks were forgotten, but she made great boiled eggs. Hers are soft in the center while the white is gently cooked through without being rubbery. Achieving this is not as easy as people think. You only have to look at the green-rimmed eggs sold in delicatessens to see that.

Most of the eggs on the market these days are from a week to a month old. The fresher ones are, of course, much better. There is no difference in taste between brown and white eggs. The pigment on the eggshells depends on the breed; for example, Rhode Island Red hens lay brown eggs, while White Leghorns lay white ones.

There are various ways of telling how fresh eggs are, both in the market and when you contemplate the eggs sitting in your refrigerator at home. Inside the round end is an air pocket that gets bigger as the egg becomes older because it loses moisture through the pores of the shell. You can tell how big the air pocket is by holding the egg up to the light or by shaking it. If it sloshes, the air pocket is large and the egg is stale. A stale egg will be light for its size. While a really fresh egg submerged in cold water will stay on the bottom, an old one will rise to the surface.

Older eggs have thinner, more watery whites. They can be used for baking but are not much good for frying or poaching. Try to poach a stale egg in boiling water; the white runs away into a string. Try to fry one, and the membrane that holds the yolk stretches and the yolk flattens.

Before they are packed, most commercially sold eggs are washed in a solution of water mixed with detergent and chlorine. Sometimes ammonia is added. The washing is done because producers feel that shoppers won't buy eggs that have dirt on them. However, the washing makes the eggs lose their flavor more quickly because their protective coating is removed. If possible, try to find a source for organic eggs if the price is not prohibitive.

Before being shipped, eggs are graded by Federal inspectors. The grades are AA, A, B, or C, depending on the stiffness and viscosity of the yolks and whites, judged by a process called "candling," by holding the egg up to a light. The lower grades are progessively runnier and more watery inside, and the shells thinner and more porous. Freshness and size are not taken into account in grading.

When buying eggs check the date on the carton and make sure it has not expired. Open the carton to see that the eggs aren't cracked. Since eggs are porous and absorb the smells of strong foods in the refrigerator, don't buy more than half a dozen at a time unless you intend to use them right away. A cool place with plenty of air, if you have one, is actually better for storing eggs than the refrigerator. Use eggs at room temperature for mayonnaise, whisking, and boiling.

Fines Herbes Omelet   YIELD: 1 Serving

3	eggs
2	tablespoons chopped
	fresh chives, tarragon,
	and/or basil
	Coarse salt and freshly
	ground white pepper to
	taste
2	tablespoons cold butter

1. Break the eggs into a bowl and add the herbs, salt, pepper, and 1 tablespoon of the butter, cut into small pieces.

2. Using an omelet pan, heat the remaining butter until it has stopped foaming and is just beginning to turn brown.

3. Pour in the eggs and stir a couple of times with the prongs of a fork. With the fork, pull the edge of the omelet toward the center of the pan and and tilt the pan to allow the eggs to run back to the sides. Do this two or three times. The center of the omelet should be runny and the bottom golden brown.

4. Fold the omelet onto a heated plate and serve.

Scrambled Eggs with Smoked Salmon in Brioche

YIELD: 6 Servings

12	brioches
12	eggs
	Coarse salt and freshly ground pepper
½	pound unsalted butter, at room temperature
¼	pound smoked salmon, diced
1	tablespoon chopped fresh dill

1. Preheat the oven to 350 degrees and heat the brioches. Meanwhile, prepare the eggs.

2. Put the eggs into a blender with salt, pepper, and 4 tablespoons of butter. Blend until frothy.

3. Heat the remaining butter in a heavy skillet over low heat. Stir the salmon and dill into the eggs and add the mixture to the skillet. Cook very slowly, stirring, until the eggs are cooked soft and not dried out. Meanwhile, remove the brioches from the oven, cut off the tops, and scoop out the insides. Keep them warm.

4. Fill the centers of the brioches with the egg mixture and cap with the brioche lids. Serve immediately.

Whipped Scrambled Eggs

YIELD: 3 to 4 Servings

4	tablespoons butter
8	large eggs
	Coarse salt and freshly ground pepper to taste

1. Melt the butter in a frying pan over low heat; do not allow it to brown.

2. Meanwhile, break the eggs into a blender. Add 2 tablespoons of melted butter and the salt and pepper. Blend until the mixture is foamy.

3. Add the eggs to the frying pan and cook over very low heat, stirring constantly with a spatula. Remove the pan frequently from the heat to prevent overcooking. When the eggs are still extremely moist remove from heat.

4. Serve at once on warmed plates. Accompany with hot bread or toast.

Pipérade

2	medium onions, sliced
3	tablespoons olive oil
2	sweet red peppers
1	sweet green pepper
3	tomatoes
	Dash of thyme
	Coarse salt and freshly ground pepper to taste
6	eggs
2	tablespoons chopped fresh parsley or basil

1. In a heavy skillet, soften the onions in the oil. Meanwhile, char the peppers and tomatoes by holding them over a gas flame with a fork and peeling off their skins. Chop and add to the onions with thyme, salt, and pepper. Stir, cover, and simmer for 15 minutes.

2. Meanwhile, beat the eggs seasoned with salt and pepper. Add to the vegetables and scramble until just set. Garnish with parsley or basil.

Huevos Rancheros

4	tablespoons olive oil
1	onion, finely chopped
1	clove garlic, minced
1	pound ripe tomatoes, peeled and chopped
1	fresh green chili, diced
1	teaspoon chili powder (or more to taste)
	Coarse salt and freshly ground pepper to taste
4	tortillas
4	eggs
¼	cup grated Cheddar or Monterey jack cheese

1. Heat 2 tablespoons oil in a frying pan. Add the onion and garlic and cook gently until the onion has softened.

2. Add the tomatoes, chili, and chili powder. Simmer about 10 minutes or until thick. Season with salt and pepper. If the sauce is too thick, thin it with a little water.

3. Heat the remaining oil in a separate pan and fry the tortillas until limp. Remove and drain on paper towels. Keep warm.

4. Fry the eggs. Place an egg on each tortilla on individual serving plates and spoon on the sauce. Sprinkle with cheese and serve.

Note: Mexicans usually use lard instead of oil.

Mayonnaise

2	egg yolks
¼	teaspoon Dijon mustard
	Coarse salt to taste
1¼	cups olive oil
	Lemon juice or vinegar to taste

1. Beat the egg yolks with a fork until thick and sticky. Add the mustard and salt and beat some more.

2. Add a few drops of oil and beat with a small whisk, gradually increasing the amount of oil until you have a smooth mayonnaise. Add the lemon juice. If the mayonnaise is too thin, add more oil.

Aïoli for Crudités

3	cloves garlic
2	egg yolks, at room temperature
	Coarse salt to taste
1	teaspoon Dijon mustard
1¼	cups olive oil, at room temperature
2	tablespoons lemon juice

1. With a mortar — preferably marble — and pestle, reduce the garlic cloves to paste. Add the egg yolks and salt. Work the yolks into the garlic. Work in the mustard.

2. Very slowly, a few dribbles at a time, add the oil and continue to turn the pestle, always in the same direction. When you have added half the oil, add the lemon juice and mix thoroughly. Add the remaining oil, dribble by dribble. If the mixture becomes too thick, thin with more lemon juice.

Note: This sauce can be made in the blender, but the result is not as rich and fruity as when it is made by hand.

Hollandaise Sauce

YIELD: Approximately 1 Cup

2	egg yolks
1	tablespoon lemon juice
1	tablespoon cold water
8	tablespoons butter, chopped
	Coarse salt and freshly ground white pepper to taste

1. In the top part of a double boiler, beat the yolks with a fork or whisk until they are thick and sticky. Add the lemon juice and water and beat some more.

2. Put a little of the butter into the saucepan and, over boiling water, stir until the butter starts to melt. Add a few more pieces. The sauce will start to thicken. Remove from the heat if it begins to cook too fast; otherwise the sauce will curdle. Keep adding the butter bit by bit until it is used up and the sauce has thickened.

3. Season with salt and pepper and serve.

Milk and Milk Products

Milk

When I was a child in England, birds used to peck through the metal bottle tops to get to the milk in the morning after the milkman had left the bottles on his rounds at 6 A.M. The bottles had colored tops. Gold was for the creamiest, and the birds always went for this first— then for the silver, red, and green. We saved the cream from the top of the milk for making fruit pies and porridge. The silver-capped milk was always shaken so that the cream would be distributed throughout the bottle, and we would use that for coffee and tea.

But those days seem far-off now. The milkman is a vanishing species, and so is the sort of farm milk he used to deliver. Milk is now so mediocre in quality that it is hardly surprising sales have dropped. Between 1970 and 1981, per capita milk consumption went from 23.1 gallons a year to 15.75 gallons. Within this figure skim milk sales have increased as people try to cut down on fat. In 1981, 32 percent of all milk consumed in America was low fat.

There are several reasons for the severe decline in milk quality. First of all, the cows used are not the best, such as Guernsey or Jersey cows, but are instead those that give twice as much milk, such as the Holstein. Unfortunately, this milk has nowhere near the richness and flavor of the other.

Pasteurizing and homogenizing have done nothing for the flavor of milk. Both harmful and beneficial bacteria are killed by pasteurizing, and vitamins are destroyed. That is why milk usually has vitamin A and D added. Homogenizing prevents the cream from separating and is intended to distribute the fat evenly throughout the milk. But it has disadvantages for cooking because it curdles easily.

Instead of coming from individual farms, milk from many different farms is pumped into tanks at the processing plant. The state producing the most milk is Wisconsin, where 17 percent of the nation's milk is processed. California is next, followed by New York.

Cows are milked twice a day by machine. The milk is pumped from the machine into a refrigerated tank. Before being driven to the plant the milk is sampled and checked by a federal inspector. Then the milk is taken in a refrigerated truck to the dairy plant where it is processed. First it is pasteurized, most commonly at 161 degrees Fahrenheit for 15 seconds to kill infectious organisms. Then some milk is homogenized. Automatic machines package the milk into plastic, glass, or paper containers, and refrigerated trucks take milk to the stores. The whole process can take one to three days, during which the milk is kept refrigerated. Processors date the cartons in most areas of the country. But the dates can often be rendered meaningless, because it is more the way the milk is stored by the supermarket after it has left the plant that accounts for freshness than does this date. The milk may have been left in cartons in the sun or may have been stored properly, but there's no way to tell. Milk should never be left at room temperature.

In New York, milk and cream can legally be sold for four days after 6 A.M. on the day it is pasteurized. But outside New York and in places where the processor sets the dates, the dates can vary from seven to twelve days. Milk can often last a week or so longer than the final date given on the carton.

When buying milk or cream, it is impossible to tell by looking at a carton whether it is "off" or not. Check the dates and, if in doubt, after you have bought the milk, smell it. Return it if it has gone bad.

Whole milk contains between 3.25 and 4 percent fat solids. Vitamins D and sometimes A are added. Skim milk, also called nonfat milk, must not have more than one-half of 1 percent fat. Low-fat or partly skimmed milk has about 2 percent fat. If the label says "protein fortified" it means that nonfat milk solids have been added to make the milk richer.

Raw milk has not been pasteurized or homogenized and can be sold only by specially licensed dairies. It usually costs twice as much as regular milk and is available in health food stores. It has a better flavor than pasteurized milk and contains useful bacteria and vitamins that pasteurizing kills. It has a shorter shelf life than pasteurized milk.

A relatively new milk has been making its appearance on the shelves of some late-night delicatessens and supermarkets — long-life or Ultra High Temperature milk. This milk, unrefrigerated, lasts for around three months. UHT milk is heated for a couple of seconds to 280 degrees Fahrenheit, then is rapidly cooled to below 45 degrees to prevent it from tasting scalded. Then it is packaged in sterile, hermetically sealed containers. It is processed under aseptic conditions with no bacteria so that it is almost like a canned food. This milk should be bought only in an emergency because it has so little flavor.

Evaporated and condensed milk have had half the water content removed. They are cooked, canned, and sterilized. Because they have been cooked, both milks develop a caramel flavor; they are richer than regular milk and can be whipped. About 40 percent of condensed milk is added sugar.

Dried milk is not very appetizing to drink but can be used in an emergency or to thicken regular milk for making yogurt or for baking.

Buttermilk has fallen out of favor, with sales dropping by over 30 percent in the last ten years. It is not made from butter, as many people think. It used to be made with the liquid left after the cream had been skimmed off the top.

Today's buttermilk is cultured buttermilk. It is made with whole or skim milk artificially fermented with a lactic acid bacteria culture and sometimes salt. The real thing is available at local farms, but the cultured buttermilk is good for making Crème Fraîche (page 201).

Nondairy milk substitutes used for coffee by people trying to cut down on cholesterol do not have saturated butterfat, but they often contain highly saturated coconut oil, which has a higher percentage of saturated fat than regular milk.

Cream

Heavy Cream

This is the richest cream, usually containing around 40 percent butterfat, though the amount varies from one part of the country to another. Day-old cream whips better than fresh. Most of the cream sold these days is ultrapasteurized. This gives it longer shelf life, but it never tastes as good as unpasteurized or even pasteurized cream.

Half-and-Half

This contains 10.5 percent fat and is really more like milk than cream. It does not whip. It is generally used in coffee or on fruit.

Light cream

Also known as coffee cream, this has a lower butterfat content than heavy cream, around 18 percent, and does not whip.

Devonshire Cream

This is imported from England to some specialty stores under the brand name St. Ivel. It is a rich, buttery cream used on scones with jam and comes from Southwest England, where the richest cream is made. It contains 60 percent fat, but the cream sold here is pasteurized and does not have the full taste of real Devonshire cream.

Crème Fraîche

This tart, sourish cream has 30 percent butterfat and is sold commercially at inflated prices. In France it is made from unpasteurized cream. A crème fraîche almost as good as the French cream can be made at home with butter-milk or Solait freeze-dried crème fraîche as a starter. Packages of Solait starter are available from the Crayon Yard Corporation, 75 Daggett Street, New Haven, Connecticut 06519. The telephone number is (203) 624-7094. A package can last for two years.

Paula Wolfert, an expert cook, uses crème fraîche instead of butter when broiling foods such as chicken, swordfish, liver, salmon, and fresh tuna. A tablespoon of crème fraîche per serving of fish or chicken is ample. It seals in the juices and has less than half the fat content of butter. It can be used, off heat, instead of butter for thickening a sauce. It is also delicious with berries. The procedure for making it is extremely simple.

Crème Fraîche
YIELD: 2 Cups

1 *pint heavy cream, at room temperature*
2 *tablespoons buttermilk or Solait crème fraîche starter*

Combine the heavy cream with the buttermilk or crème fraîche starter. Pour into a clean, warmed Thermos or glass jar. Cover tightly. If using buttermilk, keep in a warm place for 6 to 8 hours. If using crème fraîche starter, keep in a warm place for 24 hours. When the mixture has jelled and is almost firm, refrigerate. It will solidify further in the refrigerator.

This amount, made with buttermilk, will keep for ten days in the refrigerator; if made with Solait crème fraîche starter, it will keep for a month in the refrigerator.

To make more crème fraîche, add 2 tablespoons from the last batch to a cup of heavy cream. You can keep making more batches this way. After six months or so a slightly fermented taste may develop, in which case it is time to kill the batch and start another.

Nondairy Cream

This is made from palm or coconut oil. It is high in saturated fat and just as bad for people avoiding cholesterol as real cream but without the flavor of real cream. If you are on an airplane and are handed one of those small containers of cream for your coffee, read the contents. It's always good for a laugh — but you'll probably end up drinking your coffee black.

Ready-whipped cream comes in aerosol cans. Some of these do contain cream but spiked with additives; others, often called "dessert topping," are completely synthetic and artificial. They should be avoided.

Sour Cream

Commercial sour cream is made by injecting lactic acid cultures into cream. It does not taste the same as real sour cream made by allowing unpasteurized heavy cream to sour naturally. It keeps about four weeks. It contains not less than 18 percent butterfat. It can be used on cold soups such as cucumber or carrot soup and borscht, as a sauce for boiled beef, or, sometimes mixed with chives, on baked potatoes.

Sour Cream and Horseradish Sauce
YIELD: 6 to 8 Servings

1	8-ounce container sour cream
4 to 6	tablespoons freshly grated horseradish (or to taste)
	Coarse salt and freshly ground pepper to taste
1	tablespoon chopped fresh dill or parsley for garnish

1. Combine the first three ingredients in a bowl. Garnish with dill or parsley. Refrigerate until ready to use.
2. Serve with boiled beef or tongue.

Yogurt

I once watched a television program about a peasant woman who was celebrating her 130th birthday. The whole village — in Soviet Georgia, of course — had turned out to celebrate, and the woman was shown dancing energetically with a tall handsome man in a fur hat who turned out to be her son, aged 90. During a break in the celebrations, a reporter asked her the secret of her long life. "I suppose you eat a lot of yogurt?" "Oh, yes," she replied, "I eat yogurt for every meal." "And what else?" the reporter pressed on, talking through an interpreter. "What other healthy things do you eat?"

"In the morning I get up and I have a big glass of vodka that size," she answered, pointing to a tumbler on the table. "Then I have yogurt, of course, two or three cups of black coffee, and a pipe. Then I go out into the fields and work. For lunch, yogurt, a bottle of wine, meat and vegetables, then a pipe. For dinner, much the same, and I have vodka and a pipe, too." "*Three* pipes a day?" asked the incredulous interviewer. "Yes," she replied. "But I forget, I smoke a package of cigarettes while I'm working in the field."

Whether it was yogurt or not that gave her such a long life — and I suspect it was more a sense of belonging and being wanted instead of being cast out as so many old people are in our communities — the yogurt would have done her nothing but good. It is said to promote the growth of bacteria that are good for the digestive tract.

There are several kinds of commercial yogurt on the market. Whole-milk yogurt is thick and creamy. Skim-milk yogurt is lower in fat and thinner and more watery. Flavored yogurt has an enormous amount of sugar added. Swiss style has gelatin or chemical stabilizers added so that it doesn't have to be stirred if it contains fruit.

Frozen yogurt probably has lost most of the bacteria in the freezing. It has stabiliziers, emulsifiers, and artifical flavor and color. But it contains less sugar than ice cream.

Natural yogurt doesn't last as long as yogurt that contains additives such as gelatin or that has been pasteurized. The latter are no good as a starter for making your own yogurt. Commercial yogurts are stamped with an expiration date anywhere from twenty-one to fifty days after production.

Homemade Yogurt

YIELD: 2 Cups

| 2 cups milk |
| 1 cup dried milk (optional) |
| 1 package yogurt culture or |
| 1 teaspoon fresh yogurt |

1. Bring the milk close to boiling point and cool to lukewarm. Add the dried milk and stir in the culture or the fresh yogurt.

2. Pour the mixture into clean prewarmed jars, seal, and put in a warm place, such as the back of the stove, or place in a heated Thermos or a yogurt maker. Leave overnight.

3. Refrigerate yogurt when ready. It usually takes about 8 hours.

Butter

When I lived in Mexico I used to make my own butter by whipping unpasteurized cream in a blender until the cream turned to butter. The whey I used in baking bread, and the butter was the best I've ever tasted. You can do this with pasteurized cream and it makes better and fresher butter than any commercial brands.

All butter must contain 80 percent butterfat. The remaining 20 percent consists of water and milk curds. Sometimes salt is added. Most butter is colored yellow by annatto, a natural coloring. Butter producers are not required by law to state on the package if the butter is artificially colored.

Butter is graded by U.S Government inspectors. The quality depends on what cows feed and where they have grazed. The highest grade is AA, followed by grades A and B. The packages are usually marked with a grade only if it is AA. Lower grades can be made from soured cream and can have an acid or stale taste and mushy texture. Salt often disguises rancid butter, so to be sure of getting the freshest, buy unsalted (also called sweet butter). Keep sweet butter in the freezer tightly wrapped. Undivided one-pound blocks are often a better buy than butter individually wrapped in four-ounce sticks. Butter made from sweet cream (this can be salted or unsalted) says so on the package. This, graded AA, is the best.

The flavor can vary widely from one batch of butter to another because butter easily adopts the aroma of other foods to which it is exposed. I have often bought butter and found it to be rancid. Of the more widely sold brands, Land O'Lakes is one of the best.

Whipped butter spreads well because it is full of air. But it shrinks down when cooked, and you pay more for the airy bulk of it.

Clarified butter is an excellent cooking fat. Because the fat solids are removed it does not burn as easily as butter and does not go rancid. If you have too much butter and want to preserve it, this is a good way. But clarified butter (or ghee as it is called in India) does not have the rich, buttery flavor of real butter. It is often used in Indian cooking.

Ghee or Clarified Butter

½ *pound unsalted butter*

1. Melt the butter over low heat in a small saucepan, stirring with a wooden spoon, without letting it turn brown.

2. When the butter is melted, turn up heat and bring to a boil. Reduce heat to very low and simmer gently without stirring for 45 minutes or until the butter is transparent on top with golden brown milk solids underneath.

3. Strain the liquid through linen towels or a triple thickness cheesecloth. If there are any impurities, strain again. The ghee is now ready for use in cooking.

Note: Ghee will keep for two to three months in a closed jar without refrigeration.

Grains,
Flour,
and Rice

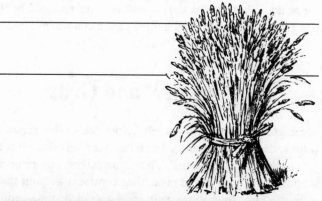

Grains, Flour, and Bread

Grains have made a comeback. Suddenly it's possible to find in a supermarket such lesser-known grains as buckwheat flour, brown rice, and even masa harina for making tortillas. For health reasons people are eating more whole grains, more bread and rice, and cutting down on meats and refined foods. Grains offer endless possibilities in the kitchen. Above all, they taste good and are cheap.

It is important when buying grains to get them from a store with a quick turnover so that you can be sure they have not become rancid. Ethnic food stores are often cheaper than supermarkets for items such as grains and are likely to do a brisk business with the neighborhood. Most supermarkets sell their grains in boxes, and these are often dated in code. If you are in any doubt, ask the date.

Grains, cereals, and grain products should be stored in a cool place in an airtight jar or tin. Whole grains should always be refrigerated because they contain the germ of the grain, which turns rancid in a warm atmosphere.

Cornmeal and Grits

Cornmeal, ground dried corn kernels, comes steel-roller-ground or stone-ground (also called water-ground). The latter is the best since it retains the nutritious germ, the core of the kernel. This cornmeal costs more because it has a shorter shelf life — it goes rancid faster than cornmeal without the germ — but if you buy in bulk you can freeze it. Indian Head, a stone-ground brand generally sold in supermarkets, is recommended. There is no difference in taste between yellow and white cornmeal — it is simply a question of aesthetics. White cornmeal comes from white corn, yellow from yellow.

Fine-ground cornmeal is the flour known as masa harina that is used for making Mexican tortillas. You can find it in Spanish specialty stores and some supermarkets. Medium-ground cornmeal is used for muffins, hush puppies, and corn bread. Coarse-ground cornmeal is recommended for Toasted Polenta (page 212), a delicious Italian dish served with specialities such as Fegato alla Veneziana (page 175), or as a snack, topped with a slice of Gorgonzola cheese. Coarse cornmeal is also used for coating foods to be fried.

Hominy or corn grits are made with corn that has been dried, the hull and germ removed. Grits are slightly coarser than meal and are an enormously popular breakfast dish in the South, boiled and served with bacon or ham for breakfast. At Hubert's restaurant in Manhattan, they are transformed into a sophisticated urban dish when made into a Grits Soufflé (page 212). The quick-cooking variety does not have the flavor or texture of regular grits.

Wheat

There are two main kinds of wheat flour in the United States. Hard wheat or gluten flour is made from a strong-grained wheat harvested in the fall in the Northeast and Canada. It is used for bread or homemade pasta — gluten is a protein that produces light yeast breads. Low-gluten soft wheat, harvested in the summer in the Middle West, is used for baking. In the South more soft than hard wheat is sold because people like it for biscuits. In the North more hard wheat gluten flour is sold because people like to make bread. National brands such as Pillsbury or Gold Medal blend their all-purpose flours to suit the region.

All-purpose white flour is milled and refined from a blend of hard and soft wheat. It does not turn rancid or moldy as does whole wheat flour. In processing, however, it loses many vitamins. Thus the introduction of "enriched" flour. Adelle Davis points out the futility of this practice in *Let's Cook It Right*. "It is as logical to say you were enriched by a burglar who robs you of 25 or more articles but drops three small ones during his getaway as to claim that flour is enriched by being robbed of 22 or more nutrients."

Bleached flour has been taken one step further and whitened artificially. Bleaching prevents it from going sour or getting weevil infestation, and some people prefer its snowy whiteness to the off-white of unbleached flour. But unbleached flour, such as that made by Hecker's from Northern wheat, has a better flavor and higher gluten content and makes much better bread.

Whole wheat flour is superior nutritionally to white because it contains 14 percent bran and 2 to 3 percent wheat germ. Some people don't like the taste of whole wheat dough. If you want a light whole wheat bread, use half unbleached white flour. The best whole wheat flour is stone ground. Steel-rolling can destroy vitamins by heat from the rollers.

Cake flour is refined, bleached flour made from soft wheat and can be useful for cakes because it is very light, but is not good for much else. Self-raising flour is simply flour with salt and baking powder added. It loses its strength within a few months.

Semolina comes somewhere between a grain and a flour. It is made from hard durum wheat and is used as a nutritious breakfast cereal, dessert, or for making pasta.

When wheat is refined to make white flour, the germ and bran are extracted. Wheat germ is sold both toasted and raw. Raw wheat germ goes rancid quickly and should be refrigerated after its container is opened. It lasts only a few weeks. Bran is the outer covering of wheat germ and is sold in health food stores and supermarkets. It is an important source of fiber. It is sold both loose and in packages.

Bulgur, a much-overlooked grain product that is becoming increasingly popular, is made from whole wheat, cracked, parboiled, and dried. It can be used raw in salad after being soaked in water (page 212) or as a stuffing for chicken when mixed with olive oil, raisins, and pine nuts. It is cheaper than rice and can be used in its place.

Bread

The state of our bread these days ranges from sad to exalted. The best-selling bread remains that pre-sliced steamed loaf with the texture of a soggy sponge. When I was driving across the country once I saw an ad for this bread. "It's batter whipped!" Whatever that means. "No human hand has ever touched our loaves!" No wonder the bread tastes like paper towels. Meanwhile, many small bakers continue to produce excellent French and Italian breads and all manner of other ethnic loaves, from Russian pumpernickel to Jewish rye. Health food stores also carry good, grainy whole wheat breads and breads made with sprouted grains. Pita breads and whole wheat English muffins are recent innovations in the supermarkets.

For years, white bread was a status symbol; dark bread was the food of the poor. The poor benefited because the nutrients had not been refined out of the flour. But recently there has been a reversal of this trend. Since white flour keeps better, the price is low. White bread, with its long shelf life, low nutritive value, and television campaigns has now become the food of the poor.

Always read the label before you buy a package of bread. Brown bread, despite the happy farm family depicted on the wrapping, may not be packed with the wholesome natural ingredients you expect but may be dyed with caramel or other dyes and laced with chemicals, antioxidants, hydrogenated fats and mold-retarding propionates.

The best place to buy bread is in the shop of a local baker whose bread you like and who bakes it himself. These days it is possible across the county to get any kind of bread you want: French baguettes and croissants, Jewish rye and bagels, pumpernickel, English muffins (a totally American invention — they don't exist in England), Indian chapattis and puris, Middle Eastern sesame pita, and all kinds of dense, fibrous health-food breads. All bread can be kept in the freezer.

If you're baking bread at home, unless you have an especially good source for buying cake yeast, dried yeast is more reliable. Cake yeast that has not been stored properly and that has been subjected to too warm temperatures may have lost its rising properties. Check the expiration date on the package of either type before buying.

Other Grains

Barley

Barley is sold hulled or with both hull and germ removed, in which case it is called pearl barley, and it comes ground coarse, medium, or fine. Whole barley is more nutritious. Barley takes about 40 minutes to cook. It goes with lamb or mutton and also makes wonderful soup.

Oats

I love oatmeal porridge for breakfast in the winter. The best is Irish or Scottish oatmeal available in good supermarkets and specialty stores. It takes longer to cook (it is simmered in water for a breakfast cereal) than Quaker oatmeal, but it has a wonderful, nutty texture. However, for those who don't have plenty of time in the morning, Quaker Oats are perfectly good and provide fiber and Vitamin B. Quaker regular oatmeal cooks faster because the oats have been sliced. Instant oatmeal is more expensive and contains additives such as sugar, salt, and artificial flavorings.

Oatmeal can be bought in large quantities and stored in the refrigerator. Health food stores often sell oatmeal loose by the pound. This is much cheaper than packaged oatmeal.

Rye

Rye flour is low in gluten and also freezes well. It is used for bread and comes in light, medium, and dark. Dark has retained more of its original bran than the lighter shades and is used for pumpernickel and rye breads.

Buckwheat

Buckwheat is not actually a grain but the seed of a grass related to rhubarb and sorrel. It is parboiled, dried, and ground to make kasha, a delicious cereal that is served with chicken or lamb. The flour is used for blinis (page 50), the buckwheat pancakes whose special taste goes with caviar.

Toasted Polenta

2½	cups water
½	pound polenta
	Coarse salt to taste

1. Bring the water to a boil in a large saucepan and add the polenta and salt. Return to a rapid boil, turn heat down, and simmer the polenta for 20 minutes, stirring regularly with a wooden spoon to remove any lumps.

2. Turn the mixture into a buttered square pan and cool. Cut into 2-to-3-inch squares and toast under broiler until browned. Serve hot.

Grits Soufflé

1½	cups water
1	cup milk
½	cup long-cooking grits
¼	cup grated Romano cheese
	Tabasco sauce to taste
	Coarse salt and freshly ground pepper to taste
4	egg yolks
5	egg whites

1. Preheat the oven to 375 degrees. Bring the water and milk to a boil, add the grits, and stir until thick. Bake, uncovered, for 15 to 20 minutes. Remove a couple of times and beat with a whisk to prevent lumps from forming.

2. Cool thoroughly and add the remaining ingredients except the egg whites. Beat the egg whites and fold gently into the batter. Pour into buttered ramekins or into a 2-quart soufflé dish and bake in a bain-marie in a preheated 425-degree oven for 10 to 15 minutes.

Tabbouleh

½	cup bulgur
2	cups boiling water
1	tomato
1	shallot
1	tablespoon chopped fresh mint
	Juice of ½ lemon
1	tablespoon olive oil
	Coarse salt and freshly ground pepper to taste

1. Pour the bulgur into a bowl. Add boiling water. Let stand for 1 hour.

2. Chop the tomato and shallot. Stir in the chopped mint and set aside.

3. Put the bulgur into a piece of cheesecloth or a triple thickness of paper towel and squeeze the water out. Put the bulgur into a bowl, add the tomato mixture, lemon juice, oil, salt, and pepper. Mix and adjust seasoning.

4. Serve with pita bread.

1	*package granular yeast*
2	*tablespoons honey*
2	*cups buttermilk*
1	*tablespoon bacon fat*
1	*tablespoon butter*
1½	*teaspoons salt*
	Approximately 6½ cups unbleached flour

1. Dissolve the yeast in ¼ cup warm water with 1 tablespoon of the honey. Set aside in a warm place to proof for 5 minutes or until the mixture becomes frothy.

2. Combine the buttermilk, bacon fat, butter, remaining honey, and salt in a saucepan. Warm over low heat until melted; do not heat above lukewarm.

3. Put 3 cups flour into a large bowl. With a wooden spoon, beat in the buttermilk mixture until smooth. Mix in the yeast. Add most of the remaining flour 1 cup at a time until the dough leaves the sides of the bowl. Turn out onto a lightly floured surface and knead about 10 to 12 minutes, adding flour as necessary to prevent the dough from sticking. The finished dough should be smooth and elastic.

4. Put the dough into a greased bowl, turn once, and cover with a cloth. Let the dough rise in a warm place until double in bulk, about 1 hour.

5. Grease two 8-by-4-inch loaf pans. Punch the dough down. Divide in half and put into the pans. Cover and let rise about 1 hour in a warm place until double in bulk.

6. Preheat the oven to 450 degrees. Bake for 10 minutes, lower heat to 350 degrees, and bake another 30 minutes. The bread should come away from the sides of the pans and sound hollow when tapped on the bottom.

7. Remove from the pans and cool on a rack.

3	cups warm milk
¾	cup molasses
½	cup butter or soft margarine
2	packages granular yeast
6	cups whole wheat flour
2	teaspoons salt

1. Mix the milk with the molasses, butter, and yeast. Set aside in a warm place to proof for 5 minutes.

2. Put 4 cups flour into a mixing bowl and make a well in the center. Beat the yeast mixture with the salt into the flour for 10 minutes. Add the rest of the flour and beat in.

3. Knead the dough on a floured board by folding it over toward you, then pushing it away with the heel of your palm. Do this for about 8 minutes or until the dough is smooth and elastic. Put it into a large greased bowl in a warm place and cover with a cloth. Allow to rise until double in bulk (about 1½ hours).

4. Grease three 8-by-4-inch loaf pans. Punch the dough down, divide into 3 loaves, and put into the pans.

5. Preheat the oven to 350 degrees. Allow the bread to rise again for another 30 minutes. Bake for about 1 hour. The bread is done when it sounds hollow when tapped on the bottom.

6. Remove from the pans and cool on a rack.

Rice

Because it is such a widely grown crop, more rice is eaten than any other food in the world. It comes in long, short, and medium grains. The sticky consistency of short grain is good for puddings, cakes, paella, and risotto. Long- and medium-grain rice becomes light and fluffy when cooked, and is served as a foil to peppery Indian curries or with gently seasoned dishes of veal, chicken, or fish.

Converted rice, a medium-length grain, has been steamed under pressure before being milled, then dried and polished so that vitamins and minerals are infused into the core. It is slightly brownish white in color and requires more liquid than unconverted white rice when cooked. It is more expensive but has a shorter cooking time and is more nutritious.

Basmati rice is an excellent long-grain rice sold in Indian shops and specialty stores. It takes about 15 minutes to cook. You must pick it over first to remove stones or unhulled bits of rice and wash it to rinse off the starch. Then soak the rice for half an hour in double its bulk in cold water. To cook it, use one part rice to three parts cold water and simmer until the rice is almost tender, about 15 minutes.

Brown rice comes with its outer coating of bran, which supplies fiber and Vitamin B. It has more vitamins and minerals than white rice. It takes about 40 to 45 minutes to cook using 3 cups water to 1 cup rice. I like to add dried seaweed, chopped carrots and onions, and some tamari soy sauce to it.

Arborio rice, sold in Italian and specialty stores and some supermarkets, is a short, stubby rice that is used for making the classic Italian risotto. It comes from Piedmont in Italy, and has a wonderful texture and flavor. For Risotto alla Milanese (page 216) it is cooked in white wine and chicken broth flavored with saffron; butter and grated Parmesan cheese are stirred in at the end of cooking. A rich and filling dish, it is served either on its own or as an accompaniment to Osso Buco, braised veal shank (page 180). When cooked, each saffron-tinted grain of rice looks as though it were made of gold.

"I wish I knew who was the genius who first grasped the fact that Piedmontese [Arborio] rice was ideally suited to slow cooking and that its particular qualities would be best appreciated in what has become the famous Milanese risotto," says Elizabeth David in *Italian Food*. "The fact that this rice can be cooked contrary to all rules, slowly, in a small amount of liquid, and emerges in a perfect state of creaminess with a very slightly resistant core in each grain gives the risotto its particular character."

Wild rice is not rice at all but a grass that grows in shallow waters and is harvested only by American Indians. Efforts are being made to cultivate it on a small scale. It is very expensive but can be stretched by being mixed with white rice. The best grains are whole and long and unbroken, sold in small packages. The special, nutty flavor of wild rice combines very well with roast game, duck, or goose.

Don't buy preseasoned rice that is sold with dry flavorings. You can season rice yourself with fresh herbs, spices, or saffron, and you won't have the peculiar chemical taste of additives.

Wild Rice
YIELD: 8 Servings

2	cups wild rice
	Boiling water
	Coarse salt and freshly ground pepper to taste
4	tablespoons butter

1. Wash the rice in cold water and place in a large pot. Pour on 4 cups boiling water. Cover and let sit for 20 minutes.

2. Bring the kettle to a boil. Drain the rice and pour in another 4 cups boiling water. Do this four times in all so that the rice cooks for a total of 1 hour and 20 minutes. Add salt with the last of the boiling water. Let sit, drain, then add pepper and butter. Keep warm, covered, in the oven or in a large double boiler.

Risotto alla Milanese
YIELD: 4 Servings

4	tablespoons butter
1	tablespoon finely chopped onion
1	tablespoon beef marrow
2	cups Arborio rice
1	cup dry white wine
	Generous pinch of saffron
	Approximately 6 cups chicken broth
	Salt to taste
4	tablespoons freshly grated Parmesan cheese
	Freshly ground pepper to taste

1. Melt 2 tablespoons of butter over medium heat and soften the onion with the marrow.

2. Pour in the rice and stir with a wooden spoon to coat the grains with butter. Let the rice cook 3 to 4 minutes, stirring frequently, so that it will absorb the butter and turn opaque.

3. Stir in the wine, then add the saffron.

4. Add the broth a ladle at a time and cook, stirring. Keep stirring and adding broth for about 20 minutes. The rice will absorb the liquid. Make sure the broth is being absorbed and there is not too much liquid on top. The bottom of the pan should be clean.

5. Test the rice for hardness. The yellow

color will deepen as it cooks. Salt the rice. Keep tasting until the rice is done.

6. Let the rice sit off heat for 3 to 4 minutes. Stir in the remaining butter. Do not return to the heat or the butter will melt without binding. Add the Parmesan cheese.

7. Spoon the rice onto individual plates and sprinkle with additional cheese and freshly ground pepper.

Pasta

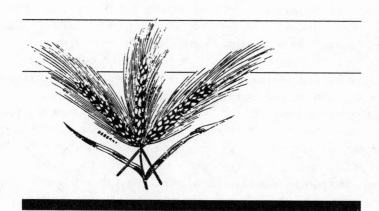

Few things are more satisfying than a plate of steaming fettuccine mixed with melting butter and Parmesan cheese, or spaghetti tossed with a simple sauce of garlic, olive oil, and parsley, and few dishes are easier to cook. You can buy your meal on the way home, cook it, and have it on the table within half an hour. No wonder there are so many new pasta shops around these days.

Not only is pasta quick to prepare, it is also cheaper than most main courses — unless you choose to serve it with truffles or caviar. Another point in its favor is that pasta is nutritious — high in energy-producing carbohydrates and low in fat. And there are endless ways of preparing it. Pasta is the perfect foil for the peppery flavor of robust salami and sausages, for fragrant pesto or thick ragù sauces. It is exhilarating with wild hare, comforting with cream. It goes wonderfully with tomatoes, anchovies, olives, and prosciutto. It can be served with delicate seafood sauces made with smoked salmon, clams, scallops, or tuna — without cheese, as purists insist. With white truffles grated on top, pasta is one of the most sublime dishes of all.

In Rome, the rage is pasta with vodka, a dish that takes only minutes to prepare and has an exotic tang imparted to it by vodka and hot peppers. Tuna mixed with lemon and parsley is another Italian favorite; it is combined with spaghetti cooked al dente and liberally sprinkled with freshly ground pepper — but no cheese. And if you have on hand a package of dried *funghi porcini*, the pungent brown mushrooms, they will give a wonderful pervasive flavor to pasta after they have been briefly soaked in warm water then sautéed in oil with garlic and parsley. Grated zucchini sautéed in butter, or ripe tomatoes, chopped and mixed with basil, make wonderful summer pasta sauces.

Pesto, the Genoese sauce of pounded basil, pine nuts, garlic, cheese, and olive oil, is good with hot or cold pasta. Once made, it keeps in the refrigerator in a sealed jar for months and is perfect for a last-minute meal. Try pesto on tortellini or cook tortellini the usual way, in butter, heavy cream and freshly grated Parmesan. Add sliced mushrooms that have been simmered in red wine and cooked until the wine has been entirely absorbed by the mushrooms.

An aromatic sauce for fusilli can be made with fennel seeds and pine nuts. Penne, short hollow pasta, are delicious with a rustic sauce of Italian sausages, mushrooms, and heavy cream.

Northern Italian dishes usually call for fresh pasta made with egg. Southern Italian cooking uses dried pasta. The variations on the shapes of the basically simple pasta dough are extraordinary. There are over six hundred shapes in

Italy — flat ribbons, long solid rods, hollow rods or cylinders, stuffed shapes, shells, butterflies, spirals, even cars. The colored pastas look attractive, but their flavor is not significantly altered by the flavorings: spinach for green pasta, tomatoes or beets for red.

If you cannot get fresh pasta and do not wish to make your own, dried can be substituted. Pasta is made from a hard wheat, "amber durum," which absorbs the minimum of water when it is cooked, and the best pasta comes from the Abruzzi region east of Rome. The dough is made of semolina, refined inner kernels ground into flour. The flour is mixed with water, sometimes with egg, and turned out in shapes and then dried.

When made to order in Northern Italy, pasta is formed into a soft dough and cut into squares for stuffing or flat ribbons. Fettuccine, linguine, tagliolini, and many others including ravioli and tortellini, which are sold fresh in America at pasta shops, are made this way.

Of the commercial brands of dried pasta, I prefer the Pastificio del Verde, Fara San Martino from Abruzzi. Sugo, DeCecco, Agnesi, and Cirio — all of them imported from Italy — are also good. Buitoni and La Rosa are my favorites among American brands.

To cook pasta, bring 4 quarts of water to a boil with a teaspoon of salt for each pound. Drop in the pasta a few at a time so that the water does not stop boiling, and stir with a fork to make sure the pasta doesn't stick. Cook dried pasta for about 7 to 9 minutes, until it is al dente, firm and resilient, so that each strand is chewy, not mushy. Freshly made pasta requires only 2 or 3 minutes. Pour in a cup of cold water to stop the cooking, and drain. Toss the pasta in sauce or butter right away or the pasta will stick together. Fresh pasta keeps for a couple of days in the refrigerator. If you are not using all of it immediately, the rest can be frozen or dried.

Another method is to cook the pasta until it is not quite al dente, drain, toss with butter and cheese, and add to your sauce. Then cook over low heat for 2 to 3 minutes, and add more cheese and sauce before serving. This way, it can be made in advance and cooked for the final few minutes before serving.

A few reminders:

• One pound of pasta easily feeds four people as a main course.

• Have ready a warmed serving bowl. Put some oil or butter in the bottom of the bowl to prevent the pasta from sticking to it. Toss with the sauce immediately.

• Grate some cheese onto the pasta right away, if the recipe calls for it, and serve the rest at the table. It is important to use good Parmesan for grating and always grate it fresh. Grated cheese sold in jars does not have the flavor or texture of freshly grated cheese and is quite useless.

• Dried pasta cooks in 7 to 9 minutes; fresh pasta takes only 2 or 3 minutes, depending on the type. In high altitudes pasta will take longer to cook because water boils at a lower temperature. Humidity and even the quality of the water will also affect the pasta. But the best pasta is always cooked al dente, firm to the bite and not mushy.

• Check the list of ingredients on the package when buying dried pasta. The best flour for pasta has a high percentage of durum wheat (semolina). If pasta is made from other flour it will be mushy, sometimes even while remaining uncooked in the middle.

Spaghetti with Oil, Garlic, and Hot Pepper Flakes

YIELD: 6 Servings

7	quarts water with 1½ tablespoons coarse salt
1	cup extra-virgin olive oil
3	cloves garlic, sliced
	Coarse salt to taste
½	teaspoon hot red pepper flakes (or more to taste)
1½	pounds spaghetti
5	tablespoons chopped fresh parsley

1. Bring the water and salt to a boil. Meanwhile, heat the oil in a large, heavy skillet. Sauté the garlic with salt until the garlic is golden.

2. Remove the skillet from the heat. Add the pepper flakes and stir for a couple of minutes to keep them from burning. Set aside.

3. Cook the spaghetti in the boiling water until very al dente, barely cooked, about 7 to 8 minutes.

4. Add the parsley to the garlic and place the pan over low heat. Drain the pasta and add to the garlic parsley mixture. Mix thoroughly and serve at once.

Spaghetti with Tuna and Parsley

YIELD: 4 Servings

1	6½-ounce can tuna packed in olive oil, drained
6	tablespoons olive oil
	Juice of 1 lemon
½	cup minced fresh parsley
	Freshly ground pepper to taste
4	quarts water with 1 tablespoon coarse salt
1	pound spaghetti

1. In a small bowl, break the tuna into pieces and add the oil, mixing with a fork. Add the lemon juice, parsley, and pepper.

2. Meanwhile, bring the water and salt to a boil. Boil the pasta for 8 to 9 minutes or until al dente. Drain.

3. Add the sauce and mix thoroughly.

Note: This needs no cheese.

Penne with Sausage, Mushrooms, Onion, and Cream

YIELD: 4 Servings

1	ounce dried *funghi porcini*
1	cup boiling water
¾	pound Italian sweet sausages
2	tablespoons olive oil
1	small onion, chopped
½	cup sliced fresh mushrooms
3	tablespoons chopped fresh parsley
1	cup heavy cream
	Coarse salt and freshly ground pepper to taste
1	pound penne

1. Cover the *funghi porcini* with 1 cup boiling water and let sit for an hour.

2. Cook the sausages in the olive oil for 15 minutes or until nearly done. Remove to a plate. Cook the onion in the same pan for 15 minutes. Add the fresh mushrooms and cook for 2 minutes more.

3. Drain the liquid from the dried mushrooms and reserve. Chop the mushrooms and add to the skillet along with the liquid. Reduce most of the liquid, stirring constantly.

4. Peel the sausages and crumble the meat. Add with the parsley to the pan. Add the cream and cook until the sauce thickens.

5. Meanwhile, cook the penne in boiling salted water about 10 minutes or until al dente. Drain, transfer to a serving bowl, and mix in the sauce.

Fusilli with Fennel Seeds

YIELD: 4 Servings

4	tablespoons fennel seeds
3	tablespoons olive oil
2	tablespoons butter
1	medium onion or 5 shallots, peeled and finely chopped
	Coarse salt and freshly ground pepper to taste
1	pound fusilli

1. Grind the fennel seeds fine in a spice grinder. Heat the oil and butter in a skillet and gently sauté the onions, without browning, until soft.

2. Add the fennel seeds and cook for 3 to 5 minutes. Do not allow them to burn. Set aside. Meanwhile, cook the fusilli in boiling salted water about 10 minutes or until al dente.

3. Toss the fusilli in the fennel sauce and serve hot or cold.

Note: Fusilli is a long dry pasta shaped like a screw. Pine nuts, chopped prosciutto, and leftovers can be added to the sauce.

Penne à la Vodka

YIELD: 4 Servings as an appetizer

¾ pound penne
1 tablespoon olive oil
2 tablespoons butter
1 onion, finely chopped
½ pound tomatoes, peeled and chopped
4 tablespoons heavy cream
Coarse salt and freshly ground pepper to taste
4 tablespoons vodka, steeped overnight or longer with 1 tablespoon hot red pepper flakes
Freshly grated Parmesan cheese to taste

1. Bring 3 quarts salted water to a boil and cook the penne until al dente.

2. Meanwhile, make the sauce. Heat the olive oil and butter in a skillet. Soften the onions without browning and add the tomatoes. Cook for about 5 minutes. Add the cream and cook for 1 minute. Season with salt and pepper. Add the vodka and simmer for 2 minutes. The vodka should evaporate slightly but not completely.

3. Toss the penne with the sauce in a heated bowl and serve with the cheese.

Note: Crushed red pepper can be steeped in vodka for 3 or 4 days. It adds a spicy taste without being fiery.

Capellini with Pesto and Bay Scallops

YIELD: 4 Servings

2 cloves garlic, crushed
Coarse salt
1 tablespoon pine nuts
1 cup fresh basil leaves
⅓ cup olive oil plus 1 tablespoon
¼ cup freshly grated Parmesan cheese
½ cup dry white wine
Juice of ½ lemon
Coarse salt and freshly ground pepper to taste
1 pound bay scallops
1 pound capellini

1. With a pestle, crush the garlic with ½ teaspoon of salt in a mortar. Add the pine nuts and gradually add the basil and ⅓ cup of the oil, a little at a time. Grind until the ingredients have been reduced to a paste.

2. Add the cheese and grind until blended. This process can be done in a blender or food processor. Scrape the pesto into a large mixing bowl and set aside.

3. In a saucepan, bring the wine, lemon juice, salt, and pepper to a boil. Add the scallops and simmer 2 or 3 minutes or until barely cooked. Drain, reserving the juice (there will be about 1 cup), and set aside.

4. Meanwhile, bring a large pot of salted water to a rolling boil. Add the tablespoon of olive oil. Add the capellini and boil, separating the strands with a long fork, about 5 to 7 minutes or until al dente.

5. Drain the capellini and immediately add to the pesto and toss thoroughly. Add the scallop cooking juice, ¼ cup at a time. Add the scallops, toss well, and correct seasoning. Serve hot or at room temperature.

Note: This pasta can be kept refrigerated in a covered bowl overnight or for two days, not more.

Cold Vermicelli with Basil and Vermouth
YIELD: 8 Servings

1	pound fresh vermicelli (or dry)
2	cups fresh basil leaves
½	cup sweet vermouth
1	clove garlic, peeled and coarsely chopped
¾	teaspoon Tabasco sauce
	Coarse salt and freshly ground pepper to taste
3	tablespoons white wine vinegar
2	teaspoons Worcestershire sauce
½	cup olive oil

1. Cook the vermicelli in boiling salted water until al dente. Rinse under cold water. Set aside.

2. In a blender, combine 1 cup of the basil leaves, vermouth, and garlic. Blend until smooth.

3. Chop the remaining basil.

4. Combine all the ingredients except the pasta in a large bowl. Mix, add the pasta, toss thoroughly, and chill.

Pasta with Ham and String Beans
YIELD: 4 Servings

1	egg
1	cup heavy cream
½	cup freshly grated Parmesan cheese
	Coarse salt and freshly ground pepper to taste
½	cup dry vermouth
1	sweet red pepper, cut in ¼-inch strips
1	cup string beans, cut julienne
1½	cups smoked ham, salt pork, or bacon, cut in small pieces
1	pound spaghetti or linguine

1. Mix the egg, cream, Parmesan, and seasonings in a bowl.

2. Place the vermouth and red pepper in a small saucepan and simmer until the vermouth has evaporated. Set aside.

3. Steam the string beans until bright green and still crisp.

4. Brown the ham in a frying pan. Remove the ham and sauté the string beans in the remaining fat.

5. Cook the pasta in a large pot of rapidly boiling water until al dente. Drain in a colander.

6. Add the egg, cream, and Parmesan mixture to the pot in which the spaghetti has cooked. Add the red pepper, smoked ham, and string beans with ham fat. Add the spaghetti, toss thoroughly, and correct the seasoning. Serve immediately in a heated serving dish.

Ravioli Malfatti

1 pound fresh spinach
½ pound ricotta cheese
1 egg, beaten
¼ teaspoon freshly grated nutmeg
1 cup freshly grated Parmesan cheese
Coarse salt and freshly ground pepper to taste

1. Remove stalks from the spinach. Wash the leaves and dry them thoroughly with paper towels. Put the leaves in a steamer and steam lightly. Remove and pat dry with paper towels. The spinach must be thoroughly dried. Chop it finely and refrigerate for 3 to 4 hours.

2. Mix the spinach with the ricotta, egg, nutmeg, Parmesan, salt, and pepper. Shape into ovals about the size of a walnut.

3. Bring a large kettle of water to a boil. Drop in the ravioli malfatti a few at a time. Poach for 3 to 4 minutes. They are cooked when they rise to the surface. Remove with a slotted spoon and keep warm. Serve with tomato sauce and freshly grated Parmesan cheese.

Note: Serve this with homemade tomato sauce. These are dumplings, not pasta.

Pasta di Taormina

(Pasta with Cauliflower)

1 medium head cauliflower, leaves removed
Juice of 1 lemon
Coarse salt to taste
½ cup extra-virgin olive oil
½ teaspoon chopped garlic
1 tablespoon chopped fresh parsley
Freshly ground pepper
¾ pound caciocavallo cheese, coarsely ground through a food mill
1½ pounds penne, pennette, or mostaccioli (or any short macaroni)
Crushed hot red pepper flakes to taste

1. Preheat the oven to 350 degrees. Boil the cauliflower in water with lemon juice and a dash of salt for 8 to 10 minutes so that it is still firm. Cool and cut in small flowerets the size of your little finger.

2. Put the olive oil in a baking pan and add the cauliflower. Sprinkle with garlic, parsley, salt, and pepper. Bake for about 6 minutes and sprinkle with the cheese while hot.

3. Meanwhile, cook the penne in 6 quarts rapidly boiling salted water for about 7 to 9 minutes or until al dente. Drain well and add to the cauliflower mixture. Coat thoroughly with the oil left in the baking pan. Toss gently but thoroughly with the cauliflower mixture.

4. Serve immediately without cheese but with crushed red pepper.

Dried Peas and Beans

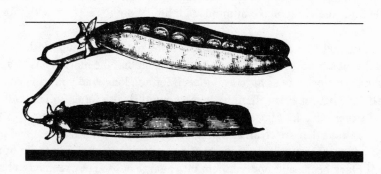

Sometimes, particularly during the cold winter months, we crave food that is sustaining and, most of all, comforting. What answers this need better than a hearty bowl of lentil soup or a cassoulet of sausages, confit d'oie, and beans? Beans are the basis of many simple, sturdy dishes, each country providing its own specialities. Black or pinto beans are used for Mexican fried beans, all colors of lentils for Indian dal, green split peas are stewed with ham hocks for Canadian pea soup. In Brazil, black beans are served with feijoada, the national dish, and in the United States brown Dutch beans become Boston baked beans.

Dried peas and beans, rich protein sources, are not merely winter foods. Cannelini beans make a wonderful, thick soup laced with green extra-vrigin olive oil that is served in Tuscany in the summer. French flageolets, soissons, and red kidney beans, mixed with oil and lemon and served at room temperature, go with light summer lunches. Chick peas ground and mixed with sesame paste, lemon, and garlic make hummus bi tahini, a dip to be eaten with pita bread.

At the market I love running my fingers through sacks of beans with their beautiful muted colors. Be sure when buying them that the market has a rapid turnover. Beans become as hard as bullets if left too long, and you can cook them all day without ever softening them enough. Health food, Indian, and Oriental stores sell a lot of beans, often cheaper than supermarkets do.

Choose beans that are clean and even sized, with no tiny pin holes. The pin holes can conceal an unpleasant surprise, as I once discovered. I brought home a sack of black beans and poured them into a large bowl. They seemed to be moving, and indeed they were. They were alive with maggots.

Besides being sold loose, beans also come in bags and in airtight boxes with a little cellophane-covered window in the front. Make sure the packages are well sealed. Sometimes beans are sold at reduced prices because they are from broken bags, and they may be stale.

Most beans you'll buy will be quite clean, but they should still be rinsed and picked over carefully to remove stones and grit before using.

All beans can be cooked about the same way. First they can be soaked in cold water for a few hours if you want to cut down the cooking time, but this is not necessary. Then they can be stewed in water with a chopped onion, garlic, carrot, celery, bouquet garni, and, if you like, a chopped chili, and parsley or fresh coriander. They usually take around an hour, depending on the beans, and should be soft yet hold their texture when done. Add salt only toward the end of cooking, otherwise the skins of the beans may split and the centers harden. Salt pork or bacon can also be simmered with the beans to add flavor, or olive oil can be added at the end. Sometimes I add tomato paste or tomatoes toward the end of cooking.

The best beans for cassoulet are the tender, slightly elongated soissons from France, but small, round, white navy beans will do very well and are cheaper. The best flageolets, which perfectly complement roast lamb, are green — they are more delicate than white. Brown Dutch beans, black-eyed peas, and dried fava beans are all delicious stewed and go with such dishes as braised or roast pork or ham. Red kidney, pinto, and black beans are used in Mexican dishes. Lentils come whole and split in red, brown, yellow, and green. Split lentils cook more quickly. Whole lentils take longer to cook but are more nutritious and hold their shape better than split lentils. Oriental adzuki beans, sweet and easy to digest, are good stewed.

Stewed White Beans

YIELD: 12 Servings

2	pounds dried white beans
2	pig's feet, split down the middle
1	10-ounce can plum tomatoes, coarsely chopped, with their juice
	Freshly ground pepper to taste
1	cup finely chopped parsley
4	cloves garlic, minced
6	tablespoons butter
	Coarse salt to taste
1	cup dried bread crumbs

1. Rinse the beans with cold water and pick over carefully. Put them in a heavy casserole with water to cover. Add the pig's feet and tomatoes. Season with pepper, cover, and simmer for about 1½ hours or until cooked, adding more water if necessary. Set aside until 30 minutes before serving.

2. Preheat the oven to 425 degrees. Stir the parsley, garlic, 4 tablespoons butter, and salt into the beans. Sprinkle with bread crumbs, dot with remaining butter, and heat through, uncovered, until sizzling.

Note: The beans may also be heated on top of the stove. Omit the bread crumbs.

Cassoulet

1	pound dry navy beans
3	carrots, chopped
2	stalks celery, chopped
2	medium onions, chopped
¼	teaspoon thyme
1	teaspoon chopped parsley
1	bay leaf
1	pound pork butt (in 1 piece)
2	chorizo sausage links
2	sweet Italian sausage links
1	kielbasa sausage ring, about 1 to 1½ pounds
	Coarse salt and freshly ground pepper to taste

1. Soak the beans overnight in water to cover.

2. Drain and rinse the beans. Combine the beans, carrots, celery, and onions in a large casserole.

3. Make a cheesecloth bundle of the thyme, parsley, and bay leaf and tie with string. Add to the casserole. Add the pork butt and water to cover all and simmer for 1½ hours.

4. Meanwhile, prepare the chorizo and Italian sausages by pricking them all over with a fork and frying over medium heat until lightly browned. Set aside.

5. Preheat the oven to 350 degrees.

6. Remove the pork butt from the casserole and cut it into ¼-inch slices. Peel the casing from the kielbasa and cut the meat into ½-inch slices. Cut the cooked chorizo and Italian sausages into ¼-inch slices. Add the pork and the sausage slices to the casserole. Stir to combine and season with salt and pepper.

7. Cover and place the casserole in the oven. Bake for 1½ hours.

8. Serve with a dry white wine and French bread.

Black Beans with Mint

1	pound black beans
1	onion, chopped
2	cloves garlic, chopped
1	green chili, minced
	Freshly ground pepper to taste
	Coarse salt to taste
4	tablespoons lard or peanut oil
3	tablespoons fresh coarsely chopped mint

1. Cook the beans in water to cover with the onion, garlic, chili, and pepper for about 2 hours or until tender. Add more water if necessary.

2. Purée the beans with their liquid in a blender. Season with salt to taste. Heat the lard or oil in a skillet and add the beans. Fry over moderately high heat, scraping the bottom of the pan frequently, until the beans are a thick, fairly dry paste with a crisp skin. Mix in the mint, stir well, and serve.

Note: These beans are excellent cold.

Black Beans and Ham

YIELD: 4 Servings

1 pound black beans
1 medium onion, coarsely chopped
1 clove garlic, minced
1 green chili, finely chopped
2 stalks celery, with leaves, chopped
Herb bouquet (parsley, bay leaf, and thyme tied in a cheesecloth)
1 ham hock
Freshly ground pepper to taste
Coarse salt to taste

1. Combine all ingredients except the salt in a large kettle with water to cover and simmer for 2 to 3 hours or until the beans are tender.

2. About 15 minutes before the beans are cooked, add the salt.

Note: This can be garnished with sour cream and fresh parsley and served with rice.

Refried Beans

YIELD: 8 Servings

¾ pound pinto beans
1 medium onion, chopped coarsely
1 bay leaf
Freshly ground pepper to taste
1 small green chili, chopped fine
Bouquet garni
Approximately 8 tablespoons lard
Coarse salt to taste
1 cup chopped romaine lettuce for garnish
8 sliced radishes for garnish

1. Cover the beans with water in a large, heavy casserole. Add the remaining ingredients except the lard, salt, and garnishes. Simmer, partly covered, for about 1½ hours or until cooked, adding more water as needed. Remove the bouquet garni.

2. Heat the lard in a frying pan and add 1 cup of the beans. Mash well and fry over high heat until sizzling. Add remaining beans, about a cup at a time. Continue frying and mashing until the purée starts to come away from the surface of the pan. It will become like a loose pancake. Cook for another 10 to 15 minutes until good and crisp.

3. Put on a serving plate, garnish with lettuce and radishes, and serve.

Note: This is good with Latin or Mexican dishes such as Humitas (page 247) or Turkey Mole (page 129).

1	cup mung dal (yellow split lentils)
6	cups water
½	teaspoon turmeric
1	teaspoon ground red chilies
1	bay leaf
1	teaspoon ground coriander seeds
6	cardamom seeds, peeled
	Coarse salt to taste
2	tablespoons ghee (Clarified Butter, page 205) or vegetable oil
2	medium onions, chopped

1. Pick over the lentils carefully to remove any grit. Put in a saucepan with the water, turmeric, chilies, bay leaf, coriander, and cardamom and simmer about 30 minutes.

2. Off heat, beat the purée with a whisk until thick. Stir in the salt.

3. Heat the ghee in a frying pan and fry the onions until golden brown. Stir into the dal, sprinkle with additional red pepper, and serve.

Vegetables

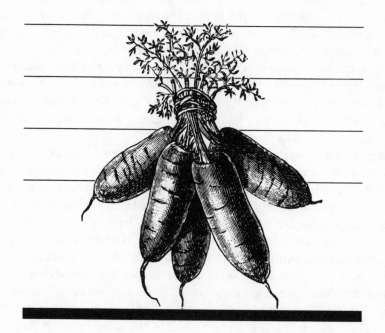

Artichokes

The artichoke is not a vegetable to be hurried over. It has to be eaten slowly, leaf by leaf, to the heart that nestles under the prickly choke at the bottom. Catherine de Medici shocked France with her passion for this vegetable, which was supposed to be an aphrodisiac, eating so much, according to one chronicler, that she nearly burst. De Chirico loved its shape so much he put it in his paintings. And yet, according to Sheila Hutchins, author of *English Recipes*, a group of British tourists not long ago returned scandalized from a holiday in Brittany complaining they had been served boiled water lilies.

One of the nicest ways of serving artichokes is simply to boil or steam them. Make a lemon butter sauce and eat the artichokes by pulling off the leaves one by one and dipping them into the sauce. When you get down to the choke, slice it off horizontally with a knife and eat the bottom, the more tender and delicious part, dipped in the sauce.

Hollandaise or vinaigrette sauce also goes with artichokes cooked this way. The insides of the artichokes can be removed and the cavity stuffed with ham and bread crumbs. Italians produce the best artichokes and cook them in the most imaginative ways. Whole ones are deep-fried à la Giudea, Jewish style, so that they emerge like huge bronzed sunflowers. Italians also slice the hearts and sauté them with vegetables or bake them with meat or fish in a rich garlicky tomato sauce. Artichokes can also be trimmed of their leaves and the hearts sliced and sautéed in olive oil with garlic for a first course or side dish.

The entire artichoke crop for the United States is grown in California around Castroville south of San Francisco, where the foggy climate suits them very well. They are in season all year round but are at their peak in April and May. When buying them, choose artichokes with tightly closed heads of bright green leaves. Avoid any that have opened-out or cracked and darkened leaves. In the winter artichokes sometimes have brownish spots on their outer leaves. These are caused by frost and should be ignored. Artichokes do not keep well and should be eaten as soon as possible after being bought.

In some specialty stores, artichokes small and tender enough to be eaten choke and all are on sale. These are delicious fried.

Artichokes served at room temperature in a vinaigrette dressing are excellent for a dinner party because they can be prepared in advance. They make wine taste sweet, so don't serve your very best with them. They are cooked when their outside leaves pull away easily.

Artichokes Vinaigrette

6	artichokes
1	cup flat-leaf parsley
2	tablespoons capers
3	shallots
2	cloves garlic
1	cup olive oil
1	tablespoon Dijon mustard
	Juice of 1 medium lemon
	Red or white wine vinegar to taste
	Coarse salt and freshly ground pepper to taste

1. Simmer the artichokes in 3 inches of water for 20 to 25 minutes or until cooked.

2. While they are cooking, make the sauce. Finely chop the parsley, capers, shallots, and garlic. Mix into the oil and add the mustard and lemon juice. Then add the vinegar, being careful not to add too much. Set aside.

3. When the artichokes are cooked, remove and invert to drain in a colander, squeezing slightly to remove the water.

4. Stir the sauce and pour about 4 tablespoons over each artichoke, leaf side up, while they are still hot.

5. Serve the artichokes at room temperature on individual plates and pass the rest of the sauce separately.

Artichoke Hearts with Fava Beans

4	artichokes
1	lemon, cut in half
	Approximately 1 cup chicken stock
6	tablespoons olive oil
2	tablespoons red wine vinegar
1	garlic clove, finely chopped
	Coarse salt and freshly ground pepper to taste
2	cups fresh fava beans, shelled (about 4 pounds)
2	tablespoons chopped fresh chives or tarragon for garnish

1. Using a sharp knife, cut the artichokes across about two-thirds of the way down. Discard the top half. Remove the green leaves from the bottom half. Rub the bottoms with the cut sides of the lemon and set aside.

2. Put enough chicken stock to come about halfway up the artichoke hearts in a pan large enough to hold them on one level. Bring to a boil and simmer, covered, for about 15 to 20 minutes or until just tender.

3. Meanwhile, make the dressing. Combine the oil, vinegar, garlic, salt, and pepper in a cup. Mix thoroughly.

3. Drain the artichoke hearts and cool. Remove and discard the choke and any tough outer leaves. Cut in half and slice thin. Put in a serving bowl and coat with the dressing.

4. Steam the fava beans for about 15 minutes or until tender. Add to the artichokes. Correct seasoning and refrigerate.

5. Serve at room temperature, garnished with chives or tarragon.

Note: This is good with cold chicken or beef.

Fried Baby Artichokes

20	baby artichokes
1	cup olive oil
	Approximately 1 cup vegetable oil
1	clove garlic, minced
	Juice of 1 lemon
	Coarse salt and freshly ground pepper to taste
	Chopped fresh parsley for garnish

1. Using a sharp knife, cut off the tops of the artichoke leaves, horizontally, about an inch or so down, so that you are left with the bottom half with about an inch of leaf. Trim the stalk and remove any discolored outer leaves.

2. With your hands, carefully spread the leaves and flatten out the artichokes slightly without breaking the leaves.

3. Heat the oil, and when it begins to smoke, add the artichokes a few at a time. Be very careful: If the oil spits onto the flame underneath, it can flame up. Keep a cover handy to hold over the artichokes if the oil spits.

4. Cook the artichokes, regulating the heat so that they become golden brown but do not burn. They should cook fast or they will not be crisp. Turn with a slotted spoon and, when done, place on a serving dish. Add the remaining artichokes.

5. When all the artichokes are cooked, add the garlic to the oil and cook without burning for a minute or two, so that the oil is flavored. Remove from heat, pour the remaining oil over the artichokes. Squeeze on the lemon juice, season with salt and pepper, sprinkle with parsley, and serve.

Note: This dish can also be served cold, but it is best when hot.

6	artichokes
1	lime
2	large carrots
6	scallions
½	cup olive oil
1	tablespoon coriander seeds
¼	cup dry white wine
1	cup chicken stock
3	garlic cloves, peeled
½	cup fresh basil

1. Cut off the stems from each artichoke with a sharp knife to make a neat, flat base. Squeeze on lime juice to prevent discoloration. Trim around the sides and base until the base is smooth and white. Place each artichoke on its side and slice off the top, leaving the base about 1½ inches deep. Remove and discard the fuzzy choke. Rub the artichoke bottom with lime and leave to soak in water until ready to use.

2. Peel the carrots and cut into ovals about 1½ inches long. Cut the scallions into 1½-inch lengths. Cut the artichoke hearts into pieces about 1 inch square.

3. Heat the oil in a deep pan and fry the artichoke hearts and carrots for about 5 minutes with the coriander seeds. Add the wine, stock, and scallions.

4. Chop the garlic finely with the basil and add to the pan. Cook for an additional 10 minutes. Turn into a bowl and allow to cool to room temperature.

Asparagus

One of the great delights of spring is steamed fresh asparagus, dipped in
melted butter and eaten with your fingers. Even though asparagus is no longer
rare (it is now grown over vast areas in California), it is still a luxury because
the season is so short. April and May are the peak months.

There are many other ways of eating asparagus besides with melted butter.
As a first course, it can be coated with a *beurre noisette* — butter that has been
heated until it turns golden brown — and sprinkled with chopped hard-
cooked eggs. Italians top it with Parmesan cheese and run it under the broiler
for a few minutes. The French do the same with Mornay sauce.

It is also good as a main course cooked with meats such as veal, brains,
sweetbreads, chicken, turkey, or ham. And asparagus is delicious with pasta —
as anyone visiting Italian restaurants when it is in season will discover. For
pasta primavera it can be cooked and mixed with other spring vegetables,
tossed with oil and vinegar, and mixed with spaghetti. Marcella Hazan, in
More Classic Italian Cooking, gives a recipe for penne or other small macaroni
with asparagus, a superb combination. The dish makes a fine first course for a
dinner party, or a main course for lunch or a light supper. An adaptation of
her recipe is given in this chapter.

Asparagus should be cooked briskly and only until it is bright green and
crisp. It should not be limp from overcooking — as it often can be in restaurants. French cooks peel it and stand it, tied in bundles, in rapidly boiling
water. It is not necessary to peel the asparagus stalks unless they are very
tough. But if you are stir-frying fairly thick asparagus, the stalks will be more
tender if peeled.

To prepare the stalks for cooking, snap off the ends at the natural point
where they break. Run them under rapidly flowing cold water. The tips cook
more quickly than the stalks, so rather than steaming, the best method is to tie
them in bundles and stand them, covered, in a couple of inches of boiling
water. Don't cook in aluminum or iron pots; these will affect the taste. Cook
only for about 5 to 10 minutes, checking from time to time for doneness.

The tips are the best part, and their condition is the key to choosing the best
fresh asparagus. If the bud is opened, it is past its prime. The bud should be
tightly furled and not limp, wilted, or going to seed. Choose firm, straight
stalks strong enough to be snapped, moist and not dry at the cut end. Their
color should be a rich green, the scales green or tinged with purple. The large
spears fat as sugar cane are as tender as the skinny ones. Buy loose asparagus,
not those already tied in bundles. This way you can be sure of choosing spears

that are all the same size that will cook evenly. About six to ten large spears per person are adequate.

What should you drink with asparagus? The sulphur in this vegetable alters the taste of wine and makes it sweeter. The wine that holds up best is a good dry Gewürtztraminer.

Asparagus with Sauce Maltaise

YIELD: 4 Servings

2	pounds fresh asparagus
2	egg yolks
1	tablespoon lemon juice
⅔	cup cold butter
	Juice of 1 small orange
	Coarse salt and freshly ground pepper to taste
	Grated peel of the orange

1. Trim the asparagus and cook. Meanwhile, make the Sauce Maltaise. Beat the egg yolks until thick and sticky, then beat in the lemon juice. Add 1 tablespoon of cold butter and thicken the mixture in the top of a double boiler.

2. When the butter has melted, add a couple more tablespoons. Continue until you have a thick, creamy sauce. Beat in the orange juice. If the sauce thins out too much, add more butter to thicken it. Do not overcook or the sauce will curdle.

3. Season with salt and pepper, then add the grated orange peel.

4. Drain the asparagus thoroughly and arrange on a serving dish. Serve the sauce separately.

Asparagus with Scallops

YIELD: 4 Servings

1½	pounds thin fresh asparagus
2	tablespoons sesame oil
2	tablespoons vegetable oil
1	pound bay scallops
1	tablespoon toasted sesame seeds
	Coarse salt and freshly ground pepper to taste

1. Trim away the woody part of the asparagus stalk. Peel the lower part of the asparagus with a potato peeler. Cut the asparagus in half crosswise.

2. Heat the oils in a large skillet. Add the asparagus, fry for 30 seconds, then add ½ cup water, taking care to avoid spattering. Stir, cover, and turn down heat. Cook for about 2 to 4 minutes or until the asparagus are cooked but still crisp and bright green.

3. Add the scallops, turn up heat, and stir-fry for about 2 to 3 minutes. Do not overcook. Sprinkle with sesame seeds, salt, and pepper and serve.

Asparagus with Penne

1½	pounds fresh asparagus
1	pound penne or other short tubular pasta
6	ounces prosciutto, cut in ¼-inch strips
2	tablespoons butter
1	cup heavy cream
	Coarse salt and freshly ground pepper to taste
	Freshly grated Parmesan cheese

1. Trim the tough end of the stalk from the asparagus. With a vegetable peeler, pare away any tough green skin from the lower half of the stalk. Rinse the asparagus in cold water.

2. Put 2 inches of water into a shallow pan and bring to a boil. Add the asparagus, cover, and cook until tender but firm.

3. Drain and, when they have cooled, cut off the tips at their base. Cut the stalks into ¾-inch pieces. Set aside.

4. Bring 4 to 5 quarts salted water to a boil and cook the pasta until al dente.

5. Meanwhile, sauté the prosciutto in a small saucepan in 1 tablespoon of the butter for about 2 minutes. Do not brown.

6. Dry the pan in which you cooked the asparagus. Add the remaining tablespoon butter and turn heat to medium. When the butter has melted add the asparagus. Toss the asparagus in the butter. Add the prosciutto and the cream, and turn heat to medium-high. Cook, stirring, for about 30 seconds, long enough to thicken the cream. Turn off heat and season with salt and pepper.

7. When the pasta is cooked, drain thoroughly and put into a heated serving bowl. Add the asparagus mixture and toss thoroughly. Grate in about ⅔ cup Parmesan and serve additional cheese at the table.

Cauliflower, Broccoli, and Brussels Sprouts

Cauliflower, broccoli, and brussels sprouts — all members of the cabbage family — go wonderfully with plain roasted meats. A mixture of all three makes a beautiful presentation for a dinner party, the cauliflower whole in the center and the other vegetables arranged around it.

The aristocrat of this group is the cauliflower, the vegetable Mark Twain called "a cabbage with a college education." A fresh cauliflower smells delicious and looks spectacular with its creamy white head nestled in the center of long green leaves (many people throw away the leaves, not realizing that they are excellent in soups or can be simply sautéed as a green vegetable). I like cauliflower whole with brown butter and capers or broken into flowerets and sautéed in oil with garlic and plum tomatoes. It is also good puréed. Cold cooked cauliflower makes a fine salad, especially with cold roast lamb.

In the Middle East and India, cauliflower is often deep-fried. First steam the flowerets, roll them in beaten egg and then in flour or fine bread crumbs. Deep-fry them in hot peanut or vegetable oil until golden. The Indians make a batter that they flavor with turmeric, which turns it a vivid and appetizing deep yellow.

When buying cauliflower, look for unblemished tightly-packed heads that feel heavy for their size. If the flowerets are loose, the cauliflower is overmature. In supermarkets the leaves are often cut off and the cauliflower covered in plastic — a pity since the leaves are a better protector. Don't buy cauliflower if it is brownish or if it has dry, curling leaves.

If cauliflower is overcooked it turns an ugly gray and becomes mushy. One way of keeping cauliflower white is to cook it in milk instead of water. Or you can squeeze lemon juice over it. When cooking it whole, trim away any discolored parts. The flowerets cook more quickly than the stalk, so make a cross in the base of the stalk so it will cook faster. Test carefully with a thin skewer to see if it is done.

Many soups, gratins, and other recipes that can be used with cauliflower can be used interchangeably with broccoli. Besides going well with lamb, broccoli is good with garlicky Italian sausages or pasta with tomato, meat, or vegetable sauce. It can also be served hot with hollandaise or cold with vinaigrette.

Broccoli is composed of flowering shoots — its name is the plural of the Italian brocco, meaning sprout or shoot — but unfortunately the commercial varieties, which come mainly from California and Arizona, are grown to enormous size, with vast heads and stems as thick as a tree trunk. The smaller the broccoli the more tender and full of flavor it will be. The flowerets should be stiff but moist. They should snap cleanly when bent. Avoid those that have yellowed. Of the types on the market, purple broccoli has the most delicate taste. As with cauliflower, care should be taken not to overcook broccoli or it will be ruined.

It is overcooking that has given brussels sprouts — and their larger relative, the cabbage — such a bad name. They should be cooked only until they are bright green and still slightly crunchy. I like them plain with butter or with caraway seeds. They are also good cold served with a tart mayonnaise.

Ideally sprouts should be no bigger than a thumbnail. The best are tiny with a sweet, nutty taste. You can find them in markets in Europe or get them from people with gardens. In America, commercial sprouts are allowed to grow so big they sometimes end up looking like small, overblown cabbages with loose, yellowing leaves. Sprouts don't keep well and should be eaten as soon as possible after being picked. Of course, avoid yellow ones. To prepare sprouts for cooking, trim off the outer coarser leaves and cut a cross in the bottom if the sprouts are large.

Caulifower, sprouts, and broccoli are all now much more widely available and for longer seasons here than they were only a few years ago. Broccoli, which is much loved by Italians and Chinese, has been popular in America only in the last few years. When this vegetable first started to appear across the country, *The New Yorker* magazine ran a cartoon showing a small child scowling down at his plate. "It's broccoli, dear," his mother is saying. The child replies, "I say it's spinach and I say the hell with it."

Cauliflower or Broccoli with Peperoncino   YIELD: 4 Servings

1	head cauliflower or broccoli
3	tablespoons walnut oil
2	tablespoons hot pepper flakes
1	sweet red pepper, chopped
	Coarse salt and freshly ground pepper to taste

1. Break the cauliflower or broccoli into flowerets and steam until barely cooked. Be careful not to overcook or it will turn mushy.

2. Heat the oil in a frying pan over low heat and add the pepper flakes and sweet red pepper. Do not heat too high, or the pepper flakes will burn and become bitter.

3. Add the cauliflower or broccoli and toss so that it is coated with the oil. Turn into a warm serving dish.

Note: This goes well with grilled lamb or chicken.

Cauliflower Cooked in Milk

YIELD: 4 Servings

1 head cauliflower
1 cup milk
1 small onion, peeled and stuck with cloves
3 tablespoons butter
1 tablespoon flour
Freshly grated nutmeg to taste
Coarse salt and freshly ground white pepper to taste
3 tablespoons freshly grated Gruyère or Parmesan cheese
Chopped fresh parsley for garnish

1. Trim the leaves from the cauliflower and leave the head whole. Heat the milk in a saucepan large enough to hold the cauliflower and bring to a boil with the cauliflower and the onion stuck with cloves. Simmer gently, covered, for about 10 minutes or until the cauliflower is tender but not overcooked. Remove from the saucepan and keep warm. Reserve the milk.

2. Melt the butter in a separate saucepan. Add the flour and cook, stirring, without browning, for about 3 minutes. Add the reserved milk and simmer for about 5 to 10 minutes or until the sauce is thick enough to coat the spoon. Season with nutmeg, salt, and pepper and pour over the cauliflower. Sprinkle with cheese and brown briefly under the broiler. Garnish with parsley and serve.

Chinese-Style Broccoli

YIELD: 4 Servings

1 head broccoli
2 tablespoons peanut or vegetable oil
1 clove garlic, finely chopped
3 scallions, chopped
1 tablespoon chopped fresh ginger
2 tablespoons oyster sauce

1. Separate the broccoli into flowerets. Cut each floweret in half.

2. Heat the oil in a large frying pan. Stir-fry the garlic, scallions, and ginger for 1 minute, then add the broccoli and stir-fry until green and crisp but tender. Add the oyster sauce; stir and cook for another minute. Serve hot.

1	10-ounce container brussels sprouts
1	tablespoon butter
	Freshly grated nutmeg to taste
1	tablespoon chopped fresh parsley
	Coarse salt and freshly ground pepper to taste

1. Steam the sprouts until bright green and still crunchy but tender. Turn them into a heated serving dish and toss with butter.

2. Grate on the nutmeg, add the parsley, and season to taste with salt and pepper.

Corn and Okra

Corn

In summer I like the simplest food and I like to cook it out of doors. The place I do this most often is at my country cottage in upstate New York in the middle of a wood next to a wildlife preserve. The road you take to get there suddenly stops at the top of the hill, and you have to abandon the car and plunge into the woods, cross a stream by stepping stones, and climb on up the mountain. The house is perched next to a waterfall. Above the waterfall there's a stream and a clearing under the trees where I have made a barbecue pit surrounded by stones.

One of my favorite foods to cook here is fresh sweet corn broiled over coals so that the kernels are slightly charred, then coated with butter and pepper. It is possible this way to eat eleven ears in one sitting if you are very greedy.

One night I was cooking ribs and corn when I noticed a pair of eyes watching us intently from behind a tree. The animal was black and white with a bushy tail, and I thought it was a badger. So I carefully left it the corn cobs and bones, and I put a bowl of milk outside the kitchen door. The next day there were two at the "badger's bar" — and soon a whole family, children and all, quietly encircled us every night waiting for leftovers.

Back in the city, I told some friends the story of our badgers. There were many smirks. Those were no badgers, I was told with glee, they were skunks. So for the next month the outdoor cooking was fraught with tension in case our new friends would become displeased with their dinner and spray us. But I'm told, apart from their not very deadly but unpleasant weapon, skunks are among the friendliest and most intelligent of animals. I'm looking forward to seeing them again.

Corn is, conveniently, at its best from June to September, the cookout months. The two kinds most commonly available are bright yellow and pearly white. I prefer the white ones: They are sweeter. In any event, corn should be eaten as fresh as possible. Like peas, once picked the sugar content of corn gradually turns to starch. For the best corn of all, start the water boiling and then go out and pick your ears of corn from the garden.

Apart from your own garden, the best corn usually comes from a roadside stand or farmers' market. Not all roadside stands are reliable, though. Some simply buy their corn from another source, and it may be as stale as that sold in some supermarkets. The best plan is to find a reliable source and keep going back to it.

Some shopkeepers partially husk the corn to show that the ears inside are plump and good. But if possible don't buy pieces already husked, because the corn will already be stale. When buying sweet corn, choose ears that have bright green husks and that look recently picked. The silk should be fresh looking and the stem end should not be dry, nor should the husks.

But pull back the husk a little before buying the corn so that you can see the state of the kernels for yourself. Make sure they are full and plump and glossy but not so full that the corn is overmature. If the corn is too young the kernels will be small and not close together. Of course, you should replace the husk to its original position once you've looked inside.

Apart from being cooked out of doors, corn can be baked in its husk in the oven, husked and boiled for 5 to 7 minutes in water, or steamed. You can also cook corn over the coals of an open fire in its husk. Dip the ears, husks intact, in water first. This prevents the husks from burning up before the kernels are cooked.

Latin Americans like to cook the kernels with onion, tomato, and raisins, then bake the mixture, wrapped in corn husks, over coals or in the oven. These, known as humitas, make a delicious snack on an outdoor grill. They are similar to the Mexican tamales.

Virgil Thomson likes to cook his corn off the cob for no longer than 3 minutes and serve it with roasted red peppers (page 279, but without the anchovies) and Roast Wild Turkey (page 128). You must not cook it longer than 3 minutes, and you must use lots and lots of pepper, he says.

Sautéed Sweet Corn

YIELD: 4 Servings

8	ears very fresh sweet corn
4	tablespoons butter
	Coarse salt and freshly
	ground pepper to taste

1. With a sharp knife, cut the corn off the cobs into a large bowl.

2. Melt the butter in a frying pan and add the corn. Add salt and pepper. Cook for 3 minutes, turning it gently with a wide spatula. Remove to a heated platter and serve at once.

Humitas

(Grated Corn with Tomatoes and Raisins)

24	ears of sweet corn
1	tablespoon butter
2	tablespoons olive oil
1	onion, finely chopped
2	tomatoes, peeled and chopped
1	bell pepper, chopped
½	cup seedless raisins
	Coarse salt and freshly ground pepper to taste
1	teaspoon sugar
2	beaten eggs

1. Make an incision across the bottom of the husks and separate the husks from the corn, trying not to damage them. Wash and drain the husks.

2. Remove the cornsilk. Grate the corn on the medium hole of a grater. Cut off any remaining kernels with a knife.

3. Melt the butter in a skillet and add the olive oil. Add the onion and cook until golden. Add the tomatoes and pepper. Cook for 10 minutes. Add the corn and cook for another 15 minutes over low heat, stirring. Add the raisins, salt, pepper, and sugar. Remove from heat and cool. Stir in the beaten eggs.

4. Overlap two husks and put a tablespoon of the mixture inside. Fold the edges of the husks in four to make an envelope. Tear strands from the cornhusks and use to tie the envelopes around the middle so they will not open when cooking.

5. Cook over hot coals for about 15 minutes, taking care not to burn them.

Note: The older the corn, the longer it needs to cook. If the corn is too dry, use a little milk to moisten it. Humitas can also be baked in a 350-degree oven.

Okra

Okra, called lady fingers in India where it is much beloved, is the central element in many African and Brazilian dishes and in the dark Creole gumbos of the South. It is a strange vegetable. It's mucilaginous quality does not appeal to all. But I adore okra, especially when it is stewed with onions and tomatoes or cooked with lamb as they do in North Africa. In Morocco they place okra and lamb with seasonings of garlic, cumin, and coriander in a *tajin*, an earthenware pot with a large conical lid. They bake the pot in the oven and eat the stew with hot flat Moroccan bread dipped into the juices.

I brought one of the *tajins* back with me, and I always use it for stews and even for cooking on top of the stove. I also cook the okra in olive oil with lemon juice and chopped garlic. No other liquid is necessary.

I like okra Southern style deep-fried in batter or rolled in cornmeal and sautéed. In the South people cook it with tomatoes and sweet corn cut from the cob and serve it with fried chicken or pork.

Okra is in season from early June to September. When buying it, choose the smallest, youngest, and brightest green pods you can find. Okra must be very fresh, not browned at the edges, and should be used right away since it is rather perishable. Avoid large okra. The seeds inside can be like pebbles.

Okra should always be washed before the ends are cut off.

Okra with Onions and Tomatoes

YIELD: 4 Servings

2	pounds okra
1	pound tomatoes
5	tablespoons olive oil
1	large onion, sliced
2	cloves garlic, chopped
	Coarse salt and freshly ground pepper to taste
	Juice of 1 lemon
3	tablespoons chopped fresh parsley or coriander

1. Wash the okra and trim the stems. Dry with paper towels.

2. Char the skins of the tomatoes by turning them over a gas flame with a fork. Remove the skins and chop the tomatoes coarsely.

3. Heat the oil in a heavy skillet. Add the onion and garlic and cook gently until soft. Add the okra and fry for 5 minutes. Add the tomatoes, salt, and pepper, cover, and simmer for about 20 to 30 minutes or until the okra is tender.

4. Add the lemon juice and parsley or coriander and cook for 10 more minutes. Serve hot or cold.

Indian Spiced Okra

1½	pounds okra
4	tablespoons peanut or vegetable oil
3	cloves garlic, minced
1	large onion, finely chopped
½	teaspoon turmeric
¼	teaspon cayenne pepper
½	teaspoon ground coriander seeds
½	teaspoon ground cumin
	Coarse salt and freshly ground pepper to taste
¼ to ½	cup water

1. Wash and trim the okra. Heat the oil in a heavy skillet and add the garlic and onion. Cook gently until soft. Add the okra and cook for 5 minutes.

2. Add the seasonings and cook for 1 minute, stirring. Add the water, cover, and cook for 15 to 20 minutes. The liquid should have evaporated, but be careful not to burn the okra.

Lamb with Okra

4	tablespoons olive oil
1	large onion, chopped
2	cloves garlic, minced
2	pounds lamb, cut into 1-inch cubes
4	cups peeled, chopped tomatoes, fresh or canned
1	tablespoon tomato paste
1	tablespoon ground cumin
1	teaspoon ground coriander
1	teaspoon paprika
	Coarse salt and freshly ground pepper to taste
½	cup water
2	pounds fresh okra, trimmed
2	tablespoons chopped fresh coriander for garnish

1. Heat the oil in a large casserole. Gently fry the onion with the garlic until soft. Add the lamb and brown.

2. Add the tomatoes and remaining ingredients except the okra and fresh coriander. Cover and simmer over low heat for 30 minutes, adding more water if the stew becomes too dry.

3. Add the okra and cook for another 30 minutes, adding more water if needed.

4. Sprinkle with coriander and serve.

Note: This is good served with rice.

Cucumbers

In Oscar Wilde's *The Importance of Being Earnest*, cucumber sandwiches were the favorite teatime dish of the formidable Lady Bracknell (played by Dame Edith Evans in the film). But alas, she never got her sandwiches in the play. The entire plate was consumed before her arrival by the greedy Algernon. And Lane, the butler, protecting Algernon, quickly removed the empty plate with the announcement that they hadn't been able to provide her treat because there wasn't a cucumber to be had for ready money in the entire town.

Cucumbers could not have been invented for a better purpose than those tiny, square, slightly salty yet sweet sandwiches served at afternoon tea on an étagère cake stand, along with fruitcake and ginger biscuits.

Unlike that of Lady Bracknell, the cucumber's position in life has been neutral. This versatile vegetable can be served in a variety of ways besides the sandwich. It is most often eaten raw, but it is also delicious stewed or baked and served coated with hollandaise, béchamel, or Mornay sauce. Cut into ovals, cucumbers can be steamed or poached and tossed with butter and herbs such as dill, tarragon, parsley, mint, basil, or chives. They may also be sautéed in butter and mixed with heavy cream or yogurt.

For salads on their own, cucumbers can be sliced very thin and sprinkled with Japanese vinegar and chopped dill, or mixed with yogurt and mint. They are also good with peppers, tomatoes, or in a mixed green salad.

Cucumbers are available year round and are at their peak in the summer. When buying them, choose those that are firm and green. Discard any that are soft or pliable or that have soft spots on the skin. Try to avoid those that feel greasy. They have been coated with paraffin as a preservative and also to give them a false, commercial shine. If you can't get cucumbers without the wax, always peel them. Choose the smallest in their size. Overmature cucumbers have large seeds and taste bitter.

Small Kirby cucumbers with pale-green-flecked skins have the most flavor. I have not come across any that are noticeably waxed, so when thoroughly washed they can be eaten with their skins. They are good in Pepper Salad (page 279).

Long green cucumbers, known as English cucumbers in the United States, are sold, generally unwaxed, encased in a plastic wrap to keep them fresh. These can usually be eaten with their peel.

It is not usually necessary to drain their liquid by salting cucumbers before you use them, although in some salads, such as the following with yogurt, their juices can make it too watery if this is not done.

Cucumbers in Yogurt

YIELD: 4 Servings

3	cucumbers
	Coarse salt
1	clove garlic, minced
3	tablespoons chopped fresh dill
1	cup plain yogurt
	Freshly ground pepper to taste

1. Peel the cucumbers and slice them thin with a mandolin or cheese parer. Salt and leave to drain for 30 minutes. Pat dry with paper towels.

2. Toss the cucumbers with the remaining ingredients. Correct seasoning and serve.

Cucumber Soup

YIELD: 4 Servings

4	cucumbers, peeled and seeded
1¼	cups plain yogurt
1¼	cups sour cream
2	cups homemade chicken stock
	Coarse salt and freshly ground pepper to taste
2	tablespoons chopped fresh mint

1. Purée the cucumbers in a blender with the yogurt and cream.

2. Mix with the chicken stock, salt, and pepper. Pour into a serving bowl or individual bowls and sprinkle with mint. Serve chilled.

4	cucumbers
2	tablespoons white wine vinegar
1	tablespoon sugar
4	tablespoons butter
4	tablespoons chopped fresh dill
	Coarse salt and freshly ground pepper to taste

1. Peel, seed, and cut the cucumbers into ½-inch pieces. Soak in vinegar for 1 hour.

2. Preheat the oven to 350 degrees. Drain the cucumbers and pat dry with paper towels.

3. Arrange the cucumbers in a buttered ovenproof dish. Sprinkle with sugar, pieces of butter, dill, salt, and pepper.

4. Cover and bake for 30 to 45 minutes or until tender.

Note: This mixture makes a fine tart when served in a pie shell. Cook the shell, then add the cooked cucumbers and heat through.

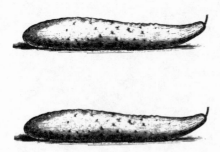

Green Cabbages

Institutional cooking has given green cabbage a bad name. There are many enterprising ways of cooking this thrifty yet superior vegetable besides prolonged boiling in salted water.

A small green cabbage is delicious quartered and lightly steamed so that it is still crunchy when cooked, then buttered and garnished with fresh chives. Cabbages of any size can be sliced and stir-fried in butter or in peanut or vegetable oil. Buttered cabbage is good with garlic, paprika, and caraway seeds, or fresh herbs such as thyme or tarragon. When stir-fried with curry spices and chopped fresh chilies it is a wonderful complement to plainly roasted chicken. It can also be cooked with bacon and caraway seeds.

Another way cabbage is good is finely shredded and cooked over low heat in a tightly covered pot with a chopped onion, a couple of tablespoons of olive oil, garlic, salt, pepper, and a tablespoon of wine vinegar. This dish goes well with pork, hamburgers, and sausages.

Green cabbage is rich in vitamin C and minerals but half of these are destroyed in cooking. Raw, it makes a fine coleslaw, shredded and coated with homemade mayonnaise mixed with a little cream and mustard. Chopped celery, walnuts, and apple can then be mixed in. This goes well with sausages, grilled meat, or ham.

Early spring is the best time for green cabbage. There are several kinds on the market: crinkly or firm dark green with fairly robust leaves, and delicate pale green, with leaves that turn almost white when cooked. Chinese cabbage, in three main varieties, is oblong with light or dark leaves and a long, thin white stem.

Bok choy looks rather like Swiss chard, with dark green leaves and white stalks. Large bok choy is good for soups; the younger, thinner bok choy is more tender and excellent for stir-frying. The leaves should be cut off the stems and cut into even-sized 2-inch pieces. The tough outer layer of the stems should be peeled. Next the base should be cut off and the stalks divided in two lengthwise with a cleaver. These should then be cut into small pieces and stir-fried.

Chinese celery cabbage comes in two varieties: short, thick, and round with light green top, and a longer, light green cabbage with broad green leaves. Both are good in soup, stir-fried with beef or chicken, or pickled.

Choose cabbages with firm, heavy heads and unblemished leaves. The trunk should not be split, dry, or soft and slimy. The firmer the cabbage, the longer it keeps. Kept in a cool place, it will last a week or more.

The following recipe is for a tart using cabbage leaves instead of pastry. It is loosely based on a recipe in Michel Guérard's *Cuisine Minceur*.

Cabbage and Onion Tart Provençal Style YIELD: 4 Servings

1	large head green cabbage, outside leaves only
2	pounds onion, chopped
2	tablespoons butter
5	tablespoons olive oil
6	anchovies, diced
¼	pound black olives, pitted and chopped
2	eggs
½	cup light cream
¼	teaspoon thyme
¼	teaspoon freshly grated nutmeg
	Coarse salt and freshly ground pepper to taste

Tomato and Caper Sauce

2	tablespoons butter
1	pound tomatoes, peeled, seeded, and chopped (or 1½ cups canned)
½	cup chicken stock
1	teaspoon tomato paste
	Coarse salt and freshly ground pepper to taste
3	tablespoons capers

1. Preheat the oven to 325 degrees. Blanch the cabbage leaves for 2 minutes in boiling water to soften them. Drain.

2. In a heavy frying pan, sauté the onions in the butter and olive oil over low heat until transparent. Mix in the anchovies and olives and set aside.

3. Beat the eggs in a bowl and add the cream, thyme, nutmeg, salt, and pepper. Add the onion mixture and stir well.

4. Arrange the cabbage leaves in a buttered baking dish so that the tops hang over the sides. Pour in the filling and close the tops over it. Cover with aluminum foil and set in a dish of hot water. Bake in the center of the oven for 1 hour or until set. Meanwhile, make the sauce.

5. To make the sauce, melt the butter in a saucepan. Stew the tomatoes, uncovered, with the chicken stock and tomato paste until thickened. Season with salt and pepper. Stir in the capers. Correct seasoning and serve hot with the cabbage and onion tart.

Stir-Fried Cabbage

1	small head cabbage
2	tablespoons peanut oil
2	cloves garlic, chopped
6	scallions, including green part, chopped
2	tablespoons chopped fresh ginger root
	Coarse salt and freshly ground pepper to taste

1. Slice the cabbage into thin 1-inch pieces against the grain with a sharp knife. Heat the oil in a wok or heavy frying pan and stir-fry the garlic, scallions, and ginger for 2 minutes.

2. Add the cabbage and season to taste. Stir-fry quickly until the color heightens and the leaves are slightly translucent. Remove and serve at once.

Note: Chinese celery cabbage and bok choy can also be cooked this way.

Creamed Cabbage

2	tablespoons butter
1	pound cabbage, coarsely chopped against the grain
1	clove garlic, minced
	Coarse salt and freshly ground pepper to taste
¼	teaspoon freshly grated nutmeg
¾	cup heavy cream

1. Melt the butter in a frying pan and add the cabbage and garlic. Cook, stirring, for about 10 minutes or until the cabbage has softened a bit but is still crunchy.

2. Season with salt, pepper, and nutmeg. Stir in the cream and cook 5 minutes more. Correct seasoning and serve.

Colcannon

1	small green cabbage, about ¾ pound
1	pound potatoes, peeled
1	onion, finely chopped
3	tablespoons butter
1	tablespoon vegetable oil
	Coarse salt and freshly ground pepper to taste

1. Quarter the cabbage and steam until barely cooked. Meanwhile, cook the potatoes until done and mash. Chop the cabbage fine and add.

2. Sauté the onion in the butter and oil until it is soft but not browned. Mix with the cabbage and potatoes and season with salt and plenty of freshly ground pepper.

3. Return the mixture to the pan and fry until brown on the bottom. Put a plate over the pan and invert to turn the mixture onto it like a pancake. Reheat the pan, adding a little more butter if necessary, and brown the mixture on the other side. Serve hot.

Note: This Irish dish is good with cold meat or ham.

Greens

In the spring the Irish have always liked to eat soup made from young nettles. It cleans the blood, they say, after the sluggish months of winter. Indeed any soup, salad, or vegetable dish made from fresh greens is more than welcome when the last snow seems to have gone and the price of leafy vegetables is no longer a bad joke.

Nettles are free and abundant in the wild (their sting is lost when they are cooked). In the market, however, spinach is the most prevalent cooking green. It can be stir-fried with other leaves, puréed with butter and cream, stuffed into pancakes, or mixed in salad. It is excellent puréed with fresh peas, made into a soufflé, or cooked with eggs for an Italian frittata.

The finest spinach in the world is Italian (anything cooked *alla fiorentina* contains spinach). Most American spinach is curly-leafed, tougher, and has less taste than the Italian, but it can still be good provided it has been picked young enough. The best is sold loose, not in cellophane bags. Open those bags and most often you'll find a pile of torn leaves and thick, tough stalks.

Fresh spinach should be bouncing, bright and squeaky, the leaves a fresh dark green, not yellow or withered. Avoid leaves riddled with insect holes or stalks that are fibrous or slimy. Spinach that has gone to seed is no good, and if it smells sour, it is old.

The leaves are always especially dirty after rain and should be thoroughly washed in several changes of water. Remove the stalks and cook them until barely wilted in the water that clings to them. Don't use aluminum or iron — the spinach will pick up an unpleasant taste.

Collard greens and kale are sturdier than spinach but can be prepared in similar ways, sautéed in butter, oil, or in bacon fat. They are especially good au gratin with béchamel sauce and served with sausages. Again, the leaves should be deep bright green, with no yellow edges or insect holes, and woody stems should be discarded.

Young beet leaves and stems are often overlooked, but these make a very good salad (if thinning your garden, use those with their little beets attached) and in cooking are interchangeable with Swiss chard and turnip greens. Swiss chard leaves should be separated from the stalks. The leaves can be cooked like regular greens, and the stalks can be braised like celery. The French rarely eat the two together.

Sorrel is a vegetable adored by the French, who use it constantly with eggs or with fish such as salmon or shad. But this vegetable is much neglected in

America, despite the fact that it is easy to grow. Its sharp lemony flavor is wonderful in salads, soups, or omelets. And it has the great advantage of being the only vegetable that purées itself when cooked.

While people are paying for greens in the stores, they are overlooking many excellent greens dismissed as weeds. Dandelion, which has been called "the tramp with the golden head," is at its best in the spring. Those bitter, tender baby leaves that are the blight of every lawn make a delicious salad tossed in vinaigrette with sizzling pieces of bacon.

Armed with a field guide, it is possible to go out to the country and find purslane for omelets or chickweed, which can be stewed in butter with onions and served with pork or ham. Brooklime, similar to watercress, grows in marshes and alongside streams.

When I was a child in Dorset our house was surrounded by nettle patches near which there was always a large clump of dock leaves, the antidote for nettle stings when rubbed vigorously onto the skin. We were constantly getting stung in our boisterous rural adventures. So, at age five, with an uncharacteristic instinct for planning ahead, I gathered as many dock leaves as I could and stashed them in the back of the medicine cabinet. My mother was extremely puzzled when she found them a week later, having literally nosed them out.

Cold Sorrel Soup

YIELD: 4 to 6 Servings

2	pounds sorrel
4	cups chicken broth
4	egg yolks
1	cup heavy cream
	Coarse salt and freshly ground white pepper to taste

1. Wash the sorrel and discard the stems. In a frying pan, cook until wilted in the water that clings to the leaves. Pass through a sieve.

2. Meanwhile, bring the chicken broth to a boil.

3. Mix the egg yolks and cream. Gradually pour into the hot broth and cook, stirring, for 10 to 15 minutes or until slightly thickened. Do not allow to boil or the mixture will curdle. Whisk in the sorrel purée and season. Chill before serving.

Stir-Fried Greens

2	pounds greens
3	tablespoons sesame, peanut, or vegetable oil
2	scallions, including green parts, chopped
1	tablespoon fresh minced ginger
1	clove garlic, minced
	Coarse salt and freshly ground pepper to taste

1. Trim the greens of any wilted leaves and tough stalks. Wash thoroughly in several changes of water if the greens are gritty. Drain and chop into 1½-inch pieces.

2. Heat the oil in a large skillet or wok. Add the scallions, ginger, and garlic and stir-fry for 1 minute. Add the greens and stir-fry for 2 or 3 minutes.

3. Season with salt and pepper and serve immediately.

Dandelion Leaves with Walnut Oil Dressing

¼	pound young dandelion leaves
1	small head Boston lettuce
1	beet, boiled and peeled
	Coarse salt and freshly ground pepper to taste
¼	pound diced smoked bacon
6	tablespoons walnut oil (see note)
3	tablespoons red wine vinegar

1. Wash the dandelions and lettuce thoroughly. Dry and place in a salad bowl.

2. Slice the beet julienne and place in the center. Season with salt and pepper.

3. Brown the pieces of bacon and add the oil long enough for it to heat through. Pour over the salad.

4. Add the vinegar to the pan and quickly bring to a boil. Pour over the salad, season with salt and pepper, and toss thoroughly. Serve at once.

Note: Use only the best French walnut oil with this salad.

Lettuce

Bibb, red leaf, green leaf, oakleaf, Boston. Those, along with that perennial best seller, iceberg, are just a few of the varieties of lettuce — much of it locally grown — that a shopper might find in neighborhood markets across the country. The greenery doesn't end there, either. The shopper who looks a little further can find arugula, spinach, beet greens, and dandelion leaves, too. Salad has become so popular that in 1981 more heads of lettuce were bought in supermarkets in the United States than were cartons of milk or loaves of bread.

If it's true, and sales figures seem to indicate that it is, that most of America's salads are composed of shredded iceberg lettuce and bottled dressing, then it seems time for many people to discover what they have been missing in iceberg's lesser-known but much tastier relatives. For instance, there are tiny Bibb lettuces from Florida or California and radicchio flown in from Italy, which are expensive but worth it. The Bibb is so delicate that it is best on its own with a simple vinaigrette. A few leaves of radicchio, a slightly bitter, ruby-red type of chicory, can be added to a green salad for color and flavor. You need only a small head — about one-quarter pound — for a salad.

Then there are the fragile, easily bruised lettuces that should be eaten within a day of being bought: green- and red-leaf lettuces, soft and crinkly, or oakleaf, harder to come by but with a gentle flavor and delicate, thin leaves. These are good for eating on their own or mixed with watercress, lemony sorrel, arugula, escarole, chicory, or dandelion leaves, which add a meaty, slightly bitter flavor. The least expensive lettuces, available in most supermarkets across the country, are Boston, romaine, and, of course, iceberg. Boston lettuce, with its floppy outer leaves and heart full of vitality, mixes well in almost any combination. Romaine, a robust, crisp lettuce, is excellent as a main course, in Caesar salad, with bacon, or with Roquefort dressing. Beware of huge heads of this lettuce; the leaves will be tough. Beware also of skinny, pale heads — they are big romaine with the outer leaves removed.

As for iceberg, it is beloved by airlines, fast-food chains, and, obviously, by many others, since it is far and away the best seller, far outflanking the tender, more tasty greens such as Bibb, Boston or red-leaf and even romaine, a better lettuce that usually sells for the same price. Why pay for iceberg when romaine costs the same?

There are several reasons for the success of iceberg. Being tightly packed and shaped like a bowling ball, it travels well and stays "fresh" longer than any other lettuce. It is less gritty than other lettuce. Iceberg should be washed, however, because of chemical sprays. Those who won't take the time to wash and dry a head of lettuce are like the housewife who wrote to a local paper saying that she objected to recipes calling for freshly ground pepper. "I am too busy to stop and grind pepper fresh for every dish," she said. Washing and drying a gritty loose-leafed lettuce takes perhaps 5 minutes more than preparing iceberg, and the results are worth every minute.

Other greens offer endless opportunities for combining different textures and flavors. Basil leaves, dill, tarragon, parsley, chives, scallions, or thin slices of Spanish onion can be mixed in. Also good are beet tops, nasturtium leaves, sorrel, watercress, dandelion, paper-thin slices of cucumber, fennel, radishes, alfalfa sprouts, or strips of green peppers.

Salads can be flavored with lemon or lime juice instead of vinegar, or mixed with walnuts or almonds, Gruyère, Roquefort, or Gorgonzola cheeses, pieces of orange, grapefruit, or even blackberries. Belgian endive also goes nicely with a green salad. Tomatoes and lettuce do not go well together; tomatoes make salad watery.

Weight is the key to choosing lettuce. A head should be firm and heavy. It doesn't matter if the outer leaves are a little wilted as long as the inside of the lettuce is firm and crisp. Avoid lettuce that has "bolted." If the weather is too hot, the inner part of the lettuce suddenly shoots up. Watch for this particularly in romaine lettuces. If there is a long stalk inside to which the inside leaves are clinging, the lettuce has bolted and the flavor won't be much good. Salad greens that have immense, tough, or yellow leaves, or soft, blackened stems are fit only for the compost heap.

Although in America salad is often served before the main course, in France it is served afterward. The vinegar in the dressing can spoil the taste of a good wine. With the salad, serve cheese such as chèvre, Camembert, or Roquefort, and bread. Many people enjoy salad greens along with grilled meats, roast chicken, and steaks, eaten — in the style of French peasants — on the same plate and swirled into the juices.

When making an oil and vinegar dressing do not slavishly follow the recipe but taste as you go, since oils and vinegars vary enormously in strength. Unless you use a lot of olive oil, you are better off buying in small quantities since it can become rancid after a while.

Lettuce should be stored in a partially open plastic bag in the refrigerator until you are ready to use it. Don't remove the leaves from the head or wash it if you are keeping it overnight or longer. Lettuce and other greens can, however, be washed and wrapped in a towel and kept in the refrigerator for six to eight hours. Wash the leaves under running cold water and drain them in a colander before drying them. Large leaves should be torn into bite-size pieces, never chopped or they start to go brown.

The drying of lettuce leads to all sorts of eccentric behavior. Some people use the dryer of their washing machine, others shake the leaves dry in a pillow case. A spin dryer specially made for the purpose is one of the simplest and most efficient methods. A wire salad basket that's swung around in the air is also effective. This is best done outside since the water sprays over the kitchen, but don't let go of the basket. One cook I know of did. From a sixteenth-floor balcony, he watched as arugula, expensive radicchio, and lettuce leaves fluttered gently to the ground below.

Mixed Green Salad
YIELD: 6 Servings

1 head Boston lettuce
2 heads endive
1 bunch arugula, spinach, or dandelion leaves
Approximately 2 tablespoons tarragon or red wine vinegar
½ teaspoon Dijon mustard
1 clove garlic, crushed
Approximately 6 tablespoons extra-virgin olive oil
Coarse salt and freshly ground pepper to taste

1. Discard any discolored outer leaves and wash the lettuce. Drain. Wash the remaining greens, removing the stalks. Drain. Pat all the greens dry with a dish towel and place in a salad bowl. Refrigerate.

2. Put the vinegar in a small bowl with the mustard and garlic. Gradually add the oil, beating with a fork so that it makes an emulsion with the mustard-vinegar mixture. Season with salt and pepper. Set aside.

3. When ready to serve, remove the salad from the refrigerator, stir the salad dressing again, and pour onto the leaves. Toss thoroughly and serve.

Bibb Lettuce and Mushroom Salad
YIELD: 6 Servings

2 heads Bibb lettuce
4 large Japanese shiitake mushrooms
3 tablespoons extra-virgin olive oil
2 tablespoons red wine vinegar
Coarse salt and freshly ground pepper to taste

1. Wash the lettuce, dry it, and put it in a salad bowl.

2. Slice the mushrooms into 1-inch pieces.

3. Heat the oil in a frying pan and fry the mushrooms until they are slightly browned. Pour the mushrooms and oil, hot, onto the lettuce. Add the vinegar, mix well, season with salt and pepper, and serve.

Note: Japanese shiitake mushrooms are available in Oriental groceries and specialty stores.

1	egg
¾	cup extra-virgin olive oil
2	teaspoons fresh dill leaves
¼	teaspoon curry powder
5	tablespoons white wine vinegar
	Coarse salt and freshly ground pepper to taste
1	bunch arugula
1	bunch watercress, leaves only
1	small head escarole, tender inner leaves only

1. Put the egg in a blender and blend for 1 minute. Gradually add the oil, drop by drop, then more rapidly, so that the mixture thickens like mayonnaise. Add the dill, curry powder, vinegar, salt, and pepper and blend thoroughly.

2. Wash and dry the leaves. Place in a salad bowl and coat with the dressing.

Mushrooms

Unlike truffles, mushrooms have been successfully cultivated. In addition to the white mushrooms sold in supermarkets across the United States, Japanese shiitake and enok mushrooms are now frequently available. And the market for wild mushrooms is growing — but their prices are high.

Mushrooms grow everywhere, says John Gottfried, a mycologist who has picked morels on Broadway and 54th Street, in Santa Monica on the palisades, and even in Central Park. But fear of getting indigestion or poisoning from the wrong mushroom rightly confines the untutored to the choices offered in the stores. The most well known of these are cultivated "white" mushrooms known also as Paris mushrooms.

These all-purpose mushrooms are tasteless. Colette wrote of them: "I am in revolt against the mushroom of Paris, an insipid creature born in the dark and incubated in humidity. I have had enough of it, bathing chopped in all the sauces it thickens. I forbid it to usurp the place of the chanterelle or the truffle; and I command it, together with its fitting companion, canned coxcombs, never to cross the threshold of my kitchen."

A better bet would be the meaty shiitake mushrooms, available fresh and dried with an ever growing market, or voluptuous, buttery oyster mushrooms with their pale fanlike leaves, or the little enok, thin with yellow stalks and good in salads. Shiitake mushrooms are sold dried in health food and Oriental stores, or fresh in many markets. They are grown on hardwood and have a rich, meaty taste. They go especially well in stir-fried Chinese dishes. Enok mushrooms, sold fresh, have long, thin stems and a small button top and are good as garnishes or in salads.

But the white mushroom has its uses and makes a pleasant dish sliced raw and coated with lemon juice, olive oil, and coriander seeds, or stuffed with butter, parsley, and garlic and baked.

Of the wild mushrooms, morels are now semi-cultivated. In Europe the mycelium is germinated and the mushrooms are then allowed to grow wild. In the United States there are five different varieties of morel. Most of them grow in California, Oregon, Washington, and Wisconsin. Like salmon or wine they vary in flavor according to where they come from or where they have been grown. But the crop is never a sure one, according to Mr. Gottfried, and no one knows exactly what variable affects the morels. During an elm-tree blight the mushrooms came up magnificently, but after the blight they didn't come back. "Next year, who knows?" said Mr. Gottfried. Morels are in season in late April through May and potentially to the beginning of July.

Morels are dark brown with honeycombed caps and a meaty taste. They are also sold dried. Dried morels should be soaked in warm water before being used, then drained and thoroughly rinsed because they are very gritty. Fresh morels can be sautéed in butter or simmered with stock.

Chanterelles, also called *girolles* in France, are bright orange, feathery trumpets with a wonderful smell. There are many different varieties of chanterelles, and these are found in Pacific rain forests and through Vancouver and Canada. Their season starts in mid-July and, depending upon where they are, lasts through December. They are found near streams. In the fall they are in season in the Pacific areas, where sometimes they can weigh up to a pound; in summer, on the East Coast they can be found in places such as Martha's Vineyard and New Hampshire. A luminescent mushroom called a jack-o'-lantern is similar but poisonous — but the difference should be obvious to anyone with a minimal training of field characteristics. Chanterelles should be cooked slowly in butter after being quickly but thoroughly rinsed to rid them of dirt. A little parsley and a couple of tablespoons of chicken stock can be added.

Boletus mushrooms, known variously as cèpes, Polish mushrooms, steinpilz, or porcini, according to their place of origin, grow in pine forests in the fall. They are rich and succulent and especially delicious cooked with garlic, parsley, and olive oil, or with prosciutto or pancetta, Italian bacon. Some of them can be as big as a side plate. Like all mushrooms, they are wonderful with fresh herbs.

Dried cèpes should be soaked first. They are often sold in specialty stores or Italian stores. Keep some on hand for impromptu pasta dishes (page 223) or to flavor sauces.

When buying mushrooms, buy a few at a time because they do not keep well. Avoid those that have started to shrivel or become slimy. Place the mushrooms in a container covered with a damp cloth. If wrapped in plastic, mushrooms can get slimy. They should be kept cool and humid. The commonly found supermarket "white" mushroom caps should be closed, not open with gills exposed. The mushrooms should have a white or creamy bloom. You are better off buying them loose so you can pick out the size you want. They should be washed before being used because some are coated with a preservative. Canned and frozen mushrooms are not recommended.

Mushrooms absorb moisture when cooked, although if salted and left for a while they will start to exude their own moisture. White mushrooms used for salads should be sprinkled with lemon juice to keep them white.

The mushrooms I discovered growing in the fireplace in the country during a particulary damp spring when I had been away were listed in the book as merely "not edible."

Mushrooms in Cream

3	tablespoons unsalted butter
¾	pound button mushrooms, sliced
	Coarse salt and freshly ground pepper to taste
1	cup heavy cream
	Chopped fresh tarragon or parsley
4	thin slices toast

1. Heat the butter in a skillet and add the mushrooms. Season with salt and pepper and cook for about 3 minutes.

2. Add the cream and simmer for 5 to 10 minutes or until the sauce has thickened. Sprinkle with herbs and serve on toast.

Funghi Porcini with Garlic and Parsley

1	pound fresh funghi porcini
4	tablespoons extra-virgin olive oil
	Coarse salt and freshly ground pepper to taste
2	cloves garlic, minced
3	tablespoons chopped fresh parsley

1. Marinate the mushrooms in the oil, salt, and pepper for 1 hour.

2. Pour the mixture into a frying pan with the garlic. Cook for about 20 minutes or until done. Sprinkle with parsley and serve.

Mushroom Soup

½	pound mushrooms, sliced
2	tablespoons butter
4	cups homemade chicken stock
½	cup heavy cream
2	tablespoons port wine
	Coarse salt and freshly ground pepper to taste
2	tablespoons chopped fresh dill or chervil

1. Sauté the mushrooms lightly in the butter for about 5 minutes. Add the chicken stock and simmer for 20 minutes.

2. Purée the mixture in a blender or food processor. If serving hot, return to the pan and reheat, then stir in the cream. Do not boil. If serving cold, add the cream and cool to room temperature.

3. When ready to serve, stir in the port, salt, pepper, and dill or chervil.

2	small Kirby cucumbers
	Coarse salt
	About 10 shiitake mushrooms, dried
1	icicle radish
3	teaspoons sesame seeds, toasted
3	teaspoons rice vinegar
	Soy sauce to taste

1. Peel the cucumbers and slice very thin. Salt and set aside.

2. Pour boiling water over the mushrooms and leave for 30 minutes. Shred the icicle radish and refrigerate in cold water.

3. Rinse the cucumbers and mushrooms under cold water and pat dry. Remove the mushroom stems and set aside to use for flavoring stocks. Slice the caps thin. Dry the icicle radish.

4. Combine the cucumbers, icicle radish, and mushroom caps in a bowl. Sprinkle with remaining ingredients to taste, toss, and serve.

Olives

Anyone who has ever wandered through Mediterranean open-air markets and seen the vats of vari-colored olives glistening in the sunlight will recognize the possibilities of the olive. Some olives are soft and fleshy, bursting open like ripe persimmons; others are firm, others are wrinkled — the varieties seem almost endless. Some are shaped like tiny apples, some approach the perfect oval, and the colors are as diverse as the shapes: purplish black, deep blue-green, straw yellow, dark-red wine, a spectrum of browns and greens from rich chocolate to chartreuse. Olives may be cured in brine, seasoned with coriander, fennel, or garlic; they may be stuffed with pimientos, almonds, anchovies, orange peel, or pearl onions. Such imaginative treatment of olives leads one to regard only with disdain the watery, fat American olives in cans, so uniform in size and lack of flavor that they lead one to suspect their spontaneous generation in the can.

In many better delicatessens and especially in ethnic markets, olives are sold loose. Often you can buy from a barrel. Among my favorites are wrinkled kalamata olives from Greece, tiny, shiny black olives from Nice, and Italian olives of all kinds, including large green Cevinol and black, wrinkled little ones from near Rome and from Morocco.

The difference between black and green olives is their ripeness. Black olives have been allowed to ripen on the tree and have more oil than olives that have been picked green. Black olives are cured in an alkaline solution and then exposed to the air. Green olives are also cured in an alkaline solution, then they are put in brine for about a year. The brine softens them and makes them palatable.

In the stores, black olives may be packed in oil and flavored with spices, garlic, or herbs. Green olives are usually kept in brine.

Olives are delicious in summertime for salade Niçoise or in mixed salads or even chopped and added to fresh tomato sauces for pasta or grilled fish. To store olives, put them in olive oil and, if you like, add a few rosemary leaves or coriander seeds for flavor.

In the Middle East and North Africa olives are an extremely important food — an integral part of many dishes. But in the West, olives are often used only for cocktail snacks or as decoration. This can change for the shopper who will go out of the way to find and experiment with quality olives.

There is, in fact, one good use to which canned olives can be put. Thinly slice a canned black olive, place it on a piece of pâté de foie gras or chicken, and say it's a truffle. Since it will have no more flavor than many brands of canned truffle, no one will know the difference.

The following recipe should be made only when tomatoes are in season. It is an excellent lunch dish served with French bread and unsalted butter.

Tomato Salad with Olives and Sardines   YIELD: 4 Servings

3	large ripe tomatoes
2	cans sardines
1	red onion
12	black oil-preserved olives
	About 4 tablespoons basil leaves, left whole
	Coarse salt and freshly ground pepper to taste
5	tablespoons extra-virgin olive oil
2	tablespoons red wine vinegar (balsamic if possible)

1. Slice the tomatoes and arrange them on a serving plate. Arrange the sardines over the top in a fan shape.

2. Thinly slice the onion and arrange over the top. Add the olives and the basil. Sprinkle with salt and pepper. Dribble on the oil and vinegar.

Onions and Green Onions

In England small boys wearing berets used to come over from France and sell long braids of onions and garlic door to door. My mother bought them whether she needed them or not, for the boys had shy little faces with large dark eyes fringed with long eyelashes. The onions they were selling came under the category of "keeping" onions, those that can be stored throughout the winter, dried, and sometimes braided. Green onions such as chives, scallions, and leeks are sold fresh and picked before their bulb has formed.

The most common keeping onions are yellow globe, boiling or all-purpose onions, and white or silverskin onions. This group is the best for cooking because their flavor stands up and their texture does not disintegrate. They also store well. All-purpose onions can be fried or used for soups, sauces, baking, and stuffing. Their skins add golden color to stock. Large brown Spanish or Bermuda onions, milder than yellow or white onions and called sweet onions, are good raw on hamburgers or for making fried onion rings.

White onions for glazing are smaller and milder than their larger relatives. Pearl onions, the smallest white onions, are used for pickling and for martinis. They are sometimes mixed with green peas. Peel little onions by dropping them into boiling water for a few minutes.

In the spring onions are milder. When they get older their flavor intensifies. Golden-skinned Vidalia onions from Georgia are so sweet they can almost be eaten like apples.

Sweet onions, including Bermuda, Spanish, and Italian, are best raw in salad or with pickled or fresh herring. They fall apart when cooked. Bermuda onions are flattish and yellow, white, or red; Spanish onions, large and yellow or white. Small red, white, or yellow Italian onions are generally not for cooking, except for fried onion rings, but are used in antipasti and salads.

Garlic, one of the most beneficent members of the onion family for its supposed ability to ward off both vampires and illnesses, goes wonderfully with just about any savory dish, particularly with lamb and Mediterranean dishes and to make the Provençal aïoli sauce (page 197). Chicken roasted with whole garlic cloves has a wonderful aroma. And elephant garlic, which has mild cloves the size of a thumb, is also delicious roasted whole on its own. In the summer fresh green garlic can be used to flavor fish or summer salads but is rarely sold commercially here. You have to grow it yourself.

Dried shallots have a delicate onion flavor that is excellent for sauces. They come in brown clusters with reddish cloves inside and are rather expensive.

When buying dried onions, avoid those that have sprouted because they have been kept in too warm an atmosphere. Heads should be firm, compact, and well shaped, never mushy, moldy, broken, or dry. If garlic cloves are soft and mushy, they are probably withered inside and unfit for use. Like onions, they should be avoided if they have sprouted. Onions keep very well for up to a year in a cool, dark place.

You are better off choosing onions loose from a bin rather than buying them in packages. This way you can get the sizes you want and you won't have any surprises when you get home. Size, however, means nothing in terms of quality. The skins should be dry and glistening. If they have open, woody necks they are probably decaying inside.

Fresh onions such as scallions, chives, and leeks should have bright green tops and white stems. They should not be wilted, browned, split, or slimy with dried-up roots.

Scallions are merely baby onions picked before they have fully formed their bulb — sometimes, though, they have formed little bulbs that, if they were not picked, would grow big enough to become onions. Scallions can be chopped and mixed into mashed potatoes or cooked like leeks and served in a vinaigrette dressing. They are also good raw.

Chives should be absolutely fresh, and the best way to insure this is to grow them on your windowsill — a simple undertaking. Avoid frozen or dehydrated chives; they have no flavor. Chives can be used on salads, in sauces, and on baked potatoes.

Leeks, the largest member of the green onion family, are surprisingly expensive in America compared with Europe, where they are cheap and easy to come by. They tend to be very gritty. To clean them, cut down almost to the end and rinse thoroughly. Soak them for about 10 minutes, and then rinse them under running water several times. They are good served at room temperature with a vinaigrette dressing, cooked in red wine, or baked in the oven in stock and butter. The green part can be used for flavoring stocks. Sometimes, however, leeks are sold with very little green part. This means they are probably old and the green tops had begun to wither and go brown.

Onions grow in warm and cool climates — those from warm climates are larger and milder than those grown where the weather is harsh. One mild spring, at the River Café in Brooklyn, chef Larry Forgione composed a dish of beautiful wild onion flowers served on a plate with tiny golden zucchini flowers, the latter stuffed with ground lamb. Looking at this dish I could see that onions are indeed members of the lily family.

Leeks in Red Wine

6	leeks
2	tablespoons olive oil
	Approximately 1 cup red wine
	Coarse salt and freshly ground pepper to taste
	Freshly grated nutmeg to taste

1. Trim the leeks and wash them thoroughly in several changes of cold water.

2. Heat the oil in a skillet and add the leeks. Add enough wine to barely cover, salt, and pepper. Cover and simmer for 15 minutes. Uncover and cook for another 5 to 10 minutes or until done. Season with nutmeg and cool.

3. Serve at room temperature.

Glazed White Onions

	Approximately 18 small white onions
	Boiling water
¼	cup butter
	Approximately 1½ cups chicken stock
1	tablespoon brown sugar
	Dash of thyme
1	bay leaf
2	tablespoons chopped fresh parsley
	Coarse salt and freshly ground pepper to taste

1. Drop the onions for a few minutes into boiling water. Drain and slip off their skins. Melt the butter in a large frying pan. Toss the onions in the butter until they are golden.

2. Add enough stock to barely cover. Add the sugar, herbs, and seasonings and simmer over moderate heat for 30 to 40 minutes or until the sauce has reduced to a caramel glaze.

3. Correct seasoning and serve.

Orange and Onion Salad

2	Spanish onions
2	oranges, peeled, pith and seeds removed, sliced thin
	Juice of 1 orange
3	tablespoons olive oil
	Lemon or lime juice to taste
	Coarse salt and freshly ground pepper to taste
2	tablespoons fresh chopped coriander
	Fresh coriander for garnish

1. Slice the onions and combine in a bowl with the oranges.

2. Mix the orange juice with olive oil, lemon or lime juice, salt, pepper, and chopped coriander. Pour over the onions and oranges, garnish with coriander, and serve.

Note: This goes with cold duck or game.

Pissaladière

(Onion Tart)

4	tablespoons butter
5	large onions, finely chopped
1	clove garlic, finely chopped
	Herb bouquet (parsley, bay leaf, and thyme tied in a cheesecloth)
	Coarse salt and freshly ground white pepper to taste
1	9-inch pie shell, baked for 10 minutes
8	canned anchovies
21	pitted black Nice olives
	Fresh thyme, if available

1. Melt the butter in a deep pan and soften the onions with the garlic. Add the herb bouquet, salt, and pepper. Cook very slowly for about 1 hour but do not allow to brown.

2. Remove the herb bouquet. Reserve the onion mixture until ready to serve.

3. Preheat the oven to 350 degrees. Put the onion mixture in a saucepan and heat through. Fill the pie shell and arrange the anchovies and olives on top and bake for 15 minutes. Sprinkle with fresh thyme and serve hot or cold.

Note: Do not put the onions into the pastry shell overnight or they will make it soggy.

Onions Baked in Their Skins

4 medium onions
Unsalted butter
Coarse salt and freshly
ground pepper to taste

1. Preheat the oven to 325 degrees.

2. Make a foil basket for the onions so that they stand up straight. Bake for 1 to 2 hours or until the onions are tender when pierced by a fork.

3. Open the onions with a fork and eat with butter, salt, and pepper. Wrap any leftovers in foil and refrigerate. Eat cold the next day with a vinaigrette dressing.

Note: Cayenne pepper or a little cinnamon is also good with hot baked onions.

Peas and Beans

Peas and green beans are at their best in early summer. Then they are in the markets in abundance, not only string beans and fresh peas, but sugar snap peas, brilliant snow peas, exotic yellow or purple string beans, fresh fava beans nestling in furry linings in oversized pods, and even skinny haricots verts, imported from France and sold at exorbitant prices. In summer, they are all good enough to eat on their own as well as fine accompaniments to meat, chicken, or fish.

Fresh peas have almost become an anachronism. Most are now frozen as soon as they are picked. Of all vegetables, there is no question that they freeze the best. But these sugary, uniform peas bear little relation to those freshly picked from the garden, as anyone who has ever tried to shell a pile without eating the whole thing can testify. The French discovered the joys of petits pois in 1660 when they were brought to France from Genoa and presented to King Louis XIV. Madame de Maintenon in one of her letters talks of the women at the French court who, "having supped with the King, and supped well," would take to their private chambers and feast on peas at the risk of indigestion. *"C'est une mode, une fureur,"* she observed.

Fresh peas should be eaten right after picking since after they are picked they immediately start converting their sugar into starch (which is why the ones on the market can be so mealy at times). These peas are best cooked the French way, in a saucepan lined with lettuce leaves with a dash of sugar, baby onions, and butter, or simply puréed. When buying fresh peas, make sure the pods are crisp, shiny, and brightly colored, not wizened or yellowed. The peas inside should be small, plump, and juicy.

Snow peas — also called mangetout — and sugar snap peas are bred to be eaten pods and all. Stir-frying or light steaming are the best ways to cook them. Sugar snap peas are plumper and sweeter than snow peas and they, too, are good steamed or stir-fried. They are good only when very young and fresh. Avoid frozen ones: They lose their crunchiness when thawed.

String or snap beans are also delicious cooked in similar ways. They come in three colors: purple, green, and yellow. The green beans are available all year round, from Mexico and Florida in the winter, from California in the summer. They are at their best in late spring and early fall. They have a stronger flavor than peas and take well to spices. They can also be steamed and served with butter or tossed while hot in oil and vinegar. They should generally be cooked al dente. Some, however, are simply too big to be lightly cooked. They are better stewed in a sauce, made perhaps of fresh tomatoes flavored with garlic and basil.

When buying string beans, make sure they are fresh enough to snap in half. They should not be soft, wilted, or pliable or have tough pods. To prepare them for cooking, trim top and bottom and remove strings if they have them.

Lima beans are occasionally sold fresh and already shelled in plastic packages in late summer and early fall. But they are dyed and have little flavor to boot. The frozen ones are just as good. Lima beans can be prepared much as fava beans are and can also be simply steamed and served with butter and fresh herbs.

Fava beans are not as well known in America as green beans. But the Italians, Spanish, and the British, who call them "broad beans," love them. They are excellent steamed and tossed in butter and served with fresh tarragon or with mint and butter or cream. When the beans come into season in Italy, Romans feast on raw fava beans with chilled young Frascati wine. The beans are spread out on newspaper, peeled, and sprinkled with grated Romano cheese.

Shelling peas and fava beans is not the bother it is made out to be. It can be done while you watch the evening news. In markets in the south of Mexico the Indian women who sell vegetables while away the time between sales shelling peas and fava beans that they place in clay pots to be emptied into the shoppers' baskets. The price for these, shelled and ready to cook, when I was last there in 1980 was less than a dime a cup.

Eating peas has always been a source of amusement for children, and it brings the old nursery rhyme to mind:

I eat my peas with honey,
I've done it all my life.
It makes the peas taste funny
But it keeps them on the knife.

Peas with Mint

2	cups shelled peas
	Dash of salt and sugar, if needed
2	tablespoons fresh mint leaves
1	tablespoon butter
	Freshly ground pepper to taste

1. Place the peas in a saucepan with ½ inch of water, salt, and sugar. Add the mint, bring to a boil and simmer, uncovered, until the peas are tender.

2. Drain, toss with butter, and sprinkle with pepper. Serve immediately.

Beans with Peas and Ginger

1	pound fresh yellow or green beans
1½	tablespoons peanut oil
1	cup shelled peas
1	tablespoon grated fresh ginger
2	tablespoons chopped fresh coriander
1	small green chili, minced (or less, according to taste)

1. Trim the beans and cut in 1-inch pieces. Heat the oil in a frying pan or wok with 1 cup water. Bring to a boil and add the beans. Cook for 5 minutes, covered.

2. Add the peas and cook for 5 minutes, uncovered. Add the ginger, coriander, and chili. Toss and cook, uncovered, until all the liquid has evaporated.

Sautéed String Beans

1	pound fresh string beans, trimmed and left whole
2	tablespoons butter
1	clove garlic, finely chopped
	Coarse salt and freshly ground pepper to taste

1. Steam the beans until bright green and still crunchy.

2. Heat the butter in a skillet and sauté the beans with the garlic. Season and serve.

2	pounds fresh fava beans
2	strips thick-cut bacon
1	tablespoon butter
	Coarse salt and freshly
	ground pepper to taste

1. Shell the beans and cut the bacon into ¼-inch pieces.

2. Fry the bacon until crisp. Meanwhile, steam or boil the beans until luminous green, 5 to 10 minutes.

3. Add the beans to the bacon with the butter, salt, and pepper. Toss thoroughly over high heat and serve sizzling.

Peppers, Eggplant, and Avocados

Peppers

Not all peppers are hot, as their name would imply. There are hundred of varieties in the genus Capsicum, ranging from sweet green bell peppers to fiery red hot chilies. Sweet red peppers are simply fully ripened green ones. Italian frying peppers are a pale green and longer, with a more powerful flavor than the round sweet bell pepper. Chili peppers can be green or red and vary in flavor from the hot cayenne and serrano peppers to the fairly mild ancho peppers.

Peppers are available year round and are at their peak in late spring and early fall. Choose those that are fresh, shiny, and unwrinkled with no soft, moist spots or cracks. Beware of greasy skins; that shine, as with cucumbers, tomatoes, and a host of vegetables and fruits, is paraffin. If peppers are coated with wax, they should always be charred and skinned.

Fresh chilies should be run under cold water and their tops, seeds, and veins removed. Then char them over a flame and scrape off the skin. This makes them soft for cooking and enhances their flavor. But when handling hot peppers be sure to wash your hands afterwards. If you get the oils in your eyes it can be extremely painful.

Dried chilies are sold both whole and ground. Large whole dried chilies can be soaked and puréed for cooking. The smaller dry ones can simply be ground.

Charred Peppers with Anchovies

YIELD: 4 Servings

4	red peppers
1	2-ounce can anchovies, undrained
½	cup extra-virgin olive oil
	Coarse salt and freshly ground pepper to taste

1. Holding the peppers with a fork, char them over a gas flame. Or, if you prefer, char them under a broiler, turning them until they are done on all sides. Wrap in paper towels and let sit for 5 to 10 minutes. When the peppers are cool enough to handle, strip away the skin and scrape off all charred particles, seeds, and fibrous parts.

2. Place the cleaned strips of pepper on a plate. Arrange the anchovies on top and pour on the olive oil and remaining oil from the anchovy can. Sprinkle with salt and pepper. Serve at room temperature.

Pepper Salad

YIELD: 4 Servings

2	green peppers, charred, peeled, seeded, and chopped
2	ripe tomatoes, chopped
1	small cucumber, peeled and chopped
1	small onion, finely chopped
1	clove garlic, minced
2	tablespoons chopped fresh coriander
½	cup extra-virgin olive oil
	Juice of 1 lemon
	Coarse salt and freshly ground pepper to taste

1. Combine the peppers, tomatoes, cucumber, onion, and garlic in a bowl. If the tomatoes are too juicy, pour off the juice and reserve for soups or sauces.

2. Add the coriander. Mix the oil and lemon juice and season with salt and pepper. Toss the salad with the dressing and refrigerate for 30 minutes before serving.

Note: This goes with grilled or fried fish or meats.

Chili con Carne

6   dried red chilies
2   cups boiling water
1   tablespoon olive oil
2   pounds stewing beef, cut into ½-inch cubes
2   bay leaves
1   tablespoon ground cumin
2   cloves garlic, peeled
2   teaspoons oregano
2   tablespoons Hungarian paprika
1   teaspoon sugar
Coarse salt and freshly ground pepper to taste

1. Tear the chilies into strips and cover them with the boiling water. Let soak for 30 minutes. Drain, reserving the liquid, and set aside.

2. Heat the oil in a heavy skillet and brown the beef cubes. Add the chili-soaking liquid and bring to a boil. Add the bay leaves, turn down heat, and let simmer for 1 hour, adding more water if necessary.

3. Meanwhile, purée the remaining ingredients, including the chilies, in an electric blender. Add the purée to the meat and let simmer 30 minutes more.

Note: This is a hot chili. Serve it with red kidney beans and rice.

Eggplant

Also known as aubergine, eggplant is one of the most beautiful vegetables with its shiny purple skin and dark green leaves clustered at the stem. It is a favorite Mediterranean and Middle Eastern dish — Arabs say they know a thousand ways to prepare it. There are many shapes and colors, although the most common in our markets is the egg-shaped, deep purple variety measuring around 6 to 8 inches long. But the small ones are even better, especially those slender eggplants with paler, thinner skins usually sold in Oriental markets or Indian markets. I even came across an ivory-skinned kind that was the sweetest I have ever tasted.

When buying eggplants choose those with glossy, smooth skins, the smallest and heaviest for their size. Avoid wrinkled or pliable eggplants. They are old and will be bitter.

The flesh sometimes has bitter juices. Slice the eggplant, sprinkle the slices with salt, and leave for half an hour before cooking to leach out the juices.

Eggplant is delicious baked whole in the oven, the flesh scooped out and mashed with olive oil, lemon juice, and garlic and served as a spread or dip. Slices of eggplant are good fried in olive oil, each slice then sprinkled with chopped garlic and fresh basil. The small eggplants are extremely good stuffed and baked.

In the summer I like to barbecue brochettes of cubed eggplant, pieces of raw onion and peppers, and quartered tomatoes. I thread the vegetables on a skewer, coat them with olive oil, and grill them over hot coals. A refreshing and summery sauce can be made with yogurt, garlic, fresh basil, parsley, and lemon juice seasoned with salt and pepper and puréed in the blender. Use some of this to baste the vegetables while they are cooking and the rest as a dipping sauce.

Ratatouille is one dish I never tire of. It conjures up visions of the Mediterranean seaside, of meals eaten in some small outdoor restaurant that looks upon white-painted houses, blue sea, and blue sky.

Ratatouille

YIELD: 4 to 6 Servings

2	eggplants
	Coarse salt
4	tomatoes
2	large onions
2	sweet red or green
	peppers
2	cloves garlic
2	tablespoons olive oil
	Coarse salt and freshly
	ground pepper to taste

1. Cut the eggplants into 1-inch squares and sprinkle with salt. Leave to stand for 1 hour. Pat dry with paper towels.

2. Peel the tomatoes by pouring boiling water over them and letting them stand in it for a couple of minutes, then slipping off their skins. Chop them coarsely.

3. Slice the onions and peppers and mince the garlic. Heat the oil in a heavy-bottomed skillet. Cook the onions and the garlic, stirring, until soft but not browned. Add the peppers and the eggplant. Sauté for 10 minutes.

4. Add the tomatoes, cover, and simmer for about 30 minutes. Remove the lid for the last 10 minutes if the ratatouille is too liquid.

Fried Eggplant

YIELD: 4 Servings

2	eggplants
	Coarse salt
	Approximately ⅔ cup
	extra-virgin olive oil
⅓	cup peanut or safflower
	oil
2	cloves garlic, finely
	chopped
½	cup coarsely chopped
	fresh basil
	Freshly ground pepper to
	taste

1. Slice the eggplants thin, sprinkle with salt, and allow to stand for 30 minutes. Pat dry with paper towels.

2. Heat half the oil in a skillet and fry the eggplants a few slices at a time on both sides until browned. Add more oil, a little at a time, as needed, heating it through before adding the eggplant. Remove the slices with a slotted spoon and place on a serving platter. Do not drain.

3. Sprinkle each batch of slices with garlic, basil, and pepper. Leave for a few hours at room temperature or refrigerate overnight before serving. Serve at room temperature.

Eggplant Stuffed with Tomatoes and Pine Nuts   YIELD: 4 Servings

2	eggplants
	Coarse salt
3	tablespoons olive oil
1	onion, chopped
2	cloves garlic, minced
¾	pound tomatoes, peeled, seeded, and chopped
	Freshly ground black pepper to taste
½	teaspoon freshly ground coriander seeds
½	cup Italian Arborio rice
2	tablespoons tomato paste
½	cup pine nuts

1. Slice the eggplants in half lengthwise. With a spoon scoop out the eggplant, taking care not to break the skin. Chop the eggplant and sprinkle it and the shells with salt. Leave for 30 minutes.

2. Preheat the oven to 350 degrees. Pat the eggplant shells and eggplant dry.

3. Heat 2 tablespoons oil in a skillet and sauté the onion with the garlic until soft. Add the eggplant, tomatoes with their juice, pepper, coriander, rice, and tomato paste. Cook until the eggplant is soft.

4. Stuff into the eggplant shells and sprinkle with pine nuts. Oil a baking dish with the remaining olive oil — use more if needed. Bake 45 minutes to 1 hour.

Avocados

Although as a child I prided myself on my sophisticated taste in food, there were two things that at the age of thirteen I was not prepared for. One was snails and the other was avocado. My father's cousin, who was a wonderful cook in the French tradition, had invited my mother and me to lunch in her London house. I always felt at home there. Her house was filled with English watercolors and oil paintings, Provençal china, and bric-a-brac picked up from travels in France, and it had a cozy untidiness about it that I loved. Before the meal I was allowed to have a glass of dry sherry, considered appropriate for a girl of my age despite the fact that it made me go bright red in the face.

I was feeling slightly fuzzy when we sat down to lunch in the small, plant-filled dining room. There waiting for us as a first course was a halved, unfamiliar soft green fruit, its discouraging cavity filled with vinaigrette. The only dressing I liked at that time was a commercial brand known as "Salad Cream" that was sold in bottles.

I was told that avocados were very expensive. I shall never forget that first mouthful. No amount of bread and butter stuffed into my mouth at the same time as that soft, green fruit could hide its taste.

I don't remember when I tried avocados again (they were not often wasted on young girls in England). But like so many foods I hated at first — olives, beer, tomatoes — they soon became one of my favorites for there is nothing like those black-skinned, buttery fruits, gnarled and knobbly on the outside, smooth and delicate inside, eaten with coarse salt, pepper, and a squeeze of lemon or lime juice or with a vinaigrette dressing. In Mexico they were picked ripe and we used to peel them and spread them on homemade whole-wheat bread warm from the oven.

Unfortunately, avocados are not picked ripe in the United States. At times they are extremely disappointing, so flavorless that their only salvation is to be mashed with chilies and onion, lemon juice and oil. The best are those of the Hass variety from California, with thick, black skins, sold during the summer and fall. They have much more taste than the green-skinned ones available during the winter from Florida. When buying avocados choose only those with unbroken skins that are heavy for their size. Allow them to ripen on a windowsill. When they are ready to eat they should smell fragrant. The whole avocado, not just the round end, should be soft. If refrigerated they do not ripen.

Avocado is the only fruit that virtually guarantees a free houseplant.

Guacamole

YIELD: 4 Servings

2	ripe avocados
2	small ripe tomatoes, peeled and chopped
2	green chilies, minced
2	tablespoons finely chopped onion
¼	teaspoon ground red chili (or more to taste)
2	tablespoons chopped fresh coriander
	Coarse salt and freshly ground pepper to taste
	Juice of 1 lime
	Sprig of coriander for garnish

1. Peel the avocados and mash with the remaining ingredients except the lime juice and coriander sprig.

2. Place in a small serving bowl and squeeze the lime juice over the top to prevent the guacamole from turning brown. Decorate with a sprig of coriander and serve.

2	ripe avocados
	Juice of 1 lemon
	Coarse salt and freshly
	ground pepper to taste
2	tablespoons coarsely
	chopped chervil

1. Slice the peeled avocados thin and squeeze lemon juice over all the slices, making sure they are all covered or there will be brown patches.

2. Sprinkle with salt, pepper, and chervil and serve.

Note: A light vinaigrette dressing may be used instead of the lemon juice.

Root Vegetables

With the exception of potatoes, root vegetables such as turnips, parsnips, and rutabagas remain resolutely out of fashion. They are bulbous and knobbly and lack the refinement of their brightly colored or leafy cousins.

The second-class citizens of the vegetable world, ordinary, peasantlike, and low in price, their fate has been to be boiled and served with a perfunctory dollop of butter to scowling children or to be used for pelting people. They are offered at dinner parties only by the most confident of hosts because they are so often jeered at.

Turnips

Take the turnip, for example. This harmless, delicately flavored vegetable can arouse the darkest memories. One sensitive fellow was so traumatized as a child by the hours he spent in baleful contemplation of them that he refused to eat turnips ever again. To rid him of this prejudice, friends cubed and roasted some young white turnips with sizzling duck's fat.

The unsuspecting victim, who frequently enjoyed his food to the detriment of his waistline, commented on the excellence of the "potatoes." His wife urged him to eat more. He stared at her suspiciously for a moment. Then he poked his fork into the offending vegetable.

"These aren't potatoes! They're turnips!" he cried, pushing the plate aside. "How did you guess?" she asked. "Because you would have never allowed me a second helping if they'd been potatoes," he replied. Perhaps if they were called "navets" people would associate turnips with the best French cooking — and the great French dish *canard aux navets* — rather than the nursery table.

Young white turnips are a perfect complement to rich meats such as duck, goose, pork, ham, or sausages. They are delicious in soufflés, boiled or steamed and coated with parsley butter, puréed, glazed, or slivered and fried Japanese-style in tempura batter.

When buying turnips, look for those that are small and unwrinkled. If they are too big or cracked they may be overmature and woody. The freshest will have their green tops attached and these can be steamed or stir-fried separately. The greens should be used right away; the turnips can be kept refrigerated in a plastic bag for about a week.

Rutabagas

Another much-maligned vegetable is the rutabaga, also named yellow turnip. It is coarse-looking, large, and round with a purplish skin and covered with a shiny preservative wax coating that must be removed. But the flesh inside has a sweet, subtle yet distinctive flavor. Avoid rutabagas that are cracked or that smell too strong.

Rutabagas can be cubed and steamed or boiled, then mashed with butter. The Scottish call them neeps and mash them with potatoes and butter to eat with haggis at the New Year. Rutabagas can also be used to make a delicious soufflé to go with chicken or beef.

Celeriac

Uglier still than the rutabaga is celeriac, also known as celery root, a gnarled monster of a vegetable that, like the hero in *Beauty and the Beast,* conceals a tender heart beneath a villainous exterior. Without this root *céleri rémoulade* cannot be made.

For this delicious hors d'oeuvre, the pale white celery-flavored flesh is cut julienne and tossed in a mayonnaise dressing well seasoned with mustard. Celeriac is also good cooked and mashed, with or without potatoes. It goes wonderfully with game and with roasts, pork, ham, or chicken.

Choose the smallest and smoothest roots you can find to avoid waste. Don't buy those that have soft spots or that are too big — they will be woody inside.

Parsnips

The food writer Waverley Root, in his book *Food*, calls the parsnip "an unjustly neglected vegetable [which] lost a formerly proud position in the domain of food through the competition of the potato — an unlikely competitor, since it does not resemble the parsnip either in taste or texture."

Parsnips are at their best in midwinter. Their ivory-colored flesh adds flavor to pot-au-feu and soups. They can be mashed with potatoes and go very well with chicken, beef, or game. Those with blemishes on the skin or with split roots are perfectly good, but avoid any that have brown patches or that are pliable and wizened. Small and medium parsnips are the best; large ones can be fibrous.

Beets

Beets have a brilliant color and are an enormously versatile vegetable that is almost always served the same way — sliced in a vinegar dressing. However, beets are excellent baked in their skins for about two hours (unless very large), peeled, and served hot with salt, pepper, and butter. If you have a fireplace, bake them in the ashes.

When buying beets choose those that have at least 2 inches of stalk on top, otherwise they will lose their color when boiled. The best beets are the smallest, with smooth skins. The freshest are those sold with their leaves. These, like turnip greens, can be steamed or sautéed like spinach or chopped and stir-fried in oil with garlic.

Carrots

Carrots usually play a supporting role in meals, combined with meat or other vegetables, rather than being served on their own. Like turnips, they have made many children miserable. But they are delicious cut into rounds and simmered in water with butter, salt, and sugar, then finished with chopped parsley. A little heavy cream, brought first to a simmer, can be added at the end.

A mixture of glazed carrots and onions goes well with roast beef or lamb, as do carrots and potatoes, three-quarters cooked then sautéed in butter until crisp and garnished with parsley. They can also be sautéed with Chinese vegetables or chopped into 1-inch pieces, simmered with brown rice and onions, and served with fish or chicken, with soy sauce on the side. Baby carrots can be steamed, tossed in butter, and sprinkled with parsley. Carrots also make a delicious light soup when puréed and combined with heavy cream and chives.

Look carefully when buying carrots and avoid those that are woody or rubbery. If they are green at the top they have been exposed to the sun, and the bitter stem end will have to be cut away. Those that are sold with their tops on are fresher than those that are sold trimmed.

Potatoes

Potatoes, yams, and sweet potatoes don't suffer the stigma of the other root vegetables. In winter, potatoes fried and sprinkled with crushed juniper berries are marvelous with pork. And nothing beats the potato, sweet potato, or yam baked in a stove or fireplace and loaded with butter and freshly ground pepper.

Steamed or boiled potatoes seem a simple dish, but it is amazing how often they can go wrong; if cooked too long they become mushy. One of the best ways to cook new potatoes is to steam them. They should all be approximately the same size; otherwise the large ones won't be cooked when the small ones are ready. Test them with a thin skewer rather than the prongs of a fork, which tend to break them apart.

New potatoes should not be peeled but simply scrubbed and steamed or boiled in water with a sprig of mint, then tossed in butter and sprinkled with parsley. They also make a fine salad sliced while hot and coated with a mustardy vinaigrette dressing. The potatoes can be mixed with Spanish onion rings and black olives and fresh basil.

Do not cover cooked potatoes with a lid or they will become soft. Put them in a heated serving dish, cover them loosely with a dishcloth, and keep them in a warm place either at the back of the stove or in a warm but not hot oven.

New potatoes do not keep well. They are small and sweet and lose their flavor after a few days. It is best to buy them in small quantities. They should be small with a tender, translucent skin that scrapes off easily.

There are many varieties of potato, and those most commonly found on the market are the round white ones, the "Irish" potatoes that are all-purpose. They come mainly from the Northeast and are firm and waxy. Round-whites are superb when peeled, boiled briefly, drained, and then roasted in goose or duck fat, which gives them a wonderful crisp skin. They can also be cooked in the fat in a skillet on top of the stove.

Round-reds have a reddish-brown skin and come mainly from the Northwest. They can be used in the same way as round-whites. But beware of potatoes whose skins have been dyed red. If you notice that the water in which they have been boiled is pink, return the potatoes to the store. Dyeing, which is also undertaken on sweet potatoes, is illegal.

Russets or Idaho (russets grown in Idaho) potatoes have a thick skin and are high in starch, which gives them a fluffy texture when baked. They are also good for french fries. Long-whites, which are often called Maine or Eastern potatoes in the East, or California long-whites in the West, look like russets but have a smooth, beige skin. They are all-purpose potatoes, not as good for baking as Idahos or russets or as good for boiling as the rounds.

Potatoes can be stored in a cool place throughout the winter. Those that have been stored should not have green patches — the result of exposure to light — or sprouts. Avoid potatoes that look damp in the bag or have rotten patches. All potatoes should smell fresh and should never have loose jackets. Potatoes sold in bags are graded. U.S. Extra No.1 is the top grade; next is U.S. No.1, which is the most widely available. Graded potatoes cannot be smaller than 1⅞ inches in diameter.

When buying potatoes in early spring, before the new ones have arrived, look at them very carefully. They will have been harvested in the fall and been in storage since then. Make sure they are not spongy, soft, or starting to sprout.

Salsify

Salsify looks like a white-skinned carrot, but it tastes quite different. It is also called oyster plant because some people think it tastes like oysters. In fact it tastes more like asparagus. It is delicious puréed, sautéed in butter, or braised. Choose small ones, preferably with an inch or two of leaves on top, and avoid those that are withered or overly pliable.

Yams and Sweet Potatoes

Sweet potatoes and yams look similar and can be cooked in similar ways, but the yam is actually a climbing-vine vegetable tuber and is generally sold in Latin American markets. When buying sweet potatoes or yams, which are at their peak in fall or midwinter, choose the smallest, with smooth skins. Large ones tend to be woody and fibrous.

Yams or sweet potatoes make a festive dish sliced and baked in the oven with butter, brown sugar, cinnamon, nutmeg, and rum.

Jerusalem Artichokes

Jerusalem artichokes are knobbly and a bore to peel, but they conceal delicate flavor beneath the unprepossessing exterior. Like celeriac, their pearly flesh quickly turns brown when exposed to air.

Lemon juice should be added to the water in which they are boiled. Slice and mix with ham and toss them, while hot, in a vinaigrette dressing. They are also good in soup or mashed with butter and cream.

When buying Jerusalem artichokes, choose those with an unblemished translucent brown skin (rather like that of new potatoes). They are at their peak in autumn and winter.

Kohlrabi

Kohlrabi comes from the cabbage family but is grown for its root rather than the leaves, although the leaves can be cooked like beet or turnip greens.

The ones on the market are generally too big and must be peeled and sliced before being cooked. Small kohlrabi, if available, can be skinned and cooked whole. Kohlrabi is available from late spring to early fall and reaches its peak in the summer. The bulbs should be pale jade-green or purple, unwithered and free of gashes.

Carrot Soup

YIELD: 6 Servings

3	tablespoons butter
2	pounds carrots, diced
2	Idaho potatoes, diced
1	large onion, diced
1½	tablespoons sugar
8	cups chicken stock
	Coarse salt and freshly ground pepper to taste
½	cup finely chopped fresh parsley

1. Heat 2 tablespoons butter in a large, heavy kettle and gently sauté the carrots, potatoes, and onions over low heat for 15 minutes, covered, stirring occasionally.

2. Add the sugar, stock, salt, and pepper. Simmer gently until the vegetables are soft. Purée in a blender, but do not purée too fine. Correct seasoning.

3. Just before you are ready to serve, stir in the remaining tablespoon butter and the parsley.

4. Serve the soup in heated soup bowls.

Charred Shredded Carrots

YIELD: 4 Servings

1	pound carrots (or more if necessary to fill pan)
4	tablespoons butter
	Coarse salt and freshly ground pepper to taste

1. Shred enough carrots to fill an 8-inch cast-iron pan to the brim.

2. Place the carrots in the pan and cook over high heat. No grease or liquid will be necessary. Turn them regularly with a spatula so that the carrots will dehydrate and begin to brown evenly. When some begin to blacken and the rest are cooked and well dried out, reduce the heat and add the butter, salt, and pepper. Toss gently with a spatula to blend.

3. Serve in a heated dish.

Carrot Salad

1	pound carrots, grated
1	cup raisins
4	tablespoons olive oil
	Juice of ½ lemon
	Coarse salt and freshly
	ground pepper to taste
½	teaspon ground cumin
1	teaspoon cayenne pepper
2	tablespoons chopped
	fresh coriander or
	parsley for garnish

1. Combine the carrots and raisins in a bowl. Mix the oil and lemon juice. Season with salt, pepper, cumin, and cayenne.

3. Toss the salad and dressing thoroughly, sprinkle with coriander, and serve.

Note: Flat Arab bread (pita) goes with this hors d'oeuvre.

Celeriac with Potatoes

1	pound round-white
	potatoes
1½	pounds celeriac
	Coarse salt to taste
3	tablespoons butter
¼	cup heavy cream
	Freshly ground pepper to
	taste

1. Peel the potatoes and cut into even-sized pieces. Peel the celeriac and cut into 1-inch cubes. In separate pans, cover each with cold water, add salt, and cook the vegetables for approximately 20 minutes or until tender.

2. Purée the celery root in a food processor or blender or force through a sieve. Mash the potatoes. Mix the two with butter and cream. Season and serve.

Jerusalem Artichokes

1	pound Jerusalem
	artichokes
2	tablespoons extra-virgin
	olive oil
1	large onion, finely
	chopped
1	clove garlic, minced
1	cup peeled canned
	tomatoes, with their
	juice
2	tablespoons chopped
	fresh parsley
	Coarse salt and freshly
	ground pepper to taste

1. Peel the Jerusalem artichokes with a paring knife and set aside in cool water.

2. Heat the oil in a heavy casserole and sauté the onion and garlic until golden. Add the tomatoes and parsley and cook for 2 minutes.

3. Slice the Jerusalem artichokes into ½-inch pieces. Add to the casserole, season to taste, cover, and simmer for about 15 minutes or until tender.

Braised Jerusalem Artichokes

YIELD: 4 Servings

1½	pounds Jerusalem artichokes
2	tablespoons butter
	Coarse salt and freshly ground pepper to taste
	Approximately 2 cups chicken stock, dry cider, or water
½	cup heavy cream
	Lemon juice to taste
	Freshly grated nutmeg
2	tablespoons chopped fresh parsley

1. Peel the Jerusalem artichokes and cut into ¼-inch slices.

2. Heat the butter in a heavy frying pan and gently sauté the Jerusalem artichokes for 5 minutes.

3. Add the salt, pepper, and stock, and simmer until the Jerusalem artichokes are just tender, about 10 minutes.

4. Add the cream and continue cooking until the Jerusalem artichokes are thoroughly coated. Season with lemon juice and nutmeg. Sprinkle with parsley and serve.

Parsnip Balls

YIELD: 4 Servings

1½	pounds parsnips
2	tablespoons butter
2	tablespoons heavy cream
	Freshly grated nutmeg
	Coarse salt and freshly ground pepper to taste
2	eggs, beaten
1	cup fresh bread crumbs
	Vegetable or peanut oil for deep-frying

1. Peel the parsnips and cut them into even-sized pieces. Boil in water for 10 minutes or until tender. Drain thorougly.

2. Melt the butter and in the saucepan mash the parsnips with the butter, cream, nutmeg, salt, and pepper. Cool and beat in about 1 tablespoon of the beaten egg.

3. Form into walnut-sized balls. Dip in the remaining beaten egg and then in bread crumbs. Deep-fry in hot oil until golden. Drain on paper towels.

Note: These are good with roast chicken, beef, or lamb.

Potato Salad

1	pound new potatoes
1	cup homemade
	mayonnaise (page 196)
2	teaspoons Dijon mustard
1	small Spanish onion,
	sliced in rings
¼	cup black oil-cured olives
2	tablespoons chopped
	fresh basil
	Coarse salt and freshly
	ground pepper to taste

1. Boil the potatoes until tender. Drain and slice thick.

2. Mix the mayonnaise with the mustard. Put the potatoes into a salad bowl and coat with the mixture. Add the remaining ingredients and serve at room temperature.

Pommes Dauphinoise

1	pound round-white
	potatoes, sliced thin
½	cup heavy cream
3	tablespoons butter
	Coarse salt and freshly
	ground pepper to taste

1. Preheat the oven to 350 degrees.

2. Arrange the potatoes in layers in a buttered 9-inch baking dish, pouring on a little cream and adding butter, salt, and pepper to each layer as you go. Top with cream, salt, and pepper and bake for 30 to 45 minutes or until the potatoes are cooked and the top is browned.

Steamed New Potatoes

2	pounds small new
	potatoes
3	tablespoons unsalted
	butter
	Coarse salt and freshly
	ground pepper to taste
2	tablespoons chopped
	fresh parsley or chives

1. Thoroughly scrub the potatoes and rinse under running water. Meanwhile, bring about 4 inches of water to a boil in the bottom half of a steamer. If you don't have a steamer, boil enough salted water to cover the potatoes.

2. Cook the potatoes until they are soft when tested with a skewer. If in any doubt, taste one. They should take about 20 minutes to cook.

3. Drain the potatoes in a colander. If not serving immediately, place in a hot serving dish, cover with a dishcloth, and keep warm. Just before serving, add the butter, cut into small chunks, salt, pepper, and parsley or chives, and toss.

Rutabaga Purée

1	large rutabaga, about 1 pound
3	tablespoons butter
3	tablespoons chopped fresh chives
	Coarse salt and freshly ground pepper to taste
1	egg, beaten
¼	cup heavy cream
1	tablespoon freshly grated Parmesan cheese

1. Peel the rutabaga and cut into small, even-sized pieces about the size of a golf ball. Put in cold water to cover and simmer for about 10 minutes or until soft. Drain.

2. With a fork or an electric mixer, mash the rutabaga with 2 tablespoons butter, chives, salt, pepper, egg, and cream. Correct seasoning.

3. Sprinkle with Parmesan, dot with remaining butter, and brown under the broiler.

Turnips with Orange Sauce

	Juice of 2 oranges
1½	pounds white turnips, peeled and cut into even-sized pieces
1	cup chicken stock
	Coarse salt and freshly ground pepper to taste
	Grated rind of 1 orange

1. Put the orange juice and turnips into a saucepan. Add enough chicken stock to barely cover them. Season with salt and pepper, cover, and simmer for about 30 minutes or until tender.

2. Drain, reserving the liquid. Put the liquid into a small saucepan and boil rapidly until reduced by half. Correct seasoning. Sprinkle the grated orange rind onto the turnips and pour the sauce over them.

Note: This goes with duck, pork, or ham.

Squash

There are two basic kinds of squash, although there are varieties in each category: summer squash, which has a thin and usually edible skin, and winter squash, which has a very thick skin too tough to eat. Both are inexpensive in season.

Winter squash such as acorn, Hubbard, butternut, turban and pumpkin are among the varieties available. They are delicious with honey, brown sugar, or molasses, and they go with pork, ham, or sausages.

Acorn squash can be cut in half, dotted with butter and brown sugar, and baked in the oven. It can also be peeled, steamed, and mashed.

Winter squash should be hard and heavy, the colors on the skin pronounced. Light squashes may be old. Avoid those with cut or blemished skins.

Summer squash can be cooked in butter or with peppers, tomatoes, or cheese. Besides the common yellow crookneck or straightneck, try the pretty white pattypan. Its scalloped edges make it especially attractive when stuffed or sliced and fried with garlic in olive oil.

Zucchini are delicate, smooth-skinned green squash. Choose those that are firm and small and have brightly colored skins. Avoid those that have wrinkled skins, are blemished, or are soft and squashy to the touch.

Zucchini can be cut into 1-inch chunks and steamed or sliced thin and sautéed in olive oil and garlic and fresh chopped parsley. Or, for something different, they can be grated and then cooked in oil and garlic with lemon, or in butter and finished with cream. Herbs such as mint, coriander, chives, basil, or parsley go well with them.

Sometimes it is possible to get small ones with their blossoms still on. In Europe and Mexico the lush yellow blossoms are fried in olive oil.

Stuffed Winter Squash

1	cup pork sausage meat
1	clove garlic, chopped
1	small onion, chopped
1	cup canned Italian plum tomatoes
1	teaspoon crushed juniper berries
½	cup Arborio rice
¼	teaspoon thyme
1	teaspoon Dijon mustard
2	tablespoons chopped fresh parsley
	Coarse salt and freshly ground pepper to taste
6	medium winter squash

1. Preheat the oven to 375 degrees. Brown the sausage meat in a skillet and add the garlic and onion. Cook until soft.

2. Add the tomatoes, juniper berries, and rice, and cook for 5 minutes, stirring. Add the thyme, mustard, and parsley. Season with salt and pepper.

3. Cut the squash in half and scoop out the seeds. If the squash have very thick skin, blanch them first. Stuff the mixture into the squash halves.

4. Place the squash in a baking dish with a little water in the bottom. Cover with foil and bake for 45 minutes to 1 hour. Uncover for the last 10 minutes to brown.

Sautéed Grated Zucchini

6	small, firm zucchini
1	tablespoon olive oil
4	tablespoons butter
	Coarse salt and freshly ground pepper to taste
3	tablespoons chopped fresh basil

1. Trim the ends and grate the zucchini with a grater. Put it into a towel and squeeze out excess moisture.

2. Heat the oil and butter in a skillet. Sauté the zucchini briskly until tender, stirring occasionally. Sprinkle with salt, pepper, and basil and serve.

Tomatoes

The tomato has been disappointing its customers in recent years. Instead of a product that has ripened to a glorious red in the blazing sun, a pale and flavorless distant cousin in cellophane-covered plastic boxes has dominated the market. These tomatoes would be best used for pelting boring politicians, although, as Calvin Trillin said, they are so hard that anyone who slings them "risks being arrested for assault with intent to kill."

But when summer comes, locally grown vine-ripened tomatoes are available. And people who have grown their own find themselves with so many that their neighbors tiptoe past their garden for fear of being corralled into accepting yet another load.

There are endless ways of using tomatoes, and the two main types, plum and round, have very different uses. Round beefsteak or jubilee tomatoes are best for eating raw, for stuffing, or for broiling Provence-style sprinkled with garlic, herbs, and olive oil. They are also delicious in sandwiches made with brown bread and unsalted butter, the tomatoes sliced and sprinkled with coarse salt. As a salad, they need only olive oil and fresh basil leaves or oregano if available.

If you have a glut, tomatoes can be cooked and frozen for the winter, made into chutneys and jams, or even canned. Home canning is tricky because of the risks of botulism. This risk is less with tomatoes than other foods since most strains are strong in acid and therefore inhospitable to bacteria. Raw tomatoes can be frozen. They lose their texture but keep their flavor and can be used for cooking.

Plum tomatoes are slightly dry inside with small seeds, a thick skin, and rich flavor. These are better for stews, purées and sauces, and for drying. To peel tomatoes, pour boiling water over them, leave them for a minute or two, and slip the skins off. Cherry tomatoes, which the Europeans contend are the only vegetable grown smaller in America than in Europe, are good for hors d'oeuvres and in salads.

Green tomatoes are superb sliced and fried. They also make a remarkable chutney. When buying them, make sure they are an intense green and not pinkish. Once they start going pink, they begin to lose their tartness and their texture softens. Greengrocers, often thinking that few people want them, tend to hide green tomatoes at the bottom of the pile, so be prepared to excavate.

Mexican green tomatoes, on sale at Hispanic shops, are misnamed: They are actually a cousin of the Cape gooseberry, but their flavor is similar to that of green tomatoes. They are used in Mexican sauces, usually with chilies.

Those pale supermarket tomatoes, which come from Florida in the winter, California in the summer, have no scent because they are usually picked unripe and exposed to man-made ethylene gas to make them pink. They never do get ripe but go from rock hard to rotten. These are the ones advertised as "hard ripe, selected for slicing." The nutrition expert Beatrice Trum Hunter observes in *Consumer Beware!* that they are also often soaked in brine through which sulfur dioxide has bubbled for five days. "They can be kept undamaged for an additional month in fresh water," she writes. "Tomatoes have been kept 'fresh' with this method for as long as four years."

When buying tomatoes, choose those — if you can find them — that are a vivid red, soft but not mushy to the touch, with a pleasant scent. If they have green or yellow patches, they have been burned by the sun and should be avoided. Also shun those with leathery, dark patches. This is blossom end rot, caused by drought following a period of rainy weather.

Don't refrigerate unripe tomatoes; leave them on the windowsill to ripen. If you put them into a paper bag with an apple, banana, or ripe tomato, they will turn pink more quickly because these give off a natural ethylene gas. But still, they will never have the flavor of tomatoes properly ripened on the vine.

Watch out for greasy tomatoes. These have been sprayed with paraffin to make them shiny. In packing houses they are run over a grader and through a washing solution that contains the wax. The wax is approved by the federal Food and Drug Administration, but some people, including Mrs. Hunter, call it a potential carcinogen, citing an article by Elise Jerard in the magazine *Modern Nutrition*. In any event, it is unpleasant, and to get rid of it you must wash the tomatoes in plain, unscented kitchen soap and water. Although small growers do not have the waxing machines, be wary of expensive large tomatoes labeled organic and sold at some neighborhood greengrocers. They may be coated with this wax.

In the winter most tomatoes come from Florida and Mexico. Florida tomatoes, in season from November to the end of June, are mass-harvested and treated with gas. Mexican tomatoes, on the market from January to the end of April, have more flavor since they are picked ripe. They are also smaller. In much smaller quantity, Israeli tomatoes, grown hydroponically — in greenhouses in water containing all the necessary nutrients and without sprays — are flown to some metropolitan markets. These are vine-ripened and the best winter tomatoes available. But in general you are better off with canned tomatoes, such as the excellent Italian ones from San Marzano, in the winter.

Tomatoes are one of the easiest vegetables to grow. Apartment dwellers can grow cherry tomatoes in tubs and clay pots on a sunny balcony. Larger plants can be grown along trellises. Modern disease-resistant tomatoes are the best to grow; the soil should be prepared with compost and high-potash fertilizer.

Although tomatoes are now grown in every state except Alaska, Americans were slow to use them at first. Being a member of the Solanaceae family, which includes deadly nightshade (and potatoes, eggplant, and peppers), tomatoes were thought to be poisonous or to cause gout or cancerous growths.

In the fifteenth century, the Spanish brought the tomato from the New World to Europe, where it was viewed with great suspicion at first and used as an ornamental plant. The Italians, who called it pomo d'oro, or golden apple, because the tomatoes were small and orange-yellow, began cooking with it in the middle of the sixteenth century. In France it was thought to be an aphrodisiac and was called pomme d'amour, or love apple. Americans 100 years ago were still wary, and cooked tomatoes for at least three hours before eating them to rid them of their "poisons."

Tomato Soup

YIELD: 4 Servings

2	strips bacon
1	medium onion
2	tablespoons butter
2	pounds ripe plum tomatoes
1	tablespoon thyme (fresh if available)
1	bay leaf
	Coarse salt and freshly ground pepper to taste
4	cups chicken stock
½	cup heavy cream
	Freshly grated nutmeg

1. Chop the bacon and the onion and fry in the butter in a heavy saucepan until the onion is soft. Peel the tomatoes by pouring boiling water over them, letting them stand for a few minutes, then slipping their skins off. Add the thyme, bay leaf, salt and pepper, and tomatoes to the saucepan. Sauté for 5 minutes.

2. Add the chicken stock. Bring to a boil. Cover and simmer over low heat for 15 minutes. Stir in the cream and nutmeg to taste. Correct seasoning.

Piedmont Tomato Tart

1	8-inch pie shell, baked for 10 minutes
2	pounds plum tomatoes
½	cup cornmeal
3 to 4	tablespoons butter, preferably clarified
1	tablespoon olive oil
	Coarse salt and freshly ground pepper to taste
2	tablespoons freshly grated Parmesan cheese
3	tablespoons chopped fresh basil

1. Preheat the oven to 450 degrees.

2. Meanwhile, slice the tomatoes evenly, about ¼ inch thick. Keep the ends for soups.

3. Coat the slices with cornmeal and fry them at moderately high heat a few at a time in 2 tablespoons of the butter and the olive oil. Turn them once so that they are golden brown on both sides. Add more butter as necessary. If the butter burns, wipe out the pan and start again. Drain the tomatoes on paper towels and season with salt and pepper.

4. Arrange the tomatoes, tightly packed, in the pie shell. Sprinkle with cheese and a tablespoon or so of melted clarified butter. Bake at 450 degrees for 10 minutes, then turn the oven down to 350 degrees for an additional 30 minutes. Sprinkle with basil and serve.

Note: This pie may be served hot or cold. It can also be garnished with anchovies. Clarified butter burns less easily than regular butter; to clarify, bring the butter to a simmer and skim off the foam until the butter is clear.

Italian Stuffed Tomatoes

4	large round tomatoes
½	cup Arborio rice
¼	cup chopped fresh basil leaves
½	teaspoon sugar
¼	teaspoon oregano
	Coarse salt and freshly ground pepper to taste
1½	tablespoons olive oil

1. Preheat the oven to 400 degrees. Cut a lid off each tomato at the stalk end and reserve. With a spoon, remove the pulp and put it into a bowl. Purée the pulp in a blender or food mill.

2. Measure 1½ cups puréed pulp. Mix with the rice, basil leaves, sugar, oregano, salt, and pepper. Stuff the mixture into the tomatoes, adding the remaining tomato juice if there is room. If not, reserve the juice for soup or stock.

3. Cover the tomatoes with their lids, arrange in a greased baking dish, and sprinkle with olive oil. Bake 45 minutes to 1 hour. Test the rice. It should be cooked but still firm (al dente).

4. Serve hot or at room temperature.

Tomato Sauce

YIELD: Approximately 3 Cups

3	pounds plum tomatoes
1	large onion, chopped
4	tablespoons extra-virgin olive oil
	Coarse salt and freshly ground pepper to taste
1	tablespoon sugar
1	tablespoon oregano and/or 2 tablespoons chopped fresh basil

1. Peel the tomatoes by pouring boiling water over them, letting them sit for a minute, and then slipping their skins off.

2. In a heavy saucepan, cook the onion until soft in 1 tablespoon olive oil. Add the tomatoes with salt, pepper, sugar, and oregano and/or basil. Simmer for about 45 minutes.

3. Put the sauce into a container and cover with 1 inch of olive oil.

Note: This sauce can be frozen. It will also keep for several months sealed with the olive oil. It is good on pasta or in soups or stews.

Fried Green Tomatoes

YIELD: 4 Servings

1½	pounds green tomatoes
	Tabasco sauce
	Worcestershire sauce
¾	cup flour
	Coarse salt and freshly ground pepper to taste
½	teaspoon cayenne pepper
	Approximately ¾ cup peanut or vegetable oil

1. Cut the tomatoes into slices about ¼ inch thick. Sprinkle the slices with Tabasco and Worcestershire sauce.

2. Combine the flour with salt, pepper, and cayenne pepper. Put in a plastic bag. Add the tomato slices, a few at a time, and toss to coat with the flour. Shake off excess.

3. Heat about ¼ inch of oil in a skillet and fry the tomatoes, adding them a few at a time without overcrowding, until golden brown on each side. Drain on paper towels.

4. Serve immediately. If kept, the tomatoes will turn soggy.

Green Tomato Chutney

4	*pounds green tomatoes, sliced*
2	*large onions, sliced*
1	*cup dark brown sugar, firmly packed*
½	*cup raisins*
2	*fresh green chilies, minced*
	Coarse salt and freshly ground pepper to taste
3	*tablespoons mustard seed*
1	*tablespoon minced fresh ginger*
2½	*cups white wine vinegar*
1	*tablespoon ground coriander seeds*

1. Combine all the ingredients in a large kettle and simmer, uncovered, for about 2½ hours or until the mixture has thickened.

2. Pour into sterilized jars, seal tightly, and keep in a dark cool place for at least 6 weeks before using.

Truffles

Truffles are one of the world's greatest delicacies. In season in the fall and winter, these strange, wrinkled, brownish or black knobs should be shared only with those who are passionate about them because they are very expensive, running $35 an ounce. "The truffle is not at all a positive aphrodisiac," wrote the famous French gastronome, Brillat-Savarin, "but it can, on certain occasions, make women more tender and men more amiable."

White truffles are my favorites, and these are eaten raw, sliced very fine with a grater over risotto or over fresh pasta with cream sauce, or mixed into a green salad. They make a remarkably sensual dish that is subtle, simple, and yet very pungent, with an aroma that can fill a room.

Black truffles are superb with a salad made with new potatoes. The potatoes are peeled, sliced, and coated with an extra-virgin olive oil. You then add a few chopped shallots and plenty of chopped black truffles. They also go well with chicken or veal. The very rich in France sometimes wrap whole truffles in bacon and cook them in the oven.

Truffles, which grow on the roots of oak trees, are hunted by specially trained dogs in the regions of Tuscany, Piedmont, and Romagna in Italy, and in Périgord in France, usually by pigs, who have a passion for them. The white truffle of Italy is different from the Périgord black from France. It is bigger and stronger in flavor, and many devotees prefer it.

"In the height of the season," Elizabeth David writes in *Italian Food*, "white truffles large as tennis balls are to be seen in shops in Turin, which at the same season are wonderfully decorative with orange and brown and yellow funghi, every kind of feathered game, lovely cream cheeses and rich looking sausages."

In Bologna, the truffles are served with turkey or chicken breasts cooked in butter and covered with Parmesan cheese. They are delicious on agnellotti, the crescent-shaped dumplings that are a specialty of Piedmont.

Fresh truffles can be kept for a week or two in closed jars in raw rice, which absorbs moisture. But once they have been cut into, they deteriorate rapidly.

Eating truffles for the first time can have all the excitement of the first oyster or sea urchin or the first mouthful of caviar. On a holiday in Venice in October several years ago, I was dining with a friend who ordered a plate of pasta. He sat glumly while the waiter proceeded to scrape something that looked like wood shavings onto his plate. After the waiter had gone, he methodically pushed the pieces aside.

"I've no idea what this stuff is," he said, annoyed at the intrusion into his simple meal. I was curious and dipped in with my fork. From then on, recklessly, without regard for the cost, white truffles became the staple of all our meals in Venice.

We finally scraped enough funds together to buy a small truffle to share with friends at home. There was only enough for a tiny shaving on each plate, and everyone sat in bewilderment, trying to understand what was supposed to be so marvelous about a dish that tasted like nothing more than plain spaghetti, rather cold at that.

Their confusion illustrated an important point: At least an ounce of truffle is needed for eight people. If there isn't enough, the pronounced flavor of the truffle won't come through.

Even though truffles may be expensive, pasta is not. A delicious meal that is not prohibitively expensive can be prepared from linguini or fettuccine tossed in cream and sprinkled with truffles and freshly grated Parmesan cheese, accompanied by a salad and a bottle of Chianti.

2	3-pound chickens
1	1½-ounce jar fresh truffles
2	shallots
1	tablespoon butter
½	pound pork sausage meat
¼	cup fresh bread crumbs
½	cup milk
½	cup cognac
1	pound chestnuts, peeled
2	large mushrooms, sliced
	Coarse salt and freshly ground pepper to taste
1	teaspoon thyme
½	pound small pork sausages
1	carrot, finely chopped
1	small onion, finely chopped
1	stalk celery, finely chopped
1	sprig fresh thyme (or ½ teaspoon dried)
1	bay leaf
2	sprigs parsley
1	cup chicken stock
1	cup port wine

1. The night before, wipe the chickens dry with paper towels and insert 2 or 3 slices of truffle under the skin.

2. Preheat the oven to 350 degrees. Chop the shallots and cook them in the butter until soft. Add the sausage meat and brown, stirring to prevent it from burning. Meanwhile, soak the bread crumbs in the milk.

3. Add the bread crumbs, squeezed dry, and the cognac. Coarsely chop the chestnuts, reserving a few whole ones for decoration. Add the chestnuts, the mushrooms, and the remaining truffle, cut into small sticks. Season with salt, pepper, and thyme.

4. Stuff the chickens with the mixture and sew up the cavities with kitchen thread. Rub the chickens with salt and pepper, and cover the breasts loosely with aluminum foil. Place in a roasting pan with the sausages and roast for 30 minutes, basting frequently and turning the sausages.

5. Remove the foil and add the carrot, onion, celery, thyme, bay leaf, and parsley to the pan and cook with the chickens for 30 minutes.

6. When the chickens' juices are yellow and only faintly pink, transfer the chickens to a heated serving dish. Cover loosely with the foil and allow to rest at room temperature.

7. Skim the fat and the chopped vegetables from the pan. Add the chicken stock and bring to a slow boil. Reduce to about 1½ cups, add the port, and correct seasoning. Strain and pour over the chickens. Garnish with sausages and reserved chestnuts.

Note: Recommended are the Petrossian truffles, available at Bloomingdale's in New York.

Watercress and Radishes

Watercress is extremely useful. It lends its tart, peppery taste to salads all year round. It can be tossed with endive or tiny flowerets of broccoli and small pieces of orange, and coated with a vinaigrette dressing. Watercress perks up stocks, garnishes lamb chops or chicken, and makes a delicious summer soup. It is inexpensive but extremely perishable and doesn't usually last the night well in the refrigerator.

When buying watercress choose bunches that are bright and fresh looking and avoid those with yellowed leaves. I usually cut the stems off with a sharp knife while the watercress is still tied and then wash the leaves.

A watercress salad goes especially well with duck or pork, as does the following combination with radishes. Use fresh, sprightly radishes. The best are sold with their leaves. If they are yellowed, the radishes are stale.

There are long, sweet white radishes, also known as icicle radishes, and black radishes with white flesh.

French radishes, small and sweet, are the best of the red radishes. At the end of the day, for a snack, I used to pluck them from the garden, rinse them, and dip them into unsalted butter and pepper. It was a wonderful way to begin the evening.

Radish and Watercress Salad

YIELD: 4 Servings

1	bunch radishes
1	bunch watercress
2	tablespoons sesame seeds
1	clove garlic, crushed
½	teaspoon soy sauce
1	tablespoon red wine vinegar
2	tablespoons lemon or orange juice
¼	cup sesame oil
	Coarse salt and freshly ground pepper to taste

1. Trim the stalks from the radishes and slice the radishes thin. Trim the stalks from the watercress. Combine the radishes and watercress leaves in a salad bowl.

2. Put the sesame seeds in a small pan and brown lightly over low heat.

3. Put the seeds in a small bowl and mix together with the garlic, soy sauce, vinegar, lemon or orange juice, and sesame oil. Season and pour the mixture onto the salad vegetables, first removing the garlic.

Watercress and Broccoli Salad

YIELD: 6 to 8 Servings

2	bunches watercress
1	bunch broccoli
1	clove garlic, crushed
2	tablespoons raspberry vinegar (if available) or red wine vinegar
	Approximately ¼ cup extra-virgin olive oil
	Coarse salt and freshly ground pepper to taste

1. Trim the stalks from the watercress while the bunch is still tied. Wash the watercress and dry.

2. Trim the stalks from the broccoli and divide the flowerets into pieces the size of a thumb.

3. Combine the garlic, vinegar, oil, salt, and pepper. Mix and correct seasoning. If a stronger garlic flavor is desired, chop the garlic fine and include. Otherwise, remove the garlic clove and pour the dressing over the salad. Toss and serve.

Cold Watercress Soup

YIELD: 6 Servings

1	pound potatoes, peeled and sliced
1	pound medium yellow onions, chopped
1½	quarts chicken stock
2	bunches watercress
½	cup heavy cream
	Juice of ½ lemon
	Coarse salt and freshly ground white pepper to taste
4	tablespoons chopped fresh chives

1. Simmer the potatoes and onions in the chicken stock for 40 minutes. Trim the watercress stalks. Add the watercress, reserving a few leaves for decoration, and simmer for 5 minutes.

2. Purée the mixture in a food mill and cool overnight.

3. Stir in the cream, lemon juice, and seasoning. Serve, sprinkled with chives, in individual soup bowls.

Celery, Fennel, and Endive

Celery, fennel, and endive are all good raw or cooked. They take especially well to braising, sauteing in butter, or cooking au gratin. Celery and fennel can be used interchangeably to flavor stocks, soups, or stews or as a vegetable dish.

The French eat celery raw with sweet butter and coarse sea salt and bread; the British with Stilton or Cheddar cheese. Raw fennel is delicious sliced and served with goat's cheese, a grainy fresh Parmesan, or *alla pinzimonio* — with a lemon-and-Tuscan-olive-oil dip. Cooked, it goes especially well with pork chops or fish, enlivened with a spoonful of Pernod or anisette.

When buying celery make sure the stalks are crisp and not flexible and the leaves bright green. If the leaves have been cut off and there are stalks missing at the base, the celery is past its prime. To reconstitute tired celery, wrap it in wet paper towels and stand it in a glass of water for an hour.

Celery can be stewed with butter and lemon juice, braised in chicken stock, or cooked with bacon and canned Italian plum tomatoes and chopped onions.

Fennel looks rather like a bulbous head of celery, but it has a slight taste of anise. It is sometimes called Florence fennel so as not to confuse it with the herb fennel. It has feathery green leaves that can be used for flavoring sauces or in salads. You can't tell by looking what the flavor will be like. Sometimes heads browned on the outside are perfect inside, sometimes the pristine ones turn out to be tasteless. Fennel is not an economical vegetable. Often the outer layer is so stringy it has to be cut away. Heads can be cut into quarters and braised with tomatoes and olives à la Niçoise. Fennel can also be cooked like celery.

Endive, although it is markedly different in texture from celery or fennel, being whitish and leafy, takes especially well to braising. It was first raised in Belgium, where it was discovered that if grown in the dark, the leaves do not turn green and bitter. Endive can also be cut into ribbons and simmered in stock to cover, with butter and lemon juice. When the stock has almost evaporated, stir in a few tablespoons of heavy cream, enough to make a light sauce, and simmer for a few minutes until the liquid thickens and coats the endive leaves. Both these dishes go well with roasts and chops. It is also a fine salad vegetable mixed with greens or with pieces of orange and watercress.

In the stores, endive comes carefully wrapped in blue paper to protect it from the light. If it is exposed to the light, endive will turn brown. Choose those heads underneath that are white and smooth with no blemishes.

Celery Hearts with Parmesan Cheese

YIELD: 4 Servings

2	celery hearts
¼	pound Parmesan cheese
	Lemon juice
	Extra-virgin olive oil
	Coarse salt and freshly
	ground pepper to taste

1. Slice the celery hearts into thin crescents. Shave the Parmesan into thin flakes.

2. Mix the cheese with the celery and coat with lemon juice and olive oil. Season with salt and pepper.

Note: This is good as an hors d'oeuvre or as a salad after a main course of grilled meat.

Braised Celery Hearts or Endive

YIELD: 4 Servings

4	celery hearts or endive
1	tablespoon peanut or
	vegetable oil
2	tablespoons butter
½	cup chicken stock
	Coarse salt and freshly
	ground pepper to taste
2	tablespoons chopped
	fresh chervil or parsley

1. Preheat the oven to 350 degrees. Place the hearts or endive in a shallow flameproof dish with the remaining ingredients except the chervil or parsley.

2. Cover and bake until the celery or endive is tender and the liquid has reduced to a syrupy glaze, about 20 to 30 minutes for celery, less for endive. Sprinkle with chervil or parsley and serve.

Raw Fennel with Oil and Lemon

YIELD: 6 Servings

3	medium heads fennel
	Juice of 1 lemon
	Approximately 3
	tablespoons extra-virgin
	olive oil
	Coarse salt and freshly
	ground pepper to taste

1. Remove and discard the tough outer stalks of the fennel. Cut the fennel into thin slices. Drop the slices into 2 cups cold water to which you have added half the lemon juice.

2. Drain and dry with paper towels.

3. Combine the oil, salt, pepper, and remaining lemon juice. Toss thoroughly with the fennel and serve.

Note: Fennel can also be cut into quarters or wedges and dipped into the seasoned olive oil.

Fruit

Apples

Apples are a useful fruit, enjoyed at any time of day. Their flavor complements both delicate and rich meats. Cooked with butter and cream, apples add a fragrant touch to such meats as veal, chicken, and pheasant. Puréed or sautéed, they are delicious with robust meats such as bacon, pork, goose, ham, and sausages — especially *boudin noir* (black sausage). Apples can be mixed with prunes and stuffed into a pork loin, or combined with chestnuts and sausages for turkey. They also have the largest dessert repertory of any member of the fruit family.

Fall is the time of year for the widest choice and best quality on the market. If you buy apples in quantity, store them in a cool, dry, dark place and not touching each other. Try to avoid apples that have been coated with paraffin to make them shiny. The wax makes the skins greasy, and they must be peeled or carefully scrubbed with kitchen soap and water before eating or cooking.

It is important to choose the right apples for cooking, otherwise you can end up with a disaster. Red delicious, for example, will disintegrate into a tasteless mush. The best apples for cooking are those that are sweet without being too sweet, and firm and juicy with plenty of flavor. Use hard, crisp McIntosh, Granny Smiths, russets, semisweet Cortlands, or tart greening apples. The hard apples take longer to cook than the softer-fleshed ones. Rome apples are large, dry, and semisweet and good for baking. They can be cored, their cavities filled with sugar, butter, or raisins, and served with thick cream. Golden delicious retain their shape well when cooked, which makes them useful for open tarts, but they do not have much flavor and need a dose of cinnamon, lemon peel, or cloves to perk them up. The following recipes use apples in very different ways. Sautéed with bacon, they make a splendid late supper or breakfast dish. They make a particularly good sauce with brandy and cream for chicken. The apples baked in orange sauce are an unusual dinner-party dish and can be made a day or two in advance. Apple Charlotte is an economical and rather rich dessert, ideal for a large dinner party. It can be prepared ahead of time.

Canadian Bacon with Onion and Apple

YIELD: 4 Servings

2 to 3	tablespoons butter
1	pound thick-cut Canadian bacon
1	large white onion, cut in rings
2	medium apples, unpeeled
	Freshly ground black pepper
1	tablespoon chopped fresh parsley

1. Melt the butter in a heavy frying pan and lightly fry the bacon until golden. Remove and drain on paper towels. Keep warm.

2. Fry the onion rings in the remaining fat until soft. Add the apples, cored and cut into rings ½ inch thick. Cover and simmer for 5 to 10 minutes, shaking the pan from time to time to prevent sticking.

3. Return the bacon to the pan and heat through. Season with pepper, sprinkle with parsley, and serve.

Note: This dish is excellent with mashed potatoes or fried eggs.

Chicken with Apples

YIELD: 4 Servings

3	medium cooking apples
1½	tablespoons butter
1	teaspoon safflower or peanut oil
1	3-pound chicken, cut into serving pieces
	Coarse salt and freshly ground pepper to taste
½	cup heavy cream
¼	cup Calvados or cognac

1. Peel, core, and slice the apples ¼ inch thick. Fry in the butter in a large, heavy frying pan until golden. Remove and set aside.

2. Add the oil to the frying pan. Fry the chicken pieces until golden, turn down heat, cover, and cook over low heat about 20 minutes or until done. Remove to a heated serving dish.

3. Return the apple slices to the frying pan and heat through. Remove and arrange around the chicken. Season with salt and pepper.

4. Pour the cream into the frying pan and scrape up the cooking juices. Add the Calvados or cognac, bring to a boil, and pour the sauce over the chicken. Serve immediately.

Note: This dish is good with rice.

2	oranges
6	large apples (preferably Rome beauty)
	Juice of 1 lemon
4	tablespoons butter
½	cup sugar
¼	cup Calvados or cognac
¾	cup dry white wine
½	cup red currant jelly
½	cup heavy cream

1. Preheat the oven to 325 degrees. Carefully pare the peel from the oranges and cut julienne. Simmer the strips for 10 minutes in water. Drain, rinse, and set aside. Squeeze the juice from the oranges, strain, and set aside.

2. Peel and core the apples, put them into a bowl with water to cover, and add the lemon juice to keep them from discoloring.

3. Drain the apples. Using 2 tablespoons butter, grease a flameproof baking dish just large enough to hold the apples without crowding. Put 1 teaspoon butter in each apple. Sprinkle with sugar. Add 2 tablespoons Calvados or cognac, the white wine, and the orange juice. Bring to a simmer on top of the stove, cover loosely with foil, and put into the oven.

4. Bake 25 minutes, checking occasionally to make sure that the liquid remains at a simmer and that the apples are not overcooking. If they cook too long, they will collapse.

5. When the apples are done, arrange them on a serving dish. Add the jelly to their cooking juices and bring to a boil. Stir in remaining Calvados and the orange peel. Cook for 1 to 2 minutes or until the sauce is thick enough to coat the spoon. Pour over the apples. Serve at room temperature, with the cream in a small jug.

6	pounds apples
2	lemons
	Approximately 1 cup dark brown sugar
	Approximately 1 pound sweet butter
2	loaves homemade-type white bread, sliced

1. Preheat the oven to 350 degrees.

2. Peel and core the apples and cut them into thin slices. Melt 3 tablespooons butter in a saucepan and add the apples with the lemon juice and 2 tablespoons finely diced peel. Add brown sugar to taste (the amount depends on the sweetness of the apples) and just enough water to prevent the apples from sticking to the pan. Cook the apples for about 30 minutes or until they begin to get mushy.

3. Meanwhile, put the remaining butter in a saucepan and bring to a simmer gently, without browning. Remove the foam that rises to the surface and set the butter aside.

4. Remove the crusts from the bread. Dip the slices of bread into the butter and with them line the sides and bottom of two medium-sized ovenproof baking dishes.

5. Arrange the apples in layers in the dishes and sprinkle with sugar. The dish can be prepared to this point ahead of time.

6. Bake, uncovered, for 1 hour.

Note: This is good served with heavy cream or ice cream.

Citrus Fruits

Anyone who has ever been in countries with hot climates knows how tempting the citrus fruits are in the markets. Tiny mandarins, bright lemons and limes, sometimes complete with their green leaves to show how fresh they are, are heaped next to fragrant pyramids of oranges and grapefruit, one of each kind always sliced in half so the shopper knows what the fruit will be like inside.

Here, however, things are a little different. About one-third of our oranges and tangelos are dyed. Most citrus fruit is then coated with paraffin to give it a shine. Dyed oranges look like "orange drink." Americans, however, are so used to this unlikely hue that in certain plush hotels in Mexico oranges with green skins are served already peeled so that tourists will not see the greenness of the outer skin and think that the orange is unripe.

When buying citrus fruit the rule of thumb is always to choose the heavier fruit; they will have the most juice. Don't pick those that are withered looking, soft, or bruised, and when buying packages of fruit check carefully that they contain no rotten pieces. The best have thin skins — those with thick skins often have tiny amounts of actual fruit inside. If they are green or russeted this means nothing in relation to quality. Citrus fruits often turn partly green again afer being picked, and the natural russet color affects only the look of the fruit's skin, not its taste.

Citrus fruits can be voluntarily graded U.S. Fancy or the lesser U.S. No.1 but most fruits are not graded. All are high in Vitamin C.

Oranges from Florida (where most of our juice oranges are produced) are treated with ethylene gas and a citrus red dye No. 2 — a carcinogen for animals — before being coated with paraffin. Before being dyed the oranges are treated with detergent and fungicide. Oranges from California and Israel have an orange color, and although they are treated with paraffin they are not artificially colored. Growers in Florida contend that since few people eat orange peel very often, the amount of dye consumed is harmless. Many grapefruit, limes, and lemons are also coated with paraffin.

For juice, the better buys are thin-skinned oranges. Navel oranges, from Florida and California, have plenty of juice and peel easily. They are virtually seedless and at their peak from late fall into midspring. Thin-skinned Valencia oranges can be used both for eating and juice, but I prefer them for juice since the segments are difficult to separate. Parson Browns and Hamlins are also good juice oranges.

Eating citrus on the market include navels, temples, mandarins, tangelos, and tangerines, most of which come from California. Clementines come from crossbreeding oranges and tangerines. Temple oranges have a thick, loose skin and are between classic oranges and mandarins. Tart Seville oranges are used for marmalades and liqueurs. Tangerines, in season in winter, are a fine fruit with which to end a long, rich dinner, and their dried peel is excellent for flavoring sauces, lamb, and beef stews.

It is cheaper and better to squeeze your own orange juice than to buy expensive "freshly squeezed " juice in containers. It often has been sitting around long enough to have lost most of its vitamin C, and the price is sometimes comparable to that of a bottle of wine. Frozen orange juice is better than canned or orange juice sold in cartons, provided it has been kept properly frozen. It is much cheaper and tastes better.

Grapefruit is grown in Texas, Florida, California, and Arizona. It comes white- or pink-fleshed — with no discernable difference in taste between the two — and is usually served at breakfast cut into segments with a serrated knife. It can also be pleasant in shrimp salad or combined with sliced, fresh-cooked artichoke bottoms and shallots in a vinaigrette dressing.

The best lemons are those gorgeous specimens shown in Dutch paintings, cut and half-peeled with tempting, shiny flesh, placed next to a green glass goblet and perhaps a brace of pheasant. Almost all our lemons come from California or Florida. Limes come from Mexico, the Caribbean, Florida, and California. They are cheapest and at their peak in the summer. Choose limes or lemons that are heavy for their size, fragrant, with glossy, bright skins. The skins may be thick or thin, but they should not have soft spots or be hard and dry.

Of all citrus fruits, lemons and limes have the most uses in the kitchen. They cut the fat in fried foods, they go with fish, and they stop vegetables such as avocados and artichokes from going brown when cut. They perk up sauces and salad dressings and make a great summer drink.

After school we used to drink pitchers of limeade or lemonade to go with homemade chocolate cake. They were my favorite drinks until I discovered wine. At school concerts, my friends and I would sit in the front rows and suck lemons because we were told that it would make the oboist's mouth water. She never looked at us, so I never found out if the trick would work.

Oranges in Red Wine

6	oranges
1	cup dry red wine
1	cup water
½ to ¾	cup sugar, depending on sweetness of oranges
4	whole cloves
	Dash of freshly grated nutmeg
	Cinnamon stick
½	lemon, sliced

1. Peel the skin from 3 of the oranges and reserve. Cut away the fibrous membranes and slice all the oranges. Put the slices in a shallow dish.

2. Cut the orange peel julienne, blanch, and set aside.

3. Put the remaining ingredients in a saucepan and simmer for 10 minutes. Strain onto the oranges. Sprinkle with the orange peel and chill overnight. Serve with sugar cookies.

Homemade Lemonade or Limeade

4	cups water
5	lemons (or limes)
	Honey to taste

1. Bring the water to a boil. Meanwhile, squeeze the lemons or limes and discard any seeds.

2. Put the lemon or lime juice into a pitcher and add the water. Stir in honey until the desired sweetness has been reached. Cool and refrigerate until chilled.

Lemon Soufflé

5	eggs, separated
½	cup sugar
	Juice and grated peel of 2 lemons
1	envelope (1 tablespoon) unflavored gelatin
½	cup heavy cream
½	cup toasted slivered almonds

1. Beat the egg yolks with the sugar until lemon colored. Add the lemon juice and peel, then whisk over low heat until thick.

2. Meanwhile, dissolve the gelatin in ½ cup warm water.

3. Whip the egg whites until stiff. Whip the cream.

4. Add the gelatin to the lemon mixture and cool. Fold in the egg whites. Reserve about ¼ cup of cream for the top of the soufflé. Fold the remaining cream into the lemon mixture and pour into a 2-quart soufflé dish. Cover with remaining cream and chill until set, preferably overnight.

5. Just before serving, sprinkle with the almonds.

Grapefruit Salad

1	grapefruit
3	endive, cut in thin lengthwise slices
2	bunches watercress, leaves only (save stems for soup)
6	tablespoons olive oil
1	tablespoon white wine vinegar
	Coarse salt and freshly ground pepper to taste
2 to 3	tablespoons pomegranate seeds (optional)

1. Section and seed the grapefruit. Remove membranes and cut the sections crosswise into ½-inch slices.

2. In a large salad bowl, combine the grapefruit pieces, sliced endive, and watercress leaves.

3. Combine the oil and vinegar, add salt and pepper, and mix. Pour over the salad and toss gently but thoroughly. Sprinkle with the pomegranate seeds if desired, and serve.

Cranberries

Cranberries are the fruit of a low, creeping evergreen plant that is native to North America. They were used by the Indians for both food and medicinal purposes and were not cultivated until the nineteenth century. Now they are grown in New England and come on the market in late fall and early winter.

To test a cranberry, see if it will bounce. If is doesn't, it is overripe and mushy or not ripe at all. If buying cranberries in bags, make sure they are firm and shiny.

Cranberries can be used in many dishes in which their flavor changes completely, such as soups or stews. They are also served with turkey and used in sauces and preserves.

The following recipe makes an unusual beef stew.

Beef Stew with Cranberries

YIELD: 6 Servings

2	ounces salt pork, diced
1	tablespoon butter
1	tablespoon olive oil
4	shallots, diced
2	cloves garlic, minced
2½	pounds stewing beef, cut into 2-inch cubes
	Flour for dredging
1	pound fresh cranberries
2	cups dry red wine
1	cup beef stock
1	tablespoon brown sugar
	Bouquet garni (thyme, parsley, and bay leaf tied in cheesecloth)
	Coarse salt and freshly ground pepper to taste
¼	cup Madeira
1	tablespoon softened butter
	Chopped fresh parsley for garnish

1. In a heavy casserole, fry the salt pork in the butter and oil. Add the shallots and the garlic and cook until softened.

2. Roll the beef cubes in the flour and brown in the fat. Add the cranberries, wine, stock, sugar, bouquet garni, salt, and pepper.

3. Cover and simmer for 2 hours or until the meat is tender.

4. Remove the meat to a heated serving dish. Strain the sauce through a sieve, squeezing as much juice as you can from the cranberries. In a small saucepan, boil the cranberry sauce with the Madeira. Remove from heat and swirl in the butter. Pour onto the meat. Sprinkle with parsley and serve.

Dried Fruits

Dried fruits are at their best in the winter. Prunes, apricots, figs, apple rings, dates, pears, peaches, raisins (dried muscat grapes), currants (small, black seedless grapes), and sultanas (seedless white grapes), mostly from California, are sold loose by the pound in many markets. They can be delicious combined with meat, fish, or poultry or simply stewed on their own for a winter dessert with a dash of bourbon or rum. They are also good eaten raw.

The combination of the sweet flavor of dried fruits with meats in savory stews or pilafs has long been popular in North Africa and many Arabian countries. Lamb is simmered with prunes, apricots, and honey; you simply place the lamb in a casserole with the dried fruits, onion, garlic, spices, and a touch of honey. You can also simmer chicken with peaches, prunes, dates, or raisins as they do in Morocco. Raisins also go into pilafs.

In Sweden, roast pork loin stuffed with prunes is a favorite winter dish. The juices are scraped up to make a rich, dark sauce that is sopped up with mashed potatoes. Prunes make a superb stuffing for goose and are also good stewed with red cabbage, with rabbit, and even with eel. In France freshwater eel is stewed with prunes, brandy, and salt pork or mushrooms.

Dried fruits can be used in many imaginative ways. Dried apples and raisins can be eaten with meusli, the Swiss breakfast cereal. Pheasant or tongue can be served with raisin-and-Madeira sauce. Dried pears can be made into compote or used for flavoring sweet breads. Apricots make a tart and fragrant dessert simmered with water and puréed. They are also delightful in stuffings for lamb or chicken.

When buying dried fruit make sure it feels slightly pliant and moist. Avoid fruit that is shriveled and dry. Dates should not have sugar encrusted on the skin but should be shiny and soft. Apples should be plump, not leathery or dried out. Apricots, prunes, and raisins should be moist and shiny.

The best fruits with the most flavor are those that are naturally sun-dried without chemicals. Fruits treated with sulphur dioxide look deceptively good, often better than naturally dried fruits, because they plump up beautifully and have a bright color. Many dried fruits, especially those sold in packages in supermarkets, are exposed to sulphur dioxide and artificially dried. Some are even treated with liquid paraffin to prevent them from becoming too dried. Check the label to see if the fruit has been treated with sulphur dioxide. Dried fruits sold in health food stores are more likely to be sun-dried and untreated by chemicals. Shop for these in season, during the fall and winter months.

Roast Loin of Pork with Prunes

YIELD: 6 Servings

1	*pound dried pitted prunes*
½	*cup dry red wine*
1	*5-pound pork loin roast*
2	*cloves garlic*
1	*tablespoon dried*
	rosemary (or 2
	tablespoons fresh)
	Coarse salt and freshly
	ground pepper to taste
2	*tablespoons chopped*
	fresh parsley

1. Soak the prunes for 1 hour in the wine. Reserve the wine.

2. Preheat the oven to 375 degrees. Between each rib of pork make incisions big enough to hold 2 prunes, but do not cut right through the meat.

3. Slice the garlic and place a slice in each incision along with two prunes, a pinch of rosemary, and salt and pepper.

4. Place the loin, fat side up, on a rack in a baking pan. Roast for 2 hours or until the meat is cooked, basting frequently. Be careful not to overcook or the pork will become dry.

5. Put the roast on a heated serving dish and keep warm. Pour off as much fat as you can from the cooking juices. Place the roasting pan over high heat. Add the wine and scrape up the cooking juices. Season with salt and pepper and pour into a heated sauceboat. Garnish with chopped parsley. Pass the sauce separately.

Note: This roast goes well with Celeriac with Potatoes (page 291).

Beef Tongue with Raisin Sauce

YIELD: 6 Servings

1	*4-pound beef tongue*
2	*onions*
2	*carrots, sliced*
1	*stalk celery with leaves,*
	sliced
1	*clove garlic, crushed*
2	*tablespoons butter*
⅓	*cup raisins*
3	*tablespoons chopped*
	almonds
⅓	*cup red wine vinegar*
1	*tablespoon tomato paste*
⅓	*cup Madeira*
	Coarse salt and freshly
	ground pepper to taste

1. Simmer the tongue in water to cover with 1 onion, coarsely chopped, the carrots, celery, and garlic for about 3 hours or until tender. Turn off heat and leave the tongue in its cooking broth while you prepare the sauce.

2. Chop the remaining onion and sauté in the butter in a small pan. Add the raisins and the almonds and sauté until the almonds are golden brown.

3. Stir in the vinegar and tomato paste, then add the Madeira and ⅔ cup of the tongue stock. Simmer for 3 minutes to reduce slightly, season with salt and pepper, and keep warm.

4. Peel the tongue and slice it. Arrange the slices on a serving platter and pour the sauce over the top.

Note: This dish goes well with boiled potatoes.

Chicken with Dried Apricots

1	chicken, about 3½ pounds
2	teaspoons ground cumin
1	teaspoon paprika
	Coarse salt and freshly ground pepper to taste
1	clove garlic, crushed
¾	pound dried apricots
1	large onion, sliced
1	tablespoon butter
1	tablespoon oil

1. Rub the chicken with cumin, paprika, salt, and pepper. Place the garlic in the cavity. Set aside at room temperature for 1 hour.

2. Simmer the apricots in water to cover for 30 minutes or until plump.

3. Preheat the oven to 350 degrees. In a deep, flameproof casserole, sauté the onion in the butter and oil until soft. Add the chicken and apricots. Cover and bake in the oven for 45 minutes or until the chicken is cooked, basting frequently. Remove the lid for the final 15 minutes of cooking so that the chicken breast browns. Correct seasoning and serve.

Note: This goes well with rice and a green vegetable.

Dried Fruit Compote

½	pound each dried apples, apricots, and figs
3	cups water
6	thin slices lemon, seeds removed
⅓	cup honey
¼	cup dark rum
1	cup plain yogurt
½	cup sour cream

1. Put the fruits into a large saucepan, add the water, and bring to a boil. Reduce heat and add the lemon slices and honey. Simmer for 15 to 20 minutes or until the fruit has swollen. Add the rum and bring to a boil for 1 second, then turn off the heat.

2. Place the fruit in a bowl and allow to cool to room temperature. Serve with yogurt mixed with sour cream.

Grapes

There are two main categories of grapes: white, which are actually greenish; and black, which are purplish red. Grapes are at their peak in late summer and fall. They are brought in from Latin America during the winter and are generally more expensive at that time. Table grapes do not make good wine because they do not have enough acid, and wine grapes are generally too sour for eating.

The biggest-selling grapes in the United States are Thompson seedless. They have thin skins and practically no seeds but not much flavor. I like them tossed in sour cream with brown sugar.

Ribier, one of the best-selling black grapes, has a very thick skin and is dark blue-black and mild in taste. Emperor grapes are blander, thin skinned, and have a long shelf life.

When buying grapes make sure the stems are not dried up and that the grapes are plump, not shriveled or leaking. Sometimes grapes are sold wrapped in tissue paper to protect their bloom. Often grapes are not labeled, so you don't know what kind you are buying unless you're an expert. They should have a bloom and there should be no shriveled grapes. It doesn't matter if the bunch has lost some grapes — those remaining will probably be riper and so the sweeter for it.

Catawba and Concord grapes are generally used for wine. During Prohibition an enterprising grape grower marketed his grape juice with the announcement on the bottle: Caution, this grape juice may ferment!

Green Grapes with Sour Cream and Brown Sugar

YIELD: 4 Servings

1	pound seedless grapes
1	cup sour cream
	Brown sugar to taste
	(approximately ½ cup)

1. Put the grapes into a mixing bowl and coat with the sour cream. Add the sugar and toss. Taste and add more sugar if necessary.
2. Chill for an hour or two before serving.

Melon

Melon was the central dish in one of the happiest breakfasts I remember, served at the house of Madeleine van Breugel in Marrakesh. Marrakesh melons are famous for being the sweetest and most fragrant. Some are tiny, the size of oranges. Breakfast was served in the farmhouse courtyard outside our rooms, a table laid with gleaming silver and Moroccan pottery under thatched palm leaves. The sun speckled the table and, helped by Chulita the parrot, we ate whole melons and drank black coffee flavored with cinnamon.

There are many choices of melon in the United States. Canteloupes, watermelons, and honeydews come from Texas and California, yellow cranshaw from Mexico, Texas, and California, and once in a while fiendishly expensive charantais melons are flown in from France.

Choosing a ripe melon is not easy. All melons should be heavy for their size. Pick those that are firm without moist or bald patches, with a sweet scent, and a slight "give" when pressed at the blossom end. A melon should have clean scars at the stem end.

Cantaloupes are in season from May to September. When ripe they shed their stem naturally. If there is a ragged spot where the stem was, it was pulled off before the melon was ripe. These melons have a raised netting tracework on their skins. Under the netting the skin may be yellow, gray, or tan. If it is green the melon was unripe when picked and it won't ripen. The netting should be spread evenly over the melon with no smooth patches.

Honeydews when ripe have a dulled, somewhat wrinkled yellow skin that is slightly sticky. The flesh is green. If the skin is slick, the melon is not yet ripe. Honeydews are at their peak in the summer and early fall. The largest are the best.

Casaba melons, at their best in the fall, have a thick, furrowed yellow or green rind. They are harder than cantaloupes. The rind should be golden yellow (sometimes it is dyed and will look harsh and artificial) and the blossom end should be slightly soft. Unlike other melons, they do not have a fragrance when ripe, and they are cut from the vine. Test for ripeness by pressing the blossom end.

Watermelon is a different genus from the other melons. It belongs to the cucumber family. It grows in the South, Florida, and some Northeastern states in smaller quantities. To tell whether a watermelon is ripe, shake it. It should resound but not sound too hollow. If it does not resound at all, it is unripe. If you are buying a piece rather than a whole melon, the seeds should be evenly distributed and the flesh shiny and moist without white streaks. Two kinds are available: Sugar Abby with smooth black skins from Mexico and striped watermelons, called Tiger watermelons.

They should not be flat on one side or unevenly shaped. If the melon is green and has no smell, it was picked before it was properly ripe.

Melon Sherbet

YIELD: 4 to 6 Servings

1	honeydew melon
¼	cup port wine or more to taste
¼	cup cognac or more to taste

1. Peel and seed the melon, chop into large chunks, and put in a blender or food processor.

2. Add the port and cognac; blend until smooth.

3. Pour the mixture into a freezer container and put in the freezer for a couple of hours. When nearly frozen, remove, blend again, and refreeze.

Pears

It is difficult to get good pears. Like so many of our fruits, they are picked when they are as hard as stone. Eventually time turns them not ripe but mealy. Oscar Wilde's rude definition of America certainly applies to the pears on its table: They have passed from infancy to senility without ever going through a period of maturity.

At its best, the pear is a subtle, fragile fruit, sweet and juicy, and in its glory with a slice of Roquefort cheese and a glass of Sauterne.

Most of our pears come from California, Oregon, and Washington State. Anjou, all-purpose, is green or greenish yellow when ripe. Bartlett, the pear that makes poire Williams, the pear brandy, can also be used both for cooking and eating. It is ripe when it has turned yellow, and it has a wonderful perfume. Two russet-and-yellow pears good for cooking are the long and slender Bosc and the small Seckel pear.

The red-blushed yellow Comice is one of the best pears on the market. "It is so soft that it is best eaten with a spoon," says Waverly Root in *Food*. "It has a tenderness more appealing to gourmets than to those who have to pick it up, ship, handle and store it in fear of ruinous spoilage. It is becoming ever more rare, although some conscientious — and obstinate — growers, especially in Oregon's Hood River valley, are still producing it for the luxury market, picking each fragile fruit separately from the tree as though it might explode if jarred, and packing it carefully for the few takers appreciative enough — and wealthy enough — to pay the high cost of giving each pear individual attention during its progress from plant to palate."

Ideally, pears should be picked just before ripening. If allowed to ripen fully on the tree, their texture becomes slightly gritty. They are at their peak in fall and winter. Bartletts are the first arrivals, starting to appear on the market in late July through October. Then Seckel pears appear in September to early November, followed by Comice and Bosc and Anjou pears that are usually available throughout midwinter. Avoid buying pears in the spring. Like apples, prolonged storage makes them woolly.

It can be difficult to tell by the color if a pear is ripe because the colors vary so much from one variety to another. To tell if a pear is ripe, press it near the stem. It should give slightly more than it gives at the blossom end. If the blossom end is too soft the pear is overripe. Pears ripen from the inside out, so they are usually ready when there is only a very slight give and their fragrance has developed. Don't buy pears that are spotted or that have bruises or tears in the skin.

Since the chance of getting really ripe pears is slim, the best way to eat them is cooked. When simmered in red wine, for example, pears deepen to a rich ruby red hue and make a splendid dessert.

According to Alexandre Dumas, every Wednesday at the Court of Württemberg the traditional dish was bacon cut into little cubes and fried, then combined with pears cooked with nutmeg, pepper, and tansy leaves, and served with fried croutons. Here is a contemporary version:

Birnen, Bohnen, und Speck

YIELD: 4 Servings

(Pears, Beans, and Bacon)

6 pears
½ cup water
1 pound string beans, trimmed
6 strips thick-cut bacon
1 strip lemon peel
1 teaspoon thyme
4 tablespoons sugar
2 tablespoons red wine vinegar
Juice of ½ lemon
Coarse salt and freshly ground pepper to taste

1. Peel, core, and slice the pears. Simmer them in water for 10 minutes, then add the beans. Cook until almost done but still a vivid green. Drain.

2. Meanwhile, fry the bacon until crisp. Remove from the pan and drain on paper towels. Set aside. Add the pears and beans to the pan, toss them lightly in the fat, and add the remaining ingredients except the bacon. Cover and simmer until the beans are cooked.

3. Crumble the bacon over the pears and beans and serve.

Note: This goes well with mashed potatoes.

Baked Pears with Cream

YIELD: 4 Servings

6 pears
Juice of ½ lemon
4 tablespoons brown sugar
3 whole cloves
1 cup heavy cream, whipped

1. Preheat the oven to 325 degrees. Halve and core the pears. Sprinkle with lemon juice.

2. Put ½ inch of water in a shallow baking dish and arrange the pears in one layer. Sprinkle with sugar and cloves.

3. Bake, uncovered, for 1 hour. Discard the cloves.

4. Cool slightly and serve either with the cream on top or served separately.

Pears in Red Wine

6	pears
	Approximately 1½ cups dry red wine
3	tablespoons sugar
	Dash of cinnamon
1	cup heavy cream, lightly whipped

1. Peel and core the pears but leave their stems intact.

2. Put them into a deep, heavy casserole large enough to hold them without crowding, stems up. Pour in the wine and enough water to come up to the top of the pears. Add the sugar and cinnamon.

3. Simmer, uncovered, for 2 to 3 hours or until the liquid has reduced to a glaze. If the syrup is too liquid but the pears are cooked, remove them to a serving dish. Boil the liquid down until it is thick enough to coat the spoon. Pour over the pears and allow them to cool at room temperature.

4. Serve the cream separately.

Note: These will keep for about a week in the refrigerator.

Baked Pears

8	hard Bosc pears
8	teaspoons brown sugar
8	tablespoons butter, at room temperature
16	amaretti (Italian almond cookies)
½	cup heavy cream

1. Preheat the oven to 350 degrees.

2. Core the pears, leaving the skins on.

3. Mix the sugar and butter, and spoon into the cavities.

4. In a large baking dish, make 8 aluminum foil wells and place a pear in each. This will stop the butter mixture from running out of the cavities. Place the baking dish in a shallow pan of water. Bake the pears for 1 hour.

5. Place the cookies on a breadboard and crush finely, using a rolling pin or a thick glass.

6. To serve, arrange the pears in a serving dish and sprinkle with crushed amaretti. Pass the cream separately.

Pitted Fruits

Fruits with pits — cherries, plums, peaches, nectarines, and apricots — should be chosen with great care because much of what is in the stores these days is a better subject for an artist's canvas than for the dining table. Golden apricots appear perfect enough to be painted by Cézanne or Manet. Sink your teeth into one, however, and the flesh has the texture of mashed potato. A flawless peach also tastes like potato — raw potato — and is so hard one is afraid of cracking a tooth. And a ruby plum, plump, glossy and Victorian, brings tears to your eyes — from its sourness.

What makes these fruits such poor eating? The same problem faced by our tomatoes and avocados: They are not allowed to ripen before being picked, so usually they never do ripen properly. They rot first.

Most of our fruits with pits are from California, but peaches also come from Georgia. The California harvest is divided in two parts, "Western maturity" and "Eastern maturity." Fruits that have reached Western maturity have been allowed to ripen a little longer on the tree because they are to be sold in nearby markets. Eastern maturity is actually a euphemism for unripe fruit. The produce is harvested while still hard so it will not be damaged or rot in transit to the East Coast.

If fruits with pits don't always make wonderful eating in their raw state, however, they can be fine for cooking, even when not ripened to their peak of flavor and juiciness. They don't turn mushy, and they lend themselves to a wide variety of preparations. The mealiest of apricots become juicy and tender when laced with kirsch and baked. The most recalcitrant of peaches or nectarines can be peeled, sliced, and baked with butter and brandy, the tartest of plums stewed and made into a spectacular ice cream. All these fruits are delicious simply stewed and served with heavy cream or cooked in open-faced flaky pastry tarts. Austrians wrap them in a thin layer of pastry and poach them. They even combine with spices such as cumin, saffron, or coriander to go with meats such as chicken, pork, or lamb.

The California cherry season begins in late May and usually lasts through June. In July cherries come in from the Northwest. The most common are the deep red Bing cherries, Lambert and Tartarian cherries, and yellow-red Royal Ann cherries. Sour cherries are too sour to be eaten raw but can be very good cooked. Early Richmond, Montmorency, and English morello are the most common varieties.

The darker the cherry for its variety, the more likely it is to be ripe and juicy. Choose those that are plump and glossy without abrasions, stickiness, or bruises. Stems, if the cherries have them, should be pliable and fresh, not dry or brittle.

Apricots are in season briefly, from May to August in the West, and in the East usually only in June and July. They will ripen after being picked, but unfortunately they are often mealy and lacking juice, even when soft.

Nectarines and peaches come in two categories, freestone and cling. Cling peaches, so called because the fruit clings to the pit, are usually used for canning. Peaches may range in skin color from reddish white to deep gold. Nectarines are like smooth-skinned peaches in appearance but they have firmer flesh and are generally eaten raw. Their color goes from pinkish white to red-gold.

California is the country's leading producer of plums. The most widely available is the Santa Rosa, with a dark red skin and yellow flesh. Damsons are usually used for tarts and jellies. Greengages are good raw when properly ripe and also are good for cooking.

The best way to judge any piece of fruit is to smell it: It should have a pronounced fragrance. Test the fruits with your fingers. They should be soft. Avoid peaches or nectarines with a greenish tinge; they will never develop any aroma or taste. Hard plums will be sour because they are unripe, but they can be used for cooking. Avoid fruits with cracked, shriveled, or bruised skins.

Although the best way to be sure of getting the fruit so ripe that the juice runs down your chin when you bite into it is to grow your own trees, this isn't always the answer. When I was a child we had an enormous cherry tree outside my window that reached to the roof of the house. Every year I would watch as the cherries grew riper and riper. Then, literally overnight, they would be gone. The birds would make off with the lot. In all our years in that house, we never had a single cherry.

Plum Ice Cream

2	pounds plums
½	cup sugar
	Juice of 1 orange
1½	cups heavy cream

1. Put the plums into a saucepan with 3 tablespoons sugar, the orange juice, and 1 cup of water. Simmer until soft. Carefully remove the pits with a slotted spoon.

2. Bring the mixture to a boil with the remaining sugar and reduce to about 1½ cups. Cool.

3. In a blender, whip the cream until thick and add the plum mixture. Blend until smooth and pour into an ice-cream maker or an ice tray.

4. If using an ice tray, put it in the freezing compartment of the refrigerator, stirring occasionally to prevent icing. Freeze overnight.

Note: This ice cream is at its best served soft with sugar cookies.

Plums with Framboise

3	pounds purple Italian or freestone plums
½	pound sugar
½	cup framboise eau de vie (raspberry brandy)

1. Wash the plums, cut them in half, and remove the pits. Cook the plums with a dash of water and the sugar over low heat until soft but still intact, about 15 minutes.

2. Cool and add the framboise. Serve at room temperature.

Baked Apricots with Kirsch

2	pounds apricots
½	cup kirsch
3	tablespoons sugar

1. Preheat the oven to 350 degrees.

2. Wash the apricots and place them in a baking dish.

3. Add the kirsch and sugar and bake, covered, for 30 minutes. Serve hot or at room temperature.

Note: This is good with heavy cream, plain or whipped, or crème fraîche, and thin sugar cookies.

Glazed Baked Peaches

6	peaches
2	tablespoons butter
1 to 2	tablespoons sugar
½	cup brandy

1. Preheat the oven to 350 degrees. Drop the peaches into boiling water for a few minutes. Remove, drain, and peel off their skins while hot.

2. Grease a baking dish with the butter. Cut the peaches into slices ½ inch thick and arrange on the baking dish (a circular dish looks attractive). Sprinkle with sugar.

3. Bake for 30 minutes.

4. Heat the brandy in a small saucepan. Pour the brandy over the peaches and set alight. Serve immediately.

Note: Serve the peaches with heavy cream, whipped or plain.

Peaches with Framboise

6	peaches
2	limes
1	cup framboise (raspberry liqueur)
½	cup sugar
6 to 8	tablespoons water
½	pint raspberries (about 1 cup)
3	sprigs fresh mint

1. Drop the peaches into boiling water for a few minutes. Remove, drain, and peel off the skins while hot. Cut the peaches into thin slices.

2. Put the peaches into a bowl and squeeze the juice of the limes over them.

3. Combine the raspberry liqueur, sugar, and 6 tablespoons of water to make a syrup. Add more water if needed.

4. Pour the syrup over the peaches, add the raspberries, and decorate with the mint sprigs.

Nectarines with Raspberries and Pistachios

8	ripe nectarines
	Approximately 3 tablespoons sugar, or more to taste
½	pint raspberries (about 1 cup)
1	cup heavy cream
1	tablespoon kirsch
½	cup pistachio nuts

1. Drop the nectarines into boiling water for a few minutes. Remove, drain, and peel off the skins while hot. Cut the nectarines into slices and arrange them in a shallow serving dish. Sprinkle with sugar and place the raspberries on top.

2. Whip the cream until thick, but not stiff, and add the kirsch.

3. Pour the cream over the fruit and sprinkle with pistachio nuts.

About 1½ to 2 pounds	
	dark, red ripe cherries
	(see note)
½	*cup flour*
¼	*teaspoon salt*
3	*eggs*
2	*cups milk*
2	*tablespoons kirsch*
3	*tablespoons sugar*
1	*tablespoon powdered*
	sugar

1. Preheat the oven to 425 degrees.

2. Wash the cherries, discarding any that are imperfect.

3. Put the flour into a bowl with the salt. Break in the eggs. Beat well. Gradually add the milk and mix until smooth. Add the kirsch and sugar and beat for a few more seconds. If making batter in a blender, put the flour in after the eggs, salt, and milk.

4. Butter a baking dish, such as a 10-inch Pyrex pie plate. Arrange the cherries on the bottom and pour the batter over them. Bake for 5 minutes, then reduce heat to 350 and bake for 45 to 50 minutes or until the clafoutis is firm, puffed up, and nicely browned.

5. Sprinkle with powdered sugar and refrigerate until needed. Serve with heavy cream, whipped or plain. Clafoutis is also good served immediately, hot.

Note: Cherries are sometimes pitted for this dish, but their juices may run and cause the batter not to set. If using pitted cherries, increase the flour by 3 tablespoons. Cherry pitters are sold in most kitchen-supply shops.

Rhubarb

Rhubarb is not a fruit but the stalk of a wide-leafed plant. There are many species, and it is believed to have originated in northern Asia and been brought to Europe in the fourteenth century. Rhubarb was considered an ornamental plant, and it was not until the seventeenth century that the stalks were eaten.

When buying rhubarb, choose firm, thin stalks. There are two kinds on the market, pink hothouse rhubarb and reddish-green field rhubarb. Field rhubarb has more flavor. It is in season in late winter and early spring. Do not eat the leaves; they are toxic.

The best way to stew rhubarb is in a slow oven, uncovered, so that the pieces will remain whole, for about 20 minutes. Don't add any liquid. A little butter, brown sugar or honey, and some spices such as a few cloves, ground coriander, or cardamom seeds will add flavor. You can also put in a few mint leaves and lemon or orange peel. Serve rhubarb hot or cold with heavy cream or yogurt.

Rhubarb pie can be made by putting the raw rhubarb into a baking dish and placing the pie crust on top. By the time the pastry is cooked, the rhubarb will be cooked, too.

1½	cups flour
½	teaspoon salt
6	tablespoons butter
2	pounds rhubarb
6	tablespoons sugar

1. Sift the flour into a bowl with the salt. Add the butter and cut it up with a knife. Work the butter into the flour until it has the consistency of cornmeal.

2. Add just enough water to bind the pastry and mix it together with the blade of a knife. Shape into a ball, put into a plastic bag, and refrigerate for 1 hour or overnight, if possible.

3. Preheat the oven to 425 degrees.

4. Roll the dough out on a floured board.

5. Wash the rhubarb and slice it into 1-inch pieces. Put the rhubarb into a pie dish and sprinkle with sugar. Put a pie funnel in the middle of the dish. Cover with the pastry, decorating with leftover pieces. Sprinkle with a little sugar.

6. Bake for about 20 to 25 minutes. If the top becomes too brown, cover loosely with foil.

Note: This is good with heavy cream or crème fraîche.

Summer Berries

Summer is the time for high feasting on berries. Few desserts are better than raspberries or strawberries heaped in a bowl and served with cream. There are also blackberries, gooseberries, and red or black currants that can be made into ice creams, pies, or "fools." And there is summer pudding, the ruby red molded dome made with red currants, blackberries, and raspberries and served with crème fraîche. Gooseberry fool is another favorite; the berries are stewed and sieved, then mixed with whipped cream. And blackberry and apple pie, slightly tart yet sweet under a light glazed pastry topping, is one of the best dishes of summer.

In the summer berries of all kinds are available at local summer greenmarkets and greengrocers. But apart from strawberries and blueberries, supermarkets tend to avoid fresh berries because they are awkward to handle, easily perishable, and not very profitable.

When buying berries, look at the bottom of their container. If it is badly stained with juice, the fruit underneath the top ones may be moldy or squashed. Be particularly wary when buying raspberries. Sometimes half-pint containers are placed inside pint ones so you think you're buying more than you'll get. Also, check that the raspberries aren't moldy.

Store berries in a dark, airy place, like an English larder or the cool part of the kitchen—the refrigerator is too humid and encourages mold. The smell of strawberries and raspberries permeates other foods, too. Don't keep berries for long. Eat them as soon as possible after buying them. They should be thoroughly washed since most have been sprayed several times with insecticides.

The best cream with berries is crème fraîche. Pasteurized cream on its own, although good, lacks the slightly sour tang that brings out their flavor so well. Crème fraîche can be bought at specialty shops, but it is cheaper to make it yourself by stirring a couple of spoonfuls of yogurt or buttermilk into heavy cream and leaving it to stand in a warm place for twenty-four hours (page 201).

Also delicious on raspberries or strawberries is zabaglione, the Italian specialty of eggs and Marsala whipped to a thick froth.

In Napoleonic times Madame Tallien had 22 pounds of strawberries crushed every time she had a bath so that her skin would be soft and smooth. The strawberries in our markets are often pulpy enough to use as a skin freshener such as she would have enjoyed, but some years they can be remarkably juicy and sweet. Choose those that are plump and glossy. They should be washed just before being hulled. If you sprinkle them with sugar the juice will exude.

Raspberries, the most difficult berries to transport and the best eaten plain, are mostly from California or locally grown. Like strawberries, they make wonderful purées, particularly for ice creams.

Currants and gooseberries are not well known in America although in Europe they are abundant at the height of summer. Their cultivation was discouraged here because they can carry a fungus called *Cronartium ribicola,* which causes white pine blister rust. "In one of those improbable arrangements which makes one think of the exigencies of Lewis Carroll's *Through the Looking Glass* insects," writes Waverly Root in *Food,* "it has been decreed that *Cronartium ribicola* must spend part of its life on plants of the genus *ribes* (currants and gooseberries), to which it does no particular good but no irreparable harm either, and the rest on the white pine, which it girdles and kills."

But now these fruits are making their way back to the markets. Gooseberries, those strange little hairy, dark pink or green berries, are very juicy when cooked. They are versatile, their tart flavor going well with mackerel and also making an excellent ice cream. Gooseberry pie, Adolf Hitler's favorite dish, is second in popularity in England only to gooseberry fool. Gooseberries grow well in England because they don't like hot sun. Edward Bunyard, a fruit grower in the 1920's, describes them as "the fruit par excellence of ambulatory consumption. The freedom of the bush should be given to all visitors and the exercise of gathering, too, is beneficial to the middle aged and also stimulates their absorptive capacity."

Sweet wines such as Barsac, Château d'Yquem, Sauternes and Beaume de Venise, served chilled, are a pleasant accompaniment for summer fruit desserts. Jane Grigson in *Good Things* says that muscat was drunk in quantity in Britain during the eighteenth and nineteenth centuries, one of the great periods of gooseberry cultivation and enjoyment. "People discovered how perfectly the fragrance of muscat goes with gooseberries."

Blackberries, too, are being rediscovered in America. This tart, refreshing fruit is good with apples in a pie or with red currants and raspberries in summer pudding. British children were regularly sent off along the hedgerows of the fields to fetch dessert. A particularly memorable blackberrying outing took place one rainy summer when I went with a group of friends on a barge trip in Oxfordshire. To show that I was unafraid in front of a city friend, I started to walk across a field of cows. He was wise enough to refuse. Halfway across, the gaze of an albino bullock met my eye. He lowered his head and charged, and the rest of the herd followed. I ran as fast as I could, ducked under a strand of barbed wire, and flattened myself against a hedge rampant with glistening blackberries. The wire that was about six inches from my nose separated me from the panting herd of bullocks who stared at me across it, uncertain what to do. Finally I hurled myself backwards through the brambles with the aid of my friend who was standing anxiously on the other side, trying to distract the young bulls by yelling. Covered in scratches, with an empty bowl in our hands, we returned to the barge where our friends were sequestered with a card game. We tried to tell them our tale but they didn't even look up. "A likely story," one of them said and dealt another hand.

Strawberry Ice Cream

YIELD: About 8 Servings

2	*pints strawberries*
	(approximately 4 cups)
	Juice of 1 lemon
¾	*cup sugar*
¾	*cup water*
½	*cup heavy cream,*
	whipped

1. Purée the strawberries in a blender. Add the lemon juice and mix thoroughly.

2. Boil the sugar and water in a small saucepan for 10 to 15 minutes or until a thin syrup forms. Cool.

3. Mix the syrup into the strawberry pulp. Add the cream and mix well. Pour the mixture into two ice trays. Freeze overnight at the lowest temperature.

Note: This ice cream can also be made with puréed raspberries or with cooked, sieved gooseberries (see Gooseberry Fool, page 340).

Blackberry and Apple Pie

YIELD: 6 to 8 Servings

Shortcrust Pastry

1½	cups flour
¼	teaspoon salt
1	teaspoon sugar
¼	pound butter

Filling

2	pints blackberries
	(approximately 4 cups)
3	cooking apples
5	tablespoons sugar

Egg wash

1	egg yolk beaten with ½
	teaspoon water

1. Make the pastry. Put the flour, salt, and sugar into a bowl. Cut the butter into pieces with a knife. Rub the butter into the flour until the mixture is the consistency of cornmeal.

2. Add 3 to 4 tablespoons cold water and form the mixture into a ball. Refrigerate for 1 hour before using.

3. Preheat the oven to 425 degrees.

4. Wash the blackberries and peel, core, and slice the apples. Put a pie funnel in the middle of a buttered pie dish about 9 inches by 4 inches. Arrange the fruit in layers, sprinkling each layer with a little of the sugar.

5. On a floured board, roll out the pastry ¼ inch thick. Cover the pie with the pastry allowing about 1 inch to overlap the sides. Seal the sides down with the prongs of a fork. Make a small hole over the funnel to allow air to escape. Decorate the crust with leftover pastry pieces cut in the shapes of leaves. Glaze with the egg wash.

6. Bake the pie in the center of the oven for 15 minutes, then turn heat down to 350 degrees and bake for 30 minutes.

Gooseberry Fool

YIELD: 6 Servings

2	pints gooseberries
	(approximately 4 cups)
¾	cup sugar
1	cup whipped cream

1. Cook the gooseberries with the sugar in a saucepan for about 15 minutes or until soft. Pass through a sieve. If there is a lot of juice, set some aside. The mixture should not be too liquid. Cool the sieved gooseberries.

2. Mix the gooseberries with the whipped cream and refrigerate until ready to serve.

Summary Pudding

1	pint raspberries
	(approximately 2 cups)
2	pints red currants
	(approximately 4 cups)
1½	cups sugar
1	pint black currants or
	blueberries
	(approximately 2 cups)
1	small loaf white bread,
	sliced

1. Cook the raspberries and the red currants in a saucepan with 1 cup sugar, stirring as little as possible, for about 5 minutes or until soft. In a separate pan, cook the black currants or blueberries with the remaining ½ cup sugar, stirring as little as possible, for about 5 minutes.

2. Line a 5-cup bowl (a pudding bowl or soufflé dish will do) with slices of bread, crusts removed, leaving no gaps between the slices for the fruit juices to run out. Put in a layer of raspberry-currant mixture, then a layer of currants or blueberries, and alternate until the bowl is full. Do not add much juice. There will be about 1 cup of juice left over.

3. Cover the top with more bread and put a plate on top that just fits inside the bowl. Cover with weights and allow to stand for 24 hours in a cool place or in the refrigerator.

4. Turn the pudding out of the bowl onto a serving plate. The bread should be a deep ruby red. If there are any pale patches, pour some of the reserved juice onto them. Serve with heavy cream or crème fraîche.

Note: This pudding freezes very well.

Strawberry Fool

2	pints strawberries
	(approximately 4 cups)
3	tablespoons sugar, or
	more depending on
	sweetness of
	strawberries
1½	cups heavy cream

1. Set a few strawberries aside. Chop the rest coarsely and put them into a bowl with half the sugar. Mix and leave for 1 hour. Mash with a fork.

2. Whip the cream until thick, gradually adding the rest of the sugar.

3. Put the mixture into a bowl and top with the strawberries you have set aside.

1	bunch arugula
1	small head radicchio
1	head Boston lettuce
1	egg yolk
½	teaspoon prepared mustard
½	cup olive oil
1	clove garlic, pressed
	Coarse salt and freshly ground pepper to taste
1	tablespoon balsamic vinegar
2	tablespoons heavy cream
½	cup Gorgonzola cheese
¼	cup chopped walnuts
1	cup fresh blackberries

1. Trim the roots and stalks from the arugula. Wash the leaves. Wash the radicchio and the Boston lettuce leaves. Pat dry with a towel.

2. In a bowl large enough to contain the salad, beat the egg yolk. Mix in the mustard. Gradually add the olive oil. When absorbed, add the garlic, salt, pepper, vinegar, heavy cream, and Gorgonzola, and mix until almost smooth. Add the salad leaves and toss.

3. Arrange the salad on a plate and sprinkle on the walnuts and blackberries.

Tropical Fruits

In the middle of the winter when the weather is gray and dismal, it is very cheering to be able to bring home tropical fruits such as bright orange persimmons, red pomegranates with red seeds that gleam like rubies, fragrant pineapples, or emerald-green kiwis. Even the humble banana, fried in butter and flambéd with rum for dessert, conjures up what Baudelaire described as *"luxe, calme et volupté."*

Whenever I think of bananas I remember a Rosemary Clooney record my parents had in the Far East. The refrain went something like this:

Bunches of bananas and bottles of gin
Keep hunger out and happiness in.

I was ten years old then, and sometimes I would wake up in the middle of the night, hear the strains of the song being played downstairs, and long for the time when I could stay up, too. There was a huge banana tree next door to which our dreadful neighbors kept an Alsatian tethered. The poor dog used to bark all night. Late one evening, escorted home by the ambassador and his two sons after dinner, I heard someone yelling, "Bow wow wow! BOW WOW WOW!" followed by a stream of abuse in French. "What on earth is that?" asked the Ambassador.

"It's Daddy," I replied.

We used to pick bananas by the roadside on weekends when we'd go for picnics along a road we nicknamed "Banana Pass." There were so many our cook became extremely inventive with them, baking them in breads, using them as garnishes or stuffings, and serving them raw and sprinkled with lemon to go with curries for Sunday lunch. Bananas are also good in fruit salad with apples and oranges. There are stubby pink bananas like fingers, which make excellent eating, and green cooking ones, called plantains, to be fried and served with black beans and rice. Bananas are picked green and gradually ripen. They should not be refrigerated and should be bought in a bunch, with no breakages at the stem.

Pineapples, too, can be fried and flavored with rum, and they are also good sliced raw and sprinkled with kirsch. To buy a ripe pineapple, choose those with fragrant smell. The leaves should not be wilting, and the stalk end should not be moldy. It should yield slightly when pressed.

There has been a marked improvement in mangoes in the past year or so. Some of the ones on the market are almost as good as those you find in Caribbean countries such as Trinidad or in parts of Latin America. When the season is in full swing, there are so many that much of the crop is left to rot on the ground. They grow on large trees as high as 40 to 50 feet, and the fruit hangs from long stems. When it ripens there is usually food for everyone, and mangoes are picked off the roadside by anyone who feels like it.

Smaller mangoes can be stringy, while the larger ones are smooth and more delicate. When they are ripe they have an apricot-colored flesh. Choose those that are soft and fragrant but without any large black spots. Small speckles on the outer skin do not adversely affect the fruit inside. Unripe greenish-yellow mangoes can be allowed to ripen on the windowsill. Hard green ones will not ripen, as they have been picked too green, and blackened soft ones are over the hill. The green unripe mangoes can be made into mango chutney, skins and all, or sliced and eaten with a little salt and chili.

Ripe mangoes can be eaten for breakfast and mixed in fruit salads. To prepare them, peel away the small end of the fruit and slice the flesh away from the pit. Mixed with sugar and frozen, mango makes extremely good sherbet. In my view the only place to eat a ripe mango is in the bathtub.

The papaya is a large, oblong fruit with a thick green or yellow skin. It is heavy and soft when ripe — the best ones sometimes seem almost rotten but once cut into have a delicious soft and fragrant flesh. The skins can be green or orange, and the flesh is orange with black seeds in the middle. Papaya can be exquisite eaten for breakfast with half a lime squeezed onto the pulp. An unripe papaya will ripen if left at room temperature.

Persimmons, another subtle and delicate tropical fruit, were brought to the United States in the early nineteenth century. This fruit looks a bit like a tomato with a bright orange skin. Two varieties are available: the Hachiya, with a slightly pointed shape and bright orange color, and the Fuyu, which is flatter in shape and ready to eat while still firm. If persimmons are not ripe, they taste sour and puckery. They can be ripened at room temperature and are ready when they are soft when pressed.

The pomegranate is an ancient fruit that is used for making grenadine, the red flavoring for drinks. You can make your own by straining the juice through cheesecloth. It is a crimson fruit filled with seeds in juicy pulp that are good simply spooned out and eaten or used in cooking. They make pretty garnishes and are excellent with quail (page 124).

Pomegranates are usually picked before they are ripe because they are inclined to split if allowed to ripen on the tree. They have a tough red rind and a dark red color. The large sizes have the juiciest kernels. The fruit can be kept for several weeks at room temperature.

The Kiwi fruit from New Zealand is edible art deco, a brilliantly marketed fruit whose brown furry skin conceals a green flesh that looks like a jewel. It is a staple of nouvelle cuisine and its taste is somewhere between that of a watermelon and that of a strawberry. It is about the size of a small lime and is ready for eating when slightly soft when pressed. If unripe, it can be ripened at room temperature.

Of all exotic fruits, the one I love the most is the fig. It is not really a tropical fruit but is grown in warm climates of the Mediterranean, Asia and India, and in California. In Tangier I lived for several days on little more than figs — brown, green, black, and pink — eating a couple of pounds a day with no trouble at all, accompanied by flat bread, goat's cheese, olives, and Oustalet rosé wine. Figs also go with prosciutto as a summer first course. They are very delicate and should be chosen with care since they are expensive. They are available from May to October. There are four major kinds on the market in the United States: the Calimyrna, which has a greenish-yellow skin and sweet nutlike taste; the Black Mission, which is almost black when ripe; the Kadota, a light yellow fig; and the Smyrna, which is at its best when the fig is yellow-brown. Choose those that are plump, fragrant, and firm, but with "give." They should not be burst or leaking or smell sour.

Guavas, the fruit of the guava tree, grow mainly in tropical regions of Latin America and Asia. They are also cultivated in Hawaii, Florida, and Southern California. There are several species, which range from green to yellow-red in color and can be pear-, orange-, or fig-shaped.

Guavas can be stewed and made into jam, jelly, or pastes. Most common on the market are canned guavas, and these are traditionally eaten with cream cheese and saltine crackers, Latin-style. If fresh ones are available, choose firmer ones for cooking; for eating, choose ones that are soft when pressed.

Baked Bananas

YIELD: 4 Servings

4	bananas
	Juice of 1 lemon
3	tablespoons butter
	Brown sugar
½	cup rum

1. Peel the bananas, cut them in half, and sprinkle them with lemon juice.

2. Preheat the oven to 350 degrees. Lightly butter a baking dish and place the bananas in the dish. Dot with butter and sprinkle with brown sugar.

3. Bake for 15 to 20 minutes. Heat the rum, pour it over the bananas, and set alight, taking care to shield your face. Serve immediately.

Note: This is good with heavy cream.

Mango Chutney

8	ripe or green mangoes
1	cup red or white wine vinegar
1	cinnamon stick
½	teaspoon ground allspice
½	teaspoon ground cloves
2	tablespoons minced fresh ginger
2	cups raisins
1	cup dark brown sugar, loosely packed
1	cup water

1. Peel the mangoes if ripe; leave the skins on if green. Pit the mangoes and slice them.

2. Combine the vinegar and spices and bring to a boil. Add the mangoes, raisins, sugar, and water. Cover and simmer for 30 minutes.

3. Cool, pour into hot, sterile jars, seal, and store in a cool place.

Baked Fish with Pomegranate Seeds

1	3½-to-4 pound fish (any firm, whole white fish)
⅔	cup olive oil
	Juice of 1 lime or lemon
	Coarse salt to taste
1	medium onion, finely chopped
1	green pepper, finely chopped
1	cup walnuts, finely chopped
½	cup chopped fresh coriander or parsley
3	fresh pomegranates
	Freshly ground pepper to taste
½	cup tahini paste
1	lemon or lime, sliced
	Coriander sprigs for garnish

1. Preheat the oven to 375 degrees. Dry the fish thoroughly and place in a baking dish into which you have poured about 2 tablespoons of the oil. Squeeze the lime or lemon inside and outside the fish. Season with salt and pour on 2 tablespoons oil.

2. Heat the remaining oil in a frying pan and soften the onion and the peppers without browning. Add the walnuts and fry for 3 minutes. Spoon into a bowl and stir in the chopped coriander. Split the pomegranates, spoon out the seeds, and add to the bowl with salt and pepper. Stuff the mixture into the fish. Close the cavity with toothpicks or small skewers.

3. Bake for about 40 minutes or until the fish flakes easily when tested with a fork. Baste frequently.

4. To serve, pour on the tahini paste and garnish with lemon or lime slices and coriander sprigs.

Chocolates
and Nuts

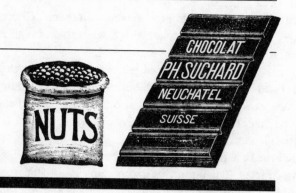

Chocolates

Forget the notion that chocolate is full of calories and sin. Think of Katharine Hepburn who, when asked the secret of her appearance, told an interviewer, "You see before you the result of a lifetime of eating chocolates." The slender actress said she particularly loved Viennese chocolate and often consumed a pound a day.

Many qualities have been attributed to chocolate since it was introduced to Europe from the New World in the sixteenth century. It was considered an aphrodisiac and a digestive, and was even thought to cure certain stomach infections. Today the strange properties of chocolate continue to intrigue doctors and scientists. Some postulate that chocolate excites a chemical in the brain called phenylethylamine producing the same reaction that is brought on by a passionate love affair. If a love affair goes wrong, they note, many people go on chocolate binges.

Mme. de Sevigné would have agreed with them. "Chocolate flatters you for a while," she wrote to her daughter. "It warms you for an instant; then, all of a sudden, it kindles a mortal fever in you."

Chocolate is made from cocoa beans that grow in large pods, mainly in Central and Latin America, each bean the size of an almond. The quality of the beans varies enormously, as is also true with coffee beans. Cheap chocolate has been blended from inferior beans and does not have as good a flavor as that from better beans.

The beans are fermented, roasted, hulled, and ground, and a red-brown liquor is extracted. The liquor, which contains about 50 percent cocoa butter, is poured into molds and allowed to set. Cocoa is a powder made from chocolate after most of the cocoa butter has been removed. Unsweetened chocolate is chocolate in its purest form and sold as baker's chocolate. Sugar, extra cocoa butter, or milk are added to make semisweet and milk chocolate.

Store chocolate in a cool, dry place at 68 to 78 degrees. For cooking, use the least sweet chocolate you can find. It will have stronger flavor. Buy it from the best confectioner's. Among recommended brands are Li-Lac, Lindt, Maillard Eagle Sweet Chocolate, Suchard Bittra, Tobler, and Van Houten. If the chocolate in the package has whitened or is "sweating," it has either been poorly stored or is stale.

Use a semisweet chocolate for icing cakes. It has a higher fat content, which makes it easier to melt. The sugar also gives the icing a sheen.

Be very careful when melting chocolate. If scorched it will turn into a solid lump. Melt in a very slow oven or in the top of a double boiler. Do not allow water to come into contact with it. A drop of water can make the chocolate stiff. Stir the chocolate with a rubber spatula. The flavor of chocolate goes wonderfully with rum, brandy, and orange liqueur.

The following dessert is a family favorite and easy to make. Fold the egg whites into the chocolate carefully, but be sure they are fully mixed. Otherwise you will get a soufflé like the one my English nanny once made. It was piebald.

Hot Chocolate Soufflé
YIELD: 4 Servings

4	ounces bitter chocolate
3	tablespoons rum or brandy
3	tablespoons sugar
6	eggs, separated
½	cup heavy cream

1. Preheat the oven to 400 degrees. In a double boiler or a slow oven, melt the chocolate carefully and stir in the rum or brandy. Add the sugar. Cool.

2. Beat 4 egg yolks and stir them into the mixture. Set the extra yolks aside for use in some other dish, such as scrambled eggs. Beat all the egg whites until they stand in peaks. Gently fold the whites into the chocolate mixture until blended.

3. Pour the mixture into a buttered 4-cup soufflé dish. Cook for 15 to 18 minutes. The soufflé should be risen but the inside center should be runny. Serve with the heavy cream passed separately.

Nuts

For me, nuts have always been synonymous with Christmastime, to be eaten by a fire along with tangerines and dates after a good dinner. The bowl that is passed around includes walnuts, hazelnuts, almonds, and those recalcitrant Brazil nuts, always the last to go because even the toughest nutcracker has difficulty opening them.

But nuts have many other uses. To go with drinks there are the expensive sweet and buttery macadamia nuts from Hawaii that come roasted in coconut oil, or peanuts or skinned almonds roasted at home and sprinkled with cayenne pepper and coarse salt. In the Middle East ground almonds or walnuts are used for thickening sauces and are cooked with lamb or chicken. Pistachios are mixed into pilaf or lend their vivid green to syrup-soaked pastries or candies. Italians make a garlicky pesto sauce for spaghetti with pine nuts and basil; Indians decorate or flavor their spicy stews and curries with cashews. Chestnuts, imported from Italy since fungus destroyed most American trees at the turn of the century, are in season during the winter and are glazed, puréed, or used for stuffing turkey or goose. And pecan pie is, of course, as American as pecan pie.

Nuts are the hard-shelled fruit of trees, but for eating purposes this category includes the peanut, which is a legume, and the Brazil nut, which is a seed. Most of the nuts sold in the United States are grown here. Almonds and pistachios come from California; walnuts and hazelnuts from California, Oregon, and Washington; macadamia nuts from California and Hawaii; and pine nuts from the Southwest — though the best pine nuts a shopper can find are imported from Italy. Peanuts come from pods that grow below the surface of the earth and are cultivated in the South. There are two main categories: the Virginia, which is long and slender, and the Spanish peanut, which is small and round.

The Brazil nut, which grows in South America, comes from trees as high as 150 feet with trunks as wide as six feet around. It is the size of a coconut and looks similar. Inside are packed the seeds that we know as Brazil nuts, little triangular-shaped shells, brown and white in color. Apparently the Amazonian hare who collects and stores the nuts for future use is responsible for their propagation. Those he forgets lie buried in the ground and eventually grow into trees that become fully grown in about nine years. When the nuts are ripe, tropical storms rip through the jungle, hurling the nuts to the ground. Each tree yields about 600 to 1,000 pounds of Brazil nuts.

Nuts are best in autumn or early winter. Buy from a store with a high turnover so the chances are they will be really fresh. If they have been sitting around for a long time they will be stale or rancid. Since most nuts sold in their shells have had their shells waxed and polished and even dyed, it is hard to tell quality by looking. But any that rattle about in the shell (except for peanuts) or are cracked, split, or stained should be avoided, and the nuts you buy should feel heavy for their size. Pine nuts easily go rancid and taste musty when stale, so buy them only from stores with a high turnover. They should always be refrigerated.

Pistachios are generally cheaper at Middle Eastern, Greek, or Indian shops, where you can find them in 2-pound bags. Store them in the refrigerator. The very best come from Sicily. Brownish ivory is the true color of the shells, with green nuts inside. The red-shelled ones have been dyed with vegetable dye, the white ones blanched.

The best walnuts grow in France and Italy. Those huge ones from California that are in our markets tend to be rather bitter. Buy walnuts early in the season while the flavor is still strong and fresh. If they are left exposed to air for too long, the kernels shrink and taste is lost.

The cashew nut grows on the pear-cashew tree, which bears a juicy red or yellow fruit. The nut is attached to the end like a large olive-colored kidney bean, and inside is the kernel, a sweet, white nut.

With the exception of peanuts, nuts sold in their shells have not usually been roasted. Shelled nuts are sold roasted, raw, or blanched, and if roasted are often salted or spiced. They are also sold whole, sliced, or in slivers, or ground. Shelled nuts should be plump with few broken pieces lurking at the bottom of the jar. Those sold in jars or cans are usually fresher than those in bags. Fresh nutmeats will snap when broken. If they are pliable, they are stale. In the future, avoid the store or brand that supplies them.

The problem with salted, roasted nuts is that they have usually been roasted in hydrogenated fats and are oversalted. Home-roasted nuts are so far superior it is worth taking the trouble to make them yourself. Spread the nuts on a baking sheet and add two or three tablespoons of vegetable or peanut oil for every pound of nuts. Toast slowly in a preheated 300-degree oven for about 20 to 30 minutes or until the nuts are golden brown. Brazil nuts need only two tablespoons oil, pine nuts need none at all. When the nuts are roasted, season with coarse salt and cayenne pepper. The nuts can also be browned in a frying pan on top of the stove.

There is no point in buying ready-ground nuts. They will have lost their aroma and can never be as fresh as those you grind yourself. Use a mortar, grinder, food mill, or even a blender to grind them yourself. It is easier to chop blanched or freshly toasted nuts while they are still hot.

Nuts should be stored in a cool, dry place, preferably the refrigerator (they can even be frozen). If the nuts are left for a length of time at high temperatures their oil turns rancid. To keep them fresh, store them in closed containers. Nuts in their shells last longer than shelled ones, unroasted longer than roasted.

Most peanuts are sold already roasted, even when in their shells. They are improved if roasted again. Since store-bought peanut butter may contain sweeteners such as sugar, honey, or dextrose, it is worth making your own. Combine the shelled roasted nuts, skins on, in the blender with a little peanut oil and coarse salt, if you like, and blend until it becomes a paste. It is a vast improvement over hydrogenated store-bought peanut butter, or indeed any store-bought peanut butter. It is also good in sauces for grilled chicken, tongue, or ham.

Deviled Almonds or Cashews
YIELD: About 3 Cups

1	pound shelled almonds or cashews
2	tablespoons peanut or vegetable oil
	Coarse salt to taste
	Cayenne pepper to taste

1. If using almonds, peel them by dropping them into boiling water and slipping off their skins.

2. Heat the oil in a frying pan. Fry the almonds or cashews until golden; drain on paper towels and sprinkle with salt and cayenne pepper.

Pesto Sauce
YIELD: 1 Cup

1	large bunch fresh basil, chopped
2	cloves garlic
4	tablespoons pine nuts
	Coarse salt to taste
2	tablespoons freshly grated Parmesan cheese
1	cup olive oil

1. Put the basil, garlic, pine nuts, salt, and cheese into a blender jar. Add about 2 tablespoons olive oil. Purée, adding more oil if necessary, until smooth.

2. Gradually add the rest of the oil, blending until you have a smooth paste.

Note: This sauce will freeze or keep in the refrigerator with a thin layer of olive oil over the top in a sealed jar.

Fish with Hazelnut Butter

1	cup toasted hazelnuts
1	tablespoon Dijon mustard
1	tablespoon white wine vinegar
	Coarse salt and freshly ground white pepper
4	ounces unsalted butter at room temperature
2	tablespoons vegetable or peanut oil
4	halibut, swordfish, or tilefish steaks
1	lemon, quartered
4	tablespoons chopped fresh chives

1. Combine the hazelnuts, mustard, vinegar, salt, pepper, and butter in the container of a blender. Blend until smooth, shape into a cylinder or square, and refrigerate.

2. Brush the fish steaks with the oil and broil until done.

3. Place the steaks on a heated plate, divide the butter into four slices, and place 1 slice on each steak. Garnish with lemon, sprinkle with chives, and serve.

Bibliography

Anderson, Kenneth, *The Pocket Guide to Coffee and Teas,* New York, Perigee Books, 1982.

Beard, James, *The New James Beard,* New York, Knopf, 1981.

Bettoja, Jo, Anna Maria, and Cornetto, *Italian Cooking in the Grand Tradition,* New York, Dial, 1982.

Brillat-Savarin, Jean-Anthelme, *The Philosopher in the Kitchen,* New York, Penguin, 1981.

———— *The Physiology of Taste,* translated by M.F.K. Fisher, New York, Knopf, 1971.

Bugialli, Giuliano, *The Fine Art of Italian Cooking,* New York, Times Books, 1977.

Child, Julia, Louisette Bertholle, and Simone Beck, *Mastering the Art of French Cooking, Volume I,* New York, Knopf, 1961.

Child, Julia, and Simone Beck, *Mastering the Art of French Cooking, Volume II,* New York, Knopf, 1970.

Claiborne, Craig, *Craig Claiborne's Favorites from The New York Times, Vol. 4,* New York, Times Books, 1978.

Conran, Terence and Caroline, *The Cook Book,* New York, Crown, 1980.

David, Elizabeth, *Classics: Mediterranean Food, French Country Cooking, Summer Cooking,* New York, Knopf, 1980.

———— *French Provincial Cooking,* London, Penguin, 1960.

———— *Italian Food,* London, Penguin, 1976.

———— *Spices, Salt and Aromatics in the English Kitchen,* London, Penguin, 1970.

Davidson, Alan, *Mediterranean Seafood,* New York, Penguin, 1980.

———— *North Atlantic Seafood,* New York, Viking, 1980.

Dumas, Alexandre, *Dictionary of Cuisine,* New York, Simon & Schuster, 1958.

Escoffier, A., *The Escoffier Cookbook,* New York, Crown, 1941.

Fisher, M.F.K., *The Art of Eating,* London, Faber & Faber, 1963.

Grigson, Jane, *Fish Cookery,* London, Penguin, 1973.

———— *Food with the Famous,* London, Penguin, 1981.

———— *Good Things,* London, Penguin, 1973.

———— *Jane Grigson's Vegetable Book,* London, Penguin, 1980.

Guérard, Michel, *Cuisine Minceur,* translated by Narcisse Chamberlain, New York, Bantam, 1977.

Hazan, Marcella, *The Classic Italian Cookbook,* New York, Knopf, 1976.

———— *More Classic Italian Cooking,* New York, Knopf, 1978.

Hess, John and Karen, *The Taste of America,* New York, Penguin, 1977.

Hillman, Howard, *The Cook's Book,* New York, Avon, 1981.

Johnston, Mireille, *Cuisine of the Sun,* New York, Random House, 1976.

Kennedy, Diana, *The Cuisines of Mexico,* New York, Harper & Row, 1972.

———— *Recipes from the Regional Cooks of Mexico,* New York, Harper & Row, 1972.

Launay, André, *Posh Food,* London, Penguin, 1964.

McDouall, Robin, *Robin McDouall's Cookery Book for the Greedy,* London, Penguin, 1965.

———— *Cooking with Wine,* London, Penguin, 1969.

McClane, A.J., *The Encyclopedia of Fish Cookery,* New York, Holt, Rinehart and Winston, 1977.

Olney, Richard, *Simple French Food,* New York, Atheneum, 1974.

Ortiz, Elizabeth Lambert, *Cooking with the Young Chefs of France,* New York, Evans, 1981.

———— *The Complete Book of Mexican Cooking,* New York, Bantam, 1968.

Roden, Claudia, *A Book of Middle Eastern Food,* New York, Vintage, 1974.

Root, Waverly, *The Food of France,* New York, Vintage, 1977.

———— *The Food of Italy,* New York, Vintage, 1977.

———— *Food,* New York, Simon & Schuster, 1980.

Sahni, Julie, *Classic Indian Cooking,* New York, Morrow, 1980.

Toklas, Alice B., *The Alice B. Toklas Cookbook,* New York, Doubleday, 1960.

Tsuji, Shizu, *Japanese Cooking: A Simple Art,* Tokyo and San Francisco, Kodansha International, 1980.

Trillin, Calvin, *Alice, Let's Eat,* New York, Vintage, 1980.

Viazzi, Alfredo, *Alfredo Viazzi's Italian Cooking,* New York, Random House, 1979.

Wolfert, Paula, *Couscous and Other Good Food from Morocco,* New York, Harper & Row, 1973.

———— *Mediterranean Cooking,* New York, Times Books, 1977.

Index